The State of
Public Manageme

D0825246

THE STATE OF PUBLIC MANAGEMENT

Edited by
Donald F. Kettl
and
H. Brinton Milward

The Johns Hopkins University Press

Baltimore and London

05 04 03 02 01 00 99 98 97 96   5 4 3 2 1

THE JOHNS HOPKINS UNIVERSITY PRESS
2715 North Charles Street
Baltimore, Maryland 21218-4319
The Johns Hopkins Press Ltd., London

Library of Congress Cataloging-in-Publication Data will be found
at the end of this book.

A catalog record for this book is available from the British
Library.

ISBN 0-8018-5275-7
ISBN 0-8018-5276-5 (pbk.)

Contents

IV. Bringing Theory and Practice Together

Preface and Acknowledgments

Public management has long been a field in search of structure. Its scholars and practitioners know what it is not: It is neither traditional public administration nor policy analysis. It borrows heavily from a host of disciplines and many different methodological approaches. It is self-evidently important. Programs not managed well are expensive and disappointing, sometimes dangerous, and always threatening to public confidence in government. But that still does not solve the basic problem of defining what public management is and how it ought to be done.

In 1991, some of the nation's leading public management scholars gathered at Syracuse University for a searching examination of these issues. That meeting produced a book, *Public Management: The State of the Art,* edited by Barry Bozeman (San Francisco: Jossey-Bass, 1993), and enthusiasm for another meeting of the group. The Robert M. La Follette Institute of Public Affairs at the University of Wisconsin-Madison convened a second National Public Management Conference in October 1993. This book includes some of the best of the papers from that meeting, as well as a smorgasbord of the thinking that defines the field. The field is undoubtedly coming of age. It has more self-awareness and self-assurance. It acknowledges its roots in a host of disciplines but, as the papers in this book demonstrate, it has jelled into something larger.

This book could not have been written without the extraordinary generosity of the La Follette Institute, directed by Peter Eisinger, and the hard work of its staff. Deserving special thanks for their contributions to the conference are Terry Shelton, Alice Honeywell, Joyce Collins, and Bonnie Cleary. They turned the three-day conference into a rich sharing of ideas. Michael Solorza assisted in compiling the materials of the book.

Other conferences will undoubtedly follow, and the study and practice of public management will certainly mature. But the chapters in this book mark important milestones. They not only explore the fascinating questions of how public programs can be managed to work better but they also chart the maturation of thinking about how this ought to be done.

The State of
Public Management

Introduction

Donald F. Kettl

Across the front page of the December 18, 1994, Sunday edition of the *New York Times* lay the remnants of an especially hectic week. Under a picture of scores of uniformed officers searching the White House grounds was the caption, "Another Bullet Strikes White House." Right next to it was a headline, "While Congress Remains Silent, Health Care Reforms Itself." Even though Congress in 1994 failed to act on health reform, massive changes were transforming the health care system. In the next column, the headline "Airline Safety Rising to Fore As a Question" began an article exploring travelers' growing nervousness about the condition of America's airlines. And the lead story, "G.O.P. Is Detailing Broad Proposals to Trim Welfare," explored how resurgent Republicans, under the leadership of Speaker-elect Newt Gingrich, were trying to carve a special piece of turf on the perennial welfare issue.

A casual reader would have seen no connection among the stories. Each one, however, underlines the recurring theme of this book: Public management matters, and it matters because the quality of public management shapes the performance of public programs. Consider the story behind each of these stories.

A closer look at the picture of the officers searching the White House reveals that the officers are wearing several different kinds of uniforms. That is because they represent several different forces, which share responsibility for guarding the president and his house. Managing the president's protection, in fact, has long proven a difficult problem. The Washington Metropolitan Police are responsible for Pennsylvania Avenue in front of the White House. The Park Police guard the perimeter, and the Secret Service takes over inside the fence. If a threat develops around the White House, whether a potential assailant waves a long knife or an armed attacker fires a semiautomatic rifle through the White House fence (both events happened in late 1994), officers must react instantly to ensure the public's and the president's safety. But they must not get in each other's way or undermine the neat boundaries of responsibility that can quickly break down in the heat of crisis. The search for coordination has long been the

Holy Grail of public management; it plays itself out every day around the White House.

In health care, reformers often think of major legislative initiatives that might nudge the system more in the direction they prefer. Even without such legislation, however, huge changes are transforming the system. A majority of Americans with private health care find themselves in "managed care" systems that limit their choice of physicians. Most doctors have signed contracts to join group practices that limit the fees they charge. Government finds itself in a rapidly changing world which it has helped shape, especially through Medicare's benefits for the elderly, but over which it has only partial control. Organizations—especially governmental organizations—have always sought to achieve their missions by trying to control the world in which they operate. As the health care case demonstrates, however, the world is increasingly less cooperative. The growth of shared responsibility for organizational missions is breaking down traditional ways of understanding what organizations do and how they do it.

These changes, however, have scarcely lessened the public's demand for high-quality services, as the airline safety headline demonstrates. The year had not been a good one for the airlines. There had been five crashes, including two each for USAir and American Eagle, and the accidents riveted the flying public's attention on issues like wing icing and the safety of commuter planes. Amid constant talk about a "Big Brother" government, too powerful and too intrusive in citizens' lives, came sharp questions about why the Federal Aviation Administration had not taken a tougher stand on airline safety. No matter how strong the public's antipathy toward government, its demand that government ensure safety in everything from air travel to fast-food hamburgers scarcely diminishes. Public trust in government programs seems to shrink even as demands for high-quality management grow.

Nowhere is the criticism of government programs stronger than in welfare. The Clinton administration promised to "end welfare as we know it." In the face of Gingrich's sweeping plan, the Clinton proposal, which had once looked radical, seemed tame. How much should the government spend on welfare? And can welfare be reformed? The program has long been part of an intricate balancing act between federal control and state flexibility. Behind the headlines of the competing welfare plans lie competing strategies for transforming the administrative side of American federalism.

There is nothing special about the stories in this copy of the *New York Times.* Any citizen anywhere could pick up a daily newspaper and find the same kind of stories. Most citizens, however, would not detect the public management thread running throughout the stories, how much they depend on effective public management, or how difficult it is to achieve the results they demand. Not only does public management matter but it matters in ways that frequently escape careful thought. It is one thing for citizens not to detect the recurring importance of public management in their daily lives; it is quite another for the officials that citizens elect to run their government to proceed frequently in ignorance of administrative reality as well.

If the rich fabric of public management issues too often escapes careful scrutiny, the implications of management—especially when done poorly—do not. Citizens and elected officials alike demand accountability. Effective management in any setting is difficult; within a democracy, with its competing forces and impossible demands, it can be daunting. Nevertheless, accountability for government's results requires careful integration of public management into the broader fabric of America's governance. On one level, nothing that elected officials decide matters until it is managed. On another level, the very foundation of citizenship in American society demands that citizens confront their expectations about government and the institutions that guide it (Ingram and Smith, 1993). All too often, citizens and elected officials alike discover public management only after disasters sear its importance into their consciousness— and only after it is much too late to remedy the problems.

The chapters in this book explore the role of public management in shaping the performance of public programs. At one time, public management theorists could content themselves by thinking that creating a bureaucracy and using "neutral competence" to shape the behavior of its bureaucrats would result in superior performance (Kaufman, 1956). But, as Guy Peters notes in his chapter, the nature of governance has changed, and that in turn has radically changed the role that traditional approaches like neutral competence can play. Furthermore, Peters persuasively illustrates the emerging central feature of public management. It is about much more than administration of programs. The questions of public management contribute mightily to the basic issues of governance—and the important questions of governance cannot be attacked without careful attention to the issues of public management.

Approaches to Public Management

Indeed, the central issue of American constitutionalism as the nation enters a new millennium is the paradox of often profound disappointment about the performance of the American governmental system coupled with scant attention to how public management shapes those results. Jeffrey L. Pressman and Aaron B. Wildavsky worried in 1973 that "there is (or there must be) a large literature about implementation in the social sciences—or so we have been told by numerous people" (p. 166). Of course, on one level, they were wrong. Students of public administration had, for generations, studied how public organizations transform policies into results. The implementation movement that Pressman and Wildavsky launched, however, changed how scholars approached the problem in two ways (Kettl, 1993).

First, implementation studies moved the issue from a focus on organizations, especially on their structures and processes, to public programs and the results they produced. The shift in research focus had profound implications. No longer could scholars look solely at organizations and their contribution to public programs. Implementation brought programs to the center and asked scholars to look at how organizations contributed to their success. Most important, the implementation movement brought questions of performance to the center of the debate for the first time. No longer could administrative scholars self-confidently assume that political decisions would produce effective results if administrators tickled and adjusted the system in the right ways. Profound performance problems, even failures, were far more prevalent than existing approaches could explain or admit. There was a "missing link" in the chain, as Erwin C. Hargrove (1975) argued, and that missing link was performance.

Second, implementation studies moved beyond a base in public administration and even beyond political science to a far broader, more interdisciplinary foundation. This was partly because the organizational focus of traditional public administration left important questions unanswered. Students of implementation also were determined to build something new from their fresh discovery of the importance of performance. In addition, scholars from other fields discovered that their interests met on the issue of making good ideas work.

From these two trends—a focus on performance more than organizational structure and process, and efforts to explore the problem from many different disciplinary bases—came the new field of public management. On one level, the difference between public administration and public management was cosmetic. Some scholars embraced "public management" because it had a livelier feel and represented fresh thinking.

Some scholars sought in public management a far more positive view of government and its programs (Neustadt, 1960; Moore and Stephens, 1991; Heymann, 1987). Implementation, for all of its appeal, played a constant note of despair. In the subtitle to Pressman and Wildavsky's 1973 book, they wondered at how government programs could work at all. Much of the implementation movement's first generation, in fact, consisted of one sad tale of failure after another (Derthick, 1972; Bardach, 1977; Elmore, 1978; Van Horn, 1979). The fledgling public management movement recognized that some programs did indeed work. Its practitioners in the new public policy programs believed fundamentally that good managers, properly trained, could make the difference between success and failure. In seeking to build success instead of to understand failure, they rejected the implementation movement. And in focusing on what managers could do instead of how organizations behaved, they rejected public administration.

Of course, both implementation and traditional public administration had much to contribute to the new debate. Implementation established the importance of the program as a fundamental unit of analysis. Public administration argued the need for a solid budgetary process, the right human resources system, and functional organizations. In their headlong rush to build something new, some public management scholars have glossed over the critical building blocks that public administrationists lovingly labored so long to build and that, even in a short time, implementation students had created.

Nevertheless, it was impossible to ignore the fact that in public management something very new was sweeping the study of governance and public policy. Public management grew haphazardly, in some cases by ignoring long-established truths and in other cases by importing fresh disciplinary ideas by the truckload. The study of public management sometimes came to resemble less an accumulation of knowledge and more a family feud. Competing academic disciplines dueled to establish bridgeheads or, worse, virtually ignored each other as they developed parallel tracks on related problems. These feuds have delayed the cross-fertilization that could have accelerated learning in the field and improved its ability to speak to the critical issues of performance.

Part II of this book examines the contributions that scholars from other disciplines—political science, sociology, economics, and psychology—have made to public management. As Laurence E. Lynn Jr. notes, the term "public management" as employed in different disciplines "is inconveniently ambiguous." John Ellwood demonstrates that political science builds on a sense of how political institutions shape policy. It contributes the ground rules; it frames conflict and how it is resolved. Linda Kaboolian argues that sociologists contribute a sense of the political culture, values about government, and, most important, an understanding about the relationship of the individual manager to governance as a whole. Sociology contributes context.

Economics, as David L. Weimer and Aidan R. Vining point out, helps managers understand the way society produces goods and how analysts can determine the most efficient allocation of resources. In addition, it suggests how to design organizations effectively and how managers themselves can find the right levers of influence. Economics contributes a sense of how to balance tools with resources.

Janet A. Weiss examines psychology's approach to management issues. She contends that psychology helps managers understand the "realistic micro-dynamics of macrostructure"—how the behavior of individuals builds to produce organizational performance. In particular, psychology can help explain what leaders at the top of a bureaucracy can do to affect behavior of managers at the bottom and, conversely, how cumulative bottom-level behavior can shape organizational performance. It moves the understanding of organizational mission away from a "thing" imposed from above to a process rooted in communication. Psychology contributes the behavioral perspective.

None of these theoretical approaches can (or does) claim to be the sole or even the most valuable approach. There are, moreover, other disciplines and approaches, including political science and public policy, that add different insights. But each discipline contributes important pieces to the complex mosaic of public management. Just as important, each of these authors recognize their reliance on scholars in other disciplines who contribute theoretical pieces they could not. Two important lessons are encapsulated in part II. First, the growing focus on the performance of governmental organizations and public programs needs to draw on a wide variety of academic disciplines for the full and richly textured picture required to improve the way government works. Second, as pregnant as these lessons might be, they are of relatively little use by themselves. Only through interdisciplinary cross-fertilization will the picture be rich enough to capture the enormous variety and complexity of true public management puzzles.

Turf Barriers

The growth of public management has been plagued by turf battles of two kinds. Some battles have swirled around academic disciplines. Other battles have centered on the turf of individual bureaucracies and programs. Perhaps the foremost lesson of traditional public administration is the need to specify goals clearly, to assign responsibility precisely, to develop tools adequately, and then to allow bureaucratic professionalism to produce results. The model has great power. It is simple and, for generations if not centuries, it has worked well.

It provides, furthermore, a good answer to the problem of bureaucratic accountability. In the traditional approach, the people elect representatives. On behalf of the people, these representatives make the law and delegate responsibility for executing the law to bureaucrats. It is the job of bureaucrats to execute the law to the highest professional standards. The precept of the traditional system is that good law will produce good and accountable results if the best bureaucrats are hired and if they are given the best tools (in structure, process, and resources) to do what needs to be done. Since the days of Woodrow Wilson (1887) and Frank J. Goodnow (1900), these principles have guided America's management of public programs.

With the dawn of the implementation movement came a series of shocks to these traditional arguments. First, it became painfully evident that even if the chain from citizens through elected officials to bureaucrats were nurtured, good performance might not result. The tales that Pressman and Wildavsky told, along with other implementation scholars, were of well-intentioned programs administered aggressively by well-meaning managers that went bad. Securing control through the chain of command did not always produce good results. With this searing realization, bureaucratic control and accountability parted paths.

Second, a closer look at these troublesome cases revealed the problem. The traditional public administration argument was built on the assumption of unity of command (each program would be delegated to a single agency, and within each agency a chain of responsibility from top to bottom would be established for results). The programs that filled the implementation literature, on the other hand, were enormously complex and violated the assumption. Grant programs might flow from a federal agency in Washington through a state government, on to local governments, and then finally to a nonprofit organization whose behavior would ultimately determine the program's success.

In short, between the end of World War II and the launch of the Great Society in the 1960s, a fundamental change in the strategy of government management—a rapid expansion in government's reliance on multiagency, intergovernmental, and public-private-nonprofit partnerships to produce government goods and services—toppled existing theory (Mosher, 1980; Salamon, 1981; Kettl, 1988). Public organizations continued to operate through authority and hierarchy, but authority and hierarchy no longer fully described the management of public programs. And with the decline of hierarchy came fresh challenges to both the descriptive and prescriptive sides of public management.

It is impossible to underestimate just how traumatic these changes have been. The failure stories of the implementation movement undercut public administration's self-confidence and made it hard for public management to build a firm foundation for better prescriptions. The realization of hierarchy's inadequacy crept slowly at best through the academic world and rarely through the practitioners' world. Along the way, it undercut long-established notions about how government could secure accountability. Public administration embarked on a long (and not-yet-finished) journey to rediscover itself. Early stages of implementation research gave way to successive waves of work that sought to move beyond failure stories (Goggin et al., 1990). Public management struggled with its own sense of direction and worried about the triumph of art over science (Lynn, 1994). Meanwhile, nonacademics like David Osborne and Ted Gaebler shook the practical world of public management with their best-seller, *Reinventing Government* (1992).

Behind the front lines of these battles, however, a surprising theoretical convergence developed. Scholars from a quite remarkable range of disciplinary backgrounds came simultaneously to this problem. They also began developing a solution: network analysis, the study of how organizations interconnect and how their interconnections affect public policy. Central to network analysis is the task of developing a better understanding of the connection between social choice—what we as a society wish to accomplish—and organizational choice—how we can structure our strategies to achieve these goals. Network analysis builds on a different foundation: *How* government manages affects *what results* it can produce.

Part III of this book examines organizational networks in both theory and practice. Beryl A. Radin examines how the U.S. Department of Agriculture's efforts to develop rural communities led it to a problem-based approach that stretched organizational boundaries. In his examination of social service organizations, Eugene Bardach finds the same thing. Both chapters make the point that effective service delivery requires not only using existing organizations as critical building blocks but also preventing their boundaries from getting in the way of getting the job done. Jeffrey L. Brudney makes the point, moreover, that neither the organizations nor the people involved in public programs need be public. Volunteer programs have become increasingly important in producing public services.

Beyond these cases lie not only important theoretical questions that require fresh answers but also intriguing new theoretical approaches that promise new insights. Barbara Koremenos and Laurence E. Lynn Jr. explore how an Illinois state department head managed to produce a government that worked better and cost less. Beyond the case study, however, they suggest that game theory—a formal approach to structuring the choices and incentives for decision makers—offers a different tack on the theoretical problems of performance. Laurence J. O'Toole Jr. takes this argument further. He asks whether formal approaches, like game theory, can in fact usefully inform public management. O'Toole finds that the great uncertainty and interdependence in implementation make adapting formal theory to public management extremely difficult. Nevertheless, he argues, it offers fresh insights about strategies to which public managers might turn.

In some respects, this section is discouraging. The authors probe largely unexplored territory and, although some are hopeful in finding managers who manage well and fresh theoretical insights that help explain why, they uncover more questions than answers. They also target important weak spots in leading theoretical explanations that seek simple explanations of complex phenomena. A far more encouraging story, however, emerges from the rich insights that come from moving beyond bureaucratic turf and organizational structure to practical problems and programmatic results. From several disciplinary perspectives, the authors demonstrate the great value of shifting the focus of research from structure and process to performance. If they cannot fully answer the tough questions of theoretical explanation, trust, confidence, and accountability, they have demonstrated that the network approach helps them formulate the questions (and their implications) far more crisply.

Uniting Theory and Practice

Of all the ideas competing to define public management, perhaps none is more important than speaking truth to power. Public management theorists are, quite simply, uncomfortable in abstract theorizing. For most students of public management, theory is a device for producing sound advice for practitioners. In that pursuit, they share a common base with traditional public administration, which for generations celebrated its ability to frame public programs and the means to manage them. John M. Bryson and his colleagues, for example, lay out in part III an analysis of major changes in both the United States and the United Kingdom. They argue that by carefully constructing a system of discussions, managers can build public support for their programs.

But even beyond the need to rebuild public support for governmental programs, government managers have been frantically struggling to reinvent, reengineer, redesign, and otherwise reform their agencies and programs. James R. Thompson and Patricia W. Ingraham examine not only the recent history of such efforts but also the fundamental and inescapable issues that drive them. By building on a case study of reform within the Internal Revenue Service, they carefully identify the different constraints that public sector managers face compared with their private sector counterparts.

Public sector management indeed is very different from private sector management. That has scarcely prevented scores of well-meaning but misdirected reformers from trying unsuccessfully to graft successful private sector reforms onto governmental agencies. In the process, they have learned painfully many of the lessons that the chapters of this book underline. Public management has come to rely on organizational arrangements of remarkable complexity, in both the ambitious goals that government pursues and in the far-flung organizational networks created to seek them. Along the way, the connection between the goals and the tools too often becomes disconnected—so much so, in fact, that any reader of any newspaper could pick up the front page, be confronted with stories of pressing importance, and not recognize the public management problems that lie at the core of each of them.

And in that discontinuity lies perhaps America's most pressing problem of governance. Too often, both citizens and policy makers dream ambitious dreams that can never be completely fulfilled. They sometimes lose faith when disappointments occur. They react by demanding more performance from government and they seek accountability through improved control, yet they search for control in programs whose very structure defies the attempt. To a huge degree, many of the American government's most profound governance problems lie rooted in the discontinuity between the ambition and the system designed to achieve it.

Management matters. It matters because citizens rightly demand high performance for the tax dollars they pay; because disappointing performance signals problems in the administrative system; because the administrative system increasingly stretches past individual government agencies into vast interconnected networks inextricably connected to society's basic institutions; and because in the end, the quality of government's performance and public faith in these institutions are inextricable. The chapters that follow do not— indeed, cannot—answer the questions definitively. But they do explore them in an imaginative way that charts their dimensions in a fresh and hopeful fashion. True to the foundations of public management, they seek solutions for harried managers, the leverage points in a complex system most likely to improve performance, and new ways to improve confidence in the institutions of government.

References

Bardach, Eugene. 1977. *The Implementation Game: What Happens after a Bill Becomes a Law.* Cambridge: MIT Press.

Derthick, Martha. 1972. *New Towns In-Town: Why a Federal Program Failed.* Washington, D.C.: Urban Institute.

Elmore, Richard. 1978. "Organizational Models of Social Program Implementation." *Public Policy* 26:185–228.

Goggin, Malcom L., Ann O'M. Bowman, James P. Lester, and Laurence J. O'Toole Jr. 1990. *Implementation Theory and Practice: Toward a Third Generation.* Glenview, Ill.: Scott, Foresman/Little, Brown.

Goodnow, Frank J. 1900. *Politics and Administration: A Study in Government.* New York: Russell & Russell.

Hargrove, Erwin C. 1975. *The Missing Link: The Study of the Implementation of Social Policy.* Washington, D.C.: Urban Institute.

Heymann, Philip B. 1987. *The Politics of Public Management.* New Haven: Yale University Press.

Ingram, Helen, and Steven Rathgeb Smith, eds. 1993. *Public Policy for Democracy.* Washington, D.C.: Brookings Institution.

Kaufman, Herbert. 1956. "Emerging Doctrines of Public Administration." *American Political Science Review* 50:1059–1073.

Kettl, Donald F. 1988. *Government by Proxy: (Mis?) Managing Federal Programs.* Washington, D.C.: Congressional Quarterly Press.

———. 1993. "Public Administration: The State of the Field," in Ada W. Finifter, ed., *Political Science: The State of the Discipline II,* pp. 407–428. Washington, D.C.: American Political Science Association.

Lynn, Laurence E., Jr. 1994. "Public Management Research: The Triumph of Art Over Science." *Journal of Policy Analysis and Management* 13 (spring): 231–259.

Moore, Mark H., and Darrel W. Stephens. 1991. *Beyond Command and Control: The Strategic Management of Police Departments.* Washington, D.C.: Police Executive Research Forum.

Mosher, Frederick C. 1980. "The Changing Responsibilities and Tactics of the Federal Government." *Public Administration Review* 40:541–548.

Neustadt, Richard. 1960. *Presidential Power: The Politics of Leadership.* New York: John Wiley & Sons.

Osborne, David, and Ted Gaebler. 1992. *Reinventing Government: How the Entrepre-*

neurial Spirit Is Transforming the Public Sector, from Schoolhouse to Statehouse, City Hall to the Pentagon. Reading, Mass.: Addison-Wesley.

Pressman, Jeffrey L., and Aaron B. Wildavsky. 1973. *Implementation: How Great Expectations in Washington Are Dashed in Oakland or, Why It's Amazing That Federal Programs Work At All, This Being a Saga of the Economic Development Administration.* Berkeley: University of California Press.

Salamon, Lester M. 1981. "Rethinking Public Management: Third-Party Government and the Changing Forms of Government Action." *Public Policy* 29:255–275.

Van Horn, Carl E. 1979. *Policy Implementation in the Federal System: National Goals and Local Implementors.* Lexington, Mass.: Lexington Books.

Wilson, Woodrow. 1887. "The Study of Administration." *Political Science Quarterly* 2:197–222.

I.

Governance and
Public Management

I.

Models of Governance for the 1990s

B. Guy Peters

Dwight Waldo (1968) once wrote that public administration has had so many identity crises that in comparison the life of the average adolescent appeared idyllic. Professor Waldo was discussing public administration as an academic discipline, but the contemporary practice of public administration displays much of the same lack of self-confidence. The questions of practice concern the structure of government, management of those structures, and the proper role of public administration in governance. Many of the old certainties about government and the role of the public service are now either totally altered or are subject to severe questioning. At least four of the old chestnuts that have guided our thinking about the public service and its role in the process of governance are no longer as canonical as they once were.[1] The first of these principles is the assumption of an apolitical civil service, and associated with that the politics/administration dichotomy and the concept of the "neutral competence" (Kaufman, 1956) within the civil service. It is increasingly clear that civil servants do have significant, if not necessarily dominant, policy roles in most contemporary governments (Peters, 1992) and that governance in most systems is probably better because they do.

The problem then becomes how to structure government in ways that recognize the reality, and even the desirability, of the enhanced policy roles for civil servants while at the same time preserving the requirements of democratic accountability. This is a difficult balance for the designers of government institutions to achieve, especially given the historical legacy of thinking about the neutrality of the civil service in Anglo-American democracies (Peters, 1993a) and public demands for enhanced accountability (Gruber, 1987;

Day and Klein, 1987). Furthermore, political leaders have come to recognize the growing policy role of civil servants and in response often have acted to try to minimize that role (Ingraham, 1987; Aberbach and Rockman, 1988). The struggle over the competence to make policy therefore is now more obvious to those working within government, as well as to citizens on the outside. The politicization of the role of the civil service, if not the members of the civil service themselves, may make the delicate balance of policy competencies mentioned above all the more difficult to achieve.

The second significant change in government relevant for this discussion is the decline of the assumption of hierarchical and rule-based management within the public service, and the authority of civil servants to implement and enforce law and policy outside the narrow confines of the public service. The neat Weberian model of management does not apply within public organizations to the extent that it once did, and in its place we encounter a variety of alternative sources of organizational power and authority. As one example, the market may be an increasingly significant standard against which to compare the structure and performance of government organizations (Lan and Rosenbloom, 1992; Hood, 1990; Boston, 1991). While the inherent differences between the public and private sectors are crucial to understanding governance (Allison, 1986), even governments on the political left have implemented a number of market-based reforms in their structures and procedures.[2]

An alternative to the market model, as well as to traditional models of bureaucracy, is the "dialectic," or participatory, organization. This model has been discussed by scholars for a number of years, but government organizations are being placed under increasing pressures to accommodate the interests of lower-level employees, as well as clients, in their decision-making processes (Barzelay, 1992). This change in management is at once a manipulative mechanism for increasing efficiency and a genuine moral commitment to participation (Thomas, 1993). Contemporary public organizations may also be expected to negotiate societal compliance with their decisions, and to negotiate compliance with contracts for service delivery, rather than directly implement programs through legal and other authoritative means. The spread of network conceptualizations in the social sciences has been paralleled by increased network practices in governance (Scharpf, 1991; Kenis and Schneider, 1991). Finally, civil servants increasingly may be expected to make their own decisions about what constitutes the public interest, and they must at times make determinations that are diametrically opposed to the stated policies and desires of their nominal political masters.[3] All of the above changes make the role of civil service managers even more difficult than it had been, and also make the role of civil servants within governments all the more ambiguous.

The third change in the assumptions about governance and the public bureaucracy concerns the permanence and stability of the organizations within government. Joining a public organization is sometimes conceptualized like joining a Japanese corporation once was: It is lifetime employment. The permanence of public organizations is frequently overestimated (Peters and Hogwood, 1988), but it has been an important partial truth about government. Increasingly this pattern of permanent organization is being attacked. The growing recognition of the dysfunctions of permanence, as well as the recognition that many of the most significant social and economic problems currently exist in the interstices of existing organizations, has led to some discussion of alternative forms of government organization. The character of the alternative organizational structures remains somewhat inchoate at present, but the discussion has begun. In particular, ideas about task forces, "czars," interdepartmental committees, and similar structures have generated options for thinking about a more flexible pattern of governance.[4]

In addition to impermanent government organizations, the personnel commitments of government also have come to be considered less permanent. Government organizations increasingly expand and contract to meet the variable demand for work, for example, in tax offices. While this style of personnel management has the potential to save governments money, it produces a number of empirical and normative questions for managers and policy makers. This change may produce even greater difficulties for citizens who may have to cope with public employees who lack the commitment to service and other public values that in most instances have characterized the civil service in democratic countries.

The last of the "chestnuts" is that the civil service should be acquiescent and respond almost entirely to the policy directives given to them by their nominal political masters. This goes beyond the question of political neutrality mentioned above. Many of the problems associated with government, and especially with the public bureaucracy, are a function of the controls imposed by political leaders seeking greater control and accountability (Walters, 1992). Government organizations are generally among the most stringently regulated organizations in any society (Wilson, 1989). Therefore, if the skills and entrepreneurship of public employees could be employed more freely, then government is likely to be able to perform more efficiently and effectively (Osborne and Gaebler, 1992). The notion of an activist and entrepreneurial civil service is anathema to many citizens and to many politicians, but it may be one way of achieving the efficiency and effectiveness in government that its critics desire.[5]

Rather than look back to these vestiges of the past, this chapter attempts to be prospective and to examine several alternative paths of development for the public service. I develop the alternative models of the state that appear to be emerging and then look at the implications of these state models for the civil service. Except for the "market model," these alternatives have not been articulated in any comprehensive fashion, and they must be extracted as "ideal types" from academic and practical discussions of governing. Further, there is some similarity of analyses and prescriptions across some of these models, although the meanings attached to them may be quite different (Roth, 1987). They all have the effect, however, of "hollowing" out the state and making it, and particularly the public service, a less significant actor in society (Peters, 1993b). This discussion is based on these developments in governance within the United States, but it also makes a number of comparative allusions. I also make some comparisons across issue areas and argue that some of these approaches to governance are better suited to particular policies than they are to others.

What is perhaps most interesting in the comparative analysis is the extent to which the alternative visions have appeared more strongly and clearly in official documents than they have in scholarly writings in many countries.[6] Although focused on alternatives, I also argue that one possible model is a vigorous restatement of *the status quo ante* and its assertion of unified public service values combined with political neutrality and managerial competence. For many civil servants, and probably for even more politicians, the "old-time religion" may still be the best way to run a government.

Visions of the State and Governance

Few governments in the Western world have remained untouched by the wave of reform that has swept through the public sector over the past several decades. The reforms that have been undertaken in most political systems may have been unprecedented, but they also have tended to be rather piecemeal and unsystematic (Savoie and Peters, 1995). This absence of clear visions and integrated strategies may explain, in part, why the results of the reforms have tended to disappoint so many of their advocates (Caiden, 1990). This chapter explicates several more integrated visions of possible futures for the state bureaucracy. The nature of each image will, in turn, influence the manner in which governance might be practiced under such a regime. If the implications of these alternative visions are more fully explored and understood, and contrasted with the conventional wisdom about governance, then there is some possibility, albeit no guarantee, of more effective planned change in government.

Our concern here with alternative visions does not mean that any one of these schemes is superior to the traditional model of the public service and its role in governance. I tend to think that is not the case, but do think that continuing reform in government is likely, and if that reform is to occur, it is more likely to be effective if it is systematic and integrated. We should also, however, remain cognizant of the internal contradictions of some of these approaches. It may be that, like Simon's discussion (1947) of the "proverbs of administration," thinking about the complexities of the public service, even when guided by a relatively strong set of theoretical assumptions, tends toward situational rather than systematic remedies.

I also look at the implications and prescriptions of each "vision" for several aspects of governing. The first of these is structure: How should the public sector be organized? The second issue is personnel: How should the members of the public sector be recruited, motivated, and managed? Third is the policy process: What should the role of the career public servant be in the policy process and, more generally, how should government seek to influence the private sector? Finally, each vision of governance contains a conception of the public interest and an overall conceptualization of what constitutes "good government."

Market Models

The most familiar, and seemingly the most popular among politicians, of the alternatives to the traditional model of administration is the market model of administration. The development of this model has several intellectual roots. The first is the analysis of the failings of conventional bureaucracies made by scholars such as Niskanen (1971), Tullock (1965), Moe (1984, 1989), Ostrom (1986), and a host of other devotees of public choice (Bendor, 1990). They argue that because of the self-interest of the organization members, especially the "bureau chiefs" at the apex, public bureaucracies tend to expand at an unjustifiable rate and to charge their sponsors (read legislatures) too much for the services produced. The permanence of bureaucrats and their monopoly of information put them at a competitive advantage when dealing with the legislature. The root of any failings in the public sector, as seen from this perspective, is the self-interest of bureaucrats.[7]

The second intellectual root of the market approach to governance in the public sector is generic management and its ally, the "new public management" (Pollitt, 1990; Massey, 1993). This corpus of analysis assumes that management is management no matter where it takes place and that instruments used to organize and motivate personnel are as applicable in the public sector as they are in the private. Thus, rather than deploring the absence of a sense of the public interest as the public choice literature often does, this approach to the public sector assumes the lack of any meaningful difference between the two sectors and then proceeds to build a series of management recommendations on that similarity.

At a relatively high intellectual plane, the recommendations of this variant of managerial thinking can be based on the ubiquity of principal-agent relationships (Perrow, 1986) and the applicability of transaction cost analysis (Williamson, 1975; Calista, 1989) in organizations, whether they are public or private. At a lower level of academic development, generic management is often the accepted doctrine of outsiders who want to export their favorite management techniques—MBO, TQM, and so forth—to the public sector.[8] At both levels of conceptualization the approach has been criticized by insiders (both scholars and practitioners) who consider management in the public sector to be a distinctive form of activity.

Structure. The market approach assumes that one of the principal problems with the traditional structure of the public sector is a reliance on large, monopolistic departments that receive little direction from the environment. The size and complexity of government organizations, combined with their delivery of unpriced goods and services, is seen especially by students of public choice to be the root of a good deal of the (perceived) inefficiency and ineffectiveness of government. These structural difficulties are accentuated by the emphasis on formal rules and authority as the guides for action within traditional public organizations, rather than depending on either market signals (Rose, 1989) or the entrepreneurial spirit of individuals to guide decisions.

The prescriptions arising from the diagnosis of the source of problems in public organizations are rather obvious. One of the central elements of reform is the decentralization of policy and implementation decisions. This decentralization can be accomplished through splitting large departments into smaller "agencies," assigning functions to lower levels of government, or using private or quasi-private organizations to deliver public services. This advice is particularly applicable when the good or service in question is marketable. In the most extreme versions of this approach, government would create multiple, competitive organizations to supply the same goods and services, with the expectation that the same competitive mechanisms presumed to work in the private sector would also work for the public sector.

The advice to divide large departments into smaller segments is less applicable to the United States than it has been to governments in other developed democracies. The U.S. government has not had to go through the exercise of creating a large number of agencies and corporate bodies as in the United Kingdom, New Zealand, and the Netherlands (Davies and Willman, 1992; Boston, 1991). The cabinet departments in the United States have traditionally granted substantial autonomy to their component agencies, and those organizations have been able to act somewhat autonomously. Of course, the admonitions of market proponents about the relationship of these agencies to market forces have not been followed very often, so the agencies were autonomous in a political sense rather than in the sense of operating as quasi-firms supplying goods and services in the marketplace. For the United States, the structural recommendations have been more in the direction of creating private and quasi-private organizations that will provide the services once provided by government. Full privatization has been more significant at the state and local level, but contracting and other instruments for introducing market forces have been significant at the federal level.

This approach has structural recommendations at the microlevel within organizations, as well as for the macrolevel of entire departments. The emphasis on entrepreneurial activity and individual responsibility encourages relatively flat organizations, with little of the layering that traditional public organizations seem to consider essential for control and consistency in decisions. Advocates of the approach presume that the leader of the organization, as well as the "bottom line" resulting from the organization's dealings with the external environment, will be more effective than would a hierarchy in producing appropriate decisions. This observation points to the importance of relatively integrated as opposed to piecemeal reforms. The structural changes without the associated changes in management are unlikely to produce the benefits presumed by the theoretical presuppositions.

Management. The managerial implications of the market model also should be rather obvious. If workers in the public sector are considered to be very much the same as workers in the private sector, then the same managerial techniques should apply. This would mean that some of the cherished traditions of personnel management within government would have to be modified. These changes are already under way in a number of personnel areas, most obviously in the reward of public officials for their participation in government. One of the traditions of public personnel systems has been that individuals in the same grade of the civil service would be paid the same amount. This notion is being replaced with a merit principle that says that people should be paid more in line with what they could earn in the market, and that better performance should be rewarded with better pay, regardless of any differences between workers that may emerge.

The emphasis on differential rewards for differential performance is especially important at the top management level of the small, relatively autonomous agencies created as a part of this approach. In several of the rewards schemes already implemented, managers are hired under contracts that contain specific performance standards. If the agency manager, and his or her organization, achieve those standards, the manager is eligible for full pay and perhaps for bonuses. If the organization does not reach these goals, then the manager may lose pay or be fired. In this model of the public sector, the manager is an entrepreneur who is responsible for what happens in the agency and is rewarded accordingly. Lower echelons within these organizations may be rewarded under similar contractual arrangements based on performance standards. The managerialist reward system in the United States, implemented as a part of the Civil Service Reform Act, is similar to those described above, depending upon bonuses at the upper echelons in exchange for some possibility of being dismissed. Merit pay programs also have been implemented at lower echelons. One of the greatest difficulties with these programs in the United States has been the failure of the political leadership to fund the bonuses and other incentives contained in the plans.

These reward schemes depend on the capacity of government to measure the performance of its employees and their organizations. Many studies have demonstrated the severe difficulties encountered in attempting to perform this seemingly simple managerial task (Metcalfe and Richards, 1990; Boston, 1992). This is especially true if performance is to be measured at the output or impact level, rather than merely at the activity level. This measurement problem means then that either performance contracts and effective managerialism will be limited to the relatively few agencies or other parts of government that provide marketable or otherwise measurable services or it must depend on a number of specious measures of performance. In either case, the capacity to implement this aspect of the market vision of the public sector appears suspect.

It should also be noted that these managerialist trends are not neutral in their effects on the perceived role of the public service. Measuring performance is substantially easier, even if still difficult, for the managerial and service delivery functions of the civil service. It is much more difficult to measure the policy advice functions. As a result of this difficulty, adoption of managerialist performance evaluations and pay schemes tends to have some bias in the direction of a more managerial and less policy-oriented role for civil servants. This may be true both because of changes in the signals coming from evaluators above and decisions on the part of the evaluated that they can maximize their own rewards by playing the managerial game.

Policy Making. The third aspect of the marketized vision of the state is the conceptualization of the manner in which public policy should be made. In particular, the question of the appropriate role of the career public servant in making policy. A fundamental contradiction appears to reside at the heart of the role that this vision assigns to the bureaucracy. On the one hand, the market approach advocates decentralizing bureaucratic functions to multiple, "entrepreneurial" agencies that would be expected to make autonomous decisions. These decisions presumably would be based either on signals received from the market or on the judgment of the entrepreneurial leadership of the organization. Breaking the bonds of bureaucracy is meant to liberate decision making and produce more risk taking and innovative activity.

On the other hand, the practitioners who have advocated this approach have expected compliance by these quasi-autonomous organizations with the policy and ideological directives coming from above. One of the consistent observations about the Reagan, Thatcher, and Mulroney governments and other similar regimes is that they have attempted to impose their own views on the civil service. Bureaucrats were seen as too committed to the growth of their own organizations, as well as perhaps too committed to serving their narrow clientele rather than "the public interest." Attempts at politicization are by no means new, but they have been more overt over the past decade. Politicization has been seen by defenders of the traditional view as the erosion of one of the most important features of merit systems and the civil service. In some ways, however, this is merely a reaffirmation of the traditional view that civil servants should be on "tap" but not on top and that the political leaders are responsible for policy. Whether or not it is a part of the traditional conceptualization, there is some inconsistency, and bureaucrats are responding to perhaps unreasonable demands.

Even if that apparent inconsistency could be resolved, there would be some additional problems for policy making arising out of the application of this approach. One of the most important of these is the problem of coordination and control. The radical decentralization of policy making to more autonomous organizations provides little opportunity for either senior bureaucrats or politicians to coordinate policy. One of the critiques of the traditional approach to governance has been that, de facto, the independence of the bureaucracy thwarted consistency across policies and often produced destructive competition (Allard, 1990). The market approach appears to exalt that competition and potential inconsistency, so long as the actions conform to the political ideals of the political leaders. It is perhaps too much to believe that the leaders of autonomous agencies would be content to be managers of these organizations and would not become concerned with policy.

Finally, at a more conceptual level, there is the problem of the role of the citizen. The market model tends to conceptualize the recipients of government programs, and the public more generally, as *consumers*. This is at once empowering and demeaning for the public. As a beneficial change, this conception provides the citizen with the same expectation of services that he or she has from a private sector firm.[9] Changes such as the Citizen's Charter in Britain and PS 2000 in Canada contain many of these elements of consumerism (Lovell, 1992). On the other hand, the citizen is now little more than a consumer, and his or her role as the holder of rights and a legal status vis-à-vis the state appears somewhat diminished. Government may be more than buying and selling, and probably should be more. If government is reduced to that level, then the citizen is a less significant figure in political theory than he or she is usually thought to be.

The Public Interest. The final component of the market vision of governance is how it defines the public interest. Although it is not clearly articulated as such, this vision does contain such a conceptualization. In the first place, government can be judged on the basis of how cheaply it can deliver public services. To achieve that goal, government may have to undertake its activities in rather unconventional ways, for example, through creating multiple competing service providers, but in the long run the public—in their role as taxpayers if not always as consumers—will be better served by services provided in this manner.

The second component of the market conceptualization of the public interest is that citizens should be considered to be consumers as well as taxpayers. Therefore, the public interest can be served by allowing citizens to exercise their free choices for services in a market. This can be accomplished both by breaking up the monopolies that traditionally have provided most public services and by providing citizens the means of exercising freer choices. The options for citizens exercising their consumer choices can be expanded by providing vouchers for services such as education and perhaps housing (Chubb and Moe, 1990). Those options might also be increased by expanding the information about the service options that is available to citizens.

Summary. As noted, the market vision has been the most popular alternative view of the relationship between state and government. It tends to consider public sector agencies as facing the same managerial and service delivery tasks as would organizations in the private sector, and it sees those agencies as being amenable to the same techniques for performing those tasks. It assumes that if the rule-based authority structure usually associated with bureaucracy is removed or deemphasized, then the creative and administrative talent of individuals working within the public sector will flower. Although usually associated with the political right, some devotees of this approach consider that its successful implementation would result in a more effective and efficient public sector, whether delivering defense or social services.

The Participatory State

A second alternative view of the state is almost the antithesis of the market approach in terms of the political ideologies of most of its advocates, but in some instances the analysis and recommendations appear remarkably similar. I have called this approach the "participatory state," but it has been discussed with a number of different names. An alternative characterization might be the "empowerment state" in which groups (presumably) excluded under more hierarchical models are permitted greater organizational involvement (Kernaghan, 1992). Like the market approach, this approach considers the hierarchical, rule-based organizations usually encountered in the public sector to be a severe impediment to effective management and governance. However, rather than concentrating attention on the upper echelons of leadership in organizations who are the proto-entrepreneurs within government, this approach concentrates on the lower echelons of workers, as well as on the clients of the organizations and even on the citizenry as a whole.

The fundamental assumption in this approach is that there is a great deal of energy and talent being underutilized at the lower echelons of hierarchies, and that the workers and clients closest to the actual production of goods and services in the public sector have the greatest amount of information about the programs. It is assumed that if those ideas and talents are harnessed, government will work better. The general prescription, therefore, is greater participation and involvement on the part of those groups within government that are commonly excluded from decision making. Somewhat predictably, the advocates of this approach tend to come more from the political left, although some from the right, interested in empowerment and self-management by clients, also advocate versions of this approach.[10]

The intellectual roots of this approach are also somewhat diverse. On the one hand, there is a body of literature that argues that involvement and participation is the best way to motivate individual employees, even if it is somewhat manipulative. Another strand of literature argues that the lower echelons of public organizations are central to the effective functioning of those organizations and that, as a simple reality, the role of "street-level bureaucrats" needs to be recognized. At a higher intellectual level, there are various strands of literature on "discursive democracy" that argue for enhanced participation by clients and workers in the identification and clarification of problems within organizations.

Structure. The structural implications of this approach are somewhat less clear than are those for the public choice approach. For this approach, process appears more important than the structures within which the processes take place. At one level, the formal patterns of organization may be irrelevant if there are other opportunities for the workers and clients to participate in decisions. There are, however, structural reforms that may make their participation easier; therefore, this approach is not entirely silent on the issue of the design of public organizations. In considering both participation and decision making, we need to note the extent to which enhanced participation by one group—either lower echelon employees or clients—may minimize the impact of the other.

The most obvious implication for structure is that, very much like the public choice approach, public organizations would be much "flatter" and have fewer tiers between the top and bottom of an organization. If the lower echelons are perceived as having a great deal to offer in decision making, and if they are highly motivated to provide good services, then hierarchical levels of control are merely impediments to good performance in an organization. The alternative implication, however, is that if clients and lower echelon employees are to be given substantial involvement in making decisions, there may be a need for greater control from above to ensure that public laws and financial restraints are adhered to faithfully.

Another structural implication of the participatory approach to governing is that there may need to be a variety of innovative structures to channel participation. This is especially true for participation by clients, but it may also be true for lower-level employees who have not been as involved in decision making as is envisioned in this approach. As governments have come to implement programs of participation for both clients and workers, a variety of councils, advisory groups, and the like have come into being. It is interesting that much of this definition of the rights of participation, albeit defined as citizenship rights, in practice becomes the rights of consumers. This again brings this approach closer to the market approach than might be expected from the political ideologies of their typical adherents.

Management. The participatory approach to governance contains somewhat more obvious implications for management within the public sector than it has for structure. The basic premise is that government organizations will function better if the lower levels of the organizations, and perhaps the clients of the organization, are included more directly in managerial decisions. At one level, this involvement might be considered to be manipulative, with top management exchanging a little bit of participation for greater productivity and loyalty from workers. While early "human relations" management had some of this manipulative character, the more contemporary advocates of participation have been more ideological and believe in the human as well as the organizational importance of participation. Even so, there can be a manipulative element in thinking that overall societal governance can be enhanced through permitting and encouraging greater social "discourse" in the process of making decisions.

Perhaps the most important feature of the participative approach is its attempt to involve societal interests in governance more explicitly. We should remember, however, that these managerial ideologies are by no means the first theoretical justifications of enhanced participation. The neocorporatist and corporate pluralist literature represents another strong strand of thinking about how to gain the advantages of the knowledge, and quiescence, of social groups (Olsen, 1986). The difference may be that this level of legitimate involvement of social interests is now becoming popular in countries with an Anglo-American political cultural legacy as well as in countries with a more Continental legacy.[11] Thus, while the market model above may denigrate the role of the citizen, this model appears to enhance the role of the citizen and to attempt to induce democratic participation in means other than voting.

Policy Making. The implications of the participatory vision of governance for policy making are for a "bottom up" versus "top down" version of the policy process.[12] That is, this vision does not assume that governments can govern best by making decisions in a centralized fashion and then implementing them through laws and relatively rigid hierarchies. Rather, the vision is one of decentralized decision making. This is true both in the sense of the lower echelons of organizations having substantial, if not determinate, impact on policy decisions and in the sense of the organizations themselves having a great deal of control over the decisions that determine their own fates. The assumption is also that decisions made in this manner will be objectively better, given the presumed higher levels of information possessed by these lower levels of the organization. In this emphasis on decentralization, the participative approach shares a good deal with the theorists, if not always the practitioners, of the public choice approach.

Given this concern with the involvement of lower-echelon workers, the participative approach is almost silent on the involvement of top-echelon bureaucrats—those usually referred to as at the "decision-making" level—in policy selections. One possible implication would be that political leaders, having somewhat greater involvement with the public, might be more suitable conduits for participatory input into decisions. On the other hand, if communications within organizations is even moderately efficient, the lower echelons should be able to send messages to the top that would then have an influence on policy. In either case, the design question is how can those usually excluded from decisions have an impact on those decisions. There is no simple answer to this problem.

The other perspective that the participatory model may have on policy making is the realistic statement that the lower echelons of the bureaucracy do have a major impact on policy in almost any political system (Lipsky, 1980; Adler and Asquith, 1981). Most decisions that governments make are not made by their political leadership, or even by the upper echelons of the civil service. Rather, they are made by the lower echelons—the street-level bureaucrats— who must make numerous decisions about particular cases every day. Not only are those decisions crucial for the actual determinations of a citizen's claim against the state for services, they are also crucial for popular perceptions of government. For most people, government is the policeman, or the tax collector, or the safety inspector, and the interactions between citizen and the representative of the state may shape the public's ideas about what government does and what it thinks about its citizens.[13] Thus, a participatory emphasis in governance may make government more popular with clients, if not necessarily more efficient in delivering services.

The Public Interest. The participatory state assumes that the public interest can be served by allowing employees and citizens the maximum involvement possible in decisions. This involvement can occur in at least three ways. First, for employees, it can occur through their enhanced capacity to make independent decisions and to have influence over the policy directions taken by their organizations. This concept of governance is sometimes considered to confer power on "street-level" bureaucrats and to make policy making a "bottom up" as opposed to "top down" process (Peters, 1993b). This is assumed to make the decisions of government objectively better, given that they will reflect the knowledge of the portions of the organization most closely in touch with the environment.

The second meaning of participation in this context is a political one. This version of the participatory state would have its decisions made through a "dialogical" process permitting citizens to exert a substantial influence over policy (Linder and Peters, 1995). Thus, the public interest will emerge through the right of citizens to say what they want and to bargain directly with other citizens with different views of appropriate public policy. This view would stand in rather sharp contrast to the "decisional" approach more common in traditional representative and bureaucratic government.

The final meaning of the public interest within the participatory state is one that is dependent on citizens themselves being involved in making some choices about policy. In this way, the participatory state is similar to the market state, given that both would prescribe allowing citizens to make more consumer choices and to give them more direct control over the programs. The manner in which these consumer choices would be exercised in the participatory state would be more political. Rather than voting in the marketplace with dollars, citizens would vote through some sort of political process. This participation might be in referenda on policy, in the style of Ross Perot, or it may be in local structures, such as school management committees in Chicago, that foster parental involvement. The fundamental point is that better decisions (procedurally if not necessarily substantively) are made through participation rather than through technocracy.

Summary. The participatory model is not as well articulated as is the public choice model. Still, it is possible to extract some of the implications of this "vision" for the role of the civil service in governing society, as well as for the nature of governance itself. This vision of governance is ideologically very different from that of public choice, as well as in its assumptions about human behavior within organizations. Even with those differences, the prescriptions for design in the two approaches are not dissimilar. In particular, the principal prescription is for decentralization and some transfer of power to the lower echelons of organizations as well as to the clients of the organizations. Further, this model recognizes the role of the bureaucracy in making public policy, although it considers this involvement more positively than does the public choice approach.

Although many of the prescriptions of the participatory approach for governance are similar to those of the market model, the meanings attached to those institutional designs for governance are markedly different. Rather than a means of creating competition among service providers so that a market can function effectively, decentralization in the participatory model is intended primarily to channel policy control to a different set of bureaucrats, or to the clients themselves. This could be thought of as the very type of agency capture that the public choice model seeks to avert (Macey, 1992). Likewise, the involvement of lower-level bureaucrats in decisions is considered positively. The alternative appears to be domination by the upper-level bureaucrats rather than by political leaders. In this model both of those elites are considered equally antithetical to the interests of clients, rather than as competitors for power.

Flexible Government

A third alternative to the traditional model of government organization is the "flexible government" model. As noted above, joining a government organization often has been conceptualized as accepting lifetime employment, assuming that the individual wants to remain in government. Likewise, forming an organization is usually thought to be creating a permanent entity, no matter how transient the reasons for the structure may appear (Kaufman, 1976). This permanence frequently is overstated, but the notion tends to guide thinking about the formation and management of the public sector.

The dysfunctions of permanence, both of employment by individuals and of organizations, are well known, and governments have begun to address them. The "flexible state" is probably the least clearly articulated of the four approaches to administration, but these ideas and practices appear to be emerging in a number of governments. Permanence has come to be considered as the source of excessive conservatism of policies and as the source of commitments to an organization more than to the policies being administered by the organization; in other words, organizations embody political interests.[14] Individuals who work for an organization may be more concerned with keeping their jobs and keeping the organization healthy in budgetary terms than in doing anything in particular, Further, a commitment to permanence tends to institutionalize prevailing conceptions of policy, and even of what the real policy problems are. In all, despite some obvious attractions, permanent government structures can present significant problems for effective and efficient governance.

In addition to the recognition of the dysfunctions of permanence, the changing nature of governance problems and the labor market have tended to produce movement away from permanence. First, an increasing number of significant problems confronted by government fall between the stools of the existing organizations. For example, although there is a Drug Enforcement Agency, a large number of other agencies—the Coast Guard, Department of Defense, the Customs Bureau, the FBI, and others—also are involved in the "War on Drugs." This widened involvement of agencies in policies has already created a fourth or fifth or nth branch of government that attempts to coordinate and control the existing organizations and policies.[15] I argue that the "policy space" and the organizational space for governments is already well populated (Hogwood and Peters, 1983) and any new initiatives are likely to confront existing organizations.

The other pressure creating impermanence in government organizations is the fundamental transformation of the labor market in most industrialized societies, with much less full-time and permanent employment and an increasing level of part-time and temporary employment. Government has already begun to adjust to these broader economic changes and has found part-time employment to be a method of saving money and enhancing organizational flexibility. Thus, even when there is a permanent organization per se, the members of that organization may be transients. This is a shift from the tradition of permanent government employment, and it has important managerial and policy implications.

Structure. The fundamental advice that this approach offers is for alternative structural arrangements within government. Rather than relying exclusively on the traditional forms of departments, agencies, and bureaus that perceive themselves to have a virtually permanent claim on a particular policy space, this approach would seek some flexibility and frequent termination of existing organizations.[16] This flexibility would be used to prevent the ossification that can afflict permanent organizations. Further, it might be expected to allow government to respond more rapidly to changing social and economic conditions. There might be, for example, less resistance to creating organizations intended to respond to novel circumstances if there were some assurance that these organizations would be terminated when their task was completed. Further, the ability to create and then destroy organizations might appeal to fiscal conservatives and critics like Niskanen who argue that permanence and bureaucratic monopolies create excessive costs as well as policy rigidities. In fact, in many ways, the organizational universe emerging from this approach would be similar to the "agencies" being created by advocates of the market approach, with the added factor that these organizations would be subject to rapid change.

As well as being structurally impermanent, these organizations might not be populated to a large degree by full-time employees who (at least in the United States) would spend most or all of their careers within the same organization. This change in career patterns is already occurring in government. For example, the proportion of total work hours put in by temporary federal employees has been gradually creeping up since the 1960s, and appears likely to continue to increase. The predictions of almost all studies of the labor market is that the trend toward temporary employment will continue in almost all segments of the economy. This trend may be applauded by fiscal conservatives who want to save money in the public sector, but it may damage other conservative values about the accountability of the civil service and its stability as a source of advice and values in an otherwise rapidly changing government.

Management. The manifest managerial implications of the temporary state are rather clear, while the latent implications are perhaps more interesting and more important. At the manifest level, this approach stresses the ability of managers to adjust their workforce requirements to match demands. As noted, this can be used as a means of saving a good deal of money for government, as well as mitigating some of the public perceptions of waste and empire-building by government organizations. Further, this approach may permit governments to respond more quickly and effectively to a crisis or to rapidly increasing demands for service, although the potential upside benefits tend to be discussed less than the cost-cutting benefits.

The latent implications of this approach include some diminution of the commitment of employees to their employers and, with that, a potential threat to the values and ethos of the public service. It now may appear somewhat idealistic to discuss the commitment of civil servants to their organizations and to the principle of public service. On the other hand, there is some evidence that civil servants have been motivated by these values and that many of them would like to continue to be so motivated. Making more public sector jobs temporary and part-time will almost certainly diminish the commitment that employees feel to their jobs and thus tend to minimize employees' motivations for excellent performance on the job. To some extent, this approach is the antithesis of the participatory state in that temporary employees would be unlikely to be interested in any real involvement with the organization. Further, their temporary status may make all of the civil service values of probity, accountability, and responsibility all the more difficult to enforce. In short, we could argue that a good deal may be sacrificed to gain some reductions in expenditures.

Policy Making. As noted above, this is the least developed of the approaches to the role of the public service in governance. In particular, the "temporary state" approach to questions of governance has little to say directly about the role of the public service in making public policy. We can, however, explore the logical implications of this approach to governing for an active policy role for the civil service. These implications appear to be potentially contradictory, with some pointing toward an enhanced role for the civil service and others seeming to reaffirm the older wisdom of a political dominance of the elected classes over policy, with civil servants being in a subordinate position.

On the one hand, by placing so much emphasis on the fragility of organizations in government, the traditional sources of organizational power arising from a common culture and commitment to the existing policies would be diminished. The old bureaucratic structures had both the advantage and disadvantage of stable personnel and with them stable policies. On the one hand, the permanent personnel provided a great deal of direction to policy and provided an experiential knowledge base for the construction of any new policy initiatives. On the other hand, this stability has been a barrier to innovations that would extend beyond the conventional wisdom about what is "feasible" in the policy area (Majone, 1989, pp. 69–94). This absence of a mortmain from the past may permit political leaders to have a stronger role in altering policies than they might otherwise have. A group of radical reformers, such as the Thatcherites or Reaganauts, would be pleased to have less of an organizational inheritance to counteract.

All the pressures from this approach do not, however, make the life of political leaders easier. By removing the anchor of large, stable organizations beneath them, the civil service elite may be able to develop their own policy ideas more autonomously. To some extent, the conception of the Senior Executive Service in the United States was that of a free-floating resource that could be used in a variety of managerial and policy advice situations. Without large, permanent organizations to encumber them in the exercise of their own conceptions of good policy, these senior officials may be able to be creative forces in policy development.

The Public Interest. As this is the least clearly articulated of the four alternative models of governance, it also has the least clearly articulated concept of the public interest. One obvious component of the idea of the public interest in this model is that lower costs for government are beneficial. If having more temporary employees will reduce costs, then the public as a whole will benefit, even if particular clients of government services are potentially disadvantaged by less knowledgeable and committed public sector employees.

A second implicit concept of the public interest is that the public will be better off with a more innovative and less ossified government. One standard complaint about government is that the organizations within government that represent interests outside the public sector fight for their turf and preserve themselves whether or not there is any real justification for their continued existence. This is a somewhat exaggerated version of the reality (Peters and Hogwood, 1988) of the permanence of government organizations, but there is still some truth in it. If change could be made as much a part of life in government as is permanence, then there will be some chance of greater creativity and, perhaps again, some opportunities for saving the public money.

Deregulating Government

The final option for changing government is to unleash the potential power and creativity of government by "deregulating government" (Wilson, 1989; Bryner, 1987). More recently this has come to be known as "reinventing government" (Osborne and Gaebler, 1992). This is almost the complete antithesis of the politics of the 1980s, which sought to reduce the activity of government and severely control those actions that remained. The politicians of the 1980s appeared to have a special dislike and distrust of the public bureaucracy, and they sought to curtail its powers over policy. The assumption of deregulating government is that if some of the constraints on action were eliminated, government could perform its current functions more efficiently, and it might be able to undertake new and creative activities to improve the collective welfare of the society. However, like the critics of government in the 1980s, there is a distrust and dislike of bureaucracy in the sense of large organizations encumbered by rules and arcane procedures.

Structure. The structural implications of this model are rather sparse. Although its advocates do not say so directly, it would appear that structures are much less important than are the procedures used to control public organizations and the people within them. It may also be that in its concerns about the ability of governments to act effectively, traditional hierarchical management is less an anathema than in other "modern" conceptions of organizations. The premise that bureaucratic structures are almost inherently undesirable is now almost the conventional wisdom, but this model argues that they are acceptable, and even desirable, in certain situations. Again, if these organizations are imbued with the right values and an entrepreneurial spirit, structure may not matter too much.

Another possible structural implication of this model is that the control agencies that political leaders have developed at the center of government are less desirable than those leaders have assumed. The reduction of centralized control would permit the individual organizations to develop and implement more of their own values than would be true when central agencies (Campbell and Szablowski, 1979) are in control. The further implications, therefore, are not too dissimilar from those coming from the market model. If bureaucratic organizations are not all bad, then the active, entrepreneurial agencies implied by the market model, for example, "Next Steps" in Britain, might be even better. The fundamental point is to get people in government to utilize their skills and energy to achieve goals.

Management. The managerial implications of this model could go in two opposite directions, in large part because management does not appear to be one of its central concerns. As noted above, this approach to governance seems to argue that traditional forms of structure and management may not be as bad as some contemporary critics would argue. This being the case, this model would tend to find hierarchical management acceptable and even desirable. That style of management would permit policy entrepreneurs, who presumably would be positioned at the top of the hierarchies, to generate action throughout the organization. This would, in turn, depend to some degree on a common organizational culture within the organization that supported the policy direction being advocated from above.

The alternative managerial implication would be for something very similar to that advocated in the participatory state model. If the creative powers of government are to be unleashed, then it may be done best by involving all levels of the organizations. Thus, if government wants to be effective and creative, it will need the commitment of all of its available resources, most importantly its employees. Like the participatory model, this approach is in contrast to the "flexible state" model, which does not assign any real importance to the involvement of employees of government.

Policy Making. The implications for policy making are somewhat clearer than are the other implications of this model. The traditional view of policy making in government is that it was the prerogative of political leaders. The "deregulating government" model would appear to assign a somewhat stronger role for the bureaucracy in making policy. The logic is that these organizations tend to be major repositories of ideas and expertise and hence should be allowed to make more decisions. To the extent that this also implies that the lower echelons of the organization, because of their expertise and close contacts with the environment, should have somewhat more influence, then this model has implications similar to those of the participatory state model.

This characterization of the deregulating government model should not be taken to mean that policy-making powers should be abrogated by political institutions in favor of the public bureaucracy. Rather, it should be taken to mean that policy making is likely to be better substantively—if not in terms of democratic theory—if there is a more active role for the bureaucracy. The policy stances adopted by this more involved bureaucracy are likely to be more interventionist than those of the more conservative governments of the past decade. Thus, in this case the choice of a model of governance will clearly have some implications for substantive policy choices. Further, this approach assumes that when discretion is exercised it will be in the direction of the public interest, rather than in the more personal direction assumed by advocates of the market model.

The Public Interest. The deregulatory model of governance assumes that the interest of the public can be served through a more activist, and a seemingly less accountable, government. The latter characterization concerning accountability is perhaps unfortunate, given that there is more of a difference about the form of accountability than about the need for that all-important feature in any democratic government. The (contradictory) assumptions of most of the attempts to control government through the use of structural and procedural devices is that without the use of such devices the public bureaucracy will either behave abusively, or it will do next to nothing. The deregulatory model, on the other hand, assumes that the civil service is composed largely of dedicated and talented individuals who want to do as good as possible a job in serving the public. This is in many ways simply a restatement of the familiar Friedrich/Finer debate over accountability.

As well as making assumptions about the role of civil servants in governance, this model makes a clear statement about the role of government in society. This role is quite different from that assigned to government by most politicians during the 1980s. The assumption is that the public interest would be better served by a more active and interventionist public sector, and that collective action is part of the solution and not part of the problem for contemporary societies. This is not a knee-jerk reaction in favor of "big government," but rather it appears to be a recognition that many of the most important problems facing society can only be solved collectively, and that this in turn implies a major role for the public bureaucracy.

Choosing among the Models

To this point we have laid out a number of alternative views of what the future may hold for public administration. To some extent, that future will be characterized by the concurrent existence of all the models, although in differing degrees of intensity. If each of these models has some utility, how can the careful scholar or practitioner choose among them? What organizational or policy characteristics may be most suitable for the use of one or the other? Contingency models have largely earned a bad name in public administration (Pitt and Smith, 1981), but this is one case in which systematic choices among the contending models of organizing may be necessary and perhaps even possible.

The market model would be most applicable for policy areas in which the goods provided are inherently marketable and have relatively few positive or negative externalities. The now-common practice of privatization of public services such as airlines, energy, and telecommunications would appear to correspond to that market logic. Some programs in which the market model has been advocated widely (e.g., education) may not in fact be appropriate venues for it, given the important social consequences of that policy area. Likewise, the market model may be most applicable in societies with a strong market ethos, such as the United States, as opposed to those that have stronger commitments to the *étatiste* tradition, such as France.

The participatory model may be most applicable in two types of situations. One would be the case in which there are large numbers of employees who have regular contacts with clients or who have other forms of frequent interaction with the relevant environment of the organization. These employees can then provide important intelligence concerning the success of programs in reaching their presumed targets and about how they are affecting their clients. The other, and to some extent opposite, type of organization would be one with a large number of professional employees who would be expected to bring substantial expertise to their jobs. Most organizations of the latter type are already managed very collegially, but that pattern might be reinforced. In both of these cases, the subject matter of the organization might best be one that does not necessitate a great deal of uniformity in order to be thought equitable by clients.

Flexible patterns of management are perhaps best suited to situations in which the policy questions and the means of ameliorating any perceived problems are poorly defined. In such a situation, government may not want to "lock in" a policy pattern prematurely but would be better advised to maintain a very flexible stance. Policy making in these situations may be more a case of managing networks than managing in a traditional, hierarchical manner. Also, flexibility may be suitable for policy areas requiring a great deal of coordination among organizations, especially when those organizations may have only a passing involvement with the issue.

Finally, almost any government program may benefit from being deregulated. Still, there may be some important differences in the applicability of the idea. First, central government services such as purchasing and personnel may benefit the most, although there are still important public values that may require some internal regulation. This is especially true for personnel functions and issues of representativeness and equity. Second, programs that involve large-scale interactions with the private sector may require some deregulation in order to interact effectively with the more entrepreneurial actors there. Finally, public programs that deal with the basic rights of citizens, or even those of noncitizens (immigrants), should not be deregulated to the extent that others are.

The above are only a few thoughts about the differential applicability of these models. A more detailed analysis, as well as some trial-and-error learning, may be required before we can advise government leaders with any certainty about how they should attempt to institutionalize reforms. That is, however, a very important consideration given the prevalence of administrative reforms and reorganizations, and the absence of clear conceptual guidance that all too often characterizes those changes in the public sector.

Conclusion: Can We Go Home Again?

We have now looked at several alternative movements away from the traditional model of administration in the public sector. Some of these models are already being implemented, while others are only in the nascent stages. In each case, the implicit or explicit comparison is made with the traditional model of administration, with its clear separation of roles between administration and politics, a hierarchical management style and structure, (largely) permanent organizations, and career civil servants.

The obvious question is whether those in government, even if they wanted to, could ever return to the comfortable system that is now past. To some degree, the emphasis on management, political reliability of the civil service, the empowerment of staff and clients, and flexibility all press toward an alteration of the tacit bargain that has existed among the participants in governance. Both sides can gain some advantages from these changes, although by far the advantages appear to run in the direction of politicians and only secondarily to the previously disadvantaged tiers within organizations. Similarly, the principal disadvantages appear to accrue to the senior levels of the civil service. Politically, then, returning to the *status quo ante* may be impossible.

If there is to be a return to the bureaucratic Garden of Eden, then there will need to be a strong restatement of the desirability of such a move. Given that the public service is not the most popular element of government in almost any polity, there is probably not a natural constituency for such a move. Therefore there will have to be political activity to produce the movement. This can be justified in part through the traditional values of neutrality and competence in the civil service, and the need to stress values such as the public service rather than thinking of government as providing services like any other "business." An end to Republican hegemony in the United States, and the waning of market ideology in a number of other Western countries,[17] may initiate public discourse on ideas of public service in a way not possible recently.

The governance role of public administration is perhaps the most significant aspect of any reassertion of the role of the public service. Again, we must contrast the role of the civil service as expressed through the "ideology" of the traditional model of governance versus the reality of its role in the model as it evolved in practice. The existence of a powerful and entrenched civil service created in essence the conditions for a strong policy role for that bureaucracy in governance. Although the market model in particular would appear to give somewhat enhanced power to the civil service, any redistribution of power would be in the role of manager rather than policy makers and advisers. Indeed, the practice of the market model has been to attempt to centralize power in the political leadership and to limit the autonomy of the presumably entrepreneurial actors created by the reforms.

The traditional model of the public service and its role in government is, however, more than merely a rationalization for civil servants to make policy. It is also a statement of basic values about matters such as accountability and responsibility, on which the alternatives, and the market model in particular, have little to say. The concept of a permanent and professional civil service providing policy advice as well as management is seen by the advocates of the traditional model as almost a sine qua non for good government. It is seen as embodying the means of providing citizens (and their politicians) the means of receiving both the best advice and the best service. While to critics the permanence of the bureaucracy is a severe problem, to its advocates it is the source of stability and reliability. It is also seen as the best means of ensuring that government can be held accountable for its actions.

We have been, to this point, discussing these four models as distinct alternatives for organizing the entire public sector. Another way to consider this set of options is to think of the possible desirable matches between particular governmental tasks and the alternative forms of organizing (Wilson, 1989). It may well be that for the provision of certain marketable services the market model is adequate and desirable, while that same model would be totally inappropriate for many social services, education being one commonly discussed exception. Likewise, the participatory model would be well suited for urban planning or for environmental issues, but would produce difficulties for many criminal justice programs. The temporary model probably would suit complex issues such as drugs as well as transient concerns such as disaster relief. While attempts at full-blown contingency theories for public administration appear to have generated relatively little benefit, we should still think about ways of making the punishment fit the crime.

Again, the purpose of this chapter is not so much to force choices among the alternative visions of governance as to make more evident the choices available to governments. To the extent that these models have been implemented in the real world (particularly the market model), they have been put forward for ideological reasons as much as from any thorough consideration of their relative merits. Each of the alternatives does have its merits, but each also may impose some costs on society and on the actors in government. Any choice of paradigms for government and administration is unlikely to be Pareto optimal, but we should be clear about what we receive and what we sacrifice when we make these judgments about governance.

Notes

1. For a discussion of the (no longer?) "conventional wisdom," see Walsh and Stewart (1992).

2. The most radical use of the variety of market-based reforms available to government was implemented by the Labour government of New Zealand.

3. This autonomous role of civil servants is not unfamiliar in the United States, but it is extremely unusual and threatening in Westminster systems. The Ponting affair in Britain and the Al-Mashat case in Canada are important examples of the importance of this change in the norms of governing in Westminster governments (Chapman, 1993; Sutherland, 1992).

4. This flexible pattern is already used widely in several European systems. See, for example, Fournier (1987) and his discussion of coordination within the French government.

5. The real question is whether the only way to achieve the necessary degree of entrepreneurship in government is to promote rather simplistic campaigns to "reinvent" the public sector.

6. Obvious examples are statements of the public choice approach in New Zealand and of the participatory model in Canada.

7. This self-interest of bureaucrats does not differentiate them from other individuals. The problem is in making the assumption that members of the public service will necessarily act in the public interest.

8. Outsiders usually want to export these techniques at a profit.

9. Those of us who deal regularly with airlines and Blue Cross-Blue Shield may consider it threatening to be treated like the customer of a private concern.

10. Jack Kemp as secretary of Housing and Urban Development in the United States is one prime example.

11. Examples would be negotiated rule making in the United States and stakeholder involvement in rewriting transportation regulations in Canada.

12. This language is usually reserved for the implementation process, but it can also be applied to the process more generally. See Peters (1993b).

13. There is some evidence, however, that although most citizens' interactions with representatives of government are positive, popular perceptions of government as an institution remain negative.

14. Interestingly, some of the public choice literature has been seeking means of designing organizations that will be conservative and will preserve the same policies over time (McCubbins, Noll, and Weingast, 1989).

15. The Gore Commission has recommended merging DEA, BATF, and the FBI to provide a more integrated version of federal law enforcement.

16. State and local governments have already made more moves in this direction with "sunset laws" and other devices that force relatively frequent reconsideration of the existence of various organizations.

17. For example, the Major government is substantially less ideological than the Thatcher government before it, the Tories may soon lose in Canada, and the right-leaning Schluter government has lost office in Denmark.

References

Aberbach, J. D., and B. A. Rockman. 1988. "Mandates or Mandarins? Control and Discretion in the Modern Administrative State." *Public Administration Review* 48:607–612.

Adler, M., and S. Asquith. 1981. *Discretion and Power.* London: Heinemann.

Allard, C. K. 1990. *Command, Control, and the Common Defense.* New Haven: Yale University Press.

Allison, G. T. 1986. "Public and Private Management: Are They Fundamentally Alike in All Unimportant Respects?" in F. S. Lane, ed., *Current Issues in Public Administration,* 3d ed. New York: St. Martin's.

Barzelay, M. 1992. *Breaking through Bureaucracy.* Berkeley: University of California Press.

Bendor, J. 1990. "Formal Models of Bureaucracy: A Review," in N. Lynn and A. Wildavsky, eds., *Public Administration: The State of the Discipline.* Chatham, N.J.: Chatham House.

Boston, J. 1991. "The Theoretical Underpinnings of State Restructuring in New Zealand," in J. Boston et al., eds., *Reshaping the State.* Auckland: Oxford University Press.

———. 1992. "Assessing the Performance of Departmental Chief Executives: Perspectives from New Zealand." *Public Administration* 70:405–428.

Bryner, G. C. 1987. *Bureaucratic Discretion.* New York: Pergamon.

Caiden, G. 1990. *Administrative Reform Comes of Age.* Berlin: Aldine de Gruyter.

Calista, D. J. 1989. "A Transaction-Cost Analysis of Implementation," in D. Palumbo and D. J. Calista, eds., *Implementation Theory.* Lexington, Mass.: Lexington Books.

Campbell, C., and G. Szablowski. 1979. *The Superbureaucrats: Structure and Behaviour in Central Agencies.* Toronto: Macmillan of Canada.

Chapman, R. A. 1993. "Reasons of State and the Public Interest: A British Variant of the Problem of Dirty Hands," in Chapman, ed., *Ethics in Public Service.* Edinburgh: University of Edinburgh Press.

Chubb, J. E., and T. Moe. 1990. *Politics, Markets, and America's Schools.* Washington, D.C.: Brookings Institution.

Davies, A., and J. Willman. 1992. *What Next? Agencies, Departments, and the Civil Service.* London: Institute for Public Policy Research.

Day, P., and R. Klein. 1987. *Accountabilities.* London: Tavistock.

Fournier, J. 1987. *La Travail gouvernmentale.* Paris: Presses Universitaires Françaises.

Gruber, J. 1987. *Controlling Bureaucracies: Dilemmas in Democratic Governance.* Berkeley: University of California Press.

Hogwood, B. W., and B. G. Peters. 1983. *Policy Dynamics.* Brighton: Harvester.

Hood, C. 1990. "De-Sir Humphreying the Westminster Model of Bureaucracy." *Governance* 3:205–214.

Ingraham, P. W. 1987. "Building Bridges or Burning Them? The President, the Appointees, and the Bureaucracy." *Public Administration Review* 47:211–223.

Kaufman, H. 1956. "Emerging Doctrines of Public Administration." *American Political Science Review* 50:1059–1073.

———. 1976. *Are Government Organizations Immortal?* Washington, DC: Brookings Institution.

Kenis, P., and V. Schneider. 1991. "Policy Networks and Policy Analysis: Scrutinizing a New Analytical Toolbox," in B. Marin and R. Mayntz, eds., *Policy Networks: Empirical Evidence and Theoretical Considerations.* Boulder, Colo.: Westview.

Kernaghan, K. 1992. "Empowerment and Public Administration: Revolutionary Advance or Passing Fancy?" *Canadian Public Administration* 35:194–214.

Lan, Z., and D. H. Rosenbloom. 1992. "Public Administration in Transition?" *Public Administration Review* 52:535–537.

Linder, S. H., and B. G. Peters. 1995. "A Design Perspective on the Structure of Public Organizations," in David Weimer, ed., *The Structure of Public Institutions.* Dordrecht: Kluwer.

Lipsky, M. 1980. *Street-Level Bureaucracy.* New York: Russell Sage Foundation.

Lovell, R. 1992. "The Citizen's Charter: The Cultural Challenge." *Public Administration* 70:395–404.

Macey, J. R. 1992. "Organizational Design and Political Control of Regulatory Agencies." *Journal of Law, Economics, and Organization* 8:93–110.

Majone, G. 1989. *Evidence, Argument, and Persuasion in the Policy Process.* New Haven: Yale University Press.

Massey, A. 1993. *Managing the Public Sector.* Aldershot: Edward Elgar.

McCubbins, M. D., R. G. Noll, and B. R. Weingast. 1989. "Structure and Process, Politics and Policy; Administrative Arrangements and the Political Control of Agencies." *Virginia Law Review* 75:431–482.

Metcalfe, L., and S. Richards. 1990. *Improving Public Management,* 2d ed. London: Sage.

Moe, T. 1984. "The New Economics of Organizations." *American Journal of Political Science* 28:739–777.

———. 1989. "The Politics of Bureaucratic Structure," in J. E. Chubb and P. E. Peterson, *Can the Government Govern?* Washington, D.C.: Brookings Institution.

Niskanen, W. 1971. *Bureaucracy and Representative Government.* Chicago: Aldine/Atherton.

Olsen, J. P. 1986. *Organized Democracy.* Oslo: Universitetsforlaget.

Osborne, D., and T. Gaebler. 1992. *Reinventing Government.* Reading, Mass.: Addison-Wesley.

Ostrom, E. 1986. "An Agenda for the Study of Institutions." *Public Choice* 48:3–25.

Perrow, C. 1986. "Economic Theories of Organization." *Theory and Society* 15:11–45.

Peters, B. G. 1992. "Public Policy and Public Bureaucracy," in D. Ashford, ed., *History and Context in Comparative Public Policy.* Pittsburgh: University of Pittsburgh Press.

———. 1993a. "Neutral Competence: A Comparative Perspective." Paper presented at the annual conference of the American Political Science Association, Washington, D.C., September 2–5.

———. 1993b. "Top-Down and Bottom-Up Visions of the Policy Process." *Politische Vierteiljahrschrift* 27:228–246.

Peters, B. G., and B. W. Hogwood. 1988. "Births, Deaths, and Marriages: Organizational Change in the U.S. Federal Bureaucracy." *American Journal of Public Administration* 18:119–133.

Pitt, D. C., and B. C. Smith. 1981. *Government Departments: An Organizational Perspective.* London: Routledge.

Pollitt, C. 1990. *Managerialism and the Public Service.* Oxford: Basil Blackwell.

Rose, R. 1989. "Charges as Contested Signals." *Journal of Public Policy* 9:261–286.

Roth, P. A. 1987. *Meaning and Method in the Social Sciences.* Ithaca, N.Y.: Cornell University Press.

Savoie, D., and B. G. Peters. 1995. "Diagnosis and Remedy in the Reform of Government," in D. Savoie and P. Thomas, eds., *Administrative Reform in Canada.* Forthcoming.

Scharpf, F. 1991. "Die Handlungsfahigkeit des Staates am Ende des zwanzigsten Jahrhunderts." *Politische Vierteiljahrschrift* 4:621–634.

Simon, H. 1947. *Administrative Behavior.* New York: Free Press.

Sutherland, S. L. 1992. "The Al-Mashat Affair: Administrative Accountability in Parliamentary Institutions." *Canadian Public Administration* 34:573–603.

Thomas, J. C. 1993. "Public Involvement and Government Effectiveness." *Administration and Society* 24:444–469.

Tullock, G. 1965. *The Politics of Bureaucracy.* Washington, D.C.: Public Affairs Press.

Waldo, D. 1968. "Scope of the Theory of Public Administration." *Annals of the American Academy of Political and Social Sciences* 8:1–26.

Walsh, K., and J. Stewart. 1992. "Change in the Management of Public Services." *Public Administration* 70:499–518.

Walters, J. 1992. "Reinventing Government: Managing the Politics of Change." *Governing* 6:11–14.

Williamson, O. E. 1975. *Markets and Hierarchies.* New York: Free Press.

Wilson, J. Q. 1989. *Bureaucracy.* New York: Free Press.

II.

Disciplinary Foundations

2.

Knowledge for Practice: Of What Use Are the Disciplines?

Laurence E. Lynn Jr.

Public management has gained wide acceptance as a term of art. Its use implies the existence of an identifiable domain of professional practice within the public sector and a subfield of teaching and research in university programs in public administration and public policy. The term is inconveniently ambiguous, however. Both the boundaries of the domain and the kinds of specialized knowledge needed for competent practice are in dispute, and there is, as yet, limited evidence of convergence.

A bit of reflection on the evolution of professions suggests why such ambiguity perdures. Andrew Abbott has analyzed the processes whereby the emerging American professions of business, law, and medicine found it convenient, beginning roughly a century ago, to affiliate with similarly emergent American research universities. Leaders of the professions recognized the need for independence and a base for certification and training. The new university would suffice, Abbott notes, because it "echoed the values of the new professions themselves: [knowledge, meritocracy, utility]" (1988, p. 207). But, he notes, "the organized professions by no means conceded control of these university [professional] schools; they were in the university but not of it" (p. 207).

The independence of professional schools, Abbott continues, had significant consequences for the university itself. Its emerging strength was based primarily on its becoming the home not only of liberal arts education but of scholarship in the natural and social sciences, the humanities, and the arts. Incidental to these central concerns, the university became "a holding company for largely autonomous [professional] faculties, usually closer to their professional associations than to a particular university." Not so incidentally, the university became "an arena of interprofessional competition" for resources, status, and influence (1988, p. 208).

And so it is today. The autonomy of professional schools, and the extent to which their teaching and research are influenced by the occupations in which their graduates practice, is everywhere a source of tension and rivalry, often benign but occasionally highly contentious, among a university's academic units and especially between its professional schools and its graduate departments in the arts and sciences.

These tensions are especially treacherous for graduate schools of public administration and public policy; indeed, the status and prestige of such schools are particularly vulnerable to internecine competition. Though once rooted in administrative law, university courses in public administration early on found more intellectual sustenance in the social sciences, especially the discipline of political science; indeed, public administration came to dominate political science for a time. The newer graduate schools of public policy are even more self-consciously extensions of the disciplines: economics, political science, statistics, and behavioral subfields concerned with organizations, decision making, and leadership. To the extent that such programs exhibit lower standards in their applied work than the standards of the disciplines, they are vulnerable to threatening criticism within the academy; tenure and promotions for their faculty may be open to challenge.

The relatively close intellectual relationship between professional schools of public administration and of public policy and the disciplines has made it difficult for these professional schools to sustain their autonomy. Autonomy is necessarily based on a unique body of "theoretical knowledge, skill, and judgment that ordinary people do not possess, may not wholly comprehend, and cannot readily evaluate" (Friedson 1994, p. 200). If that theoretical knowledge, skill, and judgment are the common possession of any number of disciplines, departments, and schools—not to mention training programs outside the academy—then no one of them can stake a strong claim to jurisdiction within the profession and to a special entitlement to research and teaching resources and to the loyalty of alumni and of practitioners in general.

For this reason, at least, many faculty associated with graduate programs in public policy—with faculty at the John F. Kennedy School of Government at Harvard University in the vanguard—have sought to create, in a manner largely unbeholden to the disciplines, a distinctive body of knowledge to guide practice and distinctive methods for its accumulation. The experience and wisdom of practitioners themselves would be the source of knowledge, with the academy playing the role of facilitator and broker.

The assertive claim of these faculty that the distinctive body of knowledge for public managerial practice was experiential and intuitive touched off a debate—really a revival of an older and largely ongoing debate—over appropriate intellectual foundations for the practice of public management. It was this debate and its implications for public management scholarship and teaching that I sought to broach in my article, "Public Management Research: The Triumph of Art over Science" (Lynn, 1994), an article that was the common starting point for the authors of chapters 3–6.

That the debate is long in the tooth becomes clear by reviewing a volume of papers presented at the twenty-fifth anniversary of the Social Science Research Building at the University of Chicago in November 1955. (It is worth noting that Leonard D. White, the Ernest De Witt Burton Distinguished Service Professor of Public Administration at the University of Chicago, was a convener.) One of the conference sessions was devoted to "The Social Scientist and the Civic Art: Politics," and one of the topics of the session was "The Social Scientist and the Administrative Art." Gordon Clapp, president of the Research and Development Corporation, offered the following answer to the question of an appropriate relationship between social scientists (basically the academy) and administrators: "We do not need proof or provable theses so much as we need questions and hypotheses which will stimulate insights among practitioners. The methodology of social science research can encourage administrators to be more self-consciously analytical and reflective about whatever art they believe they practice" (1956, p. 396).

Nearly four decades after Clapp uttered this bit of wisdom, four scholars closely associated both with the newer schools of public policy and with the emerging field of public management address a similar question in the remaining chapters of this section: How can scholarship produced within the framework of social science disciplines inform the practice of public management? Each responds in a distinctive voice and with insights of considerable interest and value.

The implication of embracing such a conclusion as Clapp's is important both for scholarship directed at informing practice and for the authority of the field's teachers and practitioners. The authority of the field, and the creation of a distinctive intellectual resource for its practitioners, will not be enhanced either by imitating scholars within the disciplines, whose goal is not to inform practice, or by abandoning the disciplines altogether in the quest for an arbitrarily unique experiential knowledge base. Rather, an authoritative field will be one able to demonstrate the capacity to assist practitioners to be more self-consciously analytical and reflective about their practice and, because they possess such skills, be more effective in their work.

References

Abbott, Andrew. 1988. *The System of Professions: An Essay on the Division of Expert Labor.* Chicago: University of Chicago Press.

Clapp, Gordon R. 1956. "The Social Scientist and the Administrative Art," in Leonard D. White, ed., *The State of the Social Sciences.* Chicago: University of Chicago Press.

Friedson, Eliot. 1994. *Professionalism Reborn: Theory, Prophecy, and Policy.* Chicago: University of Chicago Press.

Lynn, Laurence E., Jr. 1994. "Public Management Research: The Triumph of Art over Science." *Journal of Policy Analysis and Management* 13, no. 2: 231–259.

3.

Political Science

John W. Ellwood

This chapter selectively examines the political science literature to determine what, if anything, it has to offer students of public management. Its basic argument is that the output of the great gelatinous field that calls itself political science has at the same time everything and little to offer public management scholars. Everything, because politics is at the heart of public management and because political science more than any other academic field is centered on the study of political behavior, processes, and institutions. Little, because the field is much better at setting out the constraints faced by those seeking to analyze and improve public management than it is at helping those who would improve management practice.

This argument is obviously grounded on particular concepts of the fields of public management and political science. I say "fields" because students of public management and political science are bounded together not so much by a common methodology or paradigm, as is the case with most academic disciplines, as by an interest in a topic. Thus, the two fields attract scholars who employ the techniques of anthropology, economics, game theory, historiography, social psychology, and sociology. I begin, therefore, with a somewhat pedantic discussion of the nature of the two fields. The second section describes what "traditional" political science has to offer students of public management. The third section sets out the more recent approach of political economy. The final section addresses the relationship between the positive analysis of political science and the continuing normative thrust of much of public management research.

Public Management and Political Science Defined

Public Management

What is management? What is public management? And does the distinction matter? We can begin with a traditional private sector view of management: "Let us view management as an activity which performs certain functions in order to obtain the effective allocation, and utilization of human efforts and physical resources in order to accomplish some goal" (Wren, 1987, p. 4).

The dependent variable. Traditionally, students of the management of business firms have stressed efficiency in organizational settings (Drucker, 1977). Thus, Frederick Taylor defined management as "knowing exactly what you [the manager] want men to do, and then seeing that they do it in the best and cheapest way" (quoted in Wren, 1987, p. 4). An Australian scholar of management has recently defined his field as "the process through which an organization's strategy is formulated and then implemented through the organization of work, people, finance and technology" (Byrt, 1989, p. 3).

It should be noted that more recent conceptions of management have been broadened so that the dependent variable is no longer cost-minimization and profit-maximization within a for-profit firm to where the dependent variable can be any goal in any process, organization, or institution (Lynn, 1987). Under such a broad conception of management, the goal of the manager could be efficiency or the implementation of better as against worse public policies. But it could also be the political acceptance of public policies that are far from social optimums.[1]

Level of locus of analysis. In most countries, the terms management and administration are synonymous. As one summary of management education in various countries put it, "Sometimes distinctions are made between management and administration. However, these distinctions vary. In some cases administration is regarded as the higher and management as the lower level of activity. In others the opposite view is taken" (Byrt, 1989, p. 1).

Although generalizations are dangerous in this area, in practice, in the United States, management is associated with decisions and practices of those at the top levels of organizations and institutions. This is particularly true for the field of public management that is associated with programs and schools of public policy. Traditionally, public administration, like its private sector equivalent, was "devoted to the organization as the unit of analysis; how it was structured, what process and problems administrators had to solve; and how the entire process could work more efficiently" (Kettl, 1992, p. 413). But, as Kettl has pointed out, "the more-recent public management movement, by contrast, is based on the role of top administrative leaders, typically political appointees such as cabinet secretaries and agency administrators, and the strategies they set" (Kettl, 1990, p. 413).[2]

Because of this focus on top managers, the field of public management has tended to concentrate on the strategy of management. As put by two scholars who teach in the longest-running public administration program:

> Contemporary public management is something different from traditional public administration. . . . We have no brief against traditional public administration. We both remain interested in public administration, we teach aspects of public administration, and we have been public administrators. But public management is different. The chief respect in which it is different is that public management, if it is to be carried on successfully, inevitably requires a feel for strategy. Public management is broader, more integrative, and less defined by functional expertise than is public administration. Public management is, to a large extent, management of the external environment of the organization. Public administration is within the context of the organization. (Bozeman and Straussman, 1991, p. 214)

The public in public management. The defining characteristic of public management is its publicness. As put by Bozeman and Straussman, "While public and private management have much in common, the two are sharply separated by political authority. While political authority clearly influences private strategic management, it is more than simply an influence on public strategic management; it is a defining characteristic. The fact that public management is imbued with political authority means that it is essentially a different enterprise" (1991, p. 5).[3] Thus, the necessary condition for effective public management—regardless of how one chooses to define effectiveness—is political skill. We are all aware that the typical experience of the private sector manager in government is one of failure (Lynn, 1981). But what makes public management so much more difficult than private management is that, for superior management, the private-sector-sufficient management skills have to be present as well as the necessary political skill. Thus, the public manager also has to be able to motivate people, structure organizations and processes, effectively use financial resources, and (in many cases) create production processes to deliver goods and services.

Political Science

David Weimer has concisely defined political science as the discipline that is in the business of discovering "true sentences" about "the processes by which people make and execute collective choices" (Weimer, 1992, p. 240). Beyond this topical interest, however, the field is wide open. It contains anthropologists, economists, game theorists, historians, philosophers, psychologists, sociologists, and social psychologists. It also contains many who specialize in current events and institutional detail.[4] While the output of many of these scholars might not qualify as "science" in the Popperian sense, the wealth of institutional detail and history that makes up much of political science literature is frequently referred to by those who seek to apply more rigorous deductive and inductive methods to the study of politics.

A key aspect of political science is what Donald Stokes has referred to as its *copernican* perspective (Stokes, 1986). For Stokes, such a perspective means that political science is "laid out from the perspective not of a decision maker or actor but of a detached observer." This detached, positive, and descriptive perspective is in remarkable contrast to the normative or prescriptive perspective of economics—particularly microeconomics (and the other optimizing social sciences that form the basis of much of private sector management education). Because these other fields are to a great extent laid out from the perspective of a decision maker or problem solver or actor, Stokes refers to this alternative perspective as *ptolemaic* (Stokes, 1986).

A second key aspect of political science, especially when one is examining what the field has to offer students of public management, is the relationship between political science and public administration. The history of the on-again-off-again romance between political science and public administration has been well documented by Dwight Waldo (1984) and more recently by Donald Kettl (1992). Initially, public administration was central to the study of political science. As Kettl has pointed out, "The importance of administration lay at the very core of the creation of the American Political Science Association. Five of the first eleven presidents of the association came from public administration and played important roles in framing the new discipline. One of them—Woodrow Wilson—went on to even higher office" (1992, p. 409). But political science and public administration drifted apart, initially because public administrators were interested in training better public servants as well as in producing scholarly work. This desire to serve their clients led public administrators to incorporate the output of other disciplines in their training programs. Public administration was public but it was also administrative. As such, it needed to include material on personnel management, organizational behavior, budgeting, accounting, and so forth.

The conflict between the achievement of the appropriate (best) policy and the achievement of administrative efficiency—a central tenant of the (Progressive) era in which public administration became a self-conscious academic field—led to an attempted dichotomy between the study and practice of politics and administration. First set out in 1887 by Woodrow Wilson, this view of public administration called for "administrative study to discover, first, what government can properly and successfully do, and secondly, how it can do these proper things with the utmost possible efficiency and the least possible cost either of money or energy" (Wilson, 1887, p. 197). Rather than being centered on politics, Wilson and the Progressives felt that "the field of administration is a field of business . . . removed from the hurry and strife of politics. . . . The object of administrative study is to rescue executive methods from the confusion and costliness of empirical experience and set them on foundations laid deep in stable principle" (ibid.).[5] Public administration (and even public management) has never gotten over or come to terms with the Wilsonian politics-administration dichotomy. And as I suggest in the concluding section of this chapter, if policy is substituted for administration, much of the recent work building market-like incentives into public management has a Wilsonian flavor.

The desire to serve practitioners caused public administrators to de-emphasize theory. When the classical management movement failed to produce a unified set of administrative theories, it became clear to most political scientists that public administration had lost its academic core and had become simply a set of training skills. Laurence Lynn has predicted the same fate for the study of public management. Lynn's words—directed at the tendency of public management scholars to stress the art of management practice at the expense of the science of management scholarship—are equally applicable to the intellectual decline of public administration.

> In a field relieved of intellectual standards—and having no theory-building and validation traditions of its own—it is difficult to sustain meaningful intellectual communication, much less maintain relationships with adjacent fields that do have standards for evaluating the validity of arguments. An argument that "my principle is more universal, deep, timeless, powerful and resonant than yours" is unlikely to generate intellectual excitement or progress. Positions that are argued on the basis of a biased selection of case materials cannot be compared or meaningfully evaluated. (Lynn, 1994, p. 253)

Because of its intellectual decline, one is tempted to ignore public administration and public administration scholars when one is discussing what political science has to offer public management scholarship. But a significant overlap still exists between the two fields. Institutionally, political science remains the prime discipline within programs of public administration. Thus, 39 percent of the programs granting a master's degree in public administration remain located in political science departments, and political scientists account for 43 percent of the permanent faculties of the programs and schools that make up the National Association of Schools of Public Affairs and Administration (NASPAA) (Ellwood, 1985).

Intellectually, the study of public organizations remains a central interest of many political scientists. When one thinks of the "giants" of scholarly work on public bureaucracy, the list is dominated by political scientists—James Fesler, Herbert Kaufman, Norton Long, James March, Francis Rourke, Allen Schick, Herbert Simon, and James Q. Wilson. An examination of recent edited surveys of the field of public administration indicates that more than half of the authors identify themselves as political scientists (Perry, 1990; Lynn and Wildavsky, 1990). Institutional analysis, moreover, has had a rebirth within political science over the past decade (March and Olsen, 1989) as both traditional political scientists and political economists have rediscovered that institutions matter (Wilson, 1989).

Implications

Before turning to the central topic of what political science can offer students of public management, it might be best to summarize some of the implications for such a discussion from the above section.

First, modern definitions of management have gone beyond having the dependent variable be cost-minimization or profit-maximization within a hierarchical setting. The definition has been relaxed to the point that the task is to achieve a goal. That goal might be economic or organizational efficiency. It might be the implementation of public policies that improve social welfare. But it also might be reelection or public support for any policy—even a policy that causes a decline in social welfare.

This change increases the usefulness of political science for the study of public management, for the field of political science has more to say about exploiting a given political market or creating an efficient political market than about what the outcome of that market should be. This classic view has been expressed by Charles Lindblom, among others:

> We argue the superiority of the outcome from the process, not of the process from the outcome. The constancy of the economist's objection to this conclusion when applied to governmental rather than market decisions simply often reflects the fact that, while some economists are not disturbed that consumer preferences lead to allocation policies other than best respond to their tastes, when political preferences lead to governmental policies not consistent with

his informed and considered preferences, they are tempted to attribute irrationality to government. (Lindblom, 1961, pp. 323–324)

Moreover, to the extent that the goal of public management is to build political support for a policy program or for an elected administration, the extensive political science literature on public opinion, political participation, and voting behavior becomes relevant. This vast literature is grounded in theory and refutable hypotheses. If it is not normally considered relevant to the study of public management the fault lies with the management scholar who has created a politics-policy dichotomy that is almost as strong as the old public administration politics-administration dichotomy.[6]

Second, the public administration heritage within political science has meant that the study of public bureaucracy has focused on all levels of the organizational structure, including line-organizations and "street-level" bureaucracies. This is in contrast to the public management focus on top-level decision makers and staff functions.

Finally, the copernican approach of political science is more detrimental to the public management scholarship whose main goal is the improvement of management practice than to a scholarly enterprise whose goal is to improve our understanding of public management. David Weimer (1992) has reviewed the literature of contemporary political science to see what it has to offer for the improvement of practitioner skill. His general finding is, not much. To reach this conclusion, Weimer divides the political science literature into two general groups: that which is grounded in deductive theory and that which inductively seeks a description of practice. He finds that the deductive literature is limited because it is unable to treat practitioner skill as an endogenous factor. He critiques the inductive literature on the grounds that its overreliance on case studies limits its ability to be scientific in the Popperian sense. This analysis, however, only holds if one sees the purpose of public management scholarship as improving practitioner skill. If, on the other hand, the goal of public management scholarship is to improve our understanding of public management (writ large), Weimer's criticisms fall away. It is not obvious, moreover, that students of public management should have their research agendas driven by the needs of practitioners. In fact, some scholars of private sector organizational behavior have argued that the ultimate usefulness of their scholarship would increase if they ignore the short-term needs of managers and instead focus on statistically significant relationships (Brief and Dukerich, 1991).

Traditional/Inductive Political Science

Political science is one of the founding disciplines of the study of organizations. From James Madison onward, American students of government have been interested in public organizations and the nature of the leaders of those organizations. Although students of private sector organizations seem unaware of it, a large proportion of the leading scholars of organizations and organizational decision making were trained as political scientists—Mary Parker Follett, Luther Gulick, Herbert Simon, and James March. Moreover, these scholars brought (and continue to bring) to the study of all types of organizations an approach that has power and coalition building as a central focus of organizational design and managerial leadership.

Literature on Public Bureaucracies

Most of this vast traditional scholarship is inductive and much of it is based on case studies, be they historical descriptions of administrative practice (the work of Leonard White); the organization and politics of a specific jurisdiction (Wallace Sayre and Herbert Kaufman's study of the governance of New York City); or the organization, politics, and management of a specific program (Martha Derthick's studies of Social Security, disability, and "New Towns"). Other works in this tradition have analyzed the behavior of particular bureaus (the vast literature of the Bureau of the Budget is but one example) or civil servants at a particular level in the bureaucracy (Herbert Kaufman's study of bureau chiefs and the several studies of the backgrounds and beliefs of civil servants).

This literature continues to be produced. In almost all cases, it is descriptive. Sometimes its internal methodology is scientific in that hypotheses are set out and then tested. But often it is case-study driven and, therefore, is better at hypothesis generation than hypothesis testing. An almost ever-present weakness of this literature is that hypotheses are generated from and tested on the same set of data (case studies). Not since Herbert Simon decided that the findings of the classical (or generic) management school were internally inconsistent have scholars collected the various hypotheses that have been put forth from these many case studies and then used other data to determine whether the hypotheses are statistically significant. One could suggest that what this literature needs more than anything is a Simon Kuznets—someone who will do the hard work of developing the data sets that could be used to econometrically test the vast number of hypotheses that have been put forth.[7]

Yet for all its faults, this vast literature does inform. It provides institutional detail. It suggests relationships. As such, it provides the grounding for much of the model building undertaken by political economists and game theorists. An example of the usefulness of this literature to a more "scientific" scholarship is the symbiotic relationship between those who build deductive models of legislative behavior (e.g., Shepsle and Weingast) and those who have become scholars of the rules of the legislative institution. Stanley Bach, a traditional political scientist who works for the Congressional Research Service, periodically visits the political economy group at Stanford. As he describes it, what occurs at these visits is an interaction between his detailed knowledge of congressional rules and the model builders' methodological skill. They build a model and explain it to him. He reacts by saying, "that's not how it works." They then modify the model and he says, "you still haven't gotten it quite right." They again modify the model until they feel that they have achieved an appropriate balance between the model's power and its realism.

In the same way, the vast literature on public organizations informs our understanding of that aspect of public management which is driven by organizational design. Probably the best recent example of this literature is James Q. Wilson's *Bureaucracy* (1989). In many ways, this work is the culmination of Wilson's career as a teacher and scholar of public bureaucracies. It draws not only from Wilson's past scholarship and his basic course on public bureaucracies but also from some fifty dissertations that he supervised while teaching at Harvard. It thus provides a strong example of the insights that one can draw from a large number of case studies when those studies are used as data within a framework.

Wilson's framework is clearly political. As John DiIulio has pointed out, Wilson relies on the work in Chester Barnard's *The Functions of the Executive* (1938) and Phillip Selznick's *Leadership in Administration* (1957) to create a theoretical perspective. (I would add James March and Herbert Simon's *Organizations* (1958) because of its view of organizations as outcomes of a set of political compromises.) Barnard's theory of organizations is

> reflected in the three-pronged scheme that Wilson used in *The Investigators* (1978); it helped organize key parts of his Harvard bureaucracy courses; and it has now been elaborated in Bureaucracy's framework: operators (part II), managers (part III), and executives (part IV). Essentially, operators perform central or critical tasks of the organization (line-level employees, "street-level bureaucrats"), managers coordinate the activities of persons within the organization (foremen and supervisors), and executives are responsible for the maintenance of the organization (CEOs, commissioners). (DiIulio, 1991, p. 194)

This framework poses a challenge to the scholar of public management. As indicated above, public management scholarship has concentrated on political executives. But in Wilson's formulation, the lower-level operators are the key to the success of an organization. As put by DiIulio,

> In *Bureaucracy,* Wilson treats operators, managers, and executives in that order, and the order is not incidental. Rather, the order reflects one of his most fundamental and persistent ideas about the determinants of agency performance; namely, that it is mainly the nature of operators' tasks—as opposed to the styles of an agency's managers, the behavior and preferences of its executives, and the goals carved into the statutes by those who legislate and lobby over its existence—that ultimately determines "what government agencies do and why." (ibid.)

This notion, that "People matter, but organization matters also, and tasks matter most of all," is a challenge to those students of public management who stress leadership, particularly the leadership of the top managers. On the other hand, Wilson's conception supports those who believe that students of public management should spend more time studying institutional and task design.[8] Thus, Michael Barzelay's *Breaking through Bureaucracy* (1992), with its emphasis on changing institutions to create different incentives that in turn will affect task behavior, is closer to the spirit of Wilson's scholarship than Robert Behn's *Leadership Counts* (1991).

This emphasis on institutions and tasks is reflected in other recent political science scholarship on public organizations—particularly John Chubb and Terry Moe's (1990) work on the relationship of the institutional design of different types of schools and student performance, the James March and Johan Olsen (1989) work on rediscovering institutions, and the recent work of political economists. Regardless of one's judgment of the problems with the Coleman data set of educational outcomes, for our purposes the key innovation of Chubb and Moe is their merging of that data set with data on the institutional structure, processes, and tasks of different schools. On this basis, it stands as a classic "scientific" study of institutional and task design.

To the extent that one believes that institutional and task design matters, one would expect a large amount of scholarship on formal reorganizations of governmental institutions. What is remarkable is that in this area, political science has produced very little quality research. A major reason for the paucity is the fact that most major reorganizations are not adopted. Thus, what one finds in the political science literature are case studies of why reorganization X was rejected. A few case studies of reorganization exist, however, and Frederick Mosher (1967) compiled many of these and prepared an introduction that sets out hypotheses. But the basic political science finding is that in the U.S. case, reorganization does not matter in terms of managerial efficiency or the delivery of public goods or services, but it can matter in terms of a realignment of political power (Bozeman and Straussman, 1991; March and Olsen, 1989).

Wilson's reliance on the work of Phillip Selznick also has major implications for public management research. According to DiIulio,

> Wilson takes from Selznick the idea that to attract and retain persons capable of doing the work, bureaucratic organizations, public and private, must develop a "sense of mission" or "distinctive competence" defined as a widely shared view "among organization members (the bulk of whom—the operators—are on the lowest rungs of the administrative hierarchy) as to the nature, rightness, and importance of the organization's principal tasks. . . . Many organizations, especially public ones, have multiple, vague, and contradictory missions. . . . Strong organizations, however, can be defined as ones that resolve (in operational, if not logical terms) any such conflicts by how they train, reward, and manage workers.
> . . . Wilson argues that public agency leaders can be efficacious, but only by more or less dutifully obeying, not bravely commanding, the unchanged administrative and ever-changing political imperatives between which they are sandwiched. (1991, pp. 194–195)

Once again we see the traditional political science view of bureaucracy: mission, structure, tasks, and politics matter more than leadership, particularly transformational leadership. We also see the March and Simon (1958) tradition of organizations as political institutions.

Wilson's reliance on the work of Selznick also reflects a traditional political science approach to the study of political organizations. That is, the belief that organizations are something more than the aggregation of the preferences of their membership; that institutions, particularly public institutions, can be seen "not only as aggregating individual interests but also as shaping them and providing opportunities for their development" (March and Olsen, 1989, p. 120). The work of James March and Johan Olsen is frequently cited by traditional students of bureaucracy and political economists alike to justify their work on the role and influence of institutional arrangements. The reason that both groups can cite the same work is that the first half of March and Olsen's book explicates two classes of aggregating models—the rational choice models of political economy (in which preferences are fixed in the short-run) and the stochastic garbage can models. But in the less frequently cited second half of their work March and Olsen, like Wilson, stress that political organizations not only aggregate individual interests but also shape and provide opportunities to develop those interests.

> Attention to issues associated with the development of meaning and the construction of preferences has become an important part of theories of organiza-

tional choice . . . , as well as of modern institutionalist perspectives on social organization. . . . These integrative political processes in the name of popular sovereignty are distinguished by two major features that are potentially quite inconsistent with the perspective of aggregation. . . . The first is the concept of rights. The second is the idea of reasoned deliberation in search of the common good. (1989, p. 124)

Taking the second consideration first—the need for deliberation in the search for the common good—political scientists frequently hark back to *Federalist Papers* 10 and 51, authored by James Madison, where although it is recognized that political activity rests on self-interest, it is also understood that political institutions must be created that foster deliberation and attract the best citizens to governmental service.[9]

The concept of rights also has significant implications for much of the recent normative public management scholarship. Popular works, such as *Reinventing Government* (Osborne and Gaebler, 1992), and more careful scholarly treatments, such as Barzelay's *Breaking through Bureaucracy* (1992), have begun their analysis by critiquing the Progressive Era procedures that supposedly have led to a non-customer-oriented bureaucracy. The solution is to modify or replace the progressive system by a combination of devolution of the provision of the goods or services to the private sector and the creation of private sector incentives in public organizations (competition and allowing individuals to personally or organizationally gain from efficiency and attraction of customers).

What is frequently left out is that the bureaucratic rules of the Progressive Era legislation and institutions can be seen as rights (Perrow, 1986). That is, from Max Weber on, bureaucratic rules were seen as protecting the government worker and the citizen from arbitrary action in an environment where markets do not provide a check on such action by making it costly. (That is, when the owner of a privately held firm makes his dumb son the new head of the organization, he will suffer economic consequences, but when the elected official appoints the dumb son of a political friend to head an agency, it is not clear that the official will suffer.) Bureaucratic rules also protect citizen rights— the citizen is guaranteed a certain level and kind of service.

Of course the problem with a rights-based management system is that rights guaranteed through rules are hard to modify and thus quickly become a hindrance rather than a benefit in a rapidly changing environment. But the point of the benefits of rights still holds, and one can easily imagine the news reports on a computer (or, in honor of Vice President Gore, an ashtray) purchase which is made based on reputation when it turns out that the purchaser and the seller of the product are close friends.

Literature on Political Leadership

There is a long tradition in management research that leadership counts—that the top executive is the one individual that can make or break an organization (Barnard, 1938; Selznick, 1957). In political science, discussions of leadership are most often found in the subfield of presidential scholarship and in case studies of department heads and bureau chiefs. Unlike much of the organizational behavior scholarship on leadership, where attempts have been made to empirically identify underlying leadership dimensions (Bass, 1981, 1985; Bass, Avolio, and Goodheim, 1987; Yukl, 1989), political scientists have seen leadership as highly contextual. One studies individual presidencies in depth or writes detailed case studies of managers who have been successful in bringing about organizational change and innovation (Doig and Hargrove, 1987) or who have been successful in managing in impossible situations (Hargrove and Glidewell, 1990).

Such studies suffer from the $n = 1$ methodological limitation. In a recent defense of this type of analysis, Erwin Hargrove points out that "one cannot have it both ways, arguing that individuals are not important and then in the same breath arguing that the importance of individuals precludes systematic study" (1993, p. 70). In a methodological reply, Gary King agrees that

> it is certainly true that individuals are important and that presidents can be studied systematically. However, it is clear that the systematic study of individual presidents should not continue in the tradition of using the president as the unit of analysis. . . . The obvious solution is to look for ways of multiplying the number of observations—looking for additional observable implications of the same theory. For example, an obvious choice for political psychology and for decision-making research is to use the decision as the unit of analysis. (King, 1993, p. 406)

King's suggestion, of course, is exactly the reason that the Carnegie School (Simon, March, Cyert, et al.) turned away from traditional organizational behavior and focused instead on organizations as decision-making units.

The implication of the vast body of case study research on the presidency and top-level public managers is that both political science and public management research are also badly in need of their Simon Kuznets.

One of the major influences of political science literature on the study of management is the assumption that inspired leaders will outperform going-by-the-book bureaucrats. This bias is most evident in two pieces of political science scholarship that had a dramatic influence on the initial wave of public management scholarship—Richard Neustadt's *Presidential Power* (1960) and Graham Allison's *Essence of Decision* (1971).

In Neustadt's discussion of presidential management, the wheeler-dealer president who refuses to follow or give in to bureaucratic lines of authority—Franklin D. Roosevelt—is the hero, while the least admired chief executive is the most bureaucratic president—Dwight D. Eisenhower. As Jonathan Bendor and Thomas Hammond (1992) have pointed out in their critique of *Essence of Decision,* Allison clearly biases the case in favor of Model III (the political bargaining/leadership model) by setting up Model I (the rational choice model) as a straw man and by not fully setting out the virtues of Model II (the organizational process model). The historical record cited by Allison paints a picture of John F. Kennedy as a smart political decision maker who avoids bureaucratic traps. Many of the traps result from inflexible bureaucrats going by the book (following their standard operating procedures). Thus, the Russians make detection of their missile sites easy by laying them out "by the book," while the U.S. Navy almost brings on a war by following the book when it comes to how, when, and where they will intercept the Russian ships. Of course, as Bendor and Hammond point out, because Allison's work is based on a case study the reader never sees the counterfactual—the many times when bureaucratic rules and standard operating procedures rein in a cowboy president (or cabinet secretary). To the extent that Bendor and Hammond are correct, therefore, leadership scholarship, particularly if it relies on case studies, suffers from the generic limitations of case studies.

Deductive Political Science

The last four decades have seen a growth in the number of political scientists who use the methodology of microeconomics and game theory to build formal models of political activity and institutions. While the earliest work focused on constitutional arrangements and voting in clubs and committees, over the past two decades these methodologies have been applied to a wider range of political phenomena. David Weimer and Aidan Vining cover this literature in detail in chapter 5.

In 1988, Jonathan Bendor surveyed the then existing formal, or deductive, models of bureaucracy. Bendor begins his survey with Niskanen's *Bureaucracy and Representative Government* (1971). This work led to a body of scholarship that examined the power relations between a legislature and a bureau. As the literature developed, modelers explored whether bureaus that nominally are governed by legislators are able to gain favorable outcomes (and if so, why). "Most prominently, there is a running debate over the extent of bureaucratic influence in national politics. There are those who assert that agencies greatly influence policy outcomes (James Q. Wilson and William Niskanen form an otherwise odd pair), those that assert that Congress subtly controls the bureaucracy (Barry Weingast), and those who have a more pluralist view of institutional influence (Terry Moe)" (Bendor, 1988, p. 391). These initial modeling efforts were largely descriptive, but as the literature developed, particularly as principal-agent models began to be applied to the public sector, modelers were able to show deductively how different bureaucratic designs would affect incentive structures. In a series of articles, Thomas Hammond and Gary Miller (1985) "used the axiomatic approach of social choice theory by specifying intuitively reasonable criteria that any bureaucratic organization should satisfy and then investigating whether the set of criteria is internally consistent" (Bendor, 1988, 377). By showing that a set is inconsistent, Hammond and Miller established an impossibility result for organizational structures, that is, one cannot design an institution that meets all desired qualities (the desired qualities including the multiple conflicting criteria that citizens demand of their public organizations). This impossibility result leads to an organizational equivalent of Shepsle and Weingast's structurally induced equilibrium for voting rules.

Once modelers headed down this path, they began to create models that deductively showed how given organizational designs affected or created different incentive structures. One promising group of models that have incentives at their core are principal-agent models. As Terry Moe (1984) argues, one of the difficulties with applying principal-agent models to public sector activity is that the property rights to the residual (the profit, the money saved from cost-minimization, etc.) are up for grabs. But when Moe's conclusion is combined with the results of Hammond and Miller, one can turn one's attention to modeling how and why institutional arrangements induce a given set of outcomes in the struggle over the residual.

The latest and perhaps best-developed deductive formal analysis of the effects of institutional design is Gary Miller's *Managerial Dilemmas* (1992). Miller's work is discussed in detail in Weimer and Vining's chapter in this volume, but some of his results are worth noting. Miller starts from the tradition of Alchian and Demsetz (1972), finding that hierarchies are mechanisms of overcoming the market failure induced by team (or joint) production. Following the logic of principal-agent models, he then shows that the "hierarchical manipulation of incentives" can go part of the way—but only part of the way—toward correctly aligning group and individual incentives (so as to eliminate shirking, for example). But citing the Holmstrom Theorem, which sets out the rules of the possibility of perfect alignment of individual and group incentives, Miller posits that "managers who can induce norms of cooperation and trust among employees can realize more of the gains from team production than can managers who rely on formal incentive systems only." Moreover, "when cooperation in a repeated social dilemma is sustainable by rational actors as a Nash equilibrium, so are a variety of non cooperative or exploitative outcomes. Repeated play makes cooperation possible in a team, but not inevitable" (Miller, 1990, pp. 346–347).

In short, Miller has shown that in repeated noncooperative play it is possible for an organization to get stuck in a nonoptimum equilibrium. The next step in Miller's analysis is of greatest significance to public management scholars. Relying on the Folk Theorem that states that in repeated games there are many equilibria, Miller is able to reintroduce managerial skill into formal deductive models of organizational design. Specifically, he posits that

> the successful manager, recognizing the goal-oriented "rationality" of the participants, will consciously adopt strategies that get individuals to depart from the narrow self-interest maximization that constitutes a sufficient definition of rationality in markets. A successful manager will demonstrate trustworthiness; she will recognize and encourage a multiplicity of goals, including group acceptance and professional self-actualization, recognizing in these building blocks a culture of cooperation. She will train herself and subordinates in an awareness of the dangers of the social dilemma that is inherent in every hierarchy and will shape the awareness of the possibilities of escaping these dangers through the rational evolution of cooperation in the ongoing plays of the hierarchical dilemma. (1990, p. 347)

But, if the great strength of Miller's recent work is its reintroduction of managerial skill into formal deductive models, its weakness for public management is that the formal analysis does not center on the unique problems of *public* management.

One problem faced by public managers is the potential for instability of policy and organizational outcomes. In a series of papers, Terry Moe (1989, 1990, 1991) has tried to reintroduce politics into the study of public organizational design. He posits that minimum winning coalitions—even if they are all-powerful at the time of the adoption of a policy or the creation of a bureaucracy—will build due process protections into the policy and organizational design because they are rational to understand and because the coalition anticipates a future when it will be in the minority. Thus, fearing a reversal of fortune, political decision makers build inefficiencies into policies and structures.

Moe's work has led to a cottage industry of formal analyses that have studied how groups and elected officials either foster or hinder legislative and policy "drift."[10] The traditional explanation, following the logic of Moe's work, is that legislators ensure the stability of their enacted policies by building into them highly restrictive procedures and rules to govern the implementation process—at the cost of managerial and programmatic efficiency (McCubbins, Noll, and Weingast, 1989). Jonathan Macey has pointed out that there is an alternative strategy. Programs and policies can be designed in such a manner as to encourage the formation (or reconfiguration) of new interest group alignments that will maintain support for the program or institution across time (Macey, 1992). A classic example is Franklin Roosevelt's acceptance of a regressive capped wage tax for Social Security to ensure its continued political support across time.

In fact, legislators face two problems: future legislators may undo their work through legislation (this has been labeled "legislative drift") and bureaucrats may undo their work through implementation ("bureaucratic drift"). Currently Shepsle and Macey are arguing whether it is possible to create and adopt strategies to control both types of drift at the same time, with Shepsle arguing that a trade-off exists while Macey posits that the two types of drift can be simultaneously controlled through manipulation of the interest group environment (Macey, 1992; Shepsle, 1992). "The core insight of this new body of scholarship is that . . . compliance can be facilitated by crafting political institutions that constrain the ability of politicians to renege on their commitments" (Eric Patashnik, personal communication, 1993). For students of public management, such a finding again opens a mechanism for managerial and political skill.

Concluding Implications

In many ways, the literature of political science continues to positively inform students of public management. First, and most important, it continues to stress the fact that politics and publicness is at the heart of institutional, process, and policy design. In fact, those engaged in formal modeling of principal-agent relationships and noncooperative games are beginning to produce substantive findings of how institutional designs can affect incentive structures, which, in turn, can affect political and work behaviors.

Second, recent political science scholarship increasingly reinforces the notion that strategy is at the heart of the managerial function—particularly the top managerial function. Third, traditional political science continues to provide the institutional and political detail that students of public management rely on and build upon. Finally, because traditional political scientists often

Table 1

**How Satisfied Are You with the Work
and Service of the Federal Government?**

Very Dissatisfied	Somewhat Dissatisfied	Not Sure	Somewhat Satisfied	Very Satisfied
7%	22%	1%	58%	12%

Source: *USA Today,* September 12, 1985

rely on case studies, they have thought through the limitations of such research and the ways of overcoming the $n = 1$ methodological problem.

But recent political science scholarship also challenges much of the current thrust of public management research. Specifically, I am referring to that part of public management research that seeks to improve the delivery of "good" public policy through creating incentives that will make public institutions and managers more efficient and customer oriented.

The first challenge arises from the fact that political scientists are agnostic as to what is good policy. Their focus is—or should be—on politics, not on the substance of policy. Thus, for political science, if citizens are happy with the way services are delivered or if they are able to change the delivery mechanism if they are unhappy, the political market is efficient. Moreover, although most Americans are convinced that the national government is inefficient in the abstract, when it comes to their interaction with that government they seem fairly satisfied. Larry Hill reports that an SRC poll taken at the height of the Watergate crisis in 1973 found that of the 58 percent of people who reported that they had interacted with a federal agency, 72 percent were satisfied with the bureaucracy's handling of their problem (Hill, 1992). In September 1985 a *USA Today* poll asked respondents "How satisfied are you with the work and service of the federal government?" As the data in table 1 indicate, 70 percent were either very or somewhat satisfied.

To the extent that such data are accurate, one can question the political returns from improving the delivery of public service. And, if the returns are as small as I would posit, then few incentives other than managerial norms of efficiency will sustain the breaking through bureaucracy/reinventing government efforts. Certainly, the reliance on time-specific case studies allows for the real possibility that those who will benefit most from these innovations are the authors of the books. We should remember that when Pressman and Wildavsky went looking for the Oakland development projects, they were tracking down an effort that was chronicled in book form by the projects' initiators—both of whom went on to better jobs while the citizens of Oakland received little but frustration.

In fact, the political science perspective could be used to challenge the basic assumption of much of the reformist public management literature. As indicated above, much of the recent deductive formal modeling literature has reinvented or returned politics to the central core of public sector institutional design. Particularly, Terry Moe's recent work is centered around the notion that the business of government is politics rather than the efficient provision of goods and services.

In *Bureaucracy*, James Q. Wilson employs two fourfold classifications of agencies. On the political side, agencies are categorized by whether the benefits and costs of their policies are concentrated on a few individuals or groups or are widely dispersed across many citizens. On the managerial side, Wilson classifies agencies based on whether their outputs and outcomes are observable. Wilson's public sector procedural organizations are most like private sector organizations in that their outputs and outcomes are both observable. At the other extreme, and least like private profit-making firms, are what Wilson labels coping organizations where neither outputs nor outcomes are observable.[11] A cursory examination of situations where it has been suggested that the provision of goods and services could be improved tends to a focus on procedural organizations, where the activity and managerial task is most like its private sector counterpart.

To the extent that this is the case, one is tempted to ask, "Why is government engaged in the provision of these goods and services?" Of course, this opens a bigger dilemma. If government concentrates its activity on those services which, by definition, can least efficiently be provided by private or nonprofit firms, it will guarantee that its customers are less happy when they deal with it than is the case when they deal with a for-profit or nonprofit organization. The alternative, of course, is for government to do what is easy to do, but less efficiently than would be the case if it was done by for-profit firms.

Notes

1. The classic example is Franklin Roosevelt's decision to finance Social Security through a regressive wage tax because in so doing he could convince the American people that Social Security was an insurance program, thereby preventing any future Republican Congress from eliminating the program.

2. This emphasis on top-level management begins with the early bibles of the public management field—Richard Neustadt's *Presidential Power* (1960) and Graham Allison's *Essence of Decision* (1971)—and is carried through many later works such as Eugene Bardach, *The Skill Factor in Politics: Repealing the Mental Commitment Laws in California* (1972); Robert Behn, *Leadership Counts* (1991); Gordon Chase and Elizabeth Reveal, *How to Manage in the Public Sector* (1983); Philip Heymann, *The Politics of Public Management* (1987); and Douglas Yates, *The Politics of Management* (1985).

3. Hal G. Rainey and his coauthors have done the best job of summarizing the similarities and differences between public and private organizations and public and private management. For the best summary of this work, see Rainey, *Understanding and Managing Public Organizations* (1991). See also Rainey (1979, 1983, 1990); Rainey, Backoff, and Levine (1976); and Perry and Rainey (1988). For a view that holds that public and private organizations are converging, see Bozeman (1987).

4. An old RAND joke quips, Question: What's the difference between political scientists and economists? Answer: Economists read the newspaper before they come to work.

5. Donald Kettl has correctly pointed out that Wilson and his progressive followers (such as Goodnow) were not trying to remove politics writ large from the administrative process so much as they "sought to distance administration from the political spoils and scandals that had undercut administrative effectiveness, especially in the last half of the nineteenth century" (Kettl, 1992, p. 409).

6. The growth of such a politics-policy dichotomy flows from the fact that public management has grown up in schools and programs of public policy. Management was added to the curricula of these programs in order to make policy analysts more effective in the "real world." But a basic approach remains: Figure out the best policy, with *best* defined as the alternative that brings about the greatest Pareto Improvement, and then relax that alternative to take into account political realities. Of course, there is an alternative approach: Figure out the best policy, with *best* defined as the policy that will gain the greatest and most stable amount of public support, and then tinker with that policy to see what can be done to increase its positive effect on social welfare.

7. I am grateful to Eugene Smolensky for this idea.

8. In his stress on institutional design and the key role of operators, Wilson remains in the mainstream of public administration. One has the feeling that while public policy programs aim to train analytic staff and special assistants to the assistant secretary, public administration programs aim to train the operator of line-agencies.

9. The debate over whether to make public the names of congressional representatives who sign discharge petitions is a classic instance where accountability through interest aggregation (making the names public) is seen by most congressional scholars as undercutting the need to build the deliberative ability of the legislative process.

10. I am grateful to Eric Patashnik for the information behind this discussion of legislative drift.

11. For Wilson, procedural organizations are those where outputs are observable but outcomes are not observable. He labels organizations where outcomes are observable but outputs are not observable "craft" organizations.

References

Alchian, Armen, and Harold Demsetz. 1972. "Production, Information Costs, and Economic Organization." *American Economic Review* 62:777–795.

Allison, Graham T. 1971. *Essence of Decision: Explaining the Cuban Missile Crisis.* Boston: Little, Brown.

Bardach, Eugene. 1972. *The Skill Factor in Politics: Repealing the Mental Commitment Laws in California.* Cambridge: MIT Press.

Barnard, Chester. 1938. *The Functions of the Executive.* Cambridge: Harvard University Press.

Barzelay, Michael, with the collaboration of Babak J. Armajani. 1992. *Breaking through Bureaucracy: A New Vision for Managing in Government.* Berkeley: University of California Press.

Bass, Bernard M. 1981. *Handbook of Leadership: A Survey of Theory and Research.* New York: Free Press.

———. 1985. *Leadership and Performance beyond Expectations.* New York: Free Press.

Bass, Bernard M., B. J. Avolio, and L. Goodheim. 1987. "Biography and Assessment of Transformational Leadership at a World Class Level." *Journal of Management* 13:7–20.

Behn, Robert D. 1991. *Leadership Counts: Lessons for Public Managers from the Massachusetts Welfare, Training, and Employment Program.* Cambridge: Harvard University Press.

Bendor, Jonathan. 1988. "Review Article: Formal Models of Bureaucracy." *British Journal of Political Science* 18:353–395.

Bendor, Jonathan, and Thomas H. Hammond. 1992. "Rethinking Allison's Models." *American Political Science Review* 86, no. 2: 301–322.

Bozeman, Barry. 1987. *All Organizations Are Public: Bridging Public and Private Organizational Theories.* San Francisco: Jossey-Bass.

Bozeman, Barry, and Jeffrey D. Straussman. 1991. *Public Management Strategies: Guidelines for Managerial Effectiveness.* San Francisco: Jossey-Bass.

Brief, Arthur P., and Janet M. Dukerich. 1991. "Theory in Organizational Behavior: Can It Be Useful?" in Barry M. Staw and Larry L. Cummings, eds., *Research in Organizational Behavior,* 13:327–352. Greenwich, Conn.: JAI Press.

Byrt, William. 1989. "Management Education," in Byrt, ed., *Management Education: An International Survey.* London: Routledge.

Chase, Gordon, and Elizabeth C. Reveal. 1983. *How to Manage in the Public Sector.* New York: Random House.

Chubb, John E., and Terry M. Moe. 1990. *Politics, Markets, and America's Schools.* Washington, D.C.: Brookings Institution.

DiIulio, John J. 1991. "Notes on a Contrarian Scholar," from "The Public Administration of James Q. Wilson: A Symposium on *Bureaucracy.*" *Public Administration Review* 51 (May–June): 193–195.

Doig, James W., and Erwin C. Hargrove, eds. 1987. *Leadership and Innovation.* Baltimore: Johns Hopkins University Press.

Drucker, Peter F. 1977. *People and Performance: The Best of Peter Drucker on Management.* New York: Harper and Row.

Ellwood, John W. 1985. "A Morphology of Graduate Education for Public Service in the United States." A report for the "Study of Trends and Innovations in Graduate Education for Public Service," conducted by the National Association of Schools of Public Affairs and Administration.

Hammond, Thomas H., and Gary J. Miller. 1985. "A Social Choice Perspective on Expertise and Authority in Bureaucracy." *American Journal of Political Science* 29 (February).

Hargrove, Erwin C. 1993. "Presidential Personality and Leadership," in George C. Edwards, John H. Kessel, and Bert A. Rockman, eds., *Researching the Presidency: Vital Questions, New Approaches*. Pittsburgh: University of Pittsburgh Press.

Hargrove, Erwin C., and John C. Glidewell, eds. 1990. *Impossible Jobs in Public Management*. Lawrence: University Press of Kansas.

Heymann, Philip B. 1987. *The Politics of Public Management*. New Haven: Yale University Press.

Hill, Larry B. 1992. *The State of Public Bureaucracy*. Armonk, NY: M. E. Sharpe.

Kettl, Donald F. 1990. "The Perils—and Prospects—of Public Administration." *Public Administration Review* 50 (July/August): 411–419.

———. 1992. "Public Administration: The State of the Field," in Ada W. Finifter, ed., *Political Science: The State of the Discipline II*, pp. 407–428. Washington, D.C.: American Political Science Association.

King, Gary. 1993. "The Methodology of Presidential Research," in George C. Edwards, John H. Kessel, and Bert A. Rockman, eds., *Researching the Presidency: Vital Questions, New Approaches*. Pittsburgh: University of Pittsburgh Press.

Lindblom, Charles E. 1961. "Decision-Making in Taxation and Expenditures," in *Public Finances: Needs, Sources, and Utilization: A Conference of the Universities—National Bureau Committee for Economic Research*. Princeton: Princeton University Press and National Bureau of Economic Research.

Lynn, Laurence E. 1981. *Managing the Public's Business*. New York: Basic Books.

———. 1987. *Managing Public Policy*. Boston: Little, Brown.

———. 1994. "Public Management Research: The Triumph of Art over Science." *Journal of Policy Analysis and Management* 13, no. 2: 231–260.

Lynn, Naomi, and Aaron Wildavsky, eds. 1990. *Public Administration: State of the Discipline*. Chatham, N.J.: Chatham House.

Macey, Jonathan R. 1992. "Organizational Design and Political Control of Administrative Agendas." *Journal of Law, Economics, and Organization* 8, no. 1: 93–109.

March, James G. 1989. *Rediscovering Institutions: The Organizational Basis of Politics*. New York: Free Press.

March, James G., and Johan P. Olsen. 1989. *Rediscovering Institutions: The Organizational Basis of Politics*. New York: Free Press.

March, James G., and Herbert Simon. 1958. *Organizations*. New York: Wiley.

McCubbins, Matthew D., Roger G. Noll, and Barry R. Weingast. 1987. "Administrative Procedures as Instruments of Political Control." *Journal of Law, Economics, and Organization* 3, no. 2: 243–277.

———. 1989. "Structure and Process, Politics and Policy: Administrative

Arrangements and the Political Control of Agencies." *Virginia Law Review* 75:431–482.

Miller, Gary J. 1990. "Managerial Dilemmas: Political Leadership in Hierarchies," in Karen Schweers Cook and Margaret Levi, eds., *The Limits of Rationality,* pp. 324–357. Chicago: University of Chicago Press.

———. 1992. *Managerial Dilemmas: The Political Economy of Hierarchy.* New York: Cambridge University Press.

Moe, Terry. 1984. "The New Economics of Organization." *American Journal of Political Science* 78:739–777.

———. 1989. "The Politics of Bureaucratic Structure," in John Chubb and Paul E. Peterson, eds., *Can Government Govern?* Washington, D.C.: Brookings Institution.

———. 1990. "Political Institutions: The Neglected Side of the Story." *Journal of Law, Economics, and Organization* 6 (Special Issue): 213–266.

———. 1991. "Politics and the Theory of Organization." *Journal of Law, Economics, and Organization* 7:106–129.

Mosher, Frederick C. 1967. *Government Reorganization: Cases and Commentary.* Indianapolis: Bobbs-Merrill.

Neustadt, Richard E. 1960. *Presidential Power: The Politics of Leadership.* New York: Wiley.

Osborne, David, and Ted Gaebler. 1992. *Reinventing Government: How the Entrepreneurial Spirit Is Transforming the Public Sector.* Reading, Mass.: Addison-Wesley.

Perrow, Charles. 1986. *Complex Organizations: A Critical Essay,* 3d ed. New York: Random House.

Perry, James L., ed. 1990. *Handbook of Public Administration.* San Francisco: Jossey-Bass.

Perry, James L., and Hal G. Rainey. 1988. "The Public-Private Distinction in Organizational Theory: A Critique and Research Strategy." *Academy of Management Review* 13, no. 2: 182–201.

Pressman, Jeffrey L., and Aaron B. Wildavsky. 1973. *Implementation: How Great Expectations in Washington Are Dashed in Oakland or, Why It's Amazing That Federal Programs Work At All, This Being a Saga of the Economic Development Administration.* Berkeley: University of California Press.

Rainey, Hal G. 1979. "Perceptions and Incentives in Business and Government: Implications for Civil Service Reform." *Public Administration Review* 39:440–448.

———. 1983. "Public Agencies and Private Firms: Incentive Structures, Goals, and Individual Roles." *Administration and Society* 15:207–242.

———. 1990. "Public Management: Recent Developments and Current Prospects," in Naomi Lynn and Aaron Wildavsky, eds., *Public Administration: State of the Discipline.* Chatham, N.J.: Chatham House.

———. 1991. *Understanding and Managing Public Organizations.* San Francisco: Jossey-Bass.

Rainey, Hal G., Robert W. Backoff, and Charles L. Levine. 1976. "Comparing Public and Private Organizations." *Public Administration Review* 36:233–246.

Selznick, Philip. 1957. *Leadership in Administration.* New York: Harper and Row.

Shepsle, Kenneth A. 1992. "Bureaucratic Draft, Coalition Draft, and Time Consistency: A Comment on Macey." *Journal of Law, Economics, and Organization* 8, no. 1: 110–118.

Stokes, Donald E. 1986. "Political and Organizational Analysis in the Policy Curriculum." *Journal of Policy Analysis and Management* 6, no. 1: 45–55.

Waldo, Dwight. 1984. *The Administrative State: A Study of the Political Theory of American Public Administration,* 2d ed. New York: Holmes and Meier.

Weimer, David L. 1992. "Political Science, Practitioner Skill, and Public Management." *Public Administration Review* 52, no. 2: 240–245.

Wilson, James Q. 1989. *Bureaucracy: What Government Agencies Do and Why They Do It.* New York: Basic Books.

Wilson, Woodrow. 1887. "The Study of Administration." *Political Science Quarterly* 2 (June): 197–222.

Wren, Daniel. 1987. *The Evolution of Management Thought,* 3d ed. New York: Wiley.

Yates, Douglas. 1985. *The Politics of Management.* San Francisco: Jossey-Bass.

Yukl, Gary A. 1989. *Leadership in Organizations,* 2d ed. Englewood Cliffs, N.J.: Prentice-Hall.

4.

Sociology

Linda Kaboolian

The call for scholars of public management to engage the social sciences has been sounded (Lynn, 1994; Weiss, 1994). Criticism of public management research as "case-based," "descriptive," and "atheoretical" begs the question, Can the disciplines help? The answer undoubtedly is "yes, but. . . ." Yes, the disciplines can help, but help do what? Establish a new field or discipline that is credible within the academy (Bozeman, 1993)? Differentiate public management from public administration (Newland, 1994)? Or something else? To be sure, the disciplines have an obligation to produce knowledge of "dual relevance" to the worlds of theory and practice. One discipline, sociology, can contribute insights to the epistemological, methodological, and theoretical knots that have hampered research on public management.

Sociology's Origins: Theory and Practice

Sociology was founded amidst the larger debate over the nature of social phenomena and the principles governing scientific inquiry.[1] Social Darwinists and social engineers argued whether social processes were naturally occurring or socially constructed.[2] For over a century, their successors have debated the merits and imperatives of activist social science research with the goal of social reform against the more detached practice of scientific documentation, explanation, and prediction of social processes.[3] The moral obligations felt by activist sociologists to engage practical problems through the scientific study of social processes versus the moral arguments against intervention in the natural order quickly gave way to a debate over the value-neutral quality of research conducted by adherents to both camps. As a result of these debates, sociology, perhaps more than any other discipline, has reflected on philosophical and epistemological questions concerning its relationship to practice. Despite this introspection, it has had to fight hard to remain a credible social science.[4]

Sociology is the study of social processes and the relationships between the individual, social groups, and societal arrangements (Smelser, 1994). Sociologists are "intensively, endlessly, shamelessly interested in the doings" of people and their "consuming interest remains their institutions, their history, their passions" (Berger, 1963, p. 18). Like many social sciences, sociology treats individuals as actors at the same time that it locates them and embeds their actions in larger units, for example, the small group, organizations, social classes, and the political culture. Sociology treats social "things" as social constructions, however, the causal relationship between social structure and social action is still debated (Althusser, 1966; Berger and Luckmann, 1967; Giddens, 1984; Coleman, 1986). Reality is not only tangible but can be defined both objectively and subjectively (Berger and Luckmann, 1967). Nevertheless, the consequences of subjective reality can be real (Thomas, 1966).

Sociology assumes that human nature is plastic and theories of human action run along the continuum of determinism and voluntarism (Althusser, 1966; Parsons, 1951). Social action is varyingly assumed to be rational (March and Simon, 1958), contingent (Perrow, 1967), symbolic (Edelman, 1964, 1971), meaning creating (Blumer, 1969), and the outcome of unconscious processes (Lévi-Strauss, 1963). Unforeseen and unintended consequences of seemingly rational behavior (Merton, 1949a) and phenomena of seemingly chaotic behavior (Cohen, March, and Olsen, 1972; March and Olsen, 1976) all claim sociologists' attention.

The Sociology of Knowledge of Public Management

The sociology of knowledge provides a framework with which to study the production and purposes of knowledge. The forces that have influenced the type of research that has been conducted on public management problems and the difficult relationships among research, theory, and practice are illuminated by a sociological analysis.

In the status hierarchy of the academy, social sciences are wedged between the princely "hard sciences" and the seemingly expendable arts. Practice, on the other hand, needs to be informed by lessons learned and generalizable truths, if not theory, lest it lurch along, ignorant of helpful frameworks for analysis and applicable solutions (Lynn, 1994). As a result, the social sciences and the world of practice, be it public policy or public management, are in a reciprocal relationship; they need each other. The social sciences need to be legitimate and relevant. Addressing problems of the "real world" is the primary vehicle for the social sciences to achieve this (Barber, 1987, p. 2). Managers need insights and solutions to stubborn problems. Alliances with elite universities and researchers add legitimacy to managerial techniques.

Without a meaningful exchange, both endeavors risk mirroring the private sector caricatures provided by David Lodge in *Nice Work* (1988). Robyn Penrose, a university professor, is assigned to "shadow" Vic Wilcox, the senior manager of a firm facing global competition. Professor Penrose sees the industrial world from a "disciplinary" perspective:

> Industrial capitalism is phallocentric. The inventors, the engineers, the factory owners and bankers who fuelled it and maintained it, were all men. The most commonplace metonymic index of industry—the factory chimney—is also metaphorically a phallic symbol . . . tall chimneys thrusting into the sky, spewing ribbons of black smoke, buildings shaking with the rhythmic pounding of mighty engines, the railway train rushing irresistibly through the passive countryside—all this is saturated with male sexuality of a dominating and destructive kind. (p. 49)

Whereas Manager Wilcox asks:

> Does anybody know how many different products this firm made last year? . . . Nine hundred and thirty-seven. That's about nine hundred too many, in my opinion . . . every new specification means that we have to stop production, retool or reset the machines, stop a flow line, or whatever. That costs time, and time is money. Then the operatives are more likely to make mistakes when setups are constantly changing, and that leads to increased wastage. (p. 46)

The disconnection between the endeavors of "town" and "gown" parodied by Lodge appears as true for public management as it is for the private sector. The debate about the helpfulness of theory to practice and applied research to theory is an old one (Merton, 1982). Reasons for the estrangement of the disciplines from public management research are many (Lynn, 1994), however, they are not unique to public management research (Scott and Shore, 1979; Lawler et al., 1985; Kaboolian, 1994).[5]

It may be small comfort for public management researchers to know that, in addition to Lodge, there have been many critiques of the intellectual endeavors of business schools that are similar, if not identical, to those expressed about public management research. History shows us that business schools had their own debates twenty or so years ago about exactly the issues public management researchers are addressing today, and very likely for similar reasons. Organizational behavior, an interdisciplinary field, was established in business schools as a partial response to this debate. The goal of organizational behavior was to assist the move away from the generation of "craft knowledge" and toward research grounded in theoretical perspectives of the disciplines. Today, some of the best research on topics of importance to management, such as organizations, group behavior, and individual experience, is being conducted by sociologists, anthropologists, and psychologists in those departments. It is also true that some of most important theoretical development in the disciplines is being done there.

However, despite the work described above, many believe that it is hard to underestimate the formal use of research by the disciplines to understand business organizations. Mitroff (1985) tells us that in a two-by-two table of academic knowledge (high and low) and street knowledge (high and low): "Much that passes for theorizing in managerial science all too rarely rises above the level of showing that $X = X$" (1985, p. 35). Traditional academics, Mitroff argues, care for high academic knowledge and settle for low street knowledge, practitioners for the reverse, and it is rare to see research well grounded in high academic knowledge and high practitioner knowledge.

Thus, despite the incorporation of social scientists of every discipline onto the research faculties of business schools, much of the work generated by those faculties still bears the characteristics justly criticized by Lynn. Even the very question we are considering (and have considered) about public management— How do we know what we know and when we know it?—has not been fully answered by researchers of private organization management. We might then ask, Why is much of the work about management and managers—whether they are in private organizations, nonprofits, or public organizations—so "arty" and not "scientific"? Is there something about the generic field of *management* that explains this phenomenon?

One answer might be the fragmented and heterogeneous nature of the audience of managers and organizations that researchers try to address. Institutionally, the most immediate demand of professional schools is for research having practical relevance to support teaching and expand influence. Because the practitioner, rather than the disciplines, is defined as the audience, the demand for usable, relevant knowledge increases and the incentive to do theoretically relevant empirical work stays neutral, if not declines.

In addition, there is a tension between the immediate and long-term needs of the institutions. While the institutions need to be relevant to practitioners "today," they also need to be relevant "tomorrow"; that is, they need to see that research comes up with some "truths" to ensure long-term usefulness (Lynn, 1994) and hence ensure their credibility and survival. As a result, junior faculty are evaluated largely on their contribution to their disciplines. However, the immediate demands of professional school responsibilities often win out over long-term career goals. To respond to both appears to many junior faculty to be the equivalent of two full-time careers.

In addition, unlike the situation in professions such as law and medicine, the task of management is more contingent on environments and other elements, which themselves vary greatly. As a result, the practitioner and his or her function become the unifying forces for the field. This is a benefit and a curse: Although close attention to the concerns of practitioners produces compelling problem statements, Weiss warns that "progress in theory development becomes more complicated and elusive" (1994, p. 280).

While the forces that focus management research on practitioner needs are powerful, alternative foci present their own challenges. Despite Lynn's warning, which should be heeded, researchers should also be cautious about letting the disciplines unilaterally define the endeavor. Edward Lawler argues that strict adherence to the methodological and theoretical orthodoxies of the disciplines carries its own dangers.

> There seems to be a particular danger that we will do research that is more a product of the methodology than of the phenomenon being studied. Taken to its extreme, this tendency could lead to a series of theories and findings that meet the test of traditional scientific validity but that are not useful to the practitioner and, indeed, may not be useful to the theorists either, because they do not describe actual organizational behavior. They may fail to be useful because they do not inform the practitioner or the theorist about the realities of the organizational environment. Instead, they frame the issues in such a way, and report on data so far removed from the realities of the complex, interactive, ever-changing world of organization, that they are not useful as a guide to either theory or practice. (1985, pp. 3–4)

Researchers should neither let the intellectual agenda of a discipline alone set the research agenda for public management nor simply use emerging theoretical concepts in the disciplines to understand the behavior of public organizations, their executives, and other players. The former is a recipe for lack of relevance, the latter is analogous to the management yarn of the hammer in search of a nail.

Knowledge for What?

Richard Walton (1985) and others have argued that research about management should have as its ambition "dual relevance," that is, it should be useful for the development of theory as well as the improvement of practice and should be judged on this basis. "Is it useful for practice, and does it contribute to the body of scientific knowledge that is relevant to theory? If it fails either of these tests, then serious questions should be raised" (Lawler, 1985, p. 4).

One way to go about this is to ask questions of relevance to practitioners and to test, evaluate, and develop the insights of the disciplines in the course of answering those questions. Walton (1985) suggests a thought process that begins with "practical puzzles, paradoxes, or dilemmas" and asks "What is it that perplexes practitioners?" From there a researcher can formulate a theoretical puzzle and then look to see if it is a puzzle that has been solved. If it has, then the researcher must decide whether to provide an additional test.

What do practitioners need from theory? Lawler and Walton both advocate for "less uncertainty" rather than "more certainty." For this reason, Walton (1985) claims that knowledge with dual relevance is more likely to result from research designed to generate concepts, hypotheses, and theory (inductive research) than theory testing (deductive research). Lawler recommends the "fine grained research" of qualitative methods with the goal of producing "frames or ways of thinking about the world" rather than facts (1985, p. 10).

If dual relevance is the answer to the institutional needs to satisfy multiple constituencies in both the short and long term because it both generates usable knowledge and is theoretically grounded and empirically sound, why isn't more of it done?

One answer is that it is very hard to do research of dual relevance well. Also, certain characteristics of the field make it particularly hard to perform this type of research about public management. Research that is theoretically grounded and useful to both theory building and practice begs the question, What is the correct unit of analysis for the research? Is it the subindustry defined either by level of government (e.g., federal organizations) or by the core business of the organization (e.g., motor vehicle departments or welfare departments)? Unlike research on commercial organizations, in which it is logical to use as the unit of analysis an industry (e.g., the automobile industry) or a subunit of an industry (e.g., parts suppliers), it appears that for the public sector, the number of variables that describe the character of the organization and its environment are almost infinite. Thus, the answer to the question is not easily found.

Scanning what are regarded as examples of excellent research in public management provides some guidance, though not a definitive answer. The simplest form of research is the detailed case study, which does not consider the problem of unit of analysis at all. Barzelay (1993) draws attention to the detailed case study of the Social Security Disability Claims Program by Jerry

Mashaw (1983) as an exemplar. Mashaw examines the behavior of administrative law judges and provides a framework for understanding their decisions. In contrast, the methodologist Yin (1989) advises us that a stronger research design, one more likely to have the capacity to test hypotheses, compares multiple case studies.

Building on Yin's model, comparative case studies beg a related question, "What should the comparisons be based on?" Should the research design be comparisons *within an "industry,"* for example, prisons, as in DiIulio (1987); *within an industry cross-culturally,* for example, occupational safety and health agencies in the United States and Sweden, as in Kelman (1981); *within industries and across sectors of the economy,* for example, the comparison of private and public sector organizations with similar operations, as in the study of teleservice in Fountain, Kaboolian, and Kelman (1992); *across industries within the public sector,* as in Wilson (1989); *within a public sector function,* as in Sparrow's study of compliance (1994); or *across functions,* as in Kaboolian's study of service delivery (forthcoming)?

The complexity of the phenomenon we are interested in may lead us to another research strategy as we heed the warning of J. Richard Hackman that we not focus on finding unitary causes for organizational performance because "influences on performance do not come in separate, easily distinguishable packages. They come, instead, in complex tangles that often are as hard to straighten out as a backlash on a fishing reel" (1985, pp. 136–137). Organizational performance may be so overdetermined that teasing out the identification and importance of any given independent and intervening variables in comparative case studies may be a weak strategy. Hackman suggests that we "take the case study out of the classroom and put it to work in scholarly pursuits" (1985, p. 138) and provide multiple theoretical explanations for a single case. Lynn points out that this was done by Allison in the *Essence of Decision.*

The point of this review is to argue that even if we were to bring about a fruitful marriage of the field of public management and the disciplines, many research design questions remain unresolved. How, then, might we go about doing rigorous and usable research in public management?

Theory Building and Methods

Sociology offers two important concepts to aid in the production of knowledge of dual relevance: "grounded theory" and "theories of the middle range." Both concepts speak to the relationship between empirical findings and theory building. Lawler and Walton both suggest that knowledge with dual relevance can be produced by inductive research. However, it is easy for inductive research, often qualitative in nature, to assume the character of descriptive case studies that have not been found satisfactory for theory building (Lynn, 1994).

"Grounded theory" is a concept proposed by Glaser and Strauss (1967) that addresses this concern. A grounded theory is described by Strauss and Corbin as: "inductively derived from the study of the phenomenon it represents. . . . The grounded theory approach is a qualitative research method that uses a systematic set of procedures to develop an inductively derived grounded theory about a phenomenon" (1990, pp. 23, 24). At the same time, Strauss and Corbin stress the adherence of the grounded theory approach with the rules of scientific method. Qualitative research using the grounded theory approach should "enable the researcher to develop a substantive theory that meets the criteria for doing 'good' science: significance, theory-observation compatibility, generalizability, reproducibility, precision, rigor, and verification" (1990, p. 31).

The grounded theory approach is a rigorous way for qualitative researchers and, some might argue, case writers, to assist in theory generation and, ultimately, long-term relevance. Cases should not be "stories," but they should offer either the conceptual building blocks on which a framework is built that is useful to both theorists and practitioners or they should offer data for comparison against other cases for further interpretation. Nancy Roberts (forthcoming) has done just that in her interesting reinterpretation of three well-known case studies of public managers. Her analysis offers the beginning of a framework about deliberative processes that should stimulate researchers and practitioners.

Bardach suggests a similar use for the existing library of public management cases (1993). He argues that we should move toward categorization that might be useful to the generation of hypotheses that would then be testable. Bardach borrows from the physical sciences the notion of a "specimen" when considering case studies and asks, "What characteristics are generic across specimens? Is variance observable in these characteristics across the specimens?" (p. 5). Bardach says our task is an interpretive one: to disentangle the pieces and figure out what is generic, what is particularistic, and what affects the degree of outcome.

A second contribution of sociology to the production of knowledge with dual relevance is provided by Robert Merton in his criticism of attempts by the social sciences to develop a unified theory of social life. Addressing the issue of the usefulness of existing theory to explain social phenomena, Merton provides an alternative to the "abstracted empiricism of grand (social) theory"[6] and argues for the usefulness of "theories of the middle range" that "lie between the minor but necessary working hypotheses that evolve in abundance during day-to-day research and the all-inclusive systematic efforts to develop a unified theory that will explain all the observed uniformities of social behavior, social organization and social change" (1949a, p. 39).

An example of middle-range theory is Merton's theory of reference group behavior[7]—the act and consequences of an actor comparing himself or herself to others (1949a, pp. 279–440)—which is based on the empirical work of others presented in the *American Soldier* series of studies. Merton used these studies to create a framework for understanding the role of reference group identification. He then offered a set of related problems for further refinement and verification which stimulated a generation of scholars and produced a body of knowledge with dual relevance.

The importance of the concept of middle-range theories to research for dual relevance is that while middle-range theory "involves abstractions," the abstractions remain "close enough to observed data to be incorporated in propositions that permit empirical testing" (1949a, p. 39). Theories of the middle range are empirically grounded and offer the opportunity to interpret empirical work and suggest conditions under which findings do and do not hold. For these reasons, they are a useful way of using the vast data represented by the case studies currently in our archives.

Defining Research Questions

In setting an agenda for public management research that meets the criteria of dual relevance, it is necessary to select the appropriate research questions. Walton suggests that we begin with that which perplexes the practitioner and bedevils practice, and work toward theory generation. Research in public management must begin one step before: defining the practitioners of public management.

Lynn suggests focusing on "the executive function in government," noting that the topic is "quite broad because public managerial roles encompass virtually every aspect of civic and social life" (1994, p. 245). He distinguishes this topic from that of public administration, which he defines as the study of "governmental organizations." Perry and Kraemer support Lynn's distinction, defining public administration as principally concerned with "the study of characteristics that distinguish public administration from other administration . . . and political-administration system interface" (1994, p. 103).[8]

One consequence of this distinction is to focus public management research on the "role" of a public manager rather than on the character and behavior of the public bureaucracy. This focus does not preclude seeing the manager embedded in context. Lynn suggests that public management research take on the assumptions in the phrase "within a given political and institutional setting." In addition, the distinction shifts the focus from that of the long and productive tradition of research on bureaucratic administration and decision making to a wider set of tasks and behaviors.

The relationship of manager to the setting is an important one. Lynn (1994), Heymann (1987), and Moore (1994) depict the public manager as a dynamic force in reacting to and creating the circumstances surrounding their work. Building on these studies, Lynn suggests that public management research address fundamental questions about the public executive's role in designing and transforming government institutions and practices.

However, when attempting to define researchable questions, Lynn has more difficulty, noting that there is "no conceptual clarity and therefore no real map" to guide us (1994, p. 247). He summarizes "problems" offered by several authors, identifying "generic problems" that arise "in a relatively wide range of important, recurring cases" (p. 246) and a "series of conceptual approaches" that may be helpful in shaping researchable questions (pp. 247–252).

Sociology offers a possible solution in the tradition of "action research." While this term is often used to mean research that is conducted for the purposes of producing social change (Lewin, 1946), more broadly it defines a collaboration between practitioners and researchers for the production of useful knowledge.[9] In the action research tradition, the appropriate questions for public management research might be found by querying public management practitioners. The research agenda of public management might then be tempered by balancing the needs of the practitioner with the needs of the academic (Merton, 1982, p. 29). That balance need not preclude a dialogue between practitioners and researchers—the ostensible goal of the Association of Public Policy and Management (APPAM). However, at the APPAM meetings the supremacy of academics in defining research questions and research methods can be observed in the management sessions. Practitioners more often convene sessions and comment on research papers than critique the very questions propelling the work.

A Sociologist's Proposal

As a sociologist conducting research on issues of relevance to public managers, I try to distill from practitioners who attend executive programs and from midcareer students the problems that perplex them. The three types of questions (and their variants) that I hear are:

> What is my job?
> What should I be doing?
> How can (I) (my organization) perform better?

From international executives comes the question about the cultural embeddedness of the knowledge about public management based on mature democratic systems:

> What do you do when the system doesn't work like that?

In sociological terms all these questions can be recast:

> What is the role of the public sector in the production of results that are valued by members of the society?

To address this agenda, the research endeavor can be defined as the "sociology of the production of value." Several subdisciplines of sociology can inform this research. For example, public problems are defined by social construction processes, driven by political or professional concerns that often specify their solutions (Gusfield, 1981; Loeske, 1992). Organizations are one vehicle by which public value is produced and public problems are resolved. The study of organizations has been enriched by the "new institutionalism" (Powell and DiMaggio, 1991; Ferris and Tang, 1993; Kettl, 1994), network theory (Powell, 1990; Nohria and Eccles, 1992), agency theory (Pratt and Zeckhauser, 1985), transaction cost analysis (Williamson, 1982), and comparative sociology (Cole, 1989; Lincoln and Kalleberg, 1990). Social movement theory (Morris and Mueller, 1992) contributes insights about advocates and mobilization of public agendas. The political economy approach helps us understand why some meritorious actions fail while other seemingly ill-conceived efforts succeed and why the claims of some members of society are heeded and others ignored (Zald, 1970).

In addition, the value of "sociological imagination" to this endeavor cannot be overstated. C. Wright Mills wrote:

> The sociological imagination enables its possessor to understand the larger historical scene in terms of its meaning for the inner life and the external career of a variety of individuals. In enables him to take into account how individuals, in

the welter of their daily experience, often become falsely conscious of their social positions. Within that welter, the framework of modern society is sought, and within that framework the psychologies of a variety of men and women are formulated. By such means the personal uneasiness of individuals is focused upon explicit troubles and the indifference of publics is transformed into involvement with public issues. . . .

The sociological imagination enables us to grasp history and biography and the relations between the two within society. That is its task and its promise. (1959, pp. 5, 6)

Sociology begins with an understanding of the dimensions of the historical period and moves across units as grand as societies and as small as the individual self. Society, Berger (1963) argues, is "drama," dynamic, rooted in what went before but interesting for what is to come.

It is these characteristics of the discipline of sociology that can help generate the research to answer the perceptive midcareer student who challenges the syllabus of a public management course on the first day of the semester: "What," she asks, "is the long-term usefulness of the ideas you will offer in this course? Aren't all ideas about management 'fads,' time-limited in their utility?" The student then cites recent management practices such as Total Quality Management, Employee Involvement, Quality of Work Life, Zero-Based Budgeting, and Managing by Objectives as examples.

Research about public management informed by the sociological imagination provides an answer to that practitioner. An analysis of the public manager's job must be informed by an analytic framework that takes into consideration the prevailing political culture embedded with values about the role of government; the platforms of the political regime in power (perhaps tempered by the interests of subgroups); the social processes that construct or fail to construct public problems; the production paradigm of the epoch; dynamics of work groups, organizations, and networks; and the individual public manager's aspirations, motivations, and self-definition. Sociology permits the structural relationships and the meaning of the relationships among the citizen, client, polity, elected official, career bureaucrat, and worker to be understood. It is in this context that the job of a public manager to produce value and create and maintain (or not) the legitimacy of the regime can be considered and lessons gleaned that are relevant, generalizable, and dynamic.

Notes

1. It was the grand master of sociology, Émile Durkheim, in *The Rules of Sociological Method* (1938), who labeled "social facts as things" and thereby as the legitimate focus of scientific inquiry.

2. Herbert Spencer argued that sociology was to discover the laws of the universe and derive correlative laws governing society.

3. William Graham Sumner saw it as a moral imperative not to interfere with the natural order. Thorstein Veblen and William James, among others, argued for the necessity and possibility of scientifically designed social change.

4. Albion Small, the founder and long-term editor of the *American Journal of Sociology,* addressed this point one hundred years ago in the journal's mission statement: "If sociology is to be of any influence among practical men, it must be able to put its wisdom about things that interest ordinary men in a form which men of affairs will see true to life" (1985 [1895], p. xxii).

5. Public policy research also has an uneasy relationship to the social sciences. Weiss (1980) provides a set of hypotheses about why this is so. Scott and Shore (1979) examine the paradox of sociology, which has its roots in the study of practical problems but whose practitioners define policy problems in terms that speak more to sociology than to policy concerns. Lazarsfeld and Reitz (1975) also address this paradox and provide an intellectual history of the debate over "applied" research in sociology. Barber (1987) tries to generalize from the celebrated cases of social science research that have made impacts on policy areas.

6. While "theories of the middle range" was Merton's constructive alternative to Talcott Parsons, the depiction of Parsons's work quoted here is from C. Wright Mills.

7. The concept of the reference group was not Merton's invention; it was proposed by Muzafer Sherif in his *Psychology of Social Norms* (1936).

8. For a parallel and related discussion for public administration research, see Box (1994).

9. For a more detailed exposition of action research and its relationship to the positivist tradition, see Susman and Evered (1978).

References

Allison, Graham T. 1971. *The Essence of Decision.* Boston: Little, Brown.

Althusser, Louis. 1966. *For Marx.* London: New Left Books.

Argyris, Chris, and Donald A. Schon. 1978. *Organizational Learning: A Theory of Action Perspective.* Reading, Mass.: Addison-Wesley.

Barber, Bernard. 1987. *Effective Social Science: Eight Cases in Economics, Political Science, and Sociology.* New York: Russell Sage Foundation.

Bardach, Eugene. 1993. "Notes on 'Specimen Analysis' and 'Design Analysis.'" Paper presented to the Conference on Case-Based Research at the Kennedy School of Government, Harvard University, June 28.

————. 1994. "The Problem of Best Practice Research." *Journal of Policy Analysis and Management* 13, no. 2: 260–268.

Barzelay, Michael. 1993. "The Single Case Study as Intellectually Ambitious Inquiry." *Journal of Public Administration Research and Theory* 3 no. 3: 305–318.

Behn, Robert D. 1992. *Leadership Counts: Lessons for Public Managers from the Massachusetts Welfare, Training, and Employment Program.* Cambridge: Harvard University Press.

Bennis, Warren. 1985. "Observations on What We Have Learned about Useful Research," in Edward E. Lawler III, et al., *Doing Research That Is Useful for Theory and Practice,* pp. 351–357. San Francisco: Jossey-Bass.

Berger, Peter L., ed. 1963. *Invitation to Sociology: A Humanistic Perspective.* New York: Doubleday.

Berger, Peter L., and Thomas Luckmann. 1967. *The Social Construction of Reality.* New York: Doubleday.

Blau, Peter M. 1955. *The Dynamics of Bureaucracy: A Study of Interpersonal Relations in Two Government Agencies.* Chicago: University of Chicago Press.

Blumer, Herbert. 1969. *Symbolic Interactionism: Perspective and Method.* Englewood Cliffs, N.J.: Prentice-Hall.

Box, Richard. 1994. "An Examination of the Debate over Research in Public Administration," in Jay D. White and Guy B. Adams, eds., *Research in Public Administration.* Thousand Oaks, Calif.: Sage.

Bozeman, Barry, ed. 1993. *Public Management: The State of the Art.* San Francisco: Jossey-Bass.

Cohen, Michael D., James C. March, and Johan P. Olsen. 1972. "A Garbage Can Model of Organizational Choice." *Administrative Science Quarterly* 17, no. 1: 1–25.

Cole, Robert E. 1989. *Strategies for Learning: Small Group Activities in American, Japanese, and Swedish Industry.* Berkeley: University of California Press.

Coleman, James S. 1986. "Social Theory, Social Research, and a Theory of Action." *American Journal of Sociology* 91:1309–1335.

DiIulio, John J. 1987. *Governing Prisons: A Comparative Study of Correctional Management.* New York: Free Press.

————, ed. 1994. *Deregulating the Public Service.* Washington, D.C.: Brookings Institution.

Durkheim, Émile. 1938. *The Rules of Sociological Method.* Chicago: University of Chicago Press.

Edelman, Murray. 1964. *The Symbolic Uses of Politics.* Urbana: University of Illinois Press.

————. 1971. *Politics As Symbolic Action.* Chicago: Markham.

Eisenstadt, Shmuel N. 1968. "The Development of Sociological Thought," in David Sills, ed., *International Encyclopedia of the Social Sciences,* 15:23–35. New York: Macmillan and Free Press.

Ferris, James M., and Shui-Yan Tang. 1993. "The New Institutionalism and Public Administration: An Overview." *Journal of Public Administration Research and Theory* 3:4–10.

Fountain, Jane, Linda Kaboolian, and Steven Kelman. 1992. "Service to the Citizen: The Use of 800 Numbers." Paper presented at the Association for Public Policy and Management meetings in Denver, Colo., October 23.

Giddens, Anthony. 1984. *The Constitution of Society.* London: Macmillan.

Glaser, Barney G., and A. Strauss. 1967. *The Discovery of Grounded Theory.* Chicago: Aldine.

Gusfield, Joseph R. 1981. *The Culture of Public Problems.* Chicago: University of Chicago Press.

Hackman, J. Richard. 1985. "Doing Research That Makes a Difference," in Edward E. Lawler III, et al., *Doing Research That Is Useful for Theory and Practice,* pp. 126–148. San Francisco: Jossey-Bass.

Heymann, Philip B. 1987. *The Politics of Public Management.* New Haven: Yale University Press.

Kaboolian, Linda. 1994. "The Sociology of Knowledge of Public Management Research." Paper presented at the second National Public Management Research Conference, Madison, Wisc., October 2.

————. 1995. *Service Delivery in the Public Sector.* Forthcoming.

Kelman, Steven. 1981. *Regulating America, Regulating Sweden.* Cambridge: MIT Press.

Kettl, Donald F. 1994. "Deregulating at the Boundaries of Government: Would It Help?" in John J. DiIulio, ed., *Deregulating the Public Service,* pp. 175–197. Washington, D.C.: Brookings Institution.

Lawler, Edward E., III, et al. 1985. *Doing Research That Is Useful for Theory and Practice.* San Francisco: Jossey-Bass.

Lazarsfeld, Paul F., and Jeffrey G. Reitz. 1975. *An Introduction to Applied Sociology.* Amsterdam: Elsevier.

Lévi-Strauss, Claude. 1963. *Structural Anthropology.* New York: Basic Books.

Lewin, Kurt. 1946. "Action Research and Minority Problems." *Journal of Social Issues* 2:34–46.

Lincoln, James R., and Arne L. Kalleberg. 1990. *Culture, Control, and Commitment.* Cambridge: Cambridge University Press.

Lodge, David. 1988. *Nice Work.* New York: Penguin Books.

Loeske, Donileen. 1992. *The Battered Woman and Shelters: The Social Construction of Wife Abuse.* Albany: State University of New York Press.

Lynn, Laurence E. 1994. "Public Management Research: The Triumph of Art over Science." *Journal of Policy Analysis and Management* 13, no. 2: 231–259.

March, James G., and Johan P. Olsen. 1976. *Ambiguity and Choice in Organizations.* Bergen, Norway: Universitetsforlaget.

March, James G., and Herbert A. Simon. 1958. *Organizations.* New York: Wiley.

Mashaw, Jerry L. 1983. *Bureaucratic Justice: Managing Social Security Disability Claims.* New Haven: Yale University Press.

Merton, Robert K. 1949a. *Social Theory and Social Structure.* Glencoe, Ill.: Free Press.

————. 1949b. "The Role of Applied Social Science in the Formulation of Policy." *Philosophy of Science* 16, no. 2: 161–181.

————. 1982. *Social Research and the Practicing Professions.* Cambridge: Abt.

Mills, C. W. 1959. *The Sociological Imagination.* New York: Oxford University Press.

Mitroff, Ian I. 1985. "Why Our Old Pictures of the World Do Not Work Anymore," in Edward E. Lawler III, et al., eds., *Doing Research That Is Useful for Theory and Practice,* pp. 18–35. San Francisco: Jossey-Bass.

Moore, Mark H. 1994. *Creating Public Value: Strategic Management in the Public Sector.* Cambridge: Harvard University Press.

Morris, Aldon, and Carol McClurg Mueller, eds. 1992. *Frontiers in Social Movement Theory.* New Haven: Yale University Press.

Newland, Chester A. 1994. "A Field of Strangers in Search of a Discipline: Separatism of Public Management Research from Public Administration." *Public Administration Review* 54, no. 5: 486–488.

Nohria, Nitin, and Robert G. Eccles, eds. 1992. *Networks and Organizations: Structure, Form, and Action.* Cambridge: Harvard Business School Press.

Parsons, Talcott. 1951. *The Social System.* Glencoe, Ill.: Free Press.

Perrow, Charles. 1967. "A Framework for Comparative Organizational Analysis." *American Sociological Review* 32, no. 2: 194–208.

———. 1972. *Complex Organizations: A Critical Essay.* New York: Random House.

Perry, James L., and Kenneth L. Kraemer. 1994. "Research Methodology in the *Public Administration Review*," in J. White and G. Adams, eds., *Research in Public Administration.* Thousand Oaks, Calif.: Sage.

Powell, Walter W. 1990. "Neither Market nor Hierarchy: Network Forms of Organization." *Research in Organizational Behavior* 12:67–87.

Powell, Walter W., and Paul J. DiMaggio, eds. 1991. *The New Institutionalism in Organizational Studies.* Chicago: University of Chicago Press.

Pratt, John W., and Richard J. Zeckhauser. 1985. *Principals and Agents: The Structure of Business.* Boston: Harvard Business School Press.

Reiss, Albert J. 1968. "Sociology: The Field," in D. Sills, ed., *International Encyclopedia of the Social Sciences,* 15:1–23. New York: Macmillan and Free Press.

Roberts, Nancy. "Dialogue and Deliberation: An Alternative Mode of Strategy Making." *Journal of Public Administration Research and Theory.* Forthcoming.

Schelling, Thomas C. 1978. *Micromotives and Macrobehavior.* New York: W. W. Norton.

Scott, Robert A., and Arnold R. Shore. 1979. *Why Sociology Does Not Apply.* New York: Elsevier.

Senge, Peter. 1990. *The Fifth Discipline.* New York: Doubleday.

Sherif, Muzafer. 1936. *The Psychology of Social Norms.* New York: Harper and Brothers.

Small, Albion. 1985 [1895]. "The Era of Sociology." *American Journal of Sociology* 1, no. 1: 1–10. Reprinted in 100, no. 1: *ix–xv.*

Smelser, Neil J. 1994. *Sociology.* Oxford: Blackwell.

Sparrow, Malcolm. 1994. *Imposing Duties: Government's Changing Approach to Compliance.* Westport, Conn.: Praeger Press.

Stouffer, Samuel A. 1949. *The American Soldier in World War II.* Princeton: Princeton University Press.

Strauss, A., and J. Corbin. 1990. *Basics of Qualitative Research.* Newbury Park, Calif.: Sage.

Sumner, William Graham. 1963. *Social Darwinism: Selected Essays.* Englewood Cliffs, N.J.: Prentice-Hall.

Susman, Gerald I., and Roger D. Evered. 1978. "An Assessment of the Scientific Merits of Action Research." *Administrative Science Quarterly* 23: 582–603.

Thomas, W. I. 1966. *On Social Organization and Social Personality: Selected Papers.* Chicago: University of Chicago Press.

Walton, Richard E. 1985. "Strategies with Dual Relevance," in Edward E. Lawler III, et al., eds., *Doing Research That Is Useful for Theory and Practice,* pp. 176–204. San Francisco: Jossey-Bass.

Weiss, Carol. 1980. *Social Science Research and Decision Making.* New York: Columbia University Press.

Weiss, Janet. 1994. "Public Management Research: The Interdependence of Problems and Theory." *Journal of Policy Analysis and Management* 13, no. 2: 278–285.

Williamson, Oliver. 1982. "Organizational Innovation: The Transaction-Cost Approach," in J. Ronen, ed., *Entrepreneurship,* pp. 101–134. Lexington, Mass.: Heath Lexington.

Wilson, James Q. 1989. *Bureaucracy: What Government Agencies Do and Why.* New York: Basic Books.

Yin, Robert K. 1989. *Case Study Research: Design and Methods.* Newbury Park, Calif.: Sage.

Zald, Mayer. 1970. "Political Economy: A Framework for Comparative Analysis," in Mayer Zald, ed., *Power in Organizations.* Nashville: Vanderbilt University Press.

5.

Economics

David L. Weimer and Aidan R. Vining

Four related bodies of knowledge inform the study and practice of public management. Broadest in scope is knowledge about the political processes that place demands, provide opportunities, and impose constraints on public managers. Next broadest in scope is policy analysis, which provides the conceptual foundations and craft skills for determining what government should do and how it should be done. Organizational design, a subset of policy analysis, gives insight into how the public sector can be organized to facilitate the effective delivery of goods and services. Narrowest in scope, but most directly relevant to the practice of management, is knowledge about how to carry out executive functions skillfully within existing organizational designs. We take the last two bodies of knowledge, organizational design and executive function, as the core of the craft and science of public management. In this chapter, we consider what the discipline of economics offers for research on the core of public management.

Economics has made fundamental contributions to the conceptual and technical development of policy analysis. Through the public choice perspective, it has also contributed in important ways to the understanding of political processes. But what has economics contributed directly to public management? The short answer is mainly some insight into organizational design. Of course, being academics, we are not content with giving just the short answer, especially because we see some developments in economics that may eventually contribute to our fundamental understanding of executive function.

Economists have not been shy about applying their disciplinary tools to the study of a variety of nonmarket behaviors such as crime, fertility, and rent seeking. Yet the nonmarket behavior most central to the study of the economy—that which occurs within firms, public bureaus, and other organizations that produce goods and services—has only recently become part of the mainstream of the discipline. The pioneering work of Ronald Coase (1937) on transaction costs as an explanation for the existence of firms did not attract many economists to the topic. More influential was the notion that in competitive markets only those firms would survive that acted as if they maximized profits, implicitly choosing the most efficient organizational form (Alchian, 1950). The assumed efficiency of the "what is" makes the particulars of organization seem less interesting. Concern about the optimal design of information sharing among organizational members with identical goals prompted some interest in the theory of teams (Marschak, 1955). Yet with a few very notable exceptions (Downs, 1966; Niskanen, 1971), economists tended to ignore public sector organizations, which usually are not subject to the competitive discipline that in theory drives private firms toward efficiency. Further, early explorations of behavior within firms (Cyert and March, 1963) and the structure of firms (Williamson, 1975) seemed to many economists to stray too far from the dominant neoclassical paradigm of constrained optimization by rational actors. It was only with the introduction of the principal-agent framework, which preserved the core assumptions of neoclassical economics, that questions of organizational design have moved into the mainstream of economics.

For purposes of this chapter, we delineate economics as the body of theory and related empirical research that relies on the comparison of equilibria resulting from the choices of individuals with stable preferences who act rationally to maximize their welfare. These concepts—stable preferences, rational choices by individuals, and comparable equilibria—compose the core assumptions of neoclassical economics. In its simplest and most simplistic form, neoclassical economics adds the peripheral assumptions of the budget as the only relevant constraint, perfect information, and costless market exchange. We follow Thrainn Eggertsson (1990) in classifying models that preserve the core assumptions of neoclassical economics, but relax the secondary assumptions, as belonging to neoinstitutional economics. In particular, neoinstitutional economics introduces more detailed specifications of the situational constraints that individuals face, of the types of information that they have, and of the nature of the interactions in which they engage. The increasing specificity of these peripheral assumptions pushes economic theory closer to topics of concern to students of public management.

One can imagine two routes by which economics can influence public management. First, public managers can draw concepts and analytical techniques directly from economics. By understanding the economic aphorism "the scarcest resource gets the rent," or the broadly applicable concepts of moral hazard and adverse selection, for example, a manager may be better able to avoid ineffective organizational designs. Familiarity with the techniques of benefit-cost analysis may enable a manager to pursue more skillfully what Michael Barzelay calls the post-bureaucratic paradigm emphasizing the consumer perspective, net rather than gross values, and the inclusion of nonpecuniary costs (1992, p. 121). Second, economics can indirectly influence public managers by providing the conceptual frameworks employed by public management researchers. With respect to organizational design, for instance, such concepts as sustainable competition, contestability, and credible commitment may suggest very different ways of thinking about the delivery of services. An economic theory of institutions based on equilibria in repeated games may provide a clear conceptual foundation for thinking about such elusive phenomena as leadership and organizational culture.

In this chapter, we speak more to researchers than to practitioners. Rather than attempting to catalog systematically the concepts and techniques that are potentially useful to practitioners, we provide examples of important general concepts that might usefully be transferred from various economic approaches to the substantive problems of public management. Though most of these concepts are relevant to issues of organizational design, a few may be useful in helping to better understand the executive function.

We begin by considering the concept of market failure in neoclassical economic theory. Next we review the agency theory and transaction cost branches of neoinstitutional economics. Though social choice theory is substantively more often thought of as the domain of political science, we consider its application to organizational decision making. Finally, we turn to game theoretic models of institutions, which provide a new sort of "general equilibrium" in that they can explain the existence of conventions and adherence to rules without resort to the assumption of some external authority.

Neoclassical Economic Theory

The ideal paradigm of neoclassical economics, the Arrow-Debreu (1954) general equilibrium framework, simply assumes all production occurs within technically efficient firms that maximize profits. Thus, it does not speak to questions of interest to students of public management. Yet consideration of the normative implications of violating the assumptions of the ideal neoclassical paradigm—the subject of welfare economics—does offer some concepts of relevance to organizational design. In particular, the traditional market failures (public goods, externalities, natural monopoly, and information asymmetry) can be very useful in diagnosing the sort of intraorganizational problems that public managers routinely face.

The fundamental welfare theorem, which formalizes the notion of the "invisible hand," serves as the basis for normative neoclassical economics. It says that in an idealized economy that satisfies certain assumptions about consumer preferences, production technology, the nature of goods and factor inputs, information, and the existence of competitive markets, an equilibrium in prices and quantities of goods and factors exists and that it is Pareto efficient.[1] That is, it would not be possible to find a reallocation that would make someone better off without making anyone else worse off.

Certain violations of the fundamental welfare theorem's assumptions, which can be analyzed within the neoclassical framework, represent the traditional market failures that lie at the operational heart of welfare economics. They involve situations in which rational behavior by individuals results in equilibria that are not Pareto efficient in the sense that alternative allocations can be identified that could make at least some people better off without making anyone else worse off.

An economic approach to policy analysis seeks market failures as rationales for affirmative public policy. Further, associated with each of the market failures are a number of generic "solutions" that provide starting points for designing policy alternatives. For example, in situations involving externalities, characterized by a gap between marginal private costs and marginal social costs, one generic solution is for government to impose a tax or provide a subsidy that closes the gap. Other generic solutions to externality problems include direct regulation of the activity generating the externality and allowing those who bear a negative externality to seek compensation through tort from those who generate it. Thus, framing policy problems as market failures naturally leads the analyst to candidate solutions.

Although welfare economics frames these failures in the neoclassical world of market exchange, we believe that they provide a useful conceptual resource for understanding behavior within organizations and, therefore, potentially offer insight into effective organizational design and more. The production and exchange of intermediate products among organizational members, and the production and delivery of final products to the customers of the organization, can be viewed as occurring in intraorganizational markets. This may strike some readers as a bit curious, because one explanation for the existence of hierarchical organizations is that they are responses to market failures that make spot transactions unsatisfactory. Organizations to some extent substitute hierarchies of authority for market exchange. Members subject themselves to hierarchical authority in return for an ongoing relationship that provides some package of monetary and nonmonetary compensation. Yet, because the direct exercise of authority is costly in terms of specifying, monitoring, and enforcing directives, organizations typically delegate considerable discretion to their members. Thus, in many spheres of organizational life, members are free to pursue their self-interest within very broad constraints. Their interactions can be thought of as occurring in organizational markets where expenditures of time and effort are generally the relevant prices.

This perspective makes the distinction between markets and hierarchies less significant. Markets embody some hierarchy, typically a centrally enforced system of property rights but also perhaps various regulations by government agencies. Within hierarchical organizations, considerable discretion is often delegated to people whose behavior can be understood as the pursuit of self-interest subject to various administrative constraints. Indeed, the boundaries of hierarchical organizations become blurred when the organizations contract with nonmembers for the provision of services.

We develop the organizational market failure framework more systematically elsewhere (Weimer and Vining, 1992, pp. 131–138; Vining and Weimer, 1990, 1993). We offer here only a few illustrations in an effort to convey the usefulness of this approach as a conceptual resource for diagnosing and managing organizational problems.

Achieving a Favorable Organizational Reputation

A favorable reputation is valuable to both the organization and its members. A reputation for customer service may enable a private firm to expand its market; a reputation for competence and efficiency may enable a government bureau to secure more resources and greater jurisdiction from its political sponsors. Organizational members may find their jobs easier and more pleasurable when their organization has a favorable reputation. Nevertheless, departments of motor vehicles and many other organizations we routinely encounter have difficulty establishing and maintaining favorable reputations. The reason is that reputation is a public good for the organizational members.

A private good is rivalrous (only one person can use it at a time) and excludable (a particular person has exclusive control over its use). A pure public good like organizational reputation is neither rivalrous (new members benefit from the reputation without reducing its benefits to existing members) nor excludable (short of expulsion from the organization, no member can be excluded from its benefits). The chronic problem of pure public goods is undersupply.

Members of organizations typically produce both private and public goods. The production of private goods is easy to monitor—number of cases processed, dollar value of sales, units of product delivered. The production of public goods is typically much more difficult to monitor—courtesy to customers, extra effort to solve a customer's or colleague's problem, reliability of final and intermediate products. Organizational reward systems are typically based only on private good production because of these differences in the ease of monitoring.

In order to elicit supply of an organizational public good, managers must find ways of either rewarding actions that contribute to it or penalizing actions that undermine it. Making public examples of reputation-enhancing and reputation-detracting actions that come to the manager's attention is one approach. Another approach is to make the discovery of examples more systematic through soliciting or sampling customer opinions about the quality of the performance of organizational members. In situations in which coworkers can observe each other's actions, they may be involved in the monitoring and rewarding process through such devices as "quality circles." The general point is that managers should expect organizational public goods to be undersupplied without some sort of authoritative intervention to encourage provision.

We assume that the managers of private organizations are willing to expend effort to increase the supply of organizational public goods. The managers of government bureaus with monopoly positions, however, may not be willing to put effort into increasing organizational public goods because they do not have to compete for customers. Further, civil service may make it difficult for them to create incentives to motivate workers to provide public goods. Thus, relative to private organizations, government bureaus are likely to have lower levels of organizational public goods such as a favorable reputation.

Overuse of Resources

Often, organizational resources such as secretarial capacity, the time of employees having specialized skills, and shared computer systems are overused and eventually depleted or degraded. Overuse usually occurs when the goods have the characteristic of common property: They are rivalrous but not excludable. The generic solution to common property problems is to convert them to private goods by introducing excludability through such means as establishing user prices or giving "property rights" over use to a specific person.

Consider the case of a shared computer system. It is quite possible that when the system is introduced into the organization, demand for computing at zero price is sufficiently low such that no queuing occurs. As the organization grows, however, demand grows sufficiently to create queuing and other degradations of service. A natural solution is to introduce fees to discourage relatively low valued uses so that remaining users do not bear the costs of queuing. But to be effective, the fees must be denominated in units that have some other value to organizational members. Unless unspent funds in individual computer budgets can be used for other things of value to organizational members, such as equipment or travel, they will have no incentive to spend less than the full amount on computing. Indeed, if they anticipate that subsequent allocations will depend on current spending, then they have an incentive to be sure that they spend the entire account. Although the aggregate amount of budget allocations can be set to avoid queuing, sufficient information to provide individual budgets to facilitate most valued uses is unlikely to be available. The result may be inefficiency in excess of that caused by queuing.

Government bureaus typically face more severe constraints in establishing fungible budgets than do private firms. Line-item budgeting and constraints on the conversion of unused organizational resources to private income preclude designs available to private firms. Nevertheless, one of the thrusts of "reinventing government" is to allow at least managers to have fungible budgets (Osborne and Gaebler, 1992, 119–122). As we discuss later, however, such systems suffer from a lack of credibility.

Natural resources owned as common property often are depleted. Yet the users of common property resources sometimes develop governance systems that, while not necessarily achieving efficient utilization levels, preserve the resources over extended periods. Based on the observation of a large number of common property resources, Elinor Ostrom (1990) has distilled a number of design principles that seem to characterize those that are long-enduring. For example, such factors as mutual monitoring by users, participation in the determination of appropriation rules by all users, and the fitting of appropriation rules to local conditions appear to contribute to longevity. Transferring these design principles to organizational common property suggests that allowing workgroups to set rules for their use might be a promising approach to preventing their degradation.

Undersupply of Specialized Resources

As a final illustration, consider a situation in which an organization relies on a particular member for expertise in an area such as law, accounting, or engineering. Supply of the in-house expertise may have the characteristics of a natural monopoly: Over the relevant range of demand for the expertise, the average cost of its provision is falling because demand can be accommodated by a single person. The cost of the expert's employment contract can be thought of as a fixed cost; the managerial effort and user inconvenience involved in inducing the expert to deliver the expertise can be thought of as the variable cost. Natural monopolists have an incentive to restrict supply in order to drive up price and gain rents. The monopoly supplier of organizational expertise may similarly restrict effort to enjoy an easier life or obtain rents, though the higher "price" that results may be manifested as deference, queuing, or even bribes of some sort.

In recent years, the concept of contestability has been introduced to the study of natural monopoly (Baumol, Panzar, and Willig, 1982). A monopoly is contestable if there are *potential* alternative suppliers of the good. It is not contestable if there are barriers to entry, such as costly organization-specific investments in human capital that have substantially less value in other uses. If the monopoly is contestable, then the monopolist can be expected to limit prices to discourage takeovers. If it is not, then the monopolist can raise price to maximize rent without concern about loss of the monopoly.

Increasing the contestability of supply is one strategy for managers to improve the performance of monopoly suppliers within their organizations. For example, barriers to entry may be lowered by creating circumstances, such as task forces and apprenticeships, in which the monopoly supplier reveals information to other organizational members. Resistance to such strategies often appears as "turf wars," with members who enjoy monopoly positions guarding the information and the authorities that function as barriers to entry.

In situations involving the supply of a specialized resource by a group of organizational members, the members may collude to obtain monopoly rent for the group as a whole. A well-known example is the account provided by Michel Crozier (1964) of French mechanics who used intimidation and sabotage to prevent others from acquiring or exercising expertise concerning factory machines. Managers may try to break up such cartels by weakening the social relations among the colluders, say, by dispersing them to line-units rather than keeping them as a staff function. In the creation of positions in organizations, managers should keep in mind that job classifications in union contracts and civil service regulations may help group members create barriers to entry.

Summary: The Underlying Importance of Information Asymmetry

Information asymmetry arises when some members of the organization have information that they can withhold from other members. Organizational inefficiency results if the information is withheld when providing it would reduce organizational costs by more than the cost of its provision.[2] Though we focused on pure public goods, common property problems, and natural monopoly in illustrating how market failure concepts can be useful to managers in diagnosing and correcting commonly encountered organizational pathologies, one of the other traditional market failures—information asymmetry—was implicitly involved in each of these illustrations through the assumption that monitoring of the behavior of organizational members by managers is costly. Indeed, it is the information asymmetry that generally allows the other market failures to occur in the presence of hierarchical authority that could correct them through fiat. The central thrust of neoinstitutional economics is to make assumptions about information asymmetry explicit rather than implicit.

Neoinstitutional Economics: Ownership, Information, and Transaction Costs

Neoinstitutional economics has developed along two tracks.[3] Agency theory formalizes assumptions about the distribution of property rights and information in the writing of contracts that define organizations. Transaction cost theory explicitly considers the nature of the interaction between economic agents and its relation to forms of organization for governing contracts. The formal application of these theories to practical problems of organizational design has been very limited. In the case of agency theory, the formal models have incorporated very simple assumptions and produced very general propositions, often without immediately apparent empirical application; less formal models have yielded testable implications concerning corporate structure and control that have generally been confirmed by empirical research.[4] With the possible exception of bargaining models, which have actually developed as an independent line of research, transaction cost theory has yet to develop formal models. Nevertheless, both these approaches provide useful general insight into organizational design.

Agency Theory

Organizations can be viewed as collections of explicit and implicit contracts, typically covering periods of longer duration than single transactions and generally characterized by the incomplete specification of all contingencies.[5] Agency theory deals with the design of these contracts. In particular, it focuses on the relationship between principals and agents who exercise authority on their behalf.

Although we normally think of agency theory in terms of hierarchies, with managers as principals and workers as agents, ironically one of the seminal works on agency theory considers just the opposite case. Armen Alchian and Harold Demsetz (1972) propose an explanation for the existence of firms based on the problem of shirking in team production. A situation is characterized by team production when it is costly to monitor the contributions made by each of the team members to the group output. Team members have an incentive to shirk because they each bear the full costs of their effort but only share a fraction of the output. Each team member would be better off if no one shirked than if everyone did. Realizing this, they may decide to hire a manager who can monitor their behavior to eliminate shirking. But how do they keep the manager from shirking? One solution is to write a contract that pays workers fixed amounts (wages) and gives rights to the residual of revenue over cost (profit) to the manager. Thus results a firm owned by the manager.

At about the same time, Stephen Ross (1973) introduced formal techniques for modeling principal-agent relationships.[6] The problem facing the principal is to design a contract that specifies payment to the agent as a function of observable quantities such that the agent receives some minimal expected utility and the principal's expected utility is maximized by the agent's self-interested responses to the provisions of the contract. In the simplest formulation, the output produced is a function of the agent's effort and the realization of some random variable observable only by a risk-neutral agent. The optimal contract in such situations is often of the form of a franchise: The agent pays a fee to the principal and then keeps the entire value of the output.

One of the more thoroughly explored lines of development of the formal model, which leads to more commonly observed employment contracts, has involved consideration of the consequences of assuming that agents are more risk averse than principals (Stiglitz, 1974, 1975; Holmstrom, 1982). In such cases, optimal contracts typically shift some risk to the principal, but as a consequence agents have lower effort levels than they would in the case of risk neutrality. Other extensions consider situations in which the principal can observe a signal correlated with the agent's effort (Holmstrom, 1979), multiple agents compete in tournaments (Nalebuff and Stiglitz, 1983), agents perform multiple tasks (Holmstrom and Milgrom, 1991), and agents are the principals for other agents (Laffont, 1990). For nontechnical surveys of the literature using formal principal-agent models, see Bengt Holmstrom and Jean Tirole (1989), David E. M. Sappington (1991), and Jeffrey Banks (1995).

Unfortunately, the formal principal-agent models often do not provide predictions that can be directly tested empirically (Holmstrom and Tirole, 1989, p. 105).[7] Some related empirical work does offer practical insights into organizational design. Consider, for example, Charles Knoeber's (1989) study of the broiler industry, which has been extremely successful in reducing the real price of chicken over the last thirty years. Large wholesalers, called integrators, typically employ tournaments among sets of independent growers. In each tournament, growers receive similar allotments of chicks, feed, and medicine. The price they receive per pound of delivered chicken depends on how efficiently they use the inputs relative to others in the tournament. The use of tournaments in this industry is theoretically consistent with formal principal-agent models in that the growers face common random effects due to temperature, epidemics, and experimental changes in the genetic stock of chicks. It provides a way of reducing these systematic sources of risk to growers by generating information about their relative rather than just their absolute performances.

Although some examples of the use of tournaments in the public sector can be found (Fong, 1986; Church and Heumann, 1989), tournaments might be more commonly employed to maintain competition (Weimer, 1992). Specific applications arise in the context of dual-sourcing for goods purchased by the government (Riordan and Sappington, 1989; Anton and Yao, 1990) and competitive franchising (Hazlett, 1990). The general design concept for public managers to keep in mind is that they may be able to generate useful information about production costs through ongoing tournaments among contractors, regional offices, or other groups that produce similar products.

Christopher Hall's (1986) study of claiming races suggests another general design concept: inducing the production or revelation of information through the creation of appropriable value (Weimer, 1992). A high percentage of horse races at North American tracks are claiming races in which any horse can be purchased (claimed) for a set price. By setting purses sufficiently above the claim price, some owners will be induced to enter horses worth more than the claim. The possibility of the availability of these bargains induces other buyers to monitor horses, thereby increasing the chances that switched horses will be detected and reducing the chances that owners will hold back horses in prior races to manipulate odds. Claiming thus reassures bettors about the accuracy of public information about horses.

One type of application is in the enforcement of laws. The setting of "bounties" can be used to induce decentralized enforcement. Care must be taken, however, to align the incentives closely to goals or inappropriate enforcement may result. For example, because the "citizen suit" provisions of the Clean Water

Act do not tie bounties to the magnitude of environmental damage, they appear not to be contributing to social efficiency (Greve, 1989). A more worrying example is the provision in many state forfeiture laws allowing police departments to keep all, or a large fraction of, property they seize from people accused of drug-related crimes—it creates not only an incentive to go after large asset holders rather than major offenders but also an invitation to corruption.

Another application is in the creation of rules that induce the revelation of information through forced transactions. Examples include generating information about the costs of regulations by requiring firms to make estimates of how much a regulatory standard will cost and to pay that amount to any outside contractor who can alter equipment to meet the standard (Stonstelie and Portney, 1983); and generating information about the value of natural resources for taxation purposes by requiring owners to state a value and sell the resource at that value to any claimant. Although these particular applications are not necessarily desirable, they suggest how thinking explicitly about information can lead to consideration of organizational designs that might otherwise be overlooked.

A less formal, but empirically richer, strain of agency theory focuses on the effect of different structures of property rights on organizational efficiency. It was formulated in the seminal article on agency cost by Michael Jensen and William Meckling (1976). Agency costs include "the costs of structuring, monitoring, and bonding a set of contracts among agents with conflicting interests, plus the residual loss incurred because the cost of full enforcement of contracts exceeds the benefits" (p. 305). Bonding refers to arrangements made by the agents to raise the costs of their noncompliance. For example, in the case of owners as principals and managers as agents, bonding might include the promise to have audits conducted by independent accountants or an agreement to hold stock that cannot be sold during the manager's tenure. (Blue-ribbon advisory panels and independent internal investigation units may have a similar function for public managers.) The theory has been used to produce testable hypotheses about the relationship between monitoring costs and ownership structures in such industries as property and casualty insurance (Mayers and Smith, 1988).

Agency theory also has relevance to the issue of state versus private ownership of organizations. Politicians serve as the principals for state-owned organizations. In contrast to private owners, who can claim the residual of the organization, political principals are generally prohibited by electoral competition and civil service laws from taking the residual directly as personal gain. Also unlike private owners, individual politicians cannot transfer ownership to others. This nontransferability of public organizations discourages specialization in their ownership, and less effective monitoring of management may result (De Alessi, 1983; Lott, 1987). Public agencies usually have multiple principals, so that managers may receive conflicting and unstable political demands (Moe, 1984). Further, a principal-agent relationship exists between voters and politicians, which encourages oversight to discover sensational instances of fraud, waste, and abuse that will catch the attention of voters rather than more mundane monitoring of the efficiency of routine operations. These factors suggest that, other things being equal, privately owned organizations will be more efficient than state-owned organizations.

A theoretically important "other thing" is the degree of competition that the organization faces in its product markets. One way to hold the degree of competition equal is to limit the comparison of ownership forms to organizations that sell their output in competitive markets. Doing so gives support to the hypothesis that private ownership is more efficient than public ownership (Boardman and Vining, 1989; Vining and Boardman, 1992).

Differences in the effectiveness of oversight help explain why public managers are generally given less discretion than their private counterparts. Control can be accomplished through a combination of ex ante rules and ex post oversight (Thompson and Jones, 1986). When ex post monitoring is relatively less effective, we expect greater reliance on ex ante rules such as strict prohibitions against personal expropriation of organizational resources, line-item budgets, and restrictions on patronage.

Transaction Cost Theory

As with agency theory, the focus of transaction cost theory is the contract (Williamson, 1985). But unlike agency theory, which usually treats agents as simply reacting to contracts designed by principals, transaction cost theory views the parties attempting to engage in exchange (a transaction) as contracting both the terms of the exchange and their execution. The contracting process is costly. It includes not only the structuring, monitoring, bonding, and residual loss costs of agency theory but also the costs of negotiation. At one level, transaction cost theory considers the nature of specific types of transactions. At a broader level, it is concerned with which institutional arrangements best facilitate and economize which kinds of transactions (Williamson, 1985; Maser, 1986; Heckathorn and Maser, 1987; Bryson and Ring, 1990).

Douglas Heckathorn and Steven Maser (1987) identify three important problems that contribute to the costs of contracting. First, a "cooperation problem" arises when having a contract could offer all parties gain relative to the absence of a contract. To achieve a mutually beneficial contract, however, the parties must expend transaction resources that include "(1) the prerequisites for negotiating, for example, communication channels with which to bargain, independent sources of pertinent information with which to assess competing claims, and information processing capacities; and (2) the prerequisites for enforcing contracts, for instance, the ability to monitor compliance and to sanction noncompliance" (p. 76). Second, a "division problem" arises when different mutually beneficial contracts offer different relative gains. The parties may expend both bargaining resources and effort in attempts to secure more favorable contracts for themselves. Third, a "defection problem" arises when noncompliance is in the self-interest of any of the parties. Because it is impossible to anticipate all contingencies when writing contracts, parties sometimes have opportunities to withhold contributions without being subjected to anticipated sanctions or to force renegotiation of terms through threats of noncompliance.[8]

Transactions often involve investments by one or more of the parties in specific assets, such as specialized equipment or knowledge, that have much lower value in uses other than as part of the transaction. Parties who invest in specific assets are especially vulnerable to threats of noncompliance. Therefore, they may be unwilling to enter into contracts unless they receive credible commitments that other parties will not behave opportunistically in exploiting their vulnerability. A central question of political economy is how governments can make credible commitments to convince people that their investments will not be expropriated (Rodrik and Zeckhauser, 1988; North and Weingast, 1989; Root, 1989; Riker and Weimer, 1993) and that the money supply will not be debased (Blackburn and Christensen, 1989). But the problem of credible commitment is pervasive at all levels of organization.

Let us return to the problem of establishing fungible budgets for public managers. The expenditure control budget advocated by Osborne and Gaebler (1992, pp. 119–122) allows managers to carry over unspent funds from one fiscal period to the next.[9] Transaction cost theory suggests that we should be skeptical about the expenditure control budget's use in circumstances in which the manager and the central budget office do not already have a trusting relationship. The reason is that the manager must anticipate the possibility that the budget office will expropriate the savings by reducing the base budget in the next period. If this happens, the manager would not only lose the discretionary use of the savings but she would also have revealed information about the true costs of delivering output that could weaken her bargaining position in the future. What appears to be needed is some mechanism that makes credible the commitment not to expropriate the savings. One possibility is to create a sort of "Swiss bank" that conceals information about savings from the budget office (Weimer, 1992).

The risk of opportunism has obvious relevance to privatization. Competition may be very intense when a contract for provision of some service is initially put out for bids. Once a firm has won the bid, its specific investments in knowledge about producing the service create a barrier to entry that makes the contract less contestable in the future. If loss or degradation of the service is particularly costly to public officials, then the firm will enjoy a favorable bargaining position for renegotiating contract terms. Of course, the government can act opportunistically with respect to employees and suppliers who make organizationally specific investments. Civil service tenure is one way for the government to make a credible commitment that it will not exploit workers who have invested in developing expertise that has little value outside the organization.

One of the specific assets of firms and units of government is the trust they engender by virtue of their track records in supplying goods and services. By demonstrating a general reliability, they create a barrier to contestability that is to their advantage in negotiating the terms of contracts that allow them to operate above minimum cost. Substituting monitoring capability for trust may contribute to more efficient supply. Ironically, therefore, one way to make privatization more effective may be to invest in the core analytical and managerial functions of public organizations (Vining and Weimer, 1990).

Social Choice Theory and Intraorganizational Decision Making

Social choice theory considers the relationship between individual preferences and social preferences. Arrow's General Possibility Theorem raises a fundamental limitation to collective choice: No social choice rule can satisfy minimal conditions of fairness (there is no dictatorship; all transitive preference orderings for individuals are permitted; if one alternative is preferred by every individual over another, then it is socially preferred; the choice rule is not arbitrary in that it will consistently produce the same social ordering from the same individual orderings) and simultaneously guarantee a transitive social ordering of alternatives (Arrow, 1963). Most applications of Arrow's theorem concern the characteristics of voting systems, though it applies to any social choice rule. In particular, it applies to decentralized decision making within organizations.

The Liberal Paradox of Amartya Sen (1970), which replaces the condi-

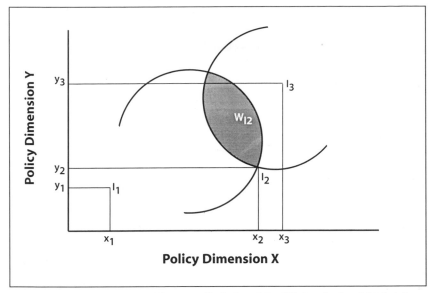

Figure 1   Disequilibrium and Structurally Induced Equilibrium in Spatial Model

tion of nondictatorship with one of minimal delegation, gives a result similar to Arrow's when applied to organizational decision making. In particular, if there are at least two individuals or organizational subunits that each have the authority to rank order at least one pair of alternatives, then no decision rule can guarantee both Pareto efficiency and transitivity of organizational choices for all combinations of individual preferences. This result can be seen as a fundamental theoretical limit to organizational performance (Hammond and Miller, 1985; Miller, 1992).

Pareto efficiency and transitivity at the level of the organization can be achieved by abandoning the condition of unrestricted preferences. One way to do this is to establish a clear corporate culture that through selective recruitment leads to members with homogeneous preferences. To do so, however, may be at the cost of excluding some types of expertise that are correlated with excluded preference profiles. For example, excluding economists from a substantive line-agency may make for a more homogeneous corporate culture but deprive the agency of expertise valuable in some circumstances. Further, as Thomas Hammond and Gary Miller (1985) point out, the fundamental limitation may reappear when decision-making authority in a government is distributed across agencies with distinct corporate cultures.

The simple spatial voting model presented in figure 1 graphically illustrates the fundamental problem of social choice and the potential role of institutional rules in overcoming it.[10] The horizontal axis represents a continuous policy dimension, say, the size of the social welfare program budget. The vertical axis represents a second continuous policy dimension, say, the size of the defense budget. The points labeled I_1, I_2, and I_3 represent the ideal, or most preferred, points for each of three legislators. Assume that each legislator prefers points that are closer rather than farther from his or her ideal point. Imagine that the status quo point is exactly the ideal point of legislator two, I_2. What do we expect to happen if a policy combination (x,y) is to be chosen by a majority rule vote?

The circular arc centered at I_1 and passing through the status quo point is an "indifference curve" for legislator one in the sense that it represents all the points that she finds equally satisfactory to the status quo. Legislator one prefers any point inside the arc because it is closer to her ideal point. The other circle arc similarly represents points of indifference to the status quo for legislator three. The intersection of these arcs, the shaded area labeled W_{12}, represents all the points that both legislator one and legislator two prefer to the status quo. Thus, if each legislator votes his or her sincere preferences, then any proposal within W_{12} would beat the status quo two votes to one.

The fundamental social choice problem arises because through a similar procedure we can find proposals that beat the new status quo. There is no equilibrium because any policy can be beaten in a majority rule vote by some alternatives. Indeed, Richard McKelvey (1976) shows that if one of the legislators has control over the agenda, he or she can, by successively proposing alternatives to the previous winning proposal, eventually secure any point in the policy space including his or her ideal point. Thus, there is either no equilibrium or one induced by giving control of the agenda to one legislator.

The institution of an "agenda setter" is one way to induce an equilibrium. Kenneth Shepsle (1979) began a line of research that explores the various institutional arrangements that can induce an equilibrium. For example, consider the delegation of authority to committees such that each one has complete authority over one of the policy dimensions. In figure 1, the points x_1, x_2, and x_3 represent the legislators' ideal points on the single dimension decided by a committee. In this case, the Median Voter Theorem gives x_2 as the equilibrium. Similarly, the committee with authority over the other policy dimension would select y_2 by majority rule vote. An equilibrium corresponding to I_2 would emerge as long as the committee structure guaranteed that only votes involving changes in one dimension at a time occurred.[11]

Spatial models provide a framework for thinking systematically about po-

litical strategy. William Riker (1986) describes "heresthetics," the art of political manipulation, in terms of agenda control, strategic voting (voting against
one's true preferences to obtain a more favorable outcome in future votes), and
the manipulation of policy dimensions. Heresthetics can help public managers
find strategies for getting more favorable results from the various political arenas in which they operate. It can also contribute to more effective organizational design.

Consider, for example, the Department of Defense's success in closing un-
necessary military bases (Weimer, 1992). Between 1976 and 1989 virtually no
military bases were closed. But in 1988, Congress delegated to a commission
the authority for formulating the set of bases to be closed. Congress further imposed a closed rule (no amendments are permitted) on the recommendations
of the commission and exempted the proposed closures from environmental
impact statement requirements that could be used to move the decisions from
the legislative to the judicial arena. As a result of these institutional changes,
bases could be closed.

Game Theoretic Models of Institutions

In common usage, institutions generally refer to the societal rules, whether
formal or informal, that constrain individual behavior. But why do people obey
the rules when violating them may be in their immediate interests? Returning
to figure 1, for instance, in the case of committee jurisdiction over policy dimensions, why is it that legislators one and three do not vote to suspend the
rules so as to be able to propose alternatives to the status quo that they find desirable? Resorting to some external authority, such as judicial interpretation of
a constitution, gives only a partial answer because it raises the question of why
the external authority is accepted. The most general theory of institutions should
explain why a set of rules is constraining without resort to some external authority. In other words, the rules constituting the institution should be self-en-
forcing in the sense that individuals voluntarily accept them.

The elements of an economic theory of institutions that meets these requirements were introduced by Andrew Schotter (1981), who views institutions, including such informal rules as conventions and norms, as equilibria in
repeated noncooperative games. A social situation is represented as a one-stage
game involving either a cooperation or coordination problem, so that the equilibrium strategies of the players lead to an outcome that is Pareto inefficient.
If this stage game is repeated indefinitely, however, then, with appropriate assumptions about the knowledge and discount rates of the players, equilibria can

result that involve varying degrees of cooperation, often including ones that achieve Pareto efficiency.[12]

By far the most commonly employed stage game is the well known Prisoners' Dilemma, characterized by an equilibrium involving "defection" by both players, whereas "cooperation" by both players would be Pareto efficient. If the game is repeated such that the players do not know the last period of play with certainty, then there may be many possible equilibria that lead to Pareto-efficient levels of cooperation, depending on their discount rates, the probability that the game continues from one period to the next, and the payoff structure of the stage game. For example, plausible assumptions often make mutual playing of the well-known "tit-for-tat" strategy (cooperate in the first period, then play the stage-game strategy that your opponent played in the previous period) an equilibrium that results in continuous cooperation.

Although most of this literature is at least one step away from modeling real institutions, one exceptional work shows the possibilities for application. Paul Milgrom, Douglass North, and Barry Weingast (1990) consider the problem of trade in the Middle Ages, which was characterized by infrequent interactions among a large number of traders. They show how a cooperative equilibrium, involving a third party who keeps records about contract compliance, can result. The record keeper corresponds closely to the historical institution of the law merchant.

David Kreps (1990) and Gary Miller (1992) make an important connection between the economic theory of institutions and leadership. They note that repeated games generally have multiple equilibria; indeed, the so-called Folk Theorem states that repeated games can even have an infinite number of equilibria. If many different equilibria are possible, then a coordination problem arises: How can the players know which strategies to play so that one of the more desirable equilibria results? An effective leader provides a vision of one of the desirable equilibria and communicates it to the members of the organization. She thus facilitates effective coordination by giving members consistent expectations about each other's behavior. Symbols may play a role in creating the shared expectations; so too might the personal interaction achieved through "management by walking around."

The importance of the credibility of managerial commitments becomes apparent in viewing organizations as repeated games. Members must anticipate not only that if they make contributions to the collective endeavor that others will as well but also that they will not be disadvantaged in future plays because they have revealed information that leaves them vulnerable to exploitation. Miller (1992), in work coauthored with Jack Knott, illustrates the importance of credible commitment through an analysis of piece-rate incentives, a contract form favored more in economic theory than in actual use. Workgroups, fearing a ratcheting down of piece rates and potential layoffs, generally create norms to limit output. The rare organization that effectively uses piece rates probably does so by convincing workers that they have job security and by giving them a role in the setting of rates. A corporate culture consisting of a set of norms about how workers will be treated may be valuable in giving credibility to the commitments by individual managers whose tenure is uncertain.

Corporate culture can also be viewed in the context of incomplete contracts (Kreps, 1990). It communicates general principles for dealing with unanticipated contingencies and provides a basis for evaluating performance ex post. Maintaining a generally valuable corporate culture may explain what otherwise appears as inappropriate managerial rigidity: Support for its principles, even when they lead to specific outcomes that are not in the best interests of the involved parties in any particular situation, may make their continued application more credible. This view of corporate culture raises a number of interesting design questions. For example, if it is important for an organization to have a single corporate culture, then should the substantive jurisdictions of public organizations be limited so that the principles constituting their corporate cultures will be appropriate for dealing with the types of unanticipated consequences they are likely to face?

Although the practical consequences of interpreting leadership and corporate culture in terms of repeated games are not yet clear, we think that this approach provides a promising conceptual foundation for generalizing about these important but elusive phenomena.

Conclusion

A variety of economic literatures, summarized in table 1, inform organizational design. The market failure framework, so central to welfare economics, can be easily applied to diagnose, and perhaps remedy, commonly encountered organizational problems. The neoinstitutional literatures focusing on agency and transaction costs bring theory a step closer to providing practical concepts for organizational design. The social choice and institutional theory literatures offer deep conceptual foundations not only for organizational design but also for some important aspects of the executive function. As these literatures are continuing to grow, they have prospects for offering more to public management in the future.

Table 1

Overview of Economic Concepts of Potential Use to Public Management Research.

Economic Approach	Central Notion	Area of Application
Neoclassical Welfare Economics	Market failures occur when violations of the assumptions of the competitive framework lead to equilibria that are not Pareto efficient	Administrative rules and incentives to increase efficiency of intra-organizational markets: solving organizational public good, common property resource, and natural monopoly problems
Neoinstitutional Economics: Agency Theory	Contracts structure the relationship between principals and agents to minimize agency cost, which is the sum of the costs of structuring, monitoring, and bonding contracts and the loss from residual discretion	Organizational design: creating incentives for the production and revelation of information that improve the efficiency of intra- and inter-organizational transactions
Neoinstitutional Economics: Transaction Cost Theory	Institutional arrangements economize on transaction cost: the sum of precontract bargaining and postcontract compliance (opportunism) costs	Organizational design: creating hostages, bonds, and other mechanisms for generating credible commitment and discouraging opportunism
Social Choice Theory	Social choice rules are prone to disequilibrium; institutional structure may induce equilibrium	Organizational design and political strategy: obtaining substantive outcomes through the manipulation of procedural rules
Economic Theory of Institutions	Institutions are equilibria in repeated games; equilibria are rarely unique	Corporate culture and leadership: creating focal points for more efficient organizational equilibria

Notes

1. Relaxing these assumptions has both positive and normative implications: It allows analysts to make predictions about the consequences of differences in institutional arrangements; it also brings into question the interpretation of efficiency in neoclassical welfare theory by treating institutional arrangements as a matter of choice rather than taking them as given (Bromley, 1989).

2. For a discussion of information asymmetry as a market failure, see Vining and Weimer (1988).

3. Neoinstitutional economics can be thought of as a subset of what has been called the "new institutional economics." The latter includes models that relax the assumption of individual rationality central to neoclassical economic theory. For example, Oliver Williamson (1985) conceives of transaction cost theory as broadly including bounded rationality and, therefore, as a part of the new institutional economics. In this chapter, because of our definition of economics, we limit our attention to that part of transaction cost theory that preserves the assumption of individual rationality.

4. Empirical research in four areas—corporate control, vertical integration, managerial compensation, and organizational structure of corporations—has been "mostly confirmatory." See Hesterly, Liebeskind, and Zenger (1990) for a review.

5. In this framework, management involves monitoring the execution of contracts and providing appropriate direction to organizational members when unspecified contingencies arise.

6. Elements of the model were introduced by Robert Wilson (1968) in the theory of syndicates and by Michael Spence and Richard Zeckhauser (1971) in their article on insurance and information.

7. We are reminded of the story of the men in a balloon who had become lost. They shouted to a man below, "Where are we?" He responded, "In a balloon." They concluded he must be an economist because he was precise but unhelpful. So far, the formal principal-agent literature has been more valuable in providing precise specifications of a variety of information asymmetries, such as hidden information and hidden action, than in informing practical issues of design.

8. The relative efficiency of giving residual rights to the various parties in situations of incomplete contracts provides an explanation for ownership of assets in organizations. See Klein, Crawford, and Alchian (1978) and Grossman and Hart (1986).

9. Robert Biller (1976) advocated the establishment of "savings banks" to allow carryover of some fraction of unspent funds to avoid the end-of-period rush to spend the budget.

10. For an excellent overview of spatial models, see Krehbiel (1988).

11. Viewing one of the committees as an agency, say, controlling the policy dimension corresponding to the speed of implementation, provides a way of thinking about the nature and stability of administrative discretion (see Hill, 1985).

12. For excellent overviews of this approach to the study of institutions, see Calvert (1995a, 1995b).

References

Alchian, Armen. 1950. "Uncertainty, Evolution, and Economic Theory." *Journal of Political Economy* 58, no. 3: 211–221.

Alchian, Armen, and Harold Demsetz. 1972. "Production, Information Costs, and Economic Organization." *American Economic Review* 62, no. 5: 777–795.

Anton, James J., and Dennis A. Yao. 1990. "Measuring the Effectiveness of Competition in Defense Procurement: A Survey of the Empirical Literature." *Journal of Policy Analysis and Management* 9, no. 1: 60–79.

Arrow, Kenneth J. 1963. *Social Choice and Individual Values,* 2d ed. New Haven: Yale University Press.

Arrow, Kenneth J., and Gerard Debreu. 1954. "Existence of an Equilibrium for a Competitive Economy." *Econometrica* 22, no. 3: 265–290.

Banks, Jeffrey S. 1995. "The Design of Institutions: An Agency Theory Perspective," in David L. Weimer, ed., *Institutional Design,* pp. 17–36. Boston: Kluwer Academic Publishing.

Barzelay, Michael. 1992. *Breaking through Bureaucracy: A New Vision for Managing in Government.* Berkeley: University of California Press.

Baumol, William J., John C. Panzar, and Robert D. Willig. 1982. *Contestable Markets and the Theory of Industry Structure.* New York: Harcourt Brace Jovanovich.

Biller, Robert P. 1976. "On Tolerating Policy and Organizational Termination: Some Design Considerations." *Policy Sciences* 7, no. 2: 133–149.

Blackburn, Keith, and Michael Christensen. 1989. "Monetary Policy and Policy Credibility: Theories and Evidence." *Journal of Economic Literature* 27, no. 1: 1–45.

Boardman, Anthony, and Aidan R. Vining. 1989. "Ownership and Performance in Competitive Environments: A Comparison of the Performance of Private, Mixed, and State-Owned Enterprises." *Journal of Law and Economics* 24, no. 3: 189–214.

Bromley, Daniel W. 1989. *Economic Interests and Institutions: The Conceptual Foundations of Public Policy.* New York: Basil Blackwell.

Bryson, John M., and Peter Smith Ring. 1990. "A Transaction-Based Approach to Policy Intervention." *Policy Sciences* 23, no. 3: 205–229.

Calvert, Randall. 1995a. "The Rational Choice Theory of Social Institutions: Cooperation, Coordination, and Communication," in Jeffrey Banks and Eric A. Hanushek, eds., *Modern Political Economy: Old Topics, New Directions,* pp. 216–267. New York: Cambridge University Press.

———. 1995b. "Rational Choice Theory of Institutions: Implications for Design," in David L. Weimer, ed., *Institutional Design,* pp. 63–94. Boston: Kluwer Academic Publishing.

Church, Thomas W., and Milton Heumann. 1989. "The Underexamined Assumptions of the Invisible Hand: Monetary Incentives as Policy Instruments." *Journal of Policy Analysis and Management* 8, no. 4: 641–657.

Coase, Ronald. 1937. "The Nature of the Firm." *Economica* 4 (November): 386–405.

Crozier, Michel. 1964. *The Bureaucratic Phenomenon.* Chicago: University of Chicago Press.

Cyert, Richard M., and James G. March. 1963. *A Behavioral Theory of the Firm.* Englewood Cliffs, N.J.: Prentice Hall.

De Alessi, Louis. 1983. "Property Rights, Transaction Costs, and X-Efficiency." *American Economic Review* 73, no. 1: 64–81.

Downs, Anthony. 1966. *Inside Bureaucracy.* Boston: Little, Brown.

Eggertsson, Thrainn. 1990. *Economic Behavior and Institutions.* New York: Cambridge University Press.

Fong, Glenn R. 1986. "The Potential for Industrial Policy: Lessons from the Very High Speed Integrated Circuit Program." *Journal of Policy Analysis and Management* 5, no. 2: 264–291.

Greve, Michael S. 1989. "Environmentalism and Bounty Hunting." *Public Interest,* no. 97 (Fall): 15–29.

Grossman, Sanford, and Oliver Hart. 1986. "The Costs and Benefits of Ownership: A Theory of Vertical and Lateral Integration." *Journal of Political Economy* 94, no. 4: 691–719.

Hall, Christopher D. 1986. "Market Enforcement of Information Asymmetry: A Study of Claiming Races." *Economic Inquiry* 24, no. 2: 271–291.

Hammond, Thomas H., and Gary J. Miller. 1985. "A Social Choice Perspective on Expertise and Authority in Bureaucracy." *American Journal of Political Science* 29, no. 1: 1–28.

Hazlett, Thomas W. 1990. "Duopolistic Competition in Cable Television: Implications for Public Policy." *Yale Journal of Regulation* 7, no. 1: 65–119.

Heckathorn, Douglas D., and Steven M. Maser. 1987. "Bargaining and the Sources of Transaction Costs: The Case of Government Regulation." *Journal of Law, Economics, and Organization* 3, no. 1: 69–98.

Hesterly, William S., Julia Liebeskind, and Todd R. Zenger. 1990. "Organizational Economics: An Impending Revolution in Organization Theory?" *Academy of Management Review* 15, no. 3: 402–420.

Hill, Jeffrey S. 1985. "Why So Much Stability? The Impact of Agency Determined Stability." *Public Choice* 46, no. 3: 275–287.

Holmstrom, Bengt. 1979. "Moral Hazard and Observability." *Bell Journal of Economics* 9, no. 2: 74–91.

———. 1982. "Moral Hazard in Teams." *Bell Journal of Economics* 13, no. 2: 324–340.

Holmstrom, Bengt, and Paul Milgrom. 1991. "Multitask Principal-Agent Analyses: Incentive Contracts, Asset Ownership, and Job Design." *Journal of Law, Economics, and Organization* 7 (Special Issue): 24–52.

Holmstrom, Bengt, and Jean Tirole. 1989. "The Theory of the Firm," in Richard Schmalensee and Robert D. Willig, eds., *Handbook of Industrial Organization,* 1:61–133. New York: North-Holland.

Jensen, Michael C., and William H. Meckling. 1976. "Theory of the Firm: Managerial Behavior, Agency Costs, and Ownership Structure." *Journal of Financial Economics* 3, no. 4: 305–360.

Klein, Benjamin, Robert G. Crawford, and Armen A. Alchian. 1978. "Vertical Integration, Appropriable Rents, and the Competitive Contracting Process." *Journal of Law and Economics* 21, no. 2: 297–326.

Knoeber, Charles R. 1989. "A Real Game of Chicken: Contracts, Tournaments, and the Production of Broilers." *Journal of Law, Economics, and Organization* 5, no. 2: 271–292.

Krehbiel, Keith. 1988. "Spatial Models of Legislative Choice." *Legislative Studies Quarterly* 13, no. 3: 259–319.

Kreps, David M. 1990. "Corporate Culture and Economic Theory," in James E. Alt and Kenneth A. Shepsle, eds., *Perspectives on Positive Political Economy,* pp. 90–143. New York: Cambridge University Press.

Laffont, Jean-Jacques. 1990. "Analysis of Hidden Gaming in a Three-Level Hierarchy." *Journal of Law, Economics, and Organization* 6, no. 2: 301–324.

Lott, John R., Jr. 1987. "The Effect of Nontransferable Property Rights on the Efficiency of Political Markets." *Journal of Public Economics* 32, no. 2: 231–246.

Marschak, Jacob. 1955. "Elements for a Theory of Teams." *Management Science* 1, no. 2: 127–137.

Maser, Steven M. 1986. "Transaction Costs in Public Administration," in Donald J. Calista, ed., *Bureaucratic and Governmental Reform,* pp. 55–71. Greenwich, Conn.: JAI Press.

Mayers, David, and Clifford W. Smith Jr. 1988. "Ownership Structure Across Lines of Property-Casualty Insurance." *Journal of Law and Economics* 31, no. 2: 351–378.

McKelvey, Richard D. 1976. "Intransitivities in Multidimensional Voting Models and Some Implications for Agenda Control." *Journal of Economic Theory* 12, no. 3: 472–482.

Milgrom, Paul R., Douglass C. North, and Barry Weingast. 1990. "The Role of Institutions in the Revival of Trade: The Law Merchant, Private Judges, and the Champagne Fairs." *Economics and Politics* 2, no. 1: 1–23.

Miller, Gary J. 1992. *Managerial Dilemmas: The Political Economy of Hierarchy.* New York: Cambridge University Press.

Moe, Terry M. 1984. "The New Economics of Organization." *American Journal of Political Science* 28, no. 4: 739–777.

Nalebuff, Barry, and Joseph E. Stiglitz. 1983. "Prizes and Incentives: Towards a General Theory of Compensation and Competition." *Bell Journal of Economics* 14, no. 1: 21–43.

Niskanen, William A., Jr. 1971. *Bureaucracy and Representative Government.* Chicago: Aldine Atherton.

North, Douglass C., and Barry R. Weingast. 1989. "Constitutions and Credible Commitments: The Evolution of the Institutions of Public Choice in 17th Century England." *Journal of Economic History* 59, no. 4: 803–832.

Osborne, David, and Ted Gaebler. 1992. *Reinventing Government: How the Entrepreneurial Spirit Is Transforming the Public Sector.* Reading, Mass.: Addison–Wesley.

Ostrom, Elinor. 1990. *Governing the Commons: The Evolution of Institutions for Collective Action.* New York: Cambridge University Press.

Riker, William H. 1986. *The Art of Political Manipulation.* New Haven: Yale University Press.

Riker, William H., and David L. Weimer. 1993. "The Economic and Political Liberalization of Socialism: The Fundamental Problem of Property Rights." *Social Philosophy and Policy* 10, no. 2: 79–102.

Riordan, Michael H., and David E. M. Sappington. 1989. "Second Sourcing." *Rand Journal of Economics* 20, no. 1: 42–58.

Rodrik, Dani, and Richard Zeckhauser. 1988. "The Dilemma of Government Responsiveness." *Journal of Policy Analysis and Management* 7, no. 4: 601–620.

Root, Hilton. 1989. "Tying the King's Hands: Credible Commitments and Royal Fiscal Policy during the Old Regime." *Rationality and Society* 1, no. 2: 240–258.

Ross, Stephen A. 1973. "The Economic Theory of Agency: The Principal's Problem." *American Economic Review* 63, no. 2: 134–139.

Sappington, David E. M. 1991. "Incentives in Principal-Agent Relationships." *Journal of Economic Perspectives* 5, no. 2: 45–66.

Schotter, Andrew. 1981. *The Economic Theory of Social Institutions.* New York: Cambridge University Press.

Sen, Amartya K. 1970. *Collective Choice and Social Welfare.* San Francisco: Holden-Day.

Shepsle, Kenneth A. 1979. "Institutional Arrangements and Equilibrium in Multidimensional Voting Models." *American Journal of Political Science* 23, no. 1: 27–69.

Spence, A. Michael, and Richard Zeckhauser. 1971. "Insurance, Information, and Individual Action." *American Economic Review* 61, no. 2: 380–387.

Stiglitz, Joseph. 1974. "Risk Sharing and Incentives in Sharecropping." *Review of Economic Studies* 41, no. 126: 219–256.

———. 1975. "Incentives, Risk, and Information: Notes Toward a Theory of Hierarchy." *Bell Journal of Economics* 6, no. 2: 552–579.

Stonstelie, Jon C., and Paul R. Portney. 1983. "Truth or Consequences: Cost Revelation and Regulation." *Journal of Policy Analysis and Management* 2, no. 2: 280–284.

Thompson, Fred, and L. R. Jones. 1986. "Controllership in the Public Sector." *Journal of Policy Analysis and Management* 5, no. 3: 547–571.

Vining, Aidan R., and Anthony Boardman. 1992. "Ownership Versus Competition: Efficiency in Public Enterprise." *Public Choice* 73, no. 2: 205–239.

Vining, Aidan R., and David L. Weimer. 1988. "Information Asymmetry Favoring Sellers: A Policy Framework." *Policy Sciences* 21, no. 4: 281–303.

———. 1990. "Government Supply and Government Production Failure: A Framework Based on Contestability." *Journal of Public Policy* 10, no. 1: pp. 1–22.

———. 1993. "Organizational Incentives and Organizational Inefficiencies." Manuscript.

Weimer, David L. 1992. "Claiming Races, Broiler Contracts, Heresthetics, and Habits: Ten Concepts for Policy Design." *Policy Sciences* 25, no. 2: 135–159.

Weimer, David L., and Aidan Vining. 1992. *Policy Analysis: Concepts and Practice,* 2d ed. Englewood Cliffs, N.J.: Prentice Hall.

Williamson, Oliver E. 1975. *Markets and Hierarchies: Analysis and Antitrust Implications.* New York: Free Press.

———. 1985. *The Economic Institutions of Capitalism.* New York: Free Press.

Wilson, Robert. 1968. "The Theory of Syndicates." *Econometrica* 36, no. 1: 119–152.

6.

Psychology

Janet A. Weiss

Research on public management covers a broad and exciting intellectual territory with relatively underdeveloped intellectual tools (Lynn, 1994; Weiss, 1994). How can managers structure and manage public agencies to produce intended policy outcomes in society? How do public officials coordinate the work of various agencies, branches, and levels of government in interaction with the private and nonprofit sectors of society to produce intended policy results? How can public policies be designed to enhance the capacity of governments and managers to produce intended policy outcomes? Questions of organization, institutional arrangements, and policies are all raised by empirical study of public management. Given that the field has been created and defined by a body of practice rather than by a body of theory, many theoretical traditions are potentially valuable in illuminating corners of this territory. Psychology offers potential contributions ranging beyond the traditional reliance on political science theoretical traditions.

Drawing theoretical perspectives from basic social science disciplines may seem odd in fields of scholarship principally concerned with the nature of practice. However, making use of several disciplines diversifies the stock of theoretical conjectures available to researchers and practitioners. Diversification is important, according to Weick's account of theorizing, because theory construction can be seen as an evolutionary process, relying on the "three processes of evolution: variation, selection, and retention" (1989, p. 519). The search for theory is triggered by problem statements (which produce variation). Theorists seek to explain or solve the problems they observe by use of theoretical conjectures. Conjectures are evaluated for their fit to the problems observed (selection). In publishing and reading the work of other scholars, some conjectures are retained by the field; others are discarded or ignored (retention). The criteria for choosing "good" problems to theorize about, for selecting conjectures worth exploring, for retaining conjectures for further work and attention can be single or multiple. Evolutionary logic predicts that the quality of theory produced in the field as a whole will vary with the diversity of the problem statements that trigger theory building, the number of and independence among the conjectures theorists invoke to explain or solve the problem, and the number and diversity of selection criteria used to test the conjectures (Weick, 1989, p. 516).

Two implications follow. First is the payoff to diversity. A richer pool of theory results when more diverse theoretical notions have the opportunity to compete for selection and retention, and when the selection and retention processes permit theoretical notions to survive for several different reasons. Possible winners are not weeded out prematurely. Creative alternatives earn the right to compete with established theoretical notions. Second is the importance of selection among conjectures. Theorizing stagnates when "virtually all conjectures and all selection criteria remain plausible and nothing gets rejected or highlighted" (Weick, 1989, p. 521). Selection and retention must be powerful enough to discriminate among conjectures.

Public management research has embraced close connections to practitioners, which leads to a strong and diverse body of problem statements (richly detailed, nuanced, true to experience), which can lead to interesting topics for theorizing. However, those close connections do not necessarily generate a strong and diverse set of possible theoretical notions (or conjectures, as Weick says). Nor do they encourage the use of diverse criteria for researchers to select among competing explanations. Indeed, we may rely too heavily on plausibility to practitioners as our criterion for selection and retention, leading us to overlook systematic influences of individuals, situations, and institutions that are not highly salient to involved participants (Weiss, 1994).

The social science disciplines are one obvious source of inspiration and variation in the conjectures we apply to public management problems. Because the various disciplines represent distinctive and, to some extent, independent sources of ideas and modes of explanation and inquiry, scholars familiar with developments in the disciplines have a more diverse inventory of conjectures to use to explain complex problems than those who have cut loose from their disciplinary moorings.

Problem statements can then be framed in ways that help to evaluate theoretical conjectures, in addition to tackling problems as defined by practitioners. Work generated by those with a primary agenda of advancing and discriminating among theoretical explanations creates a larger pool of conjectures that have been subjected to serious examination. This pool is then available to be applied to specific practitioner problems as they arise. As scholars collectively amass a more heterogeneous set of explanations for public management phenomena, the field possesses a richer, more valuable set of conjectures to apply to new and ongoing problems. I should note that this model of theoretical progress does not predict that a dominant discipline or theory will emerge to define and bind the field of public management into a coherent whole. Instead, many disciplines can supply theories of public management phenomena and the best of these will continue to coexist. Probably we will find that different disciplines are the source of successful conjectures in different niches. The survivors of the selection process will be strengthened by challenges from a variety of sources.

Why Psychology?

Nearly everyone would include political science as a prime source of disciplinary foundations in public management research, but psychology may seem far removed from the scholarship of the field. The perspective of psychology may be useful precisely because its assumptions and methods differ in some important respects from the assumptions and methods of the more familiar disciplines of political science and economics. Speaking oversimplistically, the common theme in psychology is the search for explanations of human behavior at the individual level of analysis, assumptions that behavior flows from the experience of an individual who exists within a psychological field that is a configuration of internal and external forces, and widespread (but not universal) reliance on experimental and laboratory methods for understanding the causes of human behavior. Core assumptions in other social science disciplines are considered in psychology to be open, empirical questions. For example, do individuals change their behavior in response to changes in incentives? Do individuals seek to exert power and influence over other individuals? Do individuals conform to social expectations? Under what circumstances do such assumptions describe or fail to describe human behavior? Evidence suggests that these core assumptions are often problematic and contingent. In its theoretical approach to such questions, psychology is a huge, sprawling, and heterogeneous discipline, with well-developed subfields in developmental, social, clinical, cognitive, personality, mathematical, organizational, and biological psychology.

Because of the diversity within psychology, I cannot comment comprehensively on the full range of contributions that psychology might make to the study of public management. Instead, I take a problem statement drawn from the public management literature and suggest how psychological theory and method might help us make observations and conjectures that would not be evident without that disciplinary foundation. The problem I discuss is whether a manager in a public agency can improve the performance of that agency by articulating and transmitting an organizational mission.

The Value of Mission for a Public Agency

The public management literature includes a number of endorsements of the value of an agency mission. A clear and focused mission, it is hypothesized, will enhance the capability of the public organization to accomplish its work. Among those scholars who make a similar argument are Wilson (1989), Behn (1991), Cohen (1988), Doig and Hargrove (1987), Mashaw (1983), DiIulio (1987), Heymann (1987), and Landy et al. (1990), using words such as *sense of mission, purpose, strategic thinking,* and *vision.* A statement of mission summarizes in brief and evocative language the purpose and focus of agency activity. For example, Wilson (1989) reports that the U.S. Forest Service had for many years a mission of expert, nonpartisan, and professional management of national forests for the benefit of many different users. The FBI mission, under J. Edgar Hoover, was to gather facts about possible violations of federal laws in ways that would enhance citizen confidence, obtain prosecutorial support, and make arrests that would be immune to legal challenge (Wilson, 1989, pp. 97–98). Osborne and Gaebler report that the Department of Defense office responsible for military installations has developed the mission to "provide for our customers—the soldiers, sailors, marines, and airmen who defend America— excellent places to work and live, and excellent base services" (1992, p. 134).

Why and how can the articulation of a clear mission translate into better performance? Some practitioners look at mission with considerable skepticism. After all, few employees are ignorant of the mission of the agency for which they work. Stating a mission does not change the resources available to the agency or the existence of external opponents or supporters. In the public sector, the legal mandate giving legitimacy (and resources) to the agency often includes rather detailed specification of mission. So what, if anything, does a public manager contribute by talking about mission?

Wearing the hat of a psychologist, I answer that an agency's mission may be important in framing and motivating the work of individuals within the agency. These effects are neither straightforward nor easy to get. A mission is one element in the ongoing flow of conversation, action, and interaction that surrounds people at work. Within that context, managers may launch discussion of an explicit mission for the agency, like those cited above. These discussions may offer a conceptual structure or framework for thinking about the work of the agency, as well as specific content and explicit or implicit values about what is to be done. This package of conceptual structure, content, and values is communicated to individual employees. Employees (and other involved parties, such as clients or elected officials) perceive the communication and make sense of it through the lens of their prior experience in the agency and their perception of the fit between the mission and other managerial action. They may find it credible. They may remember it. It may then influence the cognitive frameworks they use to understand subsequent events. It may become a factor in decisions they make about their work. It may influence their expectations of how other employees will carry out their work. It may affect their motivation to work. These potential effects may cumulate to raise (or lower) the level of effort employees put into their work. They may cumulate to direct effort toward some tasks and away from others. They may cumulate to strengthen coordination across employees and units of the agency. These outcomes in turn may help to improve (or lower) overall agency performance. At a number of points in this sequence of interlocking processes, the mission may fail to play a role of any significance, or may have counterproductive effects by engendering cynicism or confusion. For purposes of this chapter, I focus on the potential for positive consequences and the conditions that seem to make positive consequences more likely.

A number of lines of psychological research are helpful in understanding the steps in the chain leading from mission to organizational results. At each step, public managers are confronted with choices and challenges that make it more or less likely that any particular mission will influence the people who do the work. Although many bodies of psychological literature may be useful, I discuss three: knowledge structures in cognition, motivation, and behavioral decision making. I deliberately emphasize concepts and empirical research at the individual level of analysis, because that is psychology's most distinctive contribution. I would not like to leave readers to conclude that psychology has little to say about social interaction, its antecedents, or its consequences. This is not the case. However, space does not permit me to show why in detail.

Knowledge Structures

One way to understand an agency mission is to think of it as a knowledge structure held by an individual about the organization in which she or he works. A knowledge structure is a general, abstract representation of organized knowledge about a given concept or type of stimulus (Fiske and Taylor, 1991; Walsh, 1995). The general structure, which exists in memory, serves to organize and assimilate new information as it arrives. Existing knowledge structures shape the ways in which people perceive, understand, and remember raw data; they permit people to construct meaning out of information. Knowledge structures may be highly abstract or relatively specific. For example, people have knowledge structures about other people (such as a general concept about how a shy person behaves when meeting someone new, or more specific ones like how your spouse is likely to act when meeting one of your colleagues), about roles (knowing how judges act in court), about work (such as a teacher knowing how the first day of school is likely to unfold), and about one's self (knowing one's own reactions to the first day of classes). All types of knowledge structures shape perception, memory, and inference, making it fast and easy to process information congruent with the existing structure and making it more difficult to process disconfirming or incongruent data. They allow us to fill in the details of particular situations (correctly or incorrectly) on the basis of abstract, general knowledge. They permit individuals to make sense of very complex, ambiguous, and contradictory information environments almost instantly and without any awareness of effortful processing. Perhaps most importantly, knowledge structures reveal the inextricable links between perception and interpretation.

Psychologists have identified several types of knowledge structures with somewhat different consequences for information processing. Two of the most important are categorization and schemas. Strong reliance on categorization is evident in perception. Individuals are very likely to classify individual instances (of people, tasks, situations) as members of categories. These cognitive categories can be thought of as concentric circles with prototypes, representing the typical instance of the category, at the center, and less typical instances around the perimeter. The boundaries around the category, for all categories of any significance, tend to be fuzzy, with people having more difficulty categorizing instances that do not resemble the prototypical case (Cantor and Mischel, 1979). Some categories seem to be organized around ideal or extreme prototypes, rather than typical ones. Ideal or extreme cases may be more likely to govern categorization for goal-oriented categories with a particular purpose to them, in which the ideal example is the one that best fulfills the category's goal (Fiske and Taylor, 1991). An example of consequential categorization is that some bad things are categorized as problems, meriting attention, policy debate, and resources (Weiss, 1989). Other, equally bad things are not problems; they are regrettable facts of life.

Schemas move beyond categorization to include inferences about causal or correlational links across categories, which guide processing of incoming data. A schema is defined as a cognitive structure that represents knowledge about a concept or stimulus, including its attributes and the relations among those attributes (Hastie, 1981). Related structures, such as scripts or cognitive maps, represent sequences of events (Abelson, 1981) or causal links among concepts or stimuli (Bougon, 1992). In these structures, people both categorize and associate category members with other attributes, such as the consequences of pursuing a particular line of action. Experts develop highly elaborated cognitive schemas in which many categories are systematically linked.

Knowledge structures persist, and accumulate inertia, for several reasons. They contain their own bias that makes it easier to notice and remember consistent data and easier to ignore or discount inconsistent data. They direct attention and information processing to some sorts of data that are highly salient within the knowledge structure, and they divert attention from data expected to be less helpful. Assumptions about what merits attention are then built into organizational information seeking and storage. New data then appear to reinforce status quo assumptions, while data that might challenge those assumptions are never collected or analyzed. Knowledge structures are also anchored when individuals publicly advocate or discuss their beliefs or theories with others, which induces emotional commitment to the knowledge structure and elaborates and deepens the structure, making it less subject to disconfirmation. As a result, knowledge structures can be difficult to change.

Awareness of the importance of knowledge structures in human thinking helps us to appreciate what is happening when public managers try to forge a mission for a public agency. Individual employees at all levels in an agency have highly elaborated cognitive structures about their own work. They also have knowledge structures about what the agency does. These structures are used automatically to process daily information about work and to facilitate the completion of tasks. New and old demands are categorized, rapidly and efficiently, and these categories evoke schemas about individuals, next steps, and consequences.

Several things may happen when the leader of an agency opens up conversation about agency mission. First, existing knowledge structures may be explicitly surfaced and questioned. The extent of agreement and conflict about the agency may become evident for the first time. New categories and schemas may be proposed. From a manager's point of view, the conversation about mission might be successful if new knowledge structures emerge that serve any of three purposes: connecting individual and subunit tasks with the larger organizational mission, developing more widely shared schemas about the agency, and creating focus and a sense of priorities.

Although individuals may have elaborated knowledge structures about their tasks and work, they may have a more impoverished understanding of the agency as a whole, and of the connection between their tasks and the agency's performance. Schemas governing particular tasks are components of expertise that people acquire on the job. A good illustration is Lurigio and Carroll's (1985) study of probation officers' information processing about offenders. The researchers elicited from probation officers descriptions of the characteristic behaviors and traits of various types of offenders, and found that probation officers with substantial experience possessed a relatively small number of highly detailed schemas. These schemas included information about crimes, personal descriptions, social history, causal attributions about criminal behavior, summaries of appropriate treatment and supervision strategies, and prognosis. An example: "Burglar: early 30's, married, any race, intelligent, extensive burglary record, professional, expert. Prognosis: Very poor (set lifestyle)" (Lurigio and Carroll, 1985, p. 1115). Next they asked another sample of experienced probation officers and a comparison group of clerical staff (who lacked well-developed schemas about offenders) to evaluate four case files that included two cases that matched schemas identified in the first study and two cases that combined elements of different schemas. When evaluating cases that matched schemas, probation officers responded more quickly, with less difficulty, and more confidently than when they evaluated cases that did not match existing schemas. Clerical staff (who lacked well-developed schemas) showed no differences in processing the two kinds of cases. The probation officers were also more likely to agree with one another about specific treatment strategies and prognosis for cases that matched schemas than for cases that did not match schemas. Lurigio and Carroll concluded that the work of probation officers was structured by schemas about offenders. Their knowledge structures allowed them to evaluate specific cases faster, more confidently, and with more agreement about what actions to pursue.

If the corrections agency wanted to change the treatment of certain categories of offenders (say, drug offenders), one way to do that would be to begin a serious examination of these schemas. In particular, managers might want to encourage consideration of more comprehensive schemas that link probation officers' recommendations and the overall goals and performance of the agency. By locating the work of individuals or subunits within the larger organizational purpose, schemas about mission can develop that remind people how their work contributes to the eventual performance of the agency. This kind of schema may make salient somewhat different aspects of employees' work (aspects of most interest to clients or top managers) than schemas that are more narrowly focused on subunit or individual perspectives on the work at hand.

A second consequence of mission development may be the cultivation of shared knowledge structures. Through exposure to the same stimuli and through interaction, organizational members like the probation officers come to share knowledge structures and assumptions about their work, the agency, its political environment, mandate, and its capabilities. Shared knowledge structures in turn promote social interaction and the capacity for cooperative work. The idea that individuals know collectively is an old one. Many researchers have described knowledge structures operating at the group or organizational level of analysis (Weick, 1979; Bougon, 1992; Walsh, 1995). The concept of knowledge structure is better understood and documented at the individual level. Nevertheless, for fifty years researchers have understood that one important task of management is to develop some shared understanding about work (Barnard, 1938). These shared beliefs and assumptions constitute both a strength and a weakness: a strength in that they facilitate the processing of information and work, reducing the demand for communication to clarify each new problem or event and making predictable the activities of others; a weakness in that they make it less likely that organizational members will notice alternative points of view, or ways of understanding problems or events, or notice changing environments (such as changes in the client population or in technology) that call for new approaches to work.

One thing managers may attempt in mission development is to create shared conceptions of the organization's work. Shared conceptions may break down barriers between members of subunits in the agency who have their own ideas of what and how work is to be done. When subunit conceptions are explicitly challenged and replaced, individual employees are armed with alternative, more organizationally minded expectations that can improve internal lines of communication and cooperation.

Third, mission development may help to refocus employees or set new priorities among tasks. New knowledge structures may give priority to different aspects of complex problems. This permits perceivers to recognize the relevance of new information that they previously would have ignored or discounted, and calls attention to different dimensions of the work environment. Challenging the existing conception of mission may involve asking people to surface and examine their taken-for-granted assumptions about the definition of successful performance, what works, what doesn't work and why. Creating dissatisfaction with the status quo triggers a search for new, more satisfactory knowledge structures to guide individual effort and organizational improvement. New information about how others see the organization's mission and the growth of external demands on the organization for performance may stimulate new thinking about the kinds of performance the agency is capable of. For example, Barkdoll (1992) showed how conversations about agency mission at the Food and Drug Administration identified domains that had been systematically neglected as well as domains of rising importance due to external pressures. If conversations about mission raise such issues in a way that is persuasive to many employees, then the mission development process makes it possible to dislodge expectations and assumptions that employees have developed over many years.

Psychological research on properties of knowledge structures leads to several hypotheses about the effectiveness of the processes surrounding mission development. Mission development will be more likely to have an impact on the work of members of the organization when conversations with individual employees convey new categories and schemas for understanding the work of individuals within the agency and the performance of the agency as a whole, when new knowledge structures reveal links between the work of individuals and the performance of the agency as a whole so that individuals see the larger implications of their own work, when new knowledge structures are widely shared, and when new knowledge structures reorient the priorities and focus of individual employees and subunits to enhance their contribution to the collective mission.

Motivation

If mission development improves organizational performance, one plausible way to achieve improvements is through raising the performance of individual employees. How can mission development motivate people to work more or better? In this section, I look at potentially motivating ingredients in agency mission.

Those who see work behavior as essentially motivated by tangible rewards are most skeptical about the value of mission development. If people work according to incentives of pay and promotion, then it seems dubious that talk about agency mission will have much connection to work effort or priorities. A psychologically oriented analysis might respond to such skepticism in several ways. First, rewards do not speak for themselves; they must be interpreted and understood. Second, rewards can operate at multiple levels, including the group and organizational level. Third, some motives to work are not connected to tangible rewards at all. Let us explore these three points.

Most contemporary psychologists argue that rewards are linked to action through the filter of thought. At a minimum, people respond to rewards when they perceive the availability of the reward, perceive the connection between their behavior and the reward, and believe that they are capable of producing the behavior that will lead to the reward (Bandura, 1986). None of these perceptions happens directly or automatically, and distortions or failures of any one disrupts the link between the incentive and the intended behavior.

People must interpret and make sense of the incentives applied to them, and the process of interpretation creates the opportunity for many complications to enter the picture. Our interpretations of the incentives in our environment are governed by our past experience and by social comparison. Many perceptions of the link between performance and incentives do not grow out of direct experience; we often learn about the link between behavior and reward by observing others. "Indeed, if human behavior depended solely on personally experienced consequences, most people would not survive the hazards of early development" (Bandura, 1986, p. 283). What people observe affects their level of motivation by changing how they understand success and external incentives. Thus, a given incentive can be seen to be positive or negative depending on what one has learned from social comparison. A $50,000 salary offer may sound much better than the $40,000 you were making previously (very motivating), until you learn that your new coworker earns $70,000 (very demotivating).

People also use their experience and observations to draw inferences about the causal relationship between performance and rewards. When the causal relationships are complex—that is, when performance is not clearly and directly tied to level of reward because rewards are determined by multiple factors such as seniority, credentials, and discrimination in addition to performance—then people often perceive a weak or contingent causal link to be no link at all. This vitiates the power of rewards to induce willingness to perform at high levels.

Developing a mission is an opportunity to launch explicit conversation about how people might understand their work and the agency. Discussion of when and how success is defined and rewarded often becomes part of the process. Both employees and managers need to discuss beliefs and expectations about the connections between the mission and external rewards at managers' command. In this way, the mission development process offers opportunities to leverage the impact of rewards to foster motivation by shaping interpretations of the nexus between performance and rewards.

For external rewards to be motivating, people must do more than perceive a connection between external rewards and their own behavior. They must also believe that they are capable of producing the behavior that is to be rewarded. Competent functioning requires basic ability or skills, but also the confidence that one has the capability to use the skills (Markus et al., 1990). "Perceived self-efficacy is defined as people's judgments of their capabilities to organize and execute courses of action required to attain designated types of performances. It is concerned not with the skills one has but with judgments of what one can do with whatever skills one possesses" (Bandura, 1986, p. 391). Judgments of self-efficacy are repeatedly found to influence motivation in a variety of ways. The more efficacious people believe themselves to be, the more likely they are to persist in mastering challenges. Believing that one cannot accomplish a goal makes one more likely to give up in the face of difficulties or shy away from difficult tasks. Poor performance stems not only from deficits in skills and abilities but also from doubts, anxieties, negative expectations, pessimism, and low self-esteem (Ruvolo and Markus, 1992). Bandura's research suggests that "people are influenced more by how they read their performance successes than by the successes per se" (Bandura, 1982, p. 125). If managers have this in mind, conversations about mission can help people see themselves as more (or less) competent or efficacious. In mission development, individuals must be convinced that they and other members of the organization have the skills required to accomplish the mission. For this reason, mission development often acquires an inspirational tone, as employees are encouraged to stretch, to expect more of themselves as they acquire new skills, if necessary, to achieve higher levels of organizational performance.

Thus, mission development has a potential role to play, even if one assumes that work behavior is principally motivated by tangible incentives. It shapes how people understand the incentives at play in their work environment, develops shared understanding about the connections between incentives and the agency's mission, and provides opportunities to foster in employees the sense of efficacy necessary to capitalize on available incentives.

A second conception of motivation asks not only about the incentives operating on individuals in the work environment but also about rewards at the group, unit, or organizational level of analysis. Although self-interest is clearly important in nearly all work settings, people may also place considerable weight on the interests of their work group or their organization. In that event, the incentives operating on the individual may diminish somewhat in importance, and the incentives operating on the group or organization may become more prominent. The stronger and more salient the identification of the individual with the group or the organization, the more likely that the individual's work motivation will be influenced by the well-being of the collective. The extreme example of such identification can be found in military training in combat units, where individuals are expected to consider primarily the collective interest in assessing and pursuing lines of action.

People differ in their identification with collective interests. Some variation appears to be due to differences among individuals in self-concept and attachment to work; some of the difference appears to be attributable to differences in how organizations socialize and treat their members; and some appears to be a factor of the fit between a given individual and the organization or collective. Although individual differences are not readily influenced by the actions of managers in the mission development process, the other two sets of influences clearly can be mobilized by managers who seek to strengthen the identification of employees with the interests of the organization. Training and socialization can have the effect of encouraging members to incorporate the organization and its interests into members' sense of identity, to see the individual's interests and the collective interests as one (Van Maanen and Schein, 1979). Mission development can create a coherent story about the collective interests, which eases the task of socialization and communicates more clearly the agency's goals. Mission development may also highlight what is shared across the agency, which heightens the salience of similarities with other agency employees, discouraging competition and hostility. When the agency's managers put forward a strong statement of the organization's identity—what is distinctive, central, and enduring about the organization (Dutton et al., 1994)—in discussion of agency mission, individuals have the opportunity to see the connection between their interests and those of the agency. By making values an explicit part of mission development, managers also make it possible for employees to see when and how their values coincide with those of the agency.

None of this guarantees a good fit for every employee, of course, but it creates the opportunity for a fit to be perceived and acted upon. When this fit is achieved, it can be quite motivating. Kramer (1993) reviews evidence that increasing the salience of people's identification with the group can lead individuals to take less for themselves in order to preserve collective resources, or to cooperate with others in other ways. Individuals who identify strongly with their organization may be more likely to participate actively in organizational improvement by providing ideas for improvement or helping newcomers learn the ropes (Dutton et al., 1994). People who believe that their values are congruent with the values in their workplace tend to be more satisfied with their work, more committed to their work, and less likely to leave (Vardi et al., 1989). Kahn (1990) suggests that a good fit of values makes it more likely that people will engage deeply in their work, creating the potential for very high levels of performance. In these ways, mission development opens possibilities for managers to link individual employees' interests and identification with those of the collective.

Third, some psychological research suggests that people are motivated to work for reasons that have little connection to tangible rewards. Some psychologists distinguish between intrinsic motivation (motivation arising from desires for exploration and competence) and extrinsic motivation (motivation arising from externally directed rewards and punishments) (see, e.g., Deci and Ryan, 1985; Bandura, 1986). Considerable research suggests that applying external rewards can actually reduce the individual's intrinsic motivation to perform the work. Under some conditions, people react to rewards by *lowering* their evaluation of the activity they engaged in. The psychological mechanism is hypothesized to be this: When people attempt to understand why they perform particular tasks or exert effort, they evaluate whether their behavior is being controlled by external or internal forces. If they attribute their effort to external factors, such as being paid, they conclude that their effort was not inner-directed. If, on the other hand, they exerted the same level of effort for minimal reward, they infer that they must have done so because they wanted to. In experimental settings, this relationship has been replicated many times (see Fiske and Taylor, 1991, pp. 46–47). People given an external reward for performing what might have been understood as an intrinsically interesting task work harder and generate more activity, but they show less enjoyment of their task, make more errors, are less creative, and are likely to reduce their effort if the rewards are withdrawn. People given little reward for doing the identical tasks take more pleasure in the task, maintain their level of performance if the rewards are withdrawn, select more challenging problems to work on, and display more ingenuity and care in their work.

The appropriate conclusion from this work is not to forget about extrinsic motivators, but rather to pay attention to potential sources of intrinsic motivation. There are many. People work hard, in part because they believe in what they are doing, enjoy working together with others, and take pleasure in achievement, accomplishment, and exerting influence. McClelland (1984) calls these motives the needs for affiliation, achievement, and power. Work becomes an important arena for fulfilling these needs.

Quite a different line of research emphasizes work as an arena for understanding the self. For many people, work becomes a significant component of their self-concept and performing well validates that self-concept. Even when the psychological mechanism is something as private and idiosyncratic as the sense of self, research suggests that some work settings mobilize the "selves" of employees far more effectively than others. This is partly because the "self" is more multidimensional and fluid than most of us commonly recognize. Some self-conceptions are centrally self-defining, and chronically accessible for thinking about the self. However, many, perhaps most, self-conceptions are not so prominent or continuous in our thinking (Higgins, 1990). "They vary depending on the individual's affective or motivational state and the prevailing social conditions, and are thus more dependent on situational cues for their activation. They may be active in thought and memory under some circumstances and almost inaccessible during others" (Nurius and Markus, 1990, pp. 316–317).

Some of these more fluid self-conceptions are focused on the future, what Markus and her colleagues call the possible self. This is the self we would like to become and the self we are afraid of becoming (Markus and Nurius, 1986). Possible selves are dynamic and functional. They shape behavior in significant ways as people try to live up to their positive selves by taking action. Work experiences can activate the construction and maintenance of possible selves. Research suggests that individuals' sense of possible selves changes, partly as a function of experience, partly as a function of what the person wants for him- or herself. Both the individual and the organization benefit when an individual tries to validate a positive possible self through more or better performance. Conversely, both suffer when the work environment signals the individual that he or she is not competent, and the individual behaves to validate that deflating signal.

Mission development can provide an arena for linking organizational goals to individual tasks to an individual's sense of general competence and contribution. The possible self becomes motivating when organizational goals are explicitly and directly linked to the individual's self-concept. The individual must be able to envision in concrete ways how his or her possible self contributes to the organization's mission. Ruvolo and Markus note: "It is an individual's *specific representations* of what is possible for the self that embody and give rise to generalized feelings of efficacy, competence, control, or optimism, and that provide the means by which these global constructs have their powerful impact on behavior" (1992, p. 96). These concrete representations come in large part from the individual's work environment. Mission development creates a framework within which managers can provide models, images, and symbols available for translating organizational tasks into beliefs about the self. If individuals do not see the connection between their self-concepts and the organization's mission, the mission will not trigger the striving to validate one's self-concept through work toward the mission. One path for accomplishing this is to engage employees in discussion of exactly how any proposed mission translates into operational terms.

People also value self-integrity, the sense that they are internally coherent (Steele, 1988). When the agency's mission is aligned with what individual employees value, people may find it easier to maintain a sense of consistency and internal coherence. Earlier, I emphasized how values facilitated identification with the collective interest. But congruence between personal values and the values one furthers at work also permits individuals to derive a sense of meaning and self-affirmation from work (Maccoby, 1988; Shamir, 1991). The match of individual values to mission builds commitment to the agency and to the work. No mission will serve to validate the values of all employees, but it will signal which employees are likely to feel confirmed by the organization's mission and which feel less comfortable.

Research on goal setting is also pertinent to mission development. Locke and Latham report on an extensive program of research with the following findings: "People who try to attain specific and challenging (difficult) goals perform better on a task than people who try for specific but moderate or easy goals, vague goals such as "do your best," or no goals at all. This finding [has been] replicated in close to four hundred studies" (1990, p. 254). A mission may therefore be more effective in motivating performance when it is specific and difficult than when it is vague or easily attainable. Managers who provide concrete feedback about progress toward the mission may be more effective in motivating employees than those who do not. The mission may affect performance by channeling attention, mobilizing on-task effort, sustaining effort over time, and stimulating strategic planning (Karoly, 1993).

Behavioral Decision Making

Studies of how people make decisions may also contribute to our understanding of the impact of mission development on the employees of a public agency. Both cognitive and emotional forces are at play in decision making, and the examples in this section draw on research traditions of cognitive analysis and of motivation. One stream of work focuses on how decision problems are formulated or framed, and the consequences of settling on certain types of frames. A second stream focuses on the post hoc justification of decisions, and how the need for justification spills into choices among courses of action.

Research on decision framing has demonstrated that people's judgments can vary remarkably depending on how a decision problem is presented. Tversky and Kahneman's (1981) prospect theory focuses on decisions involving risk.

They find that choices are evaluated with respect to losses or gains from a reference position. Two important empirical results have emerged. First, the choice of reference position has a significant impact on how people evaluate decision alternatives. Second, people do not treat gains and losses as equivalent. In general, the response to losses is more extreme than the response to gains. When an outcome is framed as a gain from a reference position, people tend to make decisions that are more risk averse. When the identical outcome is framed as a loss, people tend to be willing to assume more risk to avert the loss. Although much of the research documenting this effect is done in the laboratory, some confirmation has been documented with realistic policy decisions.

This research has several implications for the mission development process. Knowing that the selection of a reference point is consequential for decision making, managers seeking to develop missions may want to begin the mission development process by creating agreement about a reference point. A manager may seek to persuade employees that the current situation is much worse than they realized, emphasizing the possibility of potential gains from an undesirable reference point. Alternatively, a manager may want to persuade employees that the status quo (or recent past) reference point has been very desirable, but that substantial losses loom on the horizon unless drastic (risky) measures are taken. The choice between these two reference points, according to behavioral decision research, may significantly alter the ways that employees respond to the alternatives facing them. For example, Gregory et al. (1993) found that people were more willing to take risks on policy options that restored losses than on those that promised future gains.

Research in a variety of managerial settings reinforces the point that decisions differ depending on whether events or problems are framed as threats or opportunities (Jackson and Dutton, 1988; Dutton, 1993), but adds a number of additional factors to take into account. Although perceived threats enhance risk taking, threats also seem to have a variety of negative cognitive and emotional effects such as anxiety, rigidity, impulsivity, concern with control, and reduced search for information (Janis, 1989; Staw et al., 1981). In comparison, perceived opportunities may reduce willingness to assume risk, but they are also associated with feelings of autonomy, challenge, competence, and a strong sense of positive possibility (Jackson and Dutton, 1988). Optimism and its associated positive feelings have been found to play very important roles in individual performance, by reducing stress, enhancing creativity, facilitating communication, sharing social support, reducing aggression, and increasing efficiency (Taylor and Brown, 1988; Isen and Baron, 1991).

Thus, using an opportunity frame can have significant consequences for subsequent action by managers and employees. For example, Freeman (1992) shows that some auto industry managers interpreted organizational downsizing through an opportunity frame, seeing it as an opportunity to redesign their organization. Other managers in the identical situation perceived it as a threat, seeing only a potential loss of resources or control. Managers who saw opportunity used different and more effective responses than managers who saw threat. Other studies reviewed by Dutton (1993) confirm that labeling events or issues as threats or opportunities has far-reaching consequences for managers and for organizational performance. Examples include university administrators responding to the decline in the 18- to 22-year-old cohort, hospital administrators responding to an impending doctors' strike, and managers of the Port Authority of New York and New Jersey responding to the presence of homeless people in their facilities.

Framing decisions in positive terms, as opportunities, can be done during mission development. In the process of devising a mission and imbuing it with content and meaning, managers nearly always state the mission affirmatively, and present employees with the opportunity for gains for themselves and for the organization. When this framing trickles down to the operational decisions under the umbrella of the overall mission, these decisions may also borrow the gloss of the opportunity frame. Although this framing may have the effect of reducing willingness to take risks, the potential benefits of sense of control, optimism, challenge, and reduced anxiety seem substantial.

Gain and loss are not the only dimensions of frames that shape subsequent decisions, although they are the most often researched dimension in psychology. Scholars of public policy have used a variety of concepts to describe the ways in which actors in policy disputes attempt to frame choice and mobilize support for one or another course of action. Stone (1993) traces the significance of using a medical (or clinical) frame to understand social phenomena, such as poor school performance or the after-effects of being raped; such a frame empowers experts at the expense of individuals and families experiencing life difficulties. Gamson and Modigliani (1987, 1989) explain public disputes about affirmative action and nuclear power by surfacing the multiple, underlying frames that structure public and elite opinion on these controversial subjects (see also Schon and Rein, 1994). Work on problem definition (e.g., Weiss, 1989) and strategic planning (Bryson, 1988) often makes the same assumption; public officials and managers craft and sell frames so that they can structure how others interpret and respond to the social demands on the government or agency. Mission development is one way that managers seek to pursue this avenue for influence with their subordinates, elected officials, clients, and other constituencies.

Psychological research on postdecisional justification also offers some insight into why mission development may be helpful in improving agency performance. Social psychologists have long argued that postdecision thinking differed from thinking prior to the moment of choice. Part of this is an internal, cognitive dilemma; people need to explain to themselves why they have chosen the option they did. Part of this is a social dilemma; people need to explain their choice to others who may be affected by the choice. In either case, justification is a necessary phase of decision behavior. Why do decisions need to be justified? As Weick explains, immediately after deciding "people temporarily face multiple, conflicting definitions of what their decision means" (1993, p. 30). The more complex the decision, the more things it may mean. To reduce their internal confusion, they justify their decision. These justifications are important to action, in that they emphasize the positive features of the chosen course, denigrate the options not chosen, and thereby reduce ambivalence and enhance commitment. Committed action is more convincing and uninhibited than ambivalent action, as Allison (1971) notes in his discussion of bureaucratic politics.

Mission development can offer to all members of the organization a set of criteria for evaluating and justifying complex decisions. If the mission has been endorsed by powerful people, it assumes credibility and legitimacy as a justification for any individual employee's choices. This makes it somewhat easier for individuals to justify choices that match the mission, both to themselves and to others. It also simplifies justification of the choice to others, as it draws on arguments that have already been widely discussed and endorsed. Because justification of some choices has become easier than justification of others, people may be more likely to make choices that do match the mission. In this way, justifications become self-fulfilling prophecies. The more people defend their decisions by referring to the mission, the more likely people are to believe that the mission is something real. The more they believe that it is real, the more likely they are to act in accordance with the mission. Through such a process, talk about mission can be translated into systematic patterns of action.

Theory Development and Disciplinary Foundations Revisited

These three lines of research have stimulated a number of questions and ideas about the consequences of redefining the mission for a public agency. Work on knowledge structures points to the importance of previous experience and observation, organized in memory, which leads to interpretation of information and action. The motivational analysis reveals the entwined emotional and cognitive stake that people bring to work. Work on motivation raises the issue of what people find satisfying, stimulating, and rewarding in their work, and how to frame work in ways that connect to values and positive self-concepts. Finally, the discussion of decision making shows that frames of reference can be actively constructed and shifted, with consequences for how people evaluate alternative courses of action and what they do subsequent to decisions. Here, too, both cognitive and emotional considerations guide people in their responses to the decision situations they confront. From these platforms, the public management researcher can construct frameworks for looking at mission development within agencies and across agencies, and identify hypotheses for further investigation.

I suggested at the beginning of this chapter that disciplinary perspectives may improve the stock of theory in public management by adding variety to the theoretical conjectures we use to explain problems. If all of our conjectures came from the world of practice, or came from a single discipline, then we would be focused but limited in our ability to explain the complex phenomena that constitute the domain of public management. Psychology may be one of the disciplines that introduces variety and independent perspectives, and thus may be useful to public management scholarship. A renewal of interest in behavioral and interpersonal dimensions of management (Lynn, 1994) moves public management research into arenas where psychological theories and evidence have distinctive advantages.

In discussing whether, when, and how mission development can improve performance in public agencies, I reviewed some of the conjectures that psychologists might offer to explain one phenomenon in public management. This exercise leads to several conclusions. First, psychology has many ideas to contribute that may help researchers understand phenomena of widespread interest in public management research. What do we know about mission development that we would not have known without consulting psychological theory or research? The contribution revolves around specifying realistic microdynamics of macrostructure. Although many of the social science disciplines emphasize the importance of institutional structures and constraints, it is often difficult to trace out the causal chain by which structure is related to actions of individuals within the institution and how those individual actions then cumulate to create organizational performance. Most of the time most policy researchers assume that structural constraints and pressures will produce effects on individuals or on larger social entities, without investigating whether and how those constraints and pressures are understood and acted upon by the people involved. Psychology as a discipline offers us some tools for analyzing how interventions at the top of an agency may affect the work of individuals at lower levels, often at considerable remove from senior managers.

Specifying the microdynamics of mission development, for example, focuses attention away from the mission and instead focuses on mission development as a process. The mere statement of a mission has relatively little power to accomplish performance improvement; the *process* of developing and communicating the mission carries the punch. To reap the potential of focus, consensus, shared values, identification, shared expectations, easy justification, common frames of reference, and the like, managers cannot simply bang out a mission and hang it on the wall. The involvement of others in exploring possible ways of understanding the agency's mission, coming to terms with the values and trade-offs implicit in any given statement of mission, talking about the mission to build awareness, translating a general statement of mission into more operational terms, communicating openly so that people come to common understandings of what the mission means, convincing others that the mission is embraced by powerful people—all these seem to be very important in moving from the mission to an improvement in organizational performance. When such microdynamics are absent, then the cynical view that the mission statement is managerial window dressing seems closer to the target.

Analysis of public management problems from a psychological perspective leaves out important dimensions. It is a partial view. A few questions about mission development that are not addressed by psychological-style analysis include: How is mission development constrained by other agencies with related or overlapping missions? What are the means by which elected officials or powerful clients constrain the freedom of agency leaders to define a mission? What happens when agency leaders are instructed by superiors to develop missions? Are the costs of mission development worth the benefits? The omissions signal that psychology, like any other discipline, achieves its advantages through a narrowing of focus.

Psychology is a valuable part of the intellectual apparatus of public management scholarship. Its contributions are most valuable when we see them as part of a broad repertoire that includes angles of insight and evidence from other disciplines and the insights of practitioners. Explanations originating in psychology have often been subjected to rigorous, sustained examination within the psychology research community. In that community, applicability to problems of management practice or public policy is not a significant criterion for acceptance. Therefore, when psychological explanations enter the pool of plausible conjectures that public management researchers call upon to understand problems of practice in public management settings, they must clear a new set of hurdles. Many psychological explanations will not be useful at all; the remainder will not be useful in all cases. Still, their presence in the pool enriches the capacity of researchers and practitioners to explain a broad range of public management phenomena.

References

Abelson, Robert P. 1981. "Psychological Status of the Script Concept." *American Psychologist* 36, no. 7: 715–729.

Allison, Graham. 1971. *Essence of Decision.* Boston: Little, Brown.

Bandura, Albert. 1982. "Self-Efficacy Mechanism in Human Agency." *American Psychologist* 37 (February): 122–147.

———. 1986. *Social Foundations of Thought and Action.* Englewood Cliffs, N.J.: Prentice-Hall.

Barkdoll, Gerald L. 1992. "Scoping versus Coping: Developing a Comprehensive Agency Vision." *Public Administration Review* 52, no. 4: 330–338.

Barnard, Chester I. 1938. *The Functions of the Executive.* Cambridge: Harvard University Press.

Barzelay, Michael. 1992. *Breaking through Bureaucracy: A New Vision for Managing in Government.* Berkeley: University of California Press.

Behn, Robert D. 1991. *Leadership Counts: Lessons for Public Managers from the Massachusetts Welfare, Training, and Employment Program.* Cambridge: Harvard University Press.

Blumenfeld, Phyllis C., John R. Mergendoller, and Pamela Puro. 1992. "Translating Motivation into Thoughtfulness," in H. H. Marshall, ed., *Redefining Student Learning,* pp. 207–239. Norwood, N.J.: Ablex.

Bougon, Michel G. 1992. "Congregate Cognitive Maps: A Unified Dynamic Theory of Organization and Strategy." *Journal of Management Studies* 29 (May): 369–389.

Bryson, John M. 1988. *Strategic Planning for Public and Nonprofit Organizations.* San Francisco: Jossey-Bass.

Cantor, Nancy, and Walter Mischel. 1979. "Prototypes in Person Perception," in L. Berkowitz, ed., *Advances in Experimental Social Psychology,* 12:3–52. New York: Academic Press.

Cohen, Steven. 1988. *The Effective Public Manager.* San Francisco: Jossey-Bass.

Deci, E. L., and R. M. Ryan. 1985. *Intrinsic Motivation and Self-Determination in Human Behavior.* New York: Plenum.

DiIulio, John J., Jr. 1987. *Governing Prisons: A Comparative Study of Correctional Management.* New York: Free Press.

Doig, Jameson W., and Erwin Hargrove, eds. 1987. *Leadership and Innovation.* Baltimore: Johns Hopkins University Press.

Dougherty, Deborah. 1992. "Interpretive Barriers to Successful Product Innovation in Large Firms." *Organization Science* 3, no. 2: 179–201.

Dutton, Jane E. 1993. "The Making of Organizational Opportunities: An Interpretive Pathway to Organizational Change," in B. M. Staw and L. L. Cummings, eds., *Research in Organizational Behavior,* 15:195–226. Greenwich, Conn.: JAI Press.

Dutton, Jane E., Janet Dukerich, and C. V. Harquail. 1994. "Organizational Images and Member Identification." *Administrative Science Quarterly* 39:239–263.

Fiske, Susan T., and Shelley E. Taylor. 1991. *Social Cognition,* 2d ed. New York: McGraw-Hill.

Freeman, Sarah Jane. 1992. "Organizational Redesign and Downsizing: A Case of Appropriated Interpretation." Ph.D. diss., University of Michigan School of Business Administration.

Gamson, William A., and Andre Modigliani. 1987. "The Changing Culture of Affirmative Action," in R. Braungart, ed., *Research in Political Sociology,* vol. 3. Greenwich, Conn.: JAI Press.

———. 1989. "Media Discourse and Public Opinion on Nuclear Power." *American Journal of Sociology* 95, no. 1: 1–37.

Gregory, Robin, Sarah Lichtenstein, and Donald MacGregor. 1993. "The Role of Past States in Determining Reference Points for Policy Decisions." *Organizational Behavior and Human Decision Processes* 55, no. 2: 195–206.

Hastie, Reid. 1981. "Schematic Principles in Human Memory," in E. T. Higgins, C. P. Herman, and M. P. Zanna, eds., *Social Cognition: The Ontario Symposium,* 1:39–88. Hillsdale, N.J.: Erlbaum.

Heymann, Philip B. 1987. *The Politics of Public Management.* New Haven: Yale University Press.

Higgins, E. Tory. 1990. "Personality, Social Psychology, and Person-Situation Relations: Standards and Knowledge Activation as a Common Language," in L. A. Pervin, ed., *Handbook of Personality: Theory and Research,* pp. 301–338. New York: Guilford Press.

Hollander, Edwin P. 1985. "Leadership and Power," in G. Lindzey and E. Aronson, eds., *Handbook of Social Psychology,* 2:485–537. New York: Random House.

Isen, Alice M., and Robert A. Baron. 1991. "Positive Affect as a Factor in Organizational Behavior," in B. M. Staw and L. L. Cummings, eds., *Research in Organizational Behavior,* 13:1–53. Greenwich, Conn.: JAI Press.

Jackson, Susan E., and Jane E. Dutton. 1988. "Discerning Threats and Opportunities." *Administrative Science Quarterly* 33:370–387.

Janis, Irving L. 1989. *Crucial Decisions: Leadership in Policymaking and Crisis Management.* New York: Macmillan.

Kahn, William A. 1990. "Psychological Conditions of Personal Engagement and Disengagement at Work." *Academy of Management Journal* 33:692–724.

Karoly, Paul. 1993. "Mechanisms of Self-Regulation: A Systems View." *Annual Review of Psychology* 44:23–52.

Kramer, Roderick. 1993. "Cooperation and Organizational Identification," in K. Murnighan, ed., *Social Psychology in Organizations,* pp. 244–269. Englewood Cliffs, N.J.: Prentice-Hall.

Landy, Marc, M. Roberts, and S. Thomas. 1990. *The Environmental Protection Agency: Asking the Wrong Questions.* New York: Oxford University Press.

Locke, Edwin A., and Gary Latham. 1990. *A Theory of Goal Setting and Task Performance.* Englewood Cliffs, N.J.: Prentice-Hall.

Lurigio, Arthur J., and John S. Carroll. 1985. "Probation Officers' Schemata of Offenders: Content, Development, and Impact on Treatment Decisions." *Journal of Personality and Social Psychology* 48, no. 5: 1112–1126.

Lynn, Laurence E. 1994. "Public Management Research: The Triumph of Art over Science." *Journal of Policy Analysis and Management* 13, no. 2: 231–259.

Maccoby, Michael. 1988. *Why Work: Motivating and Leading the New Generation.* New York: Simon and Schuster.

Markus, Hazel R., Susan Cross, and Elissa Wurf. 1990. "The Role of the Self-System in Competence," in Robert J. Sternberg and John Kolligian Jr., eds., *Competence Considered,* pp. 205–225. New Haven: Yale University Press.

Markus, Hazel R., and Paula Nurius. 1986. "Possible Selves." *American Psychologist* 41:954–969.

Mashaw, Jerry L. 1983. *Bureaucratic Justice: Managing Social Security Disability Claims.* New Haven: Yale University Press.

McClelland, David C. 1984. *Human Motivation.* Oakland, N.J.: Scott, Foresman.

Nurius, Paula S., and Hazel Markus. 1990. "Situational Variability in the Self-Concept: Appraisals, Expectancies, and Asymmetries." *Journal of Social and Clinical Psychology* 9, no. 3: 316–333.

Osborne, David, and Ted Gaebler. 1992. *Reinventing Government.* Reading, Mass.: Addison-Wesley.

Payne, John W., and James R. Bettman. 1992. "Behavioral Decision Research: A Constructive Processing Perspective." *Annual Review of Psychology* 43:87–131.

Ruvolo, Ann Patrice, and Hazel R. Markus. 1992. "Possible Selves and Performance: The Power of Self-Relevant Imagery." *Social Cognition* 10, no. 1: 95–124.

Schneider, D. J. 1991. "Social Cognition." *Annual Review of Psychology* 42:527–61.

Schon, Donald A., and Martin Rein. 1994. *Frame Reflection: Toward the Resolution of Intractable Policy Controversies.* New York: Basic Books.

Shamir, Boas. 1991. "Meaning, Self, and Motivation in Organizations." *Organization Studies* 12, no. 3: 405–424.

Staw, Barry M., Lloyd Sandelands, and Jane E. Dutton. 1981. "Threat-Rigidity Effects in Organizations: A Multi-level Analysis." *Administrative Science Quarterly* 26:501–524.

Steele, Claude M. 1988. "The Psychology of Self-Affirmation: Sustaining the Integrity of the Self." *Advances in Experimental Social Psychology* 21:261–302.

Stone, Deborah. 1993. "Clinical Authority in the Construction of Citizenship," in H. Ingram and S. Smith, eds., *Public Policy for Democracy,* pp. 45–67. Washington, D.C.: Brookings Institution.

Taylor, Shelley F., and Jonathon D. Brown. 1988. "Illusion and Well-Being: A Social Psychological Perspective on Mental Health." *Psychological Bulletin* 103, no. 2: 193–210.

Tversky, Amos, and Daniel Kahneman. 1981. "The Framing of Decisions and the Psychology of Choice." *Science* 211 (30 January): 453–458.

Van Maanen, John, and Edgar H. Schein. 1979. "Toward a Theory of Organizational Socialization," in B. Staw, ed., *Research in Organizational Behavior,* 1:209–264. Greenwich, Conn.: JAI Press.

Vardi, Yoav, Yoash Weiner, and Micha Poppa. 1989. "The Value Content of Organizational Mission as a Factor in the Commitment of Members." *Psychological Reports* 65:27–34.

Walsh, James P. 1995. "Managerial and Organizational Cognition: Notes from a Trip Down Memory Lane." *Organization Science* 6:280–321.

Weick, Karl E. 1979. "Cognitive Processes in Organizations," in B. Staw, ed., *Research in Organizational Behavior,* 1:41–74. Greenwich, Conn.: JAI Press.

———. 1989. "Theory Construction as Disciplined Imagination." *Academy of Management Review* 14:516–531.

———. 1993. "Sensemaking in Organizations: Small Structures with Large Consequences," in K. Murnighan, ed., *Social Psychology in Organizations,* pp. 10–37. Englewood Cliffs, N.J.: Prentice-Hall.

Weiss, Janet A. 1989. "The Powers of Problem Definition: The Case of Government Paperwork." *Policy Sciences* 22:97–121.

———. 1994. "Public Management Research: The Interdependence of Problems and Theory." *Journal of Policy Analysis and Management* 13, no. 2: 278–285.

Westley, Frances. 1992. "Vision Worlds: Strategic Vision as Social Interaction." *Advances in Strategic Management,* 8:271–305. Greenwich, Conn.: JAI Press.

Wilson, James Q. 1989. *Bureaucracy: What Government Agencies Do and Why They Do It.* New York: Basic Books.

Wurf, Elissa, and Hazel Markus. 1991. "Possible Selves and the Psychology of Personal Growth." *Perspectives in Personality,* vol. 3, part A, pp. 39–62.

III.

Organizational Networks in Theory and Practice

7.

Managing across Boundaries

Beryl A. Radin

Government in a complex society, by definition, is characterized by boundaries. Whether as a result of a fragmented and segmented political system, differentiation by policy issues, or because of functional imperatives, lines have been drawn that separate organizations from one another. Although these boundaries are both understandable and sometimes appropriate, the organizations created by boundaries often seem unable to respond to the changing social, political, and economic demands that are placed on them. Adaptation or even survival appears to require that public agencies look across the boundary lines that now define them.

Unlike a number of aspects of the debate on "reinventing government," the legitimacy of a boundary-spanning role or activity is widely accepted. Both the critics and the proponents of the National Performance Review, for example, cite the need to cross boundary lines. The Gore report comments:

> Unfortunately, even agencies that try harder find very real obstacles in the way of putting their customers first. Perhaps the worst is Washington's organizational chart. Time and again, agencies find it impossible to meet their customers' needs, because organizational boundaries stand in the way. . . . In a rapidly changing world, the best solution is not to keep redesigning the organizational chart; it is to melt the rigid boundaries between organizations. (Gore, 1993, p. 48)

Similarly the Brookings volume *Improving Government Performance* notes:

> How can managers solve the boundary problem? Serving citizens today means finding ways to cross jurisdictional boundaries, which requires a more deter-

Useful comments on an earlier version of this chapter were provided by Robert Agranoff, Eugene Bardach, Elizabeth Hubbard, Robert Lovan, Brint Milward, Michael O'Hare, David Sears, and Carol Weiss.

mined effort at all levels of the federal bureaucracy to cultivate government managers who are boundary spanners, managers who reach out to find colleagues in other agencies with whom they can solve problems. The need is to find ways to span multiple and cross-cutting boundaries, thereby improving government performance and responsiveness, but without sacrificing the core values that lie behind government's very existence. (DiIulio, Garvey, and Kettl, 1993, p. 60)

While there seems to be a significant level of agreement on the importance of boundary-spanning activities within contemporary management reform, there is a cacophony of voices in the academic literature regarding the dimensions and definitions of these activities. More than twenty-five years ago, James Thompson (1967) emphasized the importance of boundary-spanning structures and roles as a strategy for adjustment or adaptability for organizations that deal with heterogeneous task environments. Subsequent work, largely involving the private sector, has accentuated the relationship between boundary-spanning activities and acquisition of resources, competencies, and information necessary for an organization to survive (see Jemison, 1984). This literature has attempted to devise definitions of boundary-spanning roles (Friedman and Podolny, 1992), boundary-spanning units (At-Twaijri and Montanari, 1987), and boundary-spanning activities or behaviors (Dolinger, 1984; Schwab, Ungson, and Brown, 1985). However, there is little attention to the multiple types of boundaries that are involved in this activity such as boundaries of expertise, funding sources, regulations and policy, and professional identity (Aldrich and Whetten, 1981).

Perhaps most important, with a few exceptions, past literature in the area indicated a tendency to focus on boundary-spanning activities rather than boundary-spanning organizations (Hjern and Porter, 1981). There is little discussion of the extent to which these network organizations can achieve change, the extent of their authority, and the legitimate scope of expectations about the outcomes of their activity.

Recent work involving boundary spanning has been closely tied to analysis of organizational networks. In their interesting work titled *Organizations Working Together,* Alter and Hage emphasize four conditions that lead to interorganizational or interfirm collaboration: the willingness to cooperate, the need for expertise, the need for financial resources and sharing of risks, and the need for adaptive efficiency (1993, p. 39). The relationships that develop as a result of these conditions spawn what they describe as a three-stage model of network formation: "obligational networks (informal, loosely linked groups of organizations having relationships of preferred exchanges), promotional networks (quasi-formal clusters of organizations sharing and pooling resources to accomplish concerted action), and systemic networks (formal interorganizational units jointly producing a product or service in pursuit of a supraorganizational goal)" (p. 73). According to Alter and Hage, boundary-spanning roles are related to the embryonic stage—what they call obligational networks.

Alter and Hage's work makes visible what is an often unanalyzed or unanswered question related to interorganizational efforts: Are the loose networks that are created (e.g., the obligational and promotional networks they describe) to be viewed as transitional to other organizational forms or will they be institutionalized in their current forms? The systemic networks described by Alter and Hage are viewed as enduring bodies with division of labor and their own service-delivery systems. Similarly, it is not always clear whether the networks that are created are formed around decisions made at a single point in time (Bryson and Crosby, 1992) or move toward longer lasting relationships such as those characterized by issue networks or policy organizations (Heclo, 1979; Meltsner and Bellavita, 1983).

This chapter explores some of these issues by examining an interagency body that operates as an unusual entity in the federal government. The National Rural Development Council (NRDC) is a group that was created during the Bush administration as a part of the president's rural development initiative "to strengthen the delivery of Federal support for rural development" (Radin, 1992, p. 112). During the first two years of its life, the NRDC was known as the Monday Management Group (the MMG) and the National Rural Development Partnership was called the National Initiative on Rural Development. The Partnership was an effort begun during the Bush administration to coordinate rural development efforts among federal departments and agencies and establish collaborative relationships with states, local governments, and the private sector. It involved a number of elements within the Washington federal system as well as the creation of state rural development councils (SRDCs). By mid-1994, despite the change of administration, SRDCs were operating in twenty-nine states and in the process of organization in ten others. (To avoid confusion, the current terminology is being used in this chapter.)

The NRDC is made up of representatives from a wide range of federal departments and, in its initial charge, provided a link with the SRDCs in eight states. The NRDC focused on outcome monitoring, served as a conduit for federal officials who would act as liaisons with the states, worked with the National Governors' Association, and provided a link with the White House Working Group on Rural Development. Unlike most interagency groups with a White House connection from a previous administration, this body has been embraced by the Clinton administration. Indeed, it was cited in the Gore report as a "noteworthy initiative" (Gore, 1993, p. 49).

Focusing on the process of institutionalizing a boundary-spanning, interorganizational network in a changing policy environment, this chapter explores the developmental process involved in this effort as well as the products of the experience. The analysis examines the operation of the NRDC from three levels: the group's impact on the rural development policy area or policy system, the corporate or organizational level, and the perspective of the individuals who have participated in the group. This work is part of a multiyear and ongoing study of the rural development initiative that is funded by the Economic Research Service of the U.S. Department of Agriculture (USDA) and the Rural Policy Program of the Aspen Institute. The data used in this paper draw from observations of NRDC meetings; examination of relevant documents; confidential interviews in spring 1993 with twenty-five NRDC participants; a June 1993 seminar with NRDC members in which preliminary findings from the interviews were presented; and relevant data from a study of sixteen SRDCs.

The NRDC: A Snapshot

The NRDC, like many other interorganizational units, was born of necessity in an inchoate form that bears little resemblance to the body that exists today. The basic elements of the group took form in early 1990 when Walter Hill, the deputy undersecretary of agriculture for rural development and small communities, experienced a sense of frustration over the number of committees formed and meetings called as part of an interagency policy development task force through the Presidential Initiative on Rural Development. He observed that every time he called a meeting, different people showed up. His solution was to combine all of the committees into one group and schedule the meetings of the group every Monday morning. After about six weeks, between eighteen and twenty people showed up every time.

By September 1990, this group took on a more permanent status and was described as "a staff-level Management Group with representation from all participating Federal programs . . . [that] convened regularly to provide detailed definition to the initiative and designed a strategy for implementation" (Presidential Initiative, 1990). This group was a part of a fairly elaborate policy effort that included the subcabinet-level Economic Policy Council Working Group on Rural Development, a President's Council on Rural America, and SRDCs in eight pilot states. By December 1990, the Management Group had four management teams centered on providing organizational, staffing, and training assistance to the SRDCs.

Throughout most of 1991, the group continued to meet and expanded its membership to include senior staff from eleven departments of the federal government (approximately twenty-six agencies within them), two independent agencies, and two White House bodies. Most of the participants were career federal employees, but there was participation from political appointees as well. In addition, staff from the National Governors' Association participated in the activities. By October 1991, the group sought to clarify its role and operations through a series of three retreats. According to the facilitator for the retreats, a number of factors contributed to the effort to build consensus among the NRDC members:

> NRDC members were increasingly aware of their own development as a group. Task forces had carried out specific projects, working with the USDA Office of Rural Development and Small Communities (known as the Partnership Office). "In the past few months . . . members have sensed opportunities for enhancing their influence and operations" (Sanderson, 1991, p. 1).

> The NRDC was involved in a new, complex network of relationships. These included the White House, the Initiative Office, individual agencies and departments, and the eight pilot SRDCs.

> Players in this network were not clear about their roles and relationships and communication between the players was not viewed as satisfactory.

The three retreats sought to redefine the role and function of the NRDC, to identify specific NRDC responsibilities, and to clarify individual NRDC members' responsibilities. The specific decisions that emerged from the retreats gave organizational form to the group. Its governance was predicated on a consensus decision-making process (very infrequent informal voting when necessary but no formal motions or use of parliamentary procedure) and a steering committee composed of five members selected at large from the NRDC, including no more than one person from any department or agency. Members of the steering committee were to be selected from a slate of self-nominations by a random drawing and the chair of the NRDC would be selected in the same manner by the steering committee. By these actions, the group also sought to define some level of independence from the Partnership Office, acknowledging that the steering committee would serve as the primary link with that office, would set the NRDC meeting agenda, bring issues to the group, and establish clearer contacts with federal departments. Throughout this discussion, the NRDC members emphasized the role of the group as a body that was closely linked to the SRDCs.

The facilitator for the retreats observed that the Initiative "holds much promise as a national program. Its success largely depends on the participants' ability to manage change—change in perspective, level of operation, decision-making, and relationships" (Sanderson, 1991, p. 7). He characterized the group as a "kind of self-managing work team" that, by design, demonstrated openness and fluidity. He noted that a key role of the NRDC members is that of a boundary spanner crossing borders between agencies within a department, between departments, and between federal and state activity (pp. 8–9).

According to a progress report by one of the NRDC committees, these proposals were swiftly implemented. The report commented: "The ability to respond positively and productively to a demand for change is a good indicator of organizational success" (Outcome Monitoring Team, 1992, p. 15). The document observed that the interagency, interdepartmental character of the NRDC resulted from "a concerted effort to obtain strong participation from outside USDA" (p. 15). Not only were the vast majority of the largely political appointee participants in the subcabinet effort from outside USDA but the majority of the career NRDC members were also from agencies outside the Agriculture Department. In addition, the report noted that a large number of Washington, D.C.– based individuals had some minimal level of participation in the SRDC effort.

By March 1992, the NRDC had expanded its membership to twelve departments and more than thirty agencies, five independent agencies, and two White House bodies; it had ten project task forces; and it rotated the location of its bimonthly meetings among the participating departments. By the November 1992 presidential election, the NRDC added another activity to its agenda, the "impediments project," which was defined as an effort "to identify and redress barriers to effective government that exist as the result of federal law, regulations, and administrative practices." This would be accomplished by working closely with the SRDCs in a "bottom-up" approach where SRDCs identify their problems and NRDC representatives "seek out the facts underlying these impediments and . . . act as agents of change within their agencies to respond to the identified needs of rural communities" ("Rural Development in 1992," 1993, pp. 7, 10). While originally crafted through efforts by the eight pilot SRDCs, by late 1993 there were thirty-six states that had expressed interest or had actually formed a council.

The preelection period also spawned efforts by the Initiative to place its activities within the "new governance" framework that was being popularized by Osborne and Gaebler and was of interest to candidate Bill Clinton. Although not a project of the NRDC, a conference entitled "New Approaches to Rural Development and Changing Perspectives on Governance" was held in October 1992, sponsored by the National Academy of Public Administration in cooperation with USDA. This two-day meeting focused on the process of governance and management issues, not on rural policy.

During this period, the NRDC also expanded its membership to include other government interest groups besides the National Governors' Association, including the National League of Cities, National Association of County Officials, the National Association of Regional Councils, and other similar organizations. Other groups representing private sector interests also began to attend the NRDC meetings.

The briefing materials that were developed on the Partnership for the Clinton administration emphasized two accomplishments related to the NRDC. First, the Partnership was successful in getting seventeen federal departments and independent agencies, for the first time, to recognize that they all have a role in rural programs and meeting rural needs. And second, the Partnership encouraged federal departments and agencies, at the senior policy level, to work collectively in responding to rural needs, coordinating with each other, and building new partnerships with state, local, and tribal governments, and the private sector (National Initiative, 1993).

By September 1993, despite some initial skepticism about continuing a Bush initiative, the Clinton administration reached out to embrace the broad parameters of the Partnership and the existence of the NRDC. At the same time, the Clinton administration sought changes in the operation of the Partnership that reflected its own "imprint" and moved to support the activities in its own terms.

Rural Development Policy Change

The original design of the Bush rural initiative emphasized policy change of at least two types (Radin, 1992). The first was related to a diminished federal role in domestic policy, including block grants, deregulation, and minimization of the federal role in rural policy through changes in policy and program design as well as decreases in funding for rural programs. This view of policy change emphasized the role of the private sector in rural policy, focusing on economic development. An NRDC that devised its operations based on this set of assumptions would respond to calls by the SRDCs for formal policy and program change that could only be made in Washington.

The second approach focused exclusively on the parameters of rural policy and the USDA itself. Although by the 1990s, only 7 percent of the rural population lived in agriculturally dependent counties in the United States, the society and its political institutions continued to equate "rural" with "agriculture." For some, the Bush rural initiative was simply one of many efforts in the movement to change perceptions about the dimensions of rural America. One important part of this approach was to emphasize that rural policy change required the involvement of agencies and departments other than the USDA. In this sense, the design of the NRDC would address the need for a range of agencies to understand the ways in which their activities impacted on rural citizens.

As the NRDC and the SRDCs developed over time, the first policy agenda approach receded in importance. To a large extent, this occurred because the eight pilot SRDCs represented states that had Democratic as well as Republican governors. The SRDCs became more concerned about the areas and issues that allowed them to devise activities that could be accomplished within their own authority. Although states did send issues to the NRDC to identify policy and regulatory impediments, it was not a major activity for most of the SRDCs.

The second policy approach, by contrast, became more prominent and actually expanded in definition. It became imperative for the participants to understand the interrelationships between multiple programs. The increase in participation by federal agencies included organizations that were not usually thought to have rural components (e.g., the National Endowment for the Arts). Strategists who watched the initiative began to recognize that the shift from "agriculture" to "rural" required the cultivation of a new constituency. Increasing the membership of the NRDC to include the general-purpose government interest groups (the National Governors' Association and the League of Cities) and other interest groups became a part of the effort to educate groups that had not previously seen the relationship between their traditional concerns and those of rural residents.

For some, the initiative was viewed as a stalking horse for dramatic changes in USDA, moving the agencies and programs that could be viewed as "rural" out of the shadows and into the spotlight. This was substantiated by the Clinton appointments of Mike Espy as secretary of agriculture and Robert Nash as undersecretary for rural development and small communities (both of whom emphasized rural issues) as well as their plan for the reorganization of USDA (which also highlighted rural rather than traditional agricultural approaches).

The non-USDA federal participants in the NRDC attempted to develop strategies for linkages within their own agencies. Some of this occurred in substantive areas (e.g., emphasizing the rural dimensions of proposed regulations). Other changes developed simply because individual NRDC members were able to redefine their own responsibilities within their "home" agencies in ways that utilized their NRDC experience. This may have directly involved rural issues or may have been more generalizable; participants noted increases in their sensitivity to states as well as an increase in their own sense of efficacy and the transferability of their newly found interagency skills.

Corporate/Organizational Dimensions of the NRDC

As the previous summary of the NRDC development suggests, the evolution of the interagency group was self-conscious and open to external environmental factors that required significant change in its structure and operations. Several factors appear to have contributed to this sense of openness. First, membership in the group was never viewed in an exclusive way; indeed, the group was willing to include anyone who was interested in participating or whom they could cajole into attendance. There was some resistance to broadening the membership beyond federal agencies but this soon dissipated. Second, leadership was viewed as a shared experience. The chairs of the NRDC have been drawn from very diverse agencies (the U.S. Department of Treasury, the National Endowment for the Arts, and the Appalachian Regional Commission). Many other individuals played important leadership roles as chairs of task forces or special events.

The traditional tension between career and political appointees never surfaced as a real issue. As one participant in the process observed, "The political people were different than usual; they didn't push a political agenda." As a result, the two sets of actors operated as a team and the career people were the individuals who assumed leadership roles in the process. During 1992, campaign obligations occupied some of the political appointees, making the career staff even more important. Although the group could cloak itself in the rhetoric and symbolism of the White House, as one participant commented: "Both the White House and the Working Group [subcabinet political appointees] had a limited role. Their level of involvement and role was in promoting the initiative, giving enough recognition and credibility to move forward."

The staff of the Partnership Office was committed to openness, consultation, and cooperation. Despite some points of tension between the NRDC and the staff, most of the NRDC members believed that the personal commitment of the staff was essential to the continuation and maintenance of the group. Although the Partnership Office and much of the budget for the effort was located in the Agriculture Department, great care was taken to attempt to minimize the tendency to view the NRDC as a USDA activity. Participants in the

NRDC acknowledged the importance of an administrative function but, as one individual commented, "It's a team effort; the Partnership Office has gone the extra mile to work with the NRDC. People do not think of the NRDC as an extension of the Partnership Office staff." At the same time, one participant noted that "it's an interagency effort where one of the equals is more equal than others but does not control the process."

The design of the initiative—a combination of a bottoms-up approach (where the SRDCs have control over their own agenda) and a top-down strategy utilizing the NRDC—provided an ongoing "market" for the NRDC activities. State skepticism about the level of commitment by the federal actors, especially during the early stages of the process, pushed the interagency group to be attentive to participants in the state councils. However, both NRDC members and SRDC participants expressed concern about inadequate communication between the two nodes of activity. At various times, SRDC representatives were included in NRDC activities (e.g., several SRDC executive directors were invited to make presentations to NRDC meetings), but as one NRDC participant put it, "Councils are still perplexed about the NRDC and our expectations of each other are not realistic."

Finally, the creation of task forces provided a vehicle for individual NRDC members to exert leadership and, as well, to assume responsibility for some part of the group's activities. As the NRDC developed, its definition of tasks moved gradually away from organizational development activities (that is, providing support first to the pilot states and then to the second-generation states) to more substantive policy efforts. A number of these policy activities reflected specific aspects of the Clinton administration policy agenda. By late 1993, clusters of NRDC members (and other federal staff) interested in specific policy issues were organized. Unlike some of the original task forces, which were task specific and dissolved when their work was completed, these groups were designed as permanent entities.

Some of the changes that have occurred in the NRDC's internal structure and relationship to the SRDCs are depicted in figure 1. During Phase 1, the NRDC was a relatively empty receptacle, receiving input from the representatives of the participating federal agencies as well as from the original eight pilot SRDCs. During Phase 2, the representatives from the federal agencies participated in the NRDC as individuals, the National Governors' Association (NGA) operated both inside and outside of the organization, and the communication between the NRDC and the SRDCs was best characterized as a fluid two-way street. During Phase 3, clusters of issue groups operated within the NRDC, the NRDC itself branched out to include representatives of other in-

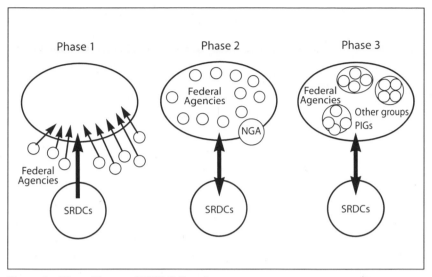

Figure 1   Three Phases of NRDC Development

terest groups, and the two-way communication between the NRDC and the SRDCs continued.

The Next Phase of NRDC Development

Four issues are now faced by the NRDC as a corporate body as it embarks on its next phase.

Conflict avoidance. To this point, the NRDC has managed to avoid or deal with conflict among its members by employing several strategies. It has not asked any of the participating agencies to change what they may view as their "core" technology (Thompson, 1967). In part this occurred because the NRDC emphasized process rather than substantive policy changes. It employed a low-visibility approach, attempting to control or buffer the group from political or other external pressures. While its offices were in USDA facilities, it operated on the margins of the department.

It is not easy to maintain this strategy. Neither participants nor their constituencies can defend an effort that does not appear to be making substantive policy change. As a result, some of the participating agencies may be asked to change regulations or program distribution patterns. The Partnership's early emphasis on process rather than outcomes was facilitated by the low-visibility strategy employed during its early phases. Low visibility was possible because the effort shied away from identification with political actors or institutions. Although the initial activity emerged from the White House, it soon became bipartisan, almost apolitical, in nature as the careerists took a predominant role. Similarly, every effort was made to avoid involvement with Congress; this was possible because the Partnership was not created through legislation and did not have a large, identifiable budget. However, this strategy was changed as support was sought from the Clinton administration and, as well, the Partnership developed some allies on the Hill.

The policy concerns that characterized the NRDC agenda did become relevant to Clinton's USDA secretary and undersecretary for rural development and small communities. As a result, some of the USDA participants in the process may associate the NRDC effort with a partisan political agenda rather than a part of a low-visibility, "professional" approach.

Formalization and the development of rules. As the NRDC grew, it found it difficult to maintain itself by utilizing the informal processes that characterized its early development. By 1993, full NRDC meetings were often attended by more than fifty individuals, making it cumbersome to have easy discussion among the participants. Task force and other reports, rather than open discussion, dominated the agendas. Differentiation of tasks and the creation of small subunits also seemed to lead to a more formal structure. In addition, expansion of the SRDCs network to nearly forty states created more and different sorts of demands on the Washington-based structures. These and other issues were discussed by the NRDC during a series of retreats in October 1993.

Relationships with the external environment. During its formative period, the NRDC's strategies created an open system where boundaries were not perceived between the group and others. Meltsner and Bellavita write that a policy organization "treats its environment as another member of the organization" (1983, p. 138). The NRDC's inclusiveness in Washington combined with its relationship to the SRDCs to spin a seamless web around the participants. The environment was not perceived as a difficult source of uncertainty because the NRDC members largely believed that they could control the interactions between the group and these "external" forces.

This sense of efficacy and openness is fragile. The change of administration in Washington brought the promise—and fear—of a new set of demands. At the same time that these shifts occurred, the SRDCs emphasized issues related to their own development and the utilization of the authority of their own members, rather than Washington-based activities. As such, it is possible that clearer boundaries will develop between the two sets of actors within the Initiative.

Institutionalization, change, and longevity. To this point, the NRDC has been able to continue because it has been able to constantly "reinvent" itself. It played the role of the "good soldier" during the early phase of the effort. It adopted an organizational development posture during the second phase, focusing on process issues. As the Clinton administration became first a possibility and then a reality, it cloaked itself and defined itself in the language of the new governance.

Today, however, the effort is less malleable than it was in earlier days. It is now visible. It has created its own internal structure. While the subunits that have been created around issue areas represent a more diversified approach to rural development questions, they also create a "baggage" and complexity that may make change more difficult than it was in the past. The NRDC represents a set of actors both in Washington and in the states with expectations about certain kinds of activities and behaviors.

If organizations move along a life cycle, then the NRDC should be approaching adulthood. What does that mean? Alter and Hage (1993) believe that networks can be institutionalized and operate in an enduring fashion (see also Agranoff, 1986; Mandell, 1988). Other depictions of networks, however, lead one to believe that they are transitional and transient. It is not yet clear how the NRDC will develop or how it will respond to both internal and external pressures for predictability and stability.

The Individuals in the NRDC

The more than sixty individuals who participate in the NRDC not only represent a wide variety of agencies and departments but also come to the group with diverse experiences. Participants in the NRDC have had educational training in many different areas; there is no single path of educational preparation for these individuals. At the same time, the group of senior career federal employees tends to be well educated; more than half of the respondents interviewed had graduate training at a master's level or beyond.

About half of the group were in career program positions while the other half were in career staff positions. Career paths of the group have involved movement between two or more federal agencies or between federal agencies and nonfederal positions. Fewer than one-third of the individuals interviewed had careers entirely in one federal agency.

While a few of the participants had job assignments in units that could be defined as boundary-spanning units, most did not. However, a number of the participants did have boundary-spanning roles in non-boundary-spanning units and had more experience with past intergovernmental and interagency efforts

than with rural issues. More than two-thirds of the respondents had been assigned by their agency to participate in the NRDC. Some were enthusiastic
about this assignment, some picked up the role from someone else in the agency,
and a few described their involvement as "just another assignment." A few individuals volunteered for the NRDC and a few were recruited for participation.
About one-third of the individuals did not know any of the other participants
before coming to an NRDC meeting. Slightly more than a third knew a few of
the people present, while very few knew a significant number of the players.

About half of the respondents began their involvement in the NRDC believing that it was a good idea. The other half were either skeptical about the
process, unsure of what it would produce, or actually negative about it. Participants who had been skeptical or unsure about the process noted that they
changed their views because people were trying to make government work;
the process had the attention of state governments; they were willing to gam-
ble on the process, liked being a part of a growing effort, and believed in the
need to network and work with other agencies; and because of the staff of the
Initiative. Asked why they continue their involvement in the NRDC, respondents gave both personal reasons ("It's fun, I like the people," "It's interesting
and challenging," "I'm impressed by the energy, it energized me") and job-re-
lated reasons ("It helps put my work in a broader context," "It fits my job description," "I need to monitor the activity").

When a group of fifty NRDC members was presented with the preliminary findings from the interviews and asked, "Why has the NRDC continued
and maintained itself over the past few years?" they emphasized seven reasons:

1. Personal commitment of the staff
2. Personal commitment of the members
3. The appeal of the rural issue
4. "We've produced something that is useful"
5. "There was White House interest"
6. It's a model to use for other issues
7. Resources are available

Similarly, when this group of NRDC participants was asked to list the
outcomes of the NRDC to date, they highlighted five issues:

1. Collaboration between Washington-based agencies and between the
    federal government and the states
2. Example of new governance, reinventing government

3. Networking, new contacts
4. The impediments process
5. Gives rural issues more visibility and sensitizes people to rural issues

Interview respondents were also asked about patterns of response and communication regarding the initiative in their home agency. Few of them reported active involvement in the process by their supervisors or colleagues. Some noted that their agency did not really understand why it should be involved and a few said their colleagues understood the process but were not interested in it. Several individuals said they were permitted to participate in the NRDC but that there was an apathetic attitude about their involvement. About one-third of the respondents had involved their field staff in some aspect of the initiative, but several people were concerned that the level of decentralization in their agency made it difficult to disseminate materials and evoke interest in the effort.

The experience of the NRDC participants provides data on several broader issues.

Participant's home base: program units or boundary-spanning units? Much of the organizational behavior literature suggests that boundary spanners are, by definition, individuals employed in boundary units (see review in At-Twaijiri and Montanari, 1987). This literature suggests that the boundary-spanning function is devised as a specialization, separate from other operations of the organization. Although a few of the NRDC participants were located in agency intergovernmental units, which were charged with developing relationships with other levels of government, most of the members were located in program or staff units that had other responsibilities as well.

This pattern suggests that boundary-spanning responsibilities may be included among an array of tasks assigned a senior careerist, not as a separate function. The role, thus, becomes one that is integral to a manager's competencies. It reinforces James Thompson's view that administration is a process flowing through the actions of various people who span and link units both within and outside the organization.

Type of person involved in boundary-spanning activity. Past studies of boundary spanners have defined personal characteristics of this individual. Miles has summarized these characteristics as flexibility, extroversion, tolerance of ambiguity, self-assurance, need for visibility, and savoir faire (quoted in Dolinger, 1984, p. 353). Meltsner and Bellavita found boundary-spanning members of the organization to be personable, high achievers, and verbal (1983, p. 211). Schwab, Ungson, and Brown suggest that people in higher-level positions deal more extensively with the external environment of the organization than do lower-level staff who are more oriented to internal operations (Schwab, Ungson and Brown (1985, p. 77).

The members of the NRDC appear to meet many of the characteristics described in these literatures. As a group, they seem to be flexible, extroverted, tolerant of ambiguity, self-assured, personable, high achieving, and verbal. They also tend to be in relatively high grades within the public service (GM 14s and 15s). However, perhaps because most are career bureaucrats, they do not demonstrate a personal need for visibility. Rather, they find meaning in the challenge of trying something new in an environment where career bureaucrats are thought to be resistant to change.

A collective profile of the NRDC member emerges in response to the question, "What have you learned as a result of your involvement in the NRDC?"

—"I got a sense of hope that government could operate well and that career officials could be positive and productive."

—"I learned that there is more creativity and professionalism in the federal bureaucracy than is usually perceived."

—"I learned about other agencies and how they do their work."

—"I learned that the federal government can play a facilitating role with states."

—"After coming out of an era of federal bashing, I learned that the leadership of the federal government is important."

—"This reinforced my belief that interagency initiatives are possible."

—"I learned about the diversity of the states."

—"I now have a new list of names and phone numbers to use as contacts."

—"I found out how devastated rural America really is."

—"I learned that there is hope for rural America, that more federal agencies are interested in rural issues than I thought."

—"I learned more about my own department as a result of this effort."

—"I learned that there is not just one model for change."

—"I found that there are other people who feel the same way that I do."

—"I recognized that people can change and grow."

—"I learned how time-consuming and expensive collaborative efforts are."

—"I learned how to run a task force."

Role conflict. The personal challenge and sense of satisfaction that was experienced by the NRDC members appears to offset some of the sources of role conflict that have been described in the literature. The individual boundary spanner, by definition, is juggling expectations from the interagency group or network and the "home" base. Friedman and Podolny have differentiated the role in terms of both content and structure and describe two types of roles: a gatekeeper (who is a conduit to the new group) and a representative (a transmitter of ideas from the "home" group) (1992, p. 32). Their work suggests that during early stages of activity the two roles are not strongly differentiated but, as time passes, differentiation between the two increases (pp. 43–44). For some researchers this set of multiple expectations creates stress; others, however, emphasize the ways in which the individual deals with the conflict—mitigating or managing its negative effects. Still others focus on the difficulty of planning and managing multiorganizational efforts (see Alter and Hage, 1993, p. 242).

Although individual NRDC members expressed concern about the response to their activities in their "home" agency, the issue does not seem to be of major concern. NRDC participants appear to be able to manage much of the role conflict that seems to go with the territory. As the appendix to this chapter suggests, NRDC members have found many ways to have an impact on their "home" agencies.

However, several members have expressed concern about the commitment of their agency to the effort, pointing to the difficulty of getting agencies and departments other than USDA to allocate money to the initiative. This promises to be even more problematic as budgets become tighter. In addition, as a new administration comes into operation, some of the NRDC members have experienced increased demands on their time and find it difficult to protect the time they would like to spend on NRDC work.

Timing, temporal dimensions. The NRDC process developed in an environment that created a window of opportunity for change. (This dynamic is similar to the policy windows described in Kingdon, 1984.) The career bureaucrats who invested in the early stages of the process were challenged in several ways. Some sought to prove that careerists were not resistant to innovation and change. Others found themselves in a situation where they believed that their abilities were not being utilized. Still others had slack time and were searching for projects in which they could expend their energies. A few participants probably used the NRDC as a way to develop contacts that might lead to job changes.

The NRDC was able to address these agendas between 1990 and 1992 as well as to make the transition to the expectations of a new administration. It is not clear whether the process is transferable to situations that do not have the same characteristics of the period in which the seeds for the NRDC were sowed, grew, and eventually bloomed.

Conclusions

At this writing, the NRDC and the National Rural Development Partnership have been accepted by the Clinton administration. It is obvious that the initiative is a relatively low-cost, low-risk investment that contains attributes that resonate with other Clinton approaches, particularly the emphasis on collaboration, responsibility assumed at the state level, and the spirit of "reinvention."

At the same time, the Clinton administration has emphasized substantive issues and areas that differ from those of the Bush administration. First, it has suggested that the SRDCs pay more attention to the diversity of the rural population within the state both in terms of membership and definition of activities. Some of the councils have been responsive to past efforts in this vein regarding the involvement of Native Americans as well as racial or ethnic minorities. Second, it has encouraged the councils to reach out to the nonprofit community, particularly community-based groups that are concerned about issues that affect rural citizens. Again, this would be done most effectively in a suggestive rather than directive manner. Finally, the Clinton administration has provided information about its policy initiatives to the councils. While it is important to support the autonomy of the councils to establish their own priorities and activities, the administration has the ability to provide information and other forms of technical assistance to the councils. This would allow the administration to emphasize its own set of approaches and issues.

This last item—information provision to the SRDCs—suggests some changes in the way that the NRDC will operate. The specialized NRDC task forces that are already developing might be more formally charged with analysis and information provision to the states around specific issues (e.g., health and welfare reform, workforce training, planning for rural communities). In this way, the current tendency for the NRDC to move into a segmented, sectoral strategy would be intensified.

However, it is not yet clear how the Clinton appointees view the relationship between their own rural development agenda and the NRDC (and the initiative as a whole). During its developmental phase, the NRDC was not colliding with other highly visible agendas. Although it had the support of the Bush USDA officials, that endorsement was more passive than active. As such, the non-USDA participants (despite some skepticism) believed there was a commitment to the interagency dimensions of the effort. If the NRDC is perceived to be a USDA effort, then the enthusiasm and participation may erode. In many ways, the initiative as a whole is still precarious and fragile.

Despite these possible problems, it is clear that the NRDC has developed its own process of operation in a creative and inventive fashion, taking advantage of the strengths of bureaucratic behavior without falling into the rigidity of many bureaucracies.

How generalizable is the NRDC experience? There are aspects of this activity that may be idiosyncratic to the rural development issue. It is a relatively low-visibility policy issue that rarely commands newspaper headlines. It was possible for the Partnership activity to develop in a protected, depoliticized environment without the attention of either interest groups or congressional players. However, much of what has occurred in the National Rural Development Partnership is generalizable to other policy areas. The effort was able to assist in broadening or redefining the rural policy issue. Other issues which are undergoing redefinition may be amenable to this type of networking, boundary-spanning strategy. The NRDC provided a mechanism for intergovernmental learning; federal staff were able to "hear" state-level concerns and perspectives. This dynamic could be utilized in other policy areas. Involvement in the NRDC gave career bureaucrats who may not have formal job descriptions as boundary spanners an opportunity to view themselves as innovators or entrepreneurs. This, too, may be used in other settings.

The NRDC activities suggest that interagency efforts can be designed to minimize turf battles by working at the margins of participating agencies and smoothing out organizational or policy problems by working in this way—thus, the relatively modest changes or outcomes found within "home agencies" of NRDC participants. Finally, the experience suggests that boundary-spanning organizations—not simply boundary-spanning activities—are both possible and productive in the federal government.

Appendix
Outcomes within Home Agency

Creation of new offices, new staffs, use of new or existing venues for discussion of rural issues

Created an office called Rural Affairs
Began discussions through impediments process
Used existing forum in department to discuss rural development issues

> Developed an internal network on rural issues
> Hired new staff for rural development
> Established a working group on rural issues within agency
> Involved higher-level staff

Holding conferences or workshops

> Held joint conferences with two or more agencies as result of initiative

Increasing visibility, giving rural issues higher priority, involvement in planning process

> Placed rural issues in key issues briefing book for first time
> Included rural issues in strategic planning process and other planning efforts
> Developed strategic plans to provide equitable assistance to rural areas
> Participation in the process gave visibility to an agency struggling to survive
> Elevated rural issues to a higher priority, higher profile in state
> Used rural issues as a selection criterion in determining priority issues for project teams
> Gave visibility to existing authority/priorities for rural issues
> Raised visibility of rural issues in normal policy-making process
> Higher agency visibility for rural development instead of agriculture
> Gave higher-level attention to concerns previously "buried" in agency

Funding issues

> New grants related to rural issues
> Refocused funding within state programming
> Set-aside source of funds for projects in council states
> Although denied, budget request for contribution to initiative gave visibility to rural development among high-level officials
> Budget always problematic

Training

> Wrote proposal for training on interagency efforts
> Developed new training programs for agency staff
> Initiated cross-training with other agencies

Increased sensitivity to rural issues, awareness of rural issues, linkages

> Involved constituency groups through panels or presentations at annual meetings
> Agency became more alert to opportunities for cooperation to serve rural areas
> Enhanced and strengthened existing links with other agencies
> Transcended traditional boundaries

Initiative provided intellectual framework for agency to use
Looked at issues beyond narrow agency boundaries
Developed positive links with GAO people
Utilized authority to encourage multicounty cooperation and geographic
   targeting
Strengthened partnerships with other agencies (e.g., cooperative agreements)
Raised awareness level
Gained knowledge about other and new programs (e.g., microloan programs)
Field staff developed awareness of rural issues

Involvement of field offices, other aspects of agency

Engaged regional office staff more extensively
Bottom-up planning process in agency allowed rural issues to come to attention
Involved field staff in councils

Research and development activities, technical assistance

Gained more research funds for rural development; provided opportunity to
   consider how research can be utilized by practitioners and officials
Wrote RFPs for research on rural development issues
Developed pilot/demonstration projects for services to rural areas
Identified "back door" approaches that help rural areas through research and
   analysis agenda and actual production of studies related to rural issues
Leveraged technical assistance budgets and programs

Changing, revising, reviewing legislation or regulations;
evaluation and monitoring

Tried to change administrative procedures
Monitored agency activities to see how rural areas are affected
Reviewed existing agency policies and authorities
Changed or modified eligibility definitions to assure that rural areas are eligible
Proposed legislative language changes to existing authority to deal with rural
   reality
Used NRDC and councils to review preliminary draft regulations

Developing new materials

Wrote brochure on support available to rural areas

References

Agranoff, Robert J. 1986. *Intergovernmental Management: Human Services Problem-Solving in Six Metropolitan Areas.* Albany: State University of New York Press.

Aldrich, Howard, and David A. Whetten. 1981. "Organization-Sets, Action-Sets, and Networks: Making the Most of Simplicity," in Paul C. Nystrom and William H. Starbuck, eds., *Handbook of Organizational Design,* vol. 1, *Adapting Organizations to Their Environments.* New York: Oxford University Press.

Alter, Catherine, and Jerald Hage. 1993. *Organizations Working Together.* Newbury Park, Calif.: Sage.

At-Twaijri, Mohamed Ibrahim Ahmad, and John R. Montanari. 1987. "The Impact of Context and Choice on the Boundary Spanning Process: An Empirical Extension." *Human Relations* 4, no. 12: 783–798.

Bryson, John M., and Barbara C. Crosby. 1992. *Leadership for the Common Good.* San Francisco: Jossey-Bass.

DiIulio, John J., Jr., Gerald Garvey, and Donald F. Kettl. 1993. *Improving Government Performance: An Owner's Manual.* Washington, D.C.: Brookings Institution.

Dolinger, Marc J. 1984. "Environmental Boundary Spanning and Information Processing Effects on Organizational Performance." *Academy of Management Journal* 27:351–368.

Friedman, Raymond A., and Joel Podolny. 1992. "Differentiation of Boundary Spanning Roles: Labor Negotiations and Implications for Role Conflict." *Administrative Science Quarterly* 37:28–47.

Gore, Albert. 1993. *Creating a Government That Works Better and Costs Less: Report of the National Performance Review.* Washington, D.C.: U.S. Government Printing Office.

Heclo, Hugh. 1979. "Issue Networks and the Executive Establishment," in Anthony King, ed., *The New American Political System,* pp. 87–124. Washington, D.C.: American Enterprise Institute for Public Policy Research.

Hjern, Benny, and David Porter. 1981. "Implementation Structures: A New Unit of Administrative Analysis." *Organization Studies* 2/3:211–227.

Jemison, David B. 1984. "The Importance of Boundary Spanning Roles in Strategic Decision-Making." *Journal of Management Studies* 21:131–152.

Kingdon, John W. 1984. *Agendas, Alternatives, and Public Policies.* Boston: Little, Brown.

Mandell, Myrna P. 1988. "Intergovernmental Management in Interorganizational Networks: A Revised Perspective." *International Journal of Public Administration* 11:393–416.

Meltsner, Arnold J., and Christopher Bellavita. 1983. *The Policy Organization.* Beverly Hills: Sage.

National Initiative on Rural America. 1993. "Briefing Book: Reinventing Government in Rural America." April 6, 1993, unpaged.

Osborne, David, and Ted Gaebler. 1992. *Reinventing Government.* Reading, Mass.: Addison-Wesley.

Outcome Monitoring Team of the MMG. 1992. "The State Rural Development Council Effort in 1991—A Progress Report." February 1992.

Presidential Initiative on Rural Development. 1990. "Summary of Progress." Washington, D.C. September 18.

Radin, Beryl A. 1992. "Rural Development Councils: An Intergovernmental Coordination Experiment." *Publius: The Journal of Federalism* 22:111–127.

"Rural Development in 1992: Annual Strategy Report to the Congress." Draft, January 8, 1993.

Sanderson, David R. 1991. "Setting the Course, A Report on the Fall 1991 Retreats of the Monday Management Group." November 27, 1991.

Schwab, Robert C., Terardo R. Ungson, and Warren Brown. 1985. "Redefining the Boundary Spanning–Environment Relationship." *Journal of Management* 11, no. 1: 75–86.

Thompson, James D. 1967. *Organizations in Action.* New York: McGraw Hill.

8.

Turf Barriers to Interagency Collaboration

Eugene Bardach

Professionals in the human services field generally agree that we should press for greater collaborative synergy across various public sector programs and agencies. For instance:

—The public health and social services professional communities look to the schools as a site to help them do case-finding for vaccinations, educate for pregnancy prevention, deliver prenatal counseling, and furnish access to students and their families for a variety of other services (Dryfoos, 1994; DeLapp, 1993; Best, 1992).

—Programs that aim to move welfare recipients into the workforce encourage state employment departments and local adult schools to provide services and programs appropriate to their clientele (Bardach, 1993; Hagen and Lurie, 1992).

—A county hospital might suppose that it could reduce demands for emergency room services from the homeless population in its catchment area if it could somehow help the social services agencies improve the shelter status of this population.

—Public works, health, and housing agencies could join the police and community groups in mounting a community-wide attack on neighborhood drug markets (Kennedy, 1990).

—The local office of child protective services may need to coordinate case management for a number of their clients and their clients' families with the probation department and the welfare department.

Human services professionals also generally agree that achieving collaborative synergies is extremely difficult. At best, the process is time-consuming. The "cycle time" is best measured in years rather than months, and these years see many individuals spending many hours apiece in planning meetings and on the telephone with one another. At worst, the process is also frustrating and divisive, both politically and personally.

Technical, legal, bureaucratic, and political barriers stand in the way of constructive collaboration. Many, though not all, can be overcome to some degree if the process of constructing collaborative capacity can draw on a modest amount of creativity and a larger amount of participant effort. This effort must, in turn, be motivated. But motivation is often blunted by the desires of many agency staff, at all levels, to protect what is loosely called "turf." Turf-protectiveness is sometimes cited as the single most important barrier to successful collaboration (Dryfoos, 1994, p. 154). In a survey of local-level participants in California collaboratives involving school-linked health and social services, 59 percent of participants said that turf had been a difficulty, compared to 24 percent who mentioned conflicting professional and group cultures, and 33 percent who mentioned personality clashes (Wagner, 1994, pp. 2–11). Analyzing why turf problems occur and how they might be overcome—in some cases, to some degree, and at some cost—is the main task of this chapter.

The first section of this chapter disposes of the threshold question of whether insufficient interagency collaboration is a problem that is big enough to attend to at all. The second section furnishes a brief vignette about four local agencies (and some of their state counterparts) in Medford, Oregon, trying to implement a collaborative service strategy under the aegis of the federal Job Opportunities and Basic Skills (JOBS) Act.[1] These efforts initially ran into severe turf problems but eventually overcame them. The third section defines "turf," sketches eight reasons that individuals in organizations care about protecting it, and attempts to locate turf barriers in the overall process of developing "interorganizational collaborative capacity" (ICC). The fourth section describes three very partial and imperfect solutions to turf problems: (1) substituting new and collaborative turf for old agency-protected turf; (2) selecting negotiators with suitable personal attributes; and (3) substituting, in interagency negotiating arenas, relatively problem-oriented participants for relatively turf-conscious participants. The conclusion underlines the importance of individual motivation and the institutional forces that shape it in any realistic understanding of how interorganizational capacity develops.

Insufficient Interagency Collaboration: How Big a Problem?

Just how big a problem might be the apparent shortfall in interagency collaboration? Unfortunately, it is impossible to say. No analogue to a theory of private market failure lays out the conditions that lead to suboptimal levels of interagency collaboration. No accounting methods are available to help us estimate the deadweight losses attributable to collaborative opportunities not taken. We cannot look at any given pair of agencies serving the same clientele, or performing related functions in some community, and take their mutual indifference—perhaps their total lack of communication—as a sign of failure. It might be. But then again, there might be many good reasons of productive efficiency, very likely obscure to outsiders, for them to keep their activities separate. Indeed, no theory is adequate to predict efficiency gains from combining productive activities (as opposed to certain financial activities) in the private sector, which is one reason why many mergers fail.

However, there are reasons to think that the losses from collaboration failures are substantial. Put aside for the moment the fact that formal incentive structures for those who run public sector bureaucracies do not sufficiently reward the improvements in performance that might flow from collaboration. Put aside, too, the constraints on productive performance attributable to political pressures. Consider only how easy it is for agencies to become prisoners of their histories. Legislative mandates are often narrow, reflecting the political climate in which their authorizing legislation was passed. And even when they do not start narrow, organizational processes are at work to narrow them indirectly. Agencies recruit professionals and experts who import and ultimately preserve a narrowed focus with regard to both means and ends. Accountability systems become enshrined, and along with them unusual attentiveness to whatever they measure. The culture of incremental budgeting carries over from year to year an expectation of what activities are to be carried out. And due to the practice of line-item budgeting, incremental budgeting also means that whatever technologies or personnel creep into one year's activities budget as the approved means to carry them out persist in subsequent years.

Meanwhile, though, the world around the agency changes. In particular, the world of policy changes. New cash entitlements, new programs, new agencies, new eligibility rules, new funding arrangements, new subsidies, and the like, arrive on the scene. This means that the clients of any single program or agency may also be the clients of one or more others, and the possibility of finding productive synergies across agencies or programs increases.

However, even when individual agencies have the will and capacity to exploit such synergies, they run into barriers at a system level. Financial management and accounting systems often do not mesh easily across agencies; and these are often held in place by eligibility rules that aim to target particular populations or categories of problems. Procedures for designing and executing interagency contracts are cumbersome and engage contracts office specialists who worry, perhaps excessively, about issues other than governmental performance, such as avoiding waste, fraud, and abuse.

The question whether we are currently very far from the optimal level of collaboration, then, is part of the larger question whether government agencies in the human services field have adapted rapidly enough to the society's changing needs. Despite the literal impossibility of answering this question empirically in any precise way, one might be forgiven for thinking that they have not.

The Problem of Start-Up Costs

It is one thing to say that we may be some distance from an optimum, quite another to say that moving closer, or even moving the entire distance, is worth the effort. If we think of this effort as a sort of investment, we can ask whether it will pay itself back with some acceptable added rate of interest in some acceptable time period. To put it a little differently, a worthwhile investment in creating what I refer to as interorganizational collaborative capacity, or ICC, should generate a discounted stream of benefits that exceeds its upfront and, if there are any, continuing costs.

This abstract formulation can be better appreciated if we think about a familiar first cousin to ICC development, to wit, bureaucratic reorganization efforts. This family resemblance is disturbing because the results of the latter are so often disappointing, while the variety of costs entailed are often underestimated (Thomas, 1993). Table 1 lays out the major categories of generic costs and benefits likely to be associated with attempts to create new ICCs. Two of the entries to which a net benefit calculation might be particularly sensitive are worthy of mention.

Consider first the time spent on setup activities (in table 1, see Costs A) by all those who become involved in the ICC development process. For the sake of illustration—but, admittedly, with no systematic evidence behind it—suppose one meeting of ten upper-middle-level managers assigned to an interagency task force charged with ICC development lasts three hours (including travel time). Multiply these thirty person-hours by fifteen meetings over eighteen months. Then double that figure to obtain the time spent in consultation back in each delegate's organizational constituency. Add another six months

Table 1

Generic Costs and Benefits of Creating
New Interorganizational Collaborative Capacity

Costs

A. Setup
1. Time spent in planning ad negotiations by all participants.
2. Time spent in home agencies and other organizations in planning, consulting, reviewing work of negotiators.
3. Time spent by officials from overhead agencies—for example, accounting, finance, information systems—in discussing, designing, testing new systems.
4. Time spent negotiating waivers and other adjustments with higher levels of government.

B. Operating
1. Administration.
2. Performance degradation of existing program due to interference from ICC.

C. Salvage
1. In event of ICC failure, disappointment, demoralization.

Benefits

A. Direct productivity effects
1. Base case: an existing program.
   a. Synergies in practice, not just on paper—value added relative to existing stand-alone operations.
   b. Correcting mismanagement or misdirection—in effect a partial "takeover" of managerial functions by a more competent agency or by an agency regarded as more ideologically reliable.

2. Alternative case: a new program.
   a. Value of synergistic alternative compared to value forgone of the next-best nonsynergistic alternative.
   b. Preventing mismanagment or direction—if effect a partial "takeover" of managerial functions by an agency regarded as more ideologically reliable.

B. Indirect spillover effects
1. Creation of new linkages among personnel across program agencies affects other programs.
2. Changes in overhead systems originating in ICC management spread to other programs.

Cost or Benefit?

A. Political support for ICC: multiple partners broaden constituency. Benefit if program is worthwhile; otherwise, cost.
B. Demonstration effect: encouraging other ICCs.

(or 1,000 hours) to develop the administrative infrastructure newly required. Add time for correspondence and telephone calls requesting waivers and other adjustments from various funding agencies (200 hours). If community meetings are required, hundreds or thousands more hours are spent by the fifty or a hundred people who attend three or four of them. Depending on the scope of the ICC's projected activities, then, the setup costs of ICCs in the human services area could conceivably run 3,000–5,000 person-hours.[2] These costs can be reduced somewhat if a locality is importing a model developed elsewhere, although the necessity to reinvent and adapt a general model for local conditions (McLaughlin, 1980) and to satisfy personal needs suggests that the reduction will not be very large.

The costs can seem large, especially to the individuals who have to attend all the meetings, read all the planning documents, and participate in all the tedious negotiations.[3] But to have meaning, the costs must be compared to the benefits they produce. These too may be large, particularly if they are amortized over several years of successful operation and, more important, over many hundreds or thousands of clients, and if the delays are not great between incurring the costs and actually producing a stream of beneficial services. Suppose, for the sake of argument, that setup costs plus a capitalized stream of continuing operation costs amount to $100,000. At a discount rate of, say, 6 percent, and a time horizon of ten years, how much benefit must be received by a pool of, say, one thousand clients or customers per year to make this break even? The answer is about $13 per client. A simple collocation arrangement or a consolidation of eligibility and intake procedures to avoid imposing the hassle of traveling and assembling documents could likely achieve this level of benefit.

Of course, some setup costs can be considerably larger than average— and they will be when the struggle over turf heats up. We now describe one turf-encumbered ICC development process that imposed costs at the outer limit of any reasonable distribution.

The Medford Meltdown and Salvage Operation

In 1988, Congress passed the Job Opportunities and Basic Skills (JOBS) Act, which offered the states matching funds to support a variety of measures to try to move AFDC recipients, particularly long-term recipients and teenagers, off welfare and into the labor force. These measures included, among other things, job search and placement, life skills education, basic education, and vocational training. State welfare agencies were to take the lead in administering the program, but they were instructed to coordinate their program activities with education agencies and with the agencies administering the Job Training and Partnership Act (JTPA).

State responses to this mandate for interagency coordination have been quite varied. Oregon has embraced it more than most other states.[4] With the encouragement of the governor and the legislature, an interagency collaborative emerged that linked the Adult and Family Services (AFS, the state welfare agency), the community colleges, the Jobs Council (the JTPA agency), and the Employment Division. Collaboration at the state level has been mirrored in each of the fifteen AFS service districts into which the state is divided, although each service district is free to work out its own collaborative design.

In 1987, a year prior to the JOBS legislation, the Medford District was one of seven districts in the state to have been chosen to implement a pilot program known as New Jobs, which in concept and in detail proved to be a precursor of JOBS. The service delivery and administrative concepts turned, like those of JOBS, on local partnership. Hence, the representatives of AFS, Rogue Community College (RCC), the Jobs Council, and Employment Division began to negotiate. These four individuals, each of whom was the highest-level official of his or her respective institution in the local area, formed the core of what eventually became known as the "Planning Committee." Around this core were assembled representatives from other public and community-based organizations with stakes in the program. These others attended Planning Committee meetings with varying degrees of regularity.

The Planning Committee began early to slide into anarchy. There was concern over how much rent RCC was intending to charge, over which agency (AFS or RCC) would have the final say on the client's movement out of basic education and into the job market, over how much financial risk RCC should assume if clients did not obtain jobs, and generally over who would get the blame if the program failed. In addition, these substantive issues were aggravated by, and to a certain degree displaced by, issues of personal standing and prerogative. Negotiations, both within Planning Committee meetings and outside them, became a medium for the expression of animosities and jealousies. Overlaid on these were suspicions arising from endemic practices of concealment and deception. Refusal to engage with the administrative problems of program design and operation destroyed any prospect of escape into the more manageable world of service issues. Nor was any help to be had from the mixing of the four "strong personalities" who represented the core agencies.

When service issues did come up, they were discussed mainly at the symbolic level and in the context of assigning blame for past failures. The representative from the Employment Division was wont to refer to welfare clients as "losers" and "second-class citizens." AFS representatives believed that failures to serve their clients effectively had much less to do with the clients than it did with the inferior quality of services delivered by the other three agencies at the table.

Outside the meetings of the Planning Committee, AFS did what it could, in many minor ways, to set the Jobs Council and RCC at odds with one another. To counter this strategy, these two organizations, together with the Employment Division, created the Southern Oregon Regional Employment Compact (SOREC), the main purpose of which was to establish a venue in which the non-AFS partners could organize a common front.

The program that was put in place did not run well. According to observers' reports of the situation in mid-1989:

—AFS caseworkers could not schedule clients for life skills classes at RCC because RCC could not or would not inform them when the classes began, when they ended, or where they were held.

—Clients were referred to Jobs Council providers on the assumption that they would receive thorough vocational assessment, but, at least in the eyes of some participants, the assessments were rudimentary and unsatisfactory.

—Clients were nominally enrolled in basic education classes at RCC, but, as one participant explained it, RCC had "no idea about how many people were actually participating. They knew that literally hundreds of them were not participating. But they really didn't have any system to track it."

—Poor information systems ensured that managers were getting no feedback about what was actually happening at ground level. The director of the Jobs Council was able to convince himself that, despite the persistent lack of progress, a "tidal wave" of people was shortly going to pass through adult basic education and job search and "crash on the shore of placements."

Two representatives from the state capital, one from AFS headquarters and one from a state office administering the JOBS contracts, were dispatched to stop the meltdown, but to no avail. The situation appeared so hopeless, and so immune to local self-help, that a two-woman team of professional mediators was brought in from Eugene in December 1990 to work with the Planning Committee. The first mediation session produced an unexpected result. The AFS branch manager in Medford expressed frustration at the end of the meeting that they had not accomplished even the first step toward solving their practical problems. He "still had no one he could telephone" in any of AFS's three partner agencies to discuss even the most minor operational problem. The participants immediately agreed to constitute a committee of operations specialists that would meet independently of the Planning Committee. They called it the "Dream Team" because it seemed that only by being visionaries and dreamers could this committee make any progress.

In the event, the Dream Team succeeded. They began by solving the easy problems, like producing a schedule of RCC life skills classes and inducing RCC to consolidate JOBS-related programming responsibilities in a single individual. They also convinced the AFS district manager to accept this concept, which she had resisted on the grounds that an RCC coordinator might jeopardize AFS caseworker accountability for, and control over, the client. By April 1991, the Dream Team had strung together enough "small wins" (Weick, 1984) and had earned enough respect from the various members of the Planning Committee, including their own hierarchical superiors, that responsibility gravitated even further in their direction. By virtue of both their successes and their self-conscious management of group dynamics, the group created an atmosphere of mutual trust and a conception of group identity.

Exactly how this gravitation process worked was subtle and was remembered somewhat differently by different participants. What is certain is that all parties were sensitive to the perception that the Operations Committee might be "usurping power." At the same time, there was a growing understanding, even among the Planning Committee members, that the Operations Committee was becoming an effective instrumentality. The Planning Committee substantially stopped meeting, and the four "strong personalities" slowly backed out of the negotiating process altogether. Perhaps more important, by virtue of retirements or resignations, all but the community college president had left the scene entirely by the time I visited Medford in June 1992. New blood also came to the Operations Committee during this period. By June 1992, the only key participant left from the era preceding the establishment of the Operations Committee was the AFS Medford branch manager.

In June 1994, I visited Medford again. The AFS branch manager from 1992 had been promoted to the position of deputy to the statewide JOBS director. Another Operations Committee member, who had earlier headed the JOBS component of the local JTPA agency, had moved into his job. The Operations Committee still functioned, though it had less to do, and a new interorganizational collaborative of line workers from the several partner agencies had emerged. This collaborative met weekly to discuss particular cases and to develop suggestions for procedural and other improvements in the way the program was working. The line workers were enthusiastic about their newfound powers and responsibilities; and there was general agreement that the program was running smoothly and effectively. The trend line in at least one important indicator of performance, cost per job placement, showed a slow but steady improvement, from $7,700 in 1990–91 to $2,516 in mid-1994.[5]

The Turf Problem

Participants in the Medford case often characterized the struggles during the meltdown phase as concerning "turf battles." But what exactly is "turf" and why do people care about it? The answer are not quite as straightforward as one might think.

I use the term *turf* to refer to the exclusive domain of activities and resources over which an agency has the right, or prerogative, to exercise operational and/or policy responsibility.[6] Thus, not every agency-related matter a manager might care about—budget, say—involves turf, at least not centrally.

Why People Care about Turf

From the manager's point of view, all other things equal, more turf is better. Consider, for instance, the stereotypical empire-building bureaucrat seeking to expand his or her domain of responsibilities and powers. This expansion brings greater prestige, ego gratification, visibility, and hence career opportunities. Expansion also brings the possibilities of a larger number of employees and larger budgets, both of which can, in some circumstances, translate into higher pay for the empire builder. A larger empire also allows for the extension of one's policy preferences into more of society's varied activities.

But concern for turf is not limited to the imperially minded. Indeed, it shows up much more commonly as a concern to protect the security of turf already occupied. Nor is the concern for turf limited to higher-level managers. Employees at all levels of the organization may have their own stakes in protecting the agency's turf. These stakes could be quite diverse, since turf, while not quite as fungible as money, is capable of being used in many different ways. Indeed, one of the underappreciated advantages of protecting agency turf is that it can serve as a great unifying force within an agency which might otherwise be strained by factionalism based on ideology, career stakes, hierarchical position, and so forth. Alas for interorganizational collaboration, this also implies that any individual or subgroup engaged in boundary-spanning activities will be regarded internally with great suspicion from many quarters.

The sources of threat to any agency's turf are numerous. The main ones are fiscal retrenchment, changes in technology, demographic shifts, and, of course, interagency collaboration. Let us see what might be at stake in turf struggles associated with this last:

Threats to job security and/or career enhancement. Collaborative work threatens caseload levels—and hence an agency's staffing levels and its employees' job security—because it raises the possibility that a collaborating agency could absorb the caseload. This might occur, for instance, in a time of fiscal stringency, if the budget bureau or a legislative appropriations committee might simply decide that "consolidation" was desirable. (Or, less plausibly, they might decide that one of the collaborators was simply so much better than the other that it deserved to get the entire job.) Loss of caseload, therefore, or indeed any other important "raw material" that the agency needs to keep on producing, is potentially a threat to jobs and careers. In the Medford case, although managers were probably not much concerned with this sort of prospect, line workers in AFS may have been. "It's a survival issue. . . . Everybody is so afraid to share the same client. . . . I want to be the end all for that client. . . . It's almost like the caseload builds how much staff you have," said the AFS district manager from the 1990–91 period.

Challenge to professional expertise. An agency's claims to professional expertise can be challenged by laymen, by rival experts within the same field, and by rival experts from outside the field. In the human services area, the technical basis of claims to professional expertise is usually weak. Hence, cross-agency collaborative projects bring together professional experts on the same turf who may very well feel vulnerable to challenges from one another. And when high-status professionals, like physicians, meet up with lower-status professionals, like social workers or teachers, there is likely to be distrust and conflict all around.

Conflict concerning facilities. Physical facilities are a form of turf, in the most literal sense. Less tangible facilities, such as an agency's letterhead, its database, and its accounting system, also count as turf. Conflict over which agency will contribute what facilities—or over how much other agencies should pay for their use, as in Medford—has symbolic implications for an agency's sense of identity and legitimacy, and occasionally, as in Medford, budgetary implications.

Loss of policy direction. Collaborators struggle over policy partly because they care about questions of value and cost. However, they also care because the outcome of such a struggle affects turf. That is, as the ICC policy orientation tilts in one direction rather than another, the "winning" agency gains more legitimacy for its particular kind of work and/or the means it uses to carry it out. In the Medford case, the AFS leadership was concerned over the employment goals of the welfare-to-work program and was leery of entrusting control over "its" clients to other entities, and particularly the community college, that might not share them.

Undermining an agency's traditional priorities. Collaboration with another agency typically implies taking on new responsibilities. These might be welcomed as an addition to turf. But they might also be seen as unwelcome competitors for agency resources with existing, and more highly valued, priorities. This pretty well characterizes the ambivalence of many community colleges about collaborating with welfare agencies in order to serve AFDC recipients.

Anxiety over accountability. Collaborators can demand accountability of one another, thereby infringing on turf. They can also distribute amongst themselves in some differential fashion the burden of accountability to outsiders (Bardach and Lesser, 1994). In this latter case, what is at issue is potential blame and credit for real or seeming program outcomes. As the director of the AFS Medford district office (circa 1990–91) explained, "The history of . . . AFS [is that they are] very accountable. . . . You didn't contract out services. . . . You were very accountable to the feds. . . . How many people did you have on your caseload. . . . We're very accountable for our dollar, we want to see what products we bring in for that dollar."

Requirements for building and maintaining consensus. Collaboration implies not just ex post accountability but also ex ante, and even continual, consensus building and mutual adjustment. This is especially difficult when agencies are dominated by professionals with different values and different theories about how the world works, for example, employment counselors and classroom teachers. In the Medford case, the consensus-building process in the Planning Committee appears to have been particularly painful.

Self-worth. Turf is defined above in institutional terms. However, institutions are in some measure the individual people who work in them and for them. Protecting an institution's turf therefore protects the self-worth of those who work for it. The process works in the other direction, too. That is, the individual derives a sense of self-worth from the turf prerogatives accorded the institution with which the individual is associated.[7]

To put it another way, individual egos have stakes in protecting institutional turf. However, not all ego stakes are stakes in turf. According to many observers of the Medford meltdown and salvage operation, the struggle was as much a reflection of "personalities and egos" as of anything else. But my inference from interviewing many informants was that these ego stakes had less to do with turf than with the prospects of "winning" or "losing" in the negotiations process.

Turf Problems in the Context of ICC Development

Interorganizational collaborative capacity is multidimensional, and turf problems do not affect all dimensions equally. In this subsection, I first explain why we should construe "interorganizational collaboration" not as a type of behavior but as a *capacity for* such behavior. I then explain the three main aspects of collaborative capacity and how turf barriers are connected to each.

When I visited Medford in June 1992, the Jobs Council and RCC were both teaching life skills classes to JOBS participants. Suppose that in 1994, when I visited again, RCC, having earlier shown itself to have been the superior provider of life skills education, had taken over both life skills classes, leaving the Jobs Council to concentrate more on job development functions. (This is a supposition contrary to fact, it should be noted.) Should we then say that collaboration had been somewhat diminished by this change? Behaviorally, there was less cross-organizational collaboration. But it also seems likely that the capacity of the two organizations to engage in collective self-evaluation and to act on the results in an amicable way had increased, with a resulting increase in overall productivity (and synergy). In my view, the increase in collaborative capacity is more significant than the decrease in ongoing collaborative behavior.

To put the matter a little differently, the most important aspects of interorganizational collaborative work exist as a state of people's minds rather than as a set of behaviors. Our conceptualization of a useful outcome variable should make use of this fact. This conceptualization squares with that of Weiss (1987).

Actually, interorganizational collaborative capacity is really made up of three somewhat different, though interrelated, capacities. One is the *operational capacity* of a system to produce service-related synergistic benefits for individual clients and for aggregations of clients. A second is the *resource-raising capacity* of a particular set of institutions or structures, that is, their collective ability to leverage resources for operational purposes either from one another or from outside the system. In most ICCs in the human services area, the most relevant resources are usually the personnel that agencies might assign to functions endorsed by the collaborative, and hence one relevant resource-raising capacity is the willingness of top managers and legislative overseers to contribute personnel. Also relevant are the variety of political resources that can be used to increase this willingness. Finally, the third important element of overall capacity is the ability of system managers and other interested parties to constitute the operational and the resource-raising capacities and to improve them over time—for ICC constantly evolves—a *"constituent" capacity,* if you will. In addition, a constituent capacity also involves an ability to act upon itself, either constructively or destructively.

In the case of the Medford ICC, the relevant operational capacity was centrally the ability of the JTPA agency to do job placement and some life skills education with AFS clients, the ability of the community college to provide basic skills and certain life skills education, and the ability of all three institutions to carry out their tasks at a high level of effectiveness. The most important element of resource-raising capacity was the state-level mandate to local agencies to engage in collaboration. As to the constituent capacity, in the Medford case this evolved more dramatically over time than the other two types of capacity, changing, as we have seen, from being dominated by conflictual and counterproductive relationships in an early period to nurturing constructive relationships in the Operations Committee in a second phase and adding, in a third phase, a capacity to integrate the contributions of line workers.[8]

Turf barriers obstruct operational capacity primarily by impeding free communication among partners and by leading them to recommend solutions to problems that reflect turf concerns more than a concern for effectiveness. They affect the resource-raising capacity of the collaborative by making the partners or potential partners less willing to contribute their resources than would be optimal. Turf barriers obstruct the development of constitutent capacity primarily by causing suspicion and mistrust among the partners. In the Medford case, clearly the most pernicious effect of turf barriers was on the constituent capacity of the Planning Committee.

Overcoming Turf Barriers

The drag of individuals' concerns about turf, and what it means to them and their colleagues personally, scarcely appears in even the best academic analyses of interagency collaboration, for example, Sharon Kagan's *Integrating Human Services: Understanding the Past to Shape the Future* (1993) and Robert Agranoff's *Intergovernmental Management: Human Services Problem-Solving in Six Metropolitan Areas* (1986). One might read Agranoff and conclude, along with him, that the various collaborative bodies that emerged in the sites he studied did improve services in some ways. But one is left to wonder how much more they might have achieved if there had not been constraints on the participants against encroaching on one another's turf. Weiss's (1987) study of cooperation among school districts within regions revealed a fair number of joint efforts. But she, too, says little about turf problems.

If the writers who think about collaboration say little about turf, the writer who says most about turf, James Q. Wilson (1989), says nothing about collaboration except that it is exceedingly unlikely. And even then, he is talking about a minimalist form of collaboration, which he calls "interagency coordination." Supporting this view, too, are Seidman and Gilmour (1986), Downs (1967), and, indeed, virtually all academic commentary. I do not intend to deviate much from this consensus. However, it is possible to observe modest amounts of interorganizational collaboration in human services, in environmental management,[9] and in other areas as well. These deviations from the norm need to be explained and, if possible, analyzed for clues as to how we might cause more such deviations.

Scholarly writing is not the only possible source of insight about turf problems and their solutions. Some excellent publications of the "how-to" variety have been produced by practitioners in human services integration (see Melaville and Blank, 1991, 1993; Chynoweth et al., 1992; Marzke et al., 1992; Farrow and Joe, 1992; Bruner, 1991). Many of these are not only practical but are analytically shrewd, and have much to teach academics interested in the question of how collaborative synergies are created across organizational boundaries. In general, however, they play down the importance of turf. The barriers to collaboration as seen through the eyes of practitioners and advocates are mainly those sorts of things that well-meaning people working hard at their jobs could overcome, for example, articulating a vision, casting aside "old ways of thinking," developing uniform eligibility and intake procedures, becoming more "customer-oriented," and the like. The advocacy bias in these materials— which is of course appropriate for advocates—thus directs analytic power to the system features that advocates can most readily change.[10] Turf-protectiveness is not one of these features.

In the absence of both a good research literature and a relevant literature of practice, the suggestions that follow here about means to overcome turf barriers to collaboration are necessarily somewhat speculative. My own research on interagency collaboration has been helpful, but it is far from completed. But even when it will have been completed, it will qualify, in social science terms, as simply exploratory.

New, Collaborative Turf

If stakes in existing turf pose barriers to collaboration, the stakes in real and prospective *new turf,*[11] turf created in the process of ICC development, act as incentives to collaborate. My approach in this subsection is to revisit each of the eight stakes that organizational actors might have in existing turf, and ask what each of these stakes might look like if they were planted in new, collaborative turf. By organizational "actors" I literally mean individuals rather than organizations; for, while only organizations "have" turf, it is only individuals who have stakes in organizational turf; and it is only individuals who can be motivated to act to create new organizational turf.

Career enhancement. It is doubtful that any of the Operations Committee participants in the Medford case saw their participation, at the time, as a way to bolster their careers. But for at least two of the three key individuals in the group, this does appear to have been one of the results. If the climate for "reinventing government," TQM, and the like is destined to improve, as I believe it will, individuals who develop the skills and contacts to work across agency boundaries and across "the seams of government," as Elmore (1986) puts it, will have enhanced their career prospects.

Professional expertise. One can acquire status by becoming knowledgeable about, if not expert in, other professional fields and disciplines, provided, at any rate, that the other profession is of higher status than one's own. This knowledge can be increased by working together with the other professionals.

Facilities. An ICC that gained access to tangible facilities of its own could prove a rather attractive opportunity for bureaucrats with an entrepreneurial streak. My observations suggest that ICC control of such facilities is relatively uncommon, but does sometimes occur, for example, in Maryland, where the Strategic Reform Initiative (SRI) that is trying to stimulate local networks to offer preventive services of an "integrated" kind to troubled families and youth has acquired a staff and place on the organization chart of state government. In this case, the state makes available for such efforts funds putatively saved by preventing out-of-home (and sometimes out-of-state) placement of children. Of course, one of the difficulties of giving the SRI office some turf of its own is that the traditional agencies can sometimes view it as "just another agency" espousing "a party line," which just happens to be "collaboration" and "integrated services."

Policy direction. As an ICC grows, it develops a policy direction. Joining with other like-minded people (and organizations) to impart a policy direction, or at least a spin, to an ICC can create a sense of collective ownership, and a resulting esprit, that is absent from more established agencies. Sometimes the policy direction does not even have to be new; it can be an existing, and even a consensual, set of policy goals that have hitherto received only lip service.

Agency priorities. If protecting existing turf is a way to protect existing priorities, then creating new collaborative turf may be a way to try to undermine those priorities in favor of something different. This is the case for

Thomas's (1994) collaborators across boundaries in the U.S. Forest Service, the U.S. Bureau of Land Management, and other agencies (see note 9 for complete details), who represent a "Young Turk" element of "ecosystem"-oriented managers turning their respective agencies away from more traditional "multiple use, sustained yield" principles of management.

Accountability. If legislators and the governor's office, or their counterparts at other governmental levels, bless efforts at collaboration, then concerns about accountability point toward collaboration rather than away from it. Such blessings have been helpful in many sites that I have visited, most notably in Oregon, where collaboration is not limited to the JOBS program but extends throughout the entire Department of Human Resources (and also, in slightly lesser degree perhaps, to the rest of state government).

Building and maintaining consensus. The Operations Committee in Medford turned out to have been welcomed by their agency superiors even as these superiors continued to be wary of the Operations Committee's collective power and possible policy direction. The Committee's ability to negotiate a consensus and, over a period of many months, to incorporate a succession of details into that consensus won it not only gratitude and praise but also (discreetly unclaimed) power and turf.

Self-worth. New, collaborative turf is just as capable as old, autonomy-protecting turf of supporting personal or group identity stakes. The stakes differ in important ways, however. While the old turf nurtures a sense of personal or group prerogative and status, the new turf creates opportunities to join with others in an innovative venture. In many cases, the challenge, the novelty, the esprit, and the discovery of other like-minded people prove very rewarding. This was so in the Medford case as well as in many other collaborative efforts my research has discovered.

Personal Attributes

The Medford case dramatizes the role that interpersonal skills and other helpful personal attributes play in creating or undermining a culture of trust.[12] An atmosphere of trust is helpful to all negotiations, of course, but ICC negotiations, involving turf problems, raise issues of personal morality not commonly encountered. It is slightly immoral to be concerned about turf, especially if the concern jeopardizes the constructive resolution of service and administrative issues. Participants in the ICC development process must disguise these concerns from one another. It would not be surprising if many a participant also disguised these concerns from himself or herself. Yet, if success is to be achieved, the concerns must be resolved, either by meeting them or by mobilizing power to defeat them. And this means that negotiators must have the diplomatic skills to elicit a certain amount of candor from one another or must be able to intuit the unarticulated needs and demands of others.

It is worth noting that, in the Medford case, the latitude to empower the more diplomatic negotiators increased when the assumption was dropped that negotiations had to be conducted by the senior officials. Shifting power to the lower ranks not only moved the more turf-conscious players out of their central roles but also expanded the sheer size of the domain of possible recruits— since, almost inevitably, there are more mid-level managers than there are senior managers.

Helpful personal attributes are not limited to skills, personality traits, or attitudes toward risk. Personal familiarity with other individuals likely to be working on the same task also counts. In a study of coordination between vocational education and JTPA agencies, Grubb and his associates discovered that, besides "personality," the factor most commonly mentioned by their informants as contributing to better coordination was "familiarity." "Very often exemplary programs were described as the creations of particularly forceful individuals, or as the result of long-time friends working together, and many of the exemplary programs to which we were directed were in rural areas where 'everyone knows each other.' The importance of networking and personal contacts was stressed repeatedly" (1989, p. 35).

Grubb et al. discount these personal relationships as mere happenstance, "because it is difficult to think of how to hire only charismatic individuals into public programs, or how to facilitate networking." (p. 35). But to require "charisma" is to set up a straw man. The same can be said of "hiring," when usually it is "selecting" from among the already hired that is needed. As to the facilitation of networking, networking is a by-product of working relationships as much as a condition for them; and in any case, it is not impossible to recruit negotiators from among those who are already enmeshed in good networks.[13] In short, if the negotiating arena comes to be stocked with people who are good at negotiating, this need not be a result of happenstance.

Institutional Position and Problem Orientation

Empowering individuals with the right problem orientations, that is, toward service and administration rather than toward turf, is probably as important as mobilizing individuals with helpful personal characteristics. How easy is it to identify such individuals, and to what extent does "the right orientation" conflict with other important attributes, such as hierarchical authority or political influence?

In the Medford case, the middle managers of the Operations Committee were less turf-conscious than the higher executives of the Planning Committee. Although the personalities on the Planning Committee were perhaps more turf-conscious than average, it is also possible that institutional position independently affects turf-consciousness, with middle managers being less turf-conscious, in at least some respects, than higher executives. Why might this be so?

First, for civil servants at least, the higher executives tend to benefit personally from their agencies' budgetary and turf positions more than do the middle managers. The higher executives' careers are more dependent on the size, responsibilities, and budgets of their agencies. Second, the middle managers will have somewhat less to lose by switching to jobs working in other agencies or even leaving government altogether.[14] Third, the very concept of middle manager is almost defined by expertise in coordination functions. Hence, for middle managers, their particular kind of turf interests may actually be advanced by the new scope for coordination activities presented by an ICC. This last point, however, suggests the directly conflicting possibility, too: A well-functioning ICC might eliminate some of the coordinating jobs that were necessary prior to the ICC. Or, only slightly less threatening, it might eliminate the need for the human capital of certain middle managers, capital that takes the form of knowledge about how to resolve certain organization-specific or program-specific administrative complexities. That is, while middle managers might be less sensitive to *agency* turf than their seniors, they might be extremely protective of the turf pertaining to their own intraagency *unit* or *function*. In the light of these distinctions to be made within the overall category of middle managers, selecting which ones to work on ICC development would be an especially sensitive task.

In cases where there is indeed a connection between seniority and turf-consciousness, why would junior managers delegated to serve on some interagency task force to explore a possible ICC risk the displeasure of their superiors by acting on their own preferences?[15] In the Medford case, a staffer at the Jobs Council who had been caught cooperating on the simple problem of designing a reporting format, was obliged by his superiors to send a memo to his negotiating partners saying: "I am not the JOBS team leader. I had assumed that function on a temporary basis only. [X] . . . is the JOBS team leader." And whatever the actual degree of risk they are running, middle managers' uncertainties may exaggerate it.[16]

Under these conditions, middle managers' willingness to compromise and their creativity in searching for effective solutions to collective problems may be diminished.[17] Moreover, they may become less willing to proceed without time-consuming delays involved in checking back with their superiors about acceptable next steps.[18]

Agency executives who want to facilitate ICC negotiations can attempt to reduce the real and perceived risk to their delegates. They can attempt to supply them with some form of mandate. In Medford, this mandate to what became the Operations Committee was a powerful one, albeit not wholly intended: The history of executive-level failure and the charged atmosphere of the mediation session gave presumptive legitimacy to almost *any* group that was ready and willing to take effective action. In other service districts in Oregon, the effective mandate to interagency work teams had come down from the highest executive level in the state in the form of the state's basic JOBS charter, a document called "Local Planning Guide: Jobs for Oregon's Future." More important perhaps, this document was backed by an evolving understanding among top administrators all across the state and across many different agencies that collaboration was indeed expected to occur.

But if agency executives are willing to furnish some sort of mandate, then there must be exceptions to the generalization above that they are too turf-conscious to have much interest in ICC development. There are indeed exceptions. Many are simply interested in having their agency do a better job and believe that an ICC can help.[19] These may function as champions. Other executives fit the mold of the stereotypical empire-building, turf-grabbing bureaucrat, referred to above, or are acting on the principle that a little turf-sacrificing collaboration now might avoid an even greater sacrifice later.

In any case, in attempting to understand the role of agency executives in furthering or obstructing ICCs, it is worth remembering that, even if no ICC could come into being without the championship of at least one agency executive, the very fact of championship emanating from one source is likely to arouse instinctive caution, born of turf-protectiveness, in potential ICC partners.

Conclusion

To understand the role turf development plays in ICC development, I have moved back and forth between two levels of analysis, the organizational and the individual. To restate and summarize:

—It is organizations, including collaboratives, that have turf.

—It is individuals who have stakes in turf, both old and new.

—Turf barriers to collaboration show up in individuals' failures to communicate and to develop trust, and in organizations' reluctance to contribute needed resources.

—The means to overcome turf barriers involve organizations or their leaders creating situations in which individuals are motivated or empowered to augment interorganizational collaborative capacity.

It is the role of individual-level motivation that has, above all, been missing from scholarly interpretations of the nature and significance of "turf." I have sought to draw attention to this dimension of "turf." In doing so, I hope to have also thrown light on processes by which individuals with a collaborationist agenda can gain the political and bureaucratic space to forward that agenda.

Notes

1. This case is drawn from my larger study of how to improve productivity in the implementation of the JOBS program (Bardach, 1993). In the course of the discussion, I also draw on material from a study in progress that focuses on interorganizational collaboration as a more generic phenomenon in contemporary American public administration. This study is supported by the State and Local Innovations Program, which is funded by the Ford Foundation and administered by the Kennedy School of Government.

2. Continuing operating costs would be lower than this. But because a good many of the continuing activities involve the same sort of planning and negotiating as occur during the setup period, the costs might not be lower than, say, one-third of the setup costs.

3. These personal costs can be reduced if the participants enjoy one another's company and enjoy the challenge of their work. Many interviewees told me that they quite enjoyed their collaborative work and that the group members self-consciously tried to encourage commitment and participation in this way.

4. For the details of this case, see Bardach (1993, chap. 3).

5. Steve Rawley, Medford AFS office, personal communication.

6. James Q. Wilson entitles chapter 10 of his well-respected *Bureaucracy: What Government Agencies Do and Why They Do It* "Turf." But this chapter is really about "autonomy," which Wilson argues matters to agency executives even more than do larger budgets. Turf, as I have defined it, is one part of autonomy, what Wilson, following Philip Selznick, calls "the external aspect of autonomy." The other part is "internal" and concerns "identity or mission—a widely shared and approved understanding of the central tasks of the agency" (1989, p. 182).

7. Turf-protectiveness may also have something to do with protecting one's ingroup against an outgroup.

8. I explicitly rule out one definition of *capacity*. This is the supposed capacity that is linked to particular organizational forms, for example, highly centralized and "rationalized" in a Weberian sense. (If I understand them correctly, Alter and Hage (1993)

advocate a Weberian model.) In fact we do not understand very well the actual capacity of particular organizational forms to carry out certain kinds of service processes. In the 1970s, an organization called the Human Ecology Institute evaluated a number of interagency collaboratives sponsored under the auspices of the U.S. Department of Health, Education, and Welfare, which were known as the Services Integration–Targets of Opportunity Projects. The Institute pronounced them failures because they did not have a certain kind of hierarchical structure (John, 1977, pp. 8–10). However, current fashion favors much "flatter" organizations—and, indeed, informal linkages between organizations (Chisholm, 1989)—and many observers might today predict failure for the very organizational forms that the Human Ecology Institute theorized were essential.

9. Craig Thomas, for instance, a doctoral student in political science at the University of California, Berkeley, has been studying collaboration in the field of ecological management among the U.S. Bureau of Land Management, the U.S. Forest Service, the National Park Service, the U.S. Bureau of Reclamation, the U.S. Fish and Wildlife Service, all their California state counterparts (e.g., the California Department of Fish and Game), and some other resource agencies (Thomas, 1994).

10. The advocacy literature probably also soft-pedals turf issues because there is a mild taboo in polite circles against a too deep discussion of these matters.

11. I have adapted this term from Craig Thomas's (1994) "cooperative turf."

12. The slow accumulation of successful experiences that were predicated on mutual trust also plays a role in creating such a culture. For the role of a momentum-building sequence of "small wins" in creating confidence in a collective enterprise, which is quite analogous to culture-building, see Weick (1984).

13. See Levin and Ferman (1985, pp. 104–105), Lax and Sebenius (1986, p. 326), and Radin (1992, p. 121). In Massachusetts, at the time that the Employment and Training Program was coming into being, the director of the Department of Public Welfare was married to the director of the Division of Employment Security, an unusually literal application of the "familiarity" principle. See Behn (1991, pp. 193, 211).

14. What has been said so far of middle managers being less turf-conscious than agency executives could also be said of professionals. It appears, for instance, that in federal resource management agencies such as the Bureau of Land Management, the Forest Service, and the Fish and Wildlife Service, individuals sharing similar professional identities and attitudes form bridges for cooperation and potential ICC development (Thomas, 1994). Line-level professionals from education and from public health agencies have also been the key players in many local school districts in California that are attempting to implement anti-tobacco programs (Balbach, 1994).

15. Of course, middle manager delegates to an interagency Operations Committee *should* strive to represent the service objectives of their own agencies as well as to search for a more encompassing set of goals. Kelman (1992) argues that "a norm stressing eventual agreement, combined with high initial commitment to one's own views" more effectively fosters a problem-solving strategy than does a setting in which participants simply had comfortable ongoing relationships with one another. He derives his argument from Ben-Yoav and Pruitt, who point to the fact that negotiators "do not find it easy to concede to an obvious solution . . . [and who then release] the creative processes that allow them to find a way to reconcile their aspirations" (Kelman, 1992, p. 195).

16. In light of the genuine perils middle managers face in these cross-pressures, a willingness to take risks is probably another helpful personal attribute. One such person is good, but two or more are better; for it takes at least a second person to create the possibility of collaborative psychological support.

17. In the best of circumstances, negotiators' flexibility is reduced when they represent constituent bodies (Lax and Sebenius, 1986, p. 311); and in some sense complex government institutions are like "constituent bodies."

18. As a further consequence, more delays and greater caution could lead to escalating suspicions that the higher executives were using the middle managers to discover other parties' bargaining strategies rather than negotiating in good faith.

19. Among agencies involved with youth and family services, for instance, there is increasing frustration over increasing problems and shrinking or stagnant budgets. Many agency leaders at least give lip service to the proposition that "None of us can do this alone."

References

Agranoff, Robert. 1986. *Intergovernmental Management: Human Services Problem-Solving in Six Metropolitan Areas.* Albany: State University of New York Press.

Alter, Catherine, and Jerald Hage. 1993. *Organizations Working Together.* Newbury Park, Calif.: Sage.

Balbach, Edith. 1994. "Interagency Collaboration in the Delivery of the California Tobacco Education Program." Ph.D. diss., Graduate School of Public Policy, University of California at Berkeley.

Bardach, Eugene. 1993. *Improving Productivity in JOBS Programs.* New York: Manpower Demonstration Research Corporation.

Bardach, Eugene, and Cara Lesser. 1994. "Accountability in Human Services Collaboratives—For What? and To Whom?" Paper presented at the Annual Research Conference of the Association for Public Policy Analysis and Management, Chicago, October 27–29.

Barzelay, Michael. 1992. *Breaking through Bureaucracy: A New Vision for Managing Government.* Berkeley: University of California Press.

Behn, Robert D. 1991. *Leadership Counts: Lessons of Public Managers from the Massachusetts Welfare, Training, and Employment Program.* Cambridge: Harvard University Press.

Best, Larry. 1992. "The School-Based Program as a Model of Services Integration." Paper presented at the Annual Research Conference of the Association for Public Policy Analysis and Management, Denver, October 29–31.

Bruner, Charles. 1991. *Thinking Collaboratively: Ten Questions and Answers to Help Policy Makers Improve Children's Services.* Washington, D.C.: Education and Human Services Consortium.

Chisholm, Donald. 1989. *Coordination without Hierarchy: Informal Structures in Multiorganizational Systems.* Berkeley: University of California Press.

Chynoweth, Judith K., Lauren Cook, Michael D. Campbell, and Barbara R. Dyer. 1992. *Experiments in Systems Change: States Implement Family Policy.* Final Report to the Ford Foundation and United Way of America. Washington, D.C.: Council of Governors' Policy Advisors.

DeLapp, Lynn R. 1993. *Putting the Pieces Together: A Status Report on Integrated Child and Family Services.* Sacramento: California State Legislature, Assembly Office of Research.

Downs, Anthony. 1967. *Inside Bureaucracy.* Boston: Little, Brown.

Dryfoos, Joy G. 1994. *Full-Service Schools: A Revolution in Health and Social Services for Children, Youth, and Families.* San Francisco: Jossey-Bass.

Elmore, Richard. 1986. "Graduate Education in Public Management: Working the Seams of Government." *Journal of Policy Analysis and Management* 6, no. 1: 69–83.

Farrow, Frank, and Tom Joe. 1992. "Financing School-Linked, Integrated Services." *The Future of Children* 2, no. 1: 56–67.

Grubb, W. Norton, Cynthia Brown, Phillip Kaufman, and John Lederer. 1989. *Innovation versus Turf: Coordination between Vocational Education and Job Training Partnership Act Programs.* Berkeley: National Center for Research in Vocational Education.

Hagen, Jan L., and Irene Lurie. 1992. *Implementing JOBS: Initial State Choices.* Albany: Nelson A. Rockefeller Institute of Government.

Honadle, Beth Walter. 1986. "Defining and Doing Capacity Building: Perspectives and Experiences," in Beth Walter Honadle and Arnold M. Howitt, eds., *Perspectives on Management Capacity Building,* pp. 9–23. Albany: State University of New York Press.

John, DeWitt. 1977. "Managing the Human Service 'System': What Have We Learned from Services Integration?" Denver: National Clearinghouse for Improving the Management of Human Services.

Kagan, Sharon L., with Peter R. Neville. 1993. *Integrating Human Services: Understanding the Past to Shape the Future.* New Haven: Yale University Press.

Kelman, Steven. 1992. "Adversary and Cooperationist Institutions for Conflict Resolution in Public Policymaking." *Journal of Policy Analysis and Management* 11, no. 2: 178–206.

Kennedy, David. 1990. *Fighting the Drug Trade in Link Valley.* Kennedy School of Government Case Program, no. C16-90-935.0. Cambridge: Harvard University.

Lax, David A., and James K. Sebenius. 1986. *The Manager as Negotiator: Bargaining for Cooperation and Competitive Gain.* New York: Free Press.

Levin, Martin A., and Barbara Ferman. 1985. *The Political Hand: Policy Implementation and Youth Employment Programs.* New York: Pergamon.

Marzke, Carolyn H., Carrie B. Chimerine, William A. Morrill, and Ellen L. Marks. 1992. *Service Integration Programs in Community Settings.* Princeton: Mathtech, Inc.

McLaughlin, Milbrey Wallin. 1980. "Evaluation and Alchemy," in John Pincus, ed., *Educational Evaluation in the Public Policy Setting,* pp. 41–47. Santa Monica: RAND Corp. R-2502-RC.

Melaville, Atelia I., and Martin J. Blank. 1991. *What It Takes: Structuring Interagency Partnerships to Connect Children and Families with Comprehensive Services.* Washington, D.C.: Education and Human Services Consortium.

————. 1993. *Together We Can: A Guide for Crafting a Profamily System of Education and Human Services.* U.S. Department of Education and U.S. Department of Health and Human Services.

Radin, Beryl. 1992. "Rural Development Councils: An Intergovernmental Coordination Experiment." *Publius: The Journal of Federalism* 22:111–127.

Reveal, Elizabeth. 1991. *Governance Options for the Systems Initiative for Children and Families.* Bala Cynwyd, Penn.: Center for Assessment and Policy Development.

Seidman, Harold, and Robert Gilmour. 1986. *Politics, Position, and Power: From the Positive to the Regulatory State.* New York: Free Press.

Thomas, Craig, 1993. "Reorganizing Public Organizations: Alternatives, Objectives, and Evidence." *Journal of Public Administration Research and Theory* 3, no. 4: 457–486.

————. 1994. "Protecting Cooperative Turf: Interagency Strategies for Managing Human Impacts on Native Species in California." Paper presented at the 1994 annual meeting of the Western Political Science Association, Albuquerque, March 10–12.

Wagner, Mary. 1994. *Collaborative Planning for School-Linked Services: An Evaluation of California's Health Start Planning Grants.* Menlo Park, Calif.: SRI International.

Weick, Karl. 1984. "Small Wins: Redefining the Scale of Social Problems." *American Psychologist* 39:40–49.

Weiss, Janet A. 1987. "Pathways to Cooperation among Public Agencies." *Journal of Policy Analysis and Management* 7, no. 1: 94–117.

Wilson, James Q. 1989. *Bureaucracy: What Government Agencies Do and Why They Do It.* New York: Basic Books.

9.

Designing and Implementing Volunteer Programs

Jeffrey L. Brudney

Although nonprofit organizations are the fortunate recipients of most of citizen volunteers' time, commitment, and skills, a significant amount of this activity is directed to the public sector. Volunteers are active in many public service domains, including education, health, recreation, and culture and the arts. According to a national Gallup Organization survey conducted in 1990, 28 percent of the volunteer work assignments were in government agencies; on a full-time equivalent basis, more than one-quarter (26%) of all time volunteered went to government (Hodgkinson et al., 1992, p. 7). Available evidence shows, moreover, that the level of volunteer involvement in public service delivery is increasing. For example, a Gallup survey taken in 1985 found that approximately one in five volunteers contributed time to government (Gallup, 1986, p. 5), compared to one in four in the 1990 survey. Economist Burton A. Weisbrod (1988, p. 202) estimates that the number of full-time equivalent volunteers to government grew by 50 percent between 1977 and 1985, a trend borne out in surveys of local governments. Studies by the National Association of Counties (NACo) suggest that 93 percent of these units use volunteers in some capacity (labor valued at $1.8 billion in 1992 alone), and that the number of volunteers in county government programs has doubled since 1990 (Barnes, 1994).

NACo President Barbara Sheen Todd explains that "in times of tight budget constraints, increasing demands for service and mounting citizen skepticism about government as a whole, promoting the development of local government volunteer programs only makes sense" (Barnes, 1994, p. 26). While the advantages of volunteer involvement, such as the potential for cost-savings, more efficient allocation of organizational resources, and broader extension of services, have been duly noted by government officials and academic researchers alike, the implications of the approach for public management have largely eluded sustained scrutiny. Accordingly, this chapter elaborates the central managerial challenges posed by volunteer involvement in service delivery and presents strategies designed to anticipate and surmount them. The foundation for the analysis consists of an integrative model of volunteer programs housed in and sponsored by government agencies. The model identifies and links the key aspects of volunteer-based service delivery, and elucidates methods that public organizations and managers can use to attain the benefits and avoid the pitfalls of the approach.

Volunteers: Costs and Benefits for Public Agencies

The labor of volunteers may be "free," but like any approach to the delivery of public services, citizen involvement entails costs for host organizations. Volunteers must be located and recruited to government. Citizens bring a huge variety of needs and motivations to be realized through donating time and a bewildering array of schedules and work preferences to be integrated and coordinated. They often lack background or training in the public sector and familiarity with its norms and values. In their sincere desire to "help," volunteers do not usually show great patience for prescribed forms, paperwork, and channels judged symptomatic (and problematic) of "bureaucracy," which nevertheless lie at the heart of agency requirements to document workload, proper treatment, due process, and, ultimately, requests for funding. With the customary inducements used for paid employees of remuneration, promotions, and perquisites normally irrelevant to them on the one hand, and the common sanctioning mechanisms of chain of command, discipline, and dismissal less effectual on the other, volunteers can prove trying to even the best of conventional managerial techniques.

In short, volunteer programs raise serious obstacles to effective public management. Yet, the approach also offers substantial compensating advantages to government agencies in three primary areas: economic benefits, responsiveness benefits, and organizational benefits.

Economic Benefits

The advantages of volunteer programs which have excited the most attention center on economic and productivity gains to public organizations. Since a well-designed and well-operated volunteer program encumbers expenditures of its own—for example, for recruitment and training, evaluation and recognition, facilities and supplies, liability insurance and reimbursement of out-of-pocket expenses—claims of overzealous proponents that volunteers are the "answer" to deficits in public budgets are misleading. In fact, unless cuts are exacted elsewhere in agency funding, volunteer involvement will normally add, at least marginally, to spending.

From an economic perspective, what the approach offers instead is marked savings in labor and fringe benefit costs that can help public organizations to hold down outlays in achieving a given level of services, or boost service quality or amount for a fixed level of expenditures—that is, increased cost-effectiveness. The chief economic advantage is the expense forgone of compensating citizens monetarily for donations of time, talents, and energy that can greatly expand the capability of public agencies. Since labor and fringe benefit costs account for a significant proportion of government spending, a volunteer program holds the promise of a healthy economic return to sponsoring organizations. In area after area of governmental activity—law enforcement, economic development, parks and recreation, libraries, health and human services, natural resources, programs for the elderly, culture and the arts, and so forth—volunteers have greatly assisted public organizations in extending the reach and scope of services at minimal cost. The typical experience of most government organizations that enlist volunteers is that the amount of hours donated, the economic valuation of their labor, and the types of activities performed far outweigh the public dollars committed. Funding for a volunteer program can finance services valued at several multiples of actual dollar outlays (Brudney, 1990b).

In addition to raising the level of organizational productivity directly through donating their own time and talents, volunteers can also affect the productivity of paid staff members. By assuming a portion of agency work responsibilities, volunteers relieve pressures on beleaguered employees. When volunteer involvement allows these staff to devote greater care and attention to the tasks for which professional training and expertise qualify them and less to mundane duties, human resources are allocated more efficiently, with consequent improvements in agency performance. This advantage is a common rationale for volunteer programs; it is particularly noteworthy in law enforcement, where police officers most often work in criminal investigation and apprehension, while citizen volunteers (and neighborhood groups) handle routine surveillance and reporting (see, e.g., Sundeen and Siegel, 1986). Conversely, volunteers might assume technical assignments for which employees lack requisite skills or experience, for example, legal assistance, computer programming, or actuarial planning.

A volunteer contingent offers public organizations further economic benefits. Although experts caution that volunteering should not be treated as a credentialing process for paid employment, trained volunteers are an attractive and convenient source of proven recruits. President Clinton has repeatedly cited as an advantage of his national and community service program that it will generate a huge new corps of police officer and teacher trainees with the skills to enter the paid labor force. At present, the federal government as well as several state and local personnel systems accept appropriate volunteer work as experience for regular positions.

Finally, volunteers contribute to the resource base necessary for government organizations to engage in innovation and to accommodate emergencies and peak-load periods. Without first having to obtain start-up funding for a demonstration or pilot program, an agency can experiment with a new initiative quickly and inexpensively by applying the labor and talents of its volunteers. The speed and alacrity with which a volunteer program can be put into operation are inspiring: For example, within a few short weeks of a court order in Alabama amending traditional practices for training election poll workers, volunteers were in the field carrying out the judicial mandate (Montjoy and Brudney, 1991). Such an option is not free, of course, but it does allow an organization to test promising changes and alternatives in policies, procedures, or services without abundant funding or great delay. Emergency situations, such as natural or man-made disasters, can provoke an even more dramatic response from volunteers. Especially in a climate of fiscal stringency, the resource flexibility afforded by a volunteer program should not be overlooked.

Responsiveness Benefits

Several authorities maintain that volunteers bring unique qualities to public service that can improve agency responsiveness to clients and the larger community. For instance, E. Gil Clary (1987) argues that more readily than paid employees, volunteers are able to build relationships with clients characterized by acceptance, approval, empathy, care, regard, respect, understanding, and trust. A prominent theme in the volunteerism literature is that citizens help to "humanize" the delivery of services by lending them a more personalized and informal quality (see, e.g., Fisher and Cole, 1993; Naylor, 1985). Not only does the emotional support provided by volunteers help to raise clients' self-esteem and self-confidence but it also increases the willingness to accept the tangible assistance offered by government organizations and to put it to good use.

Volunteer involvement can enhance the responsiveness of public organizations in other ways. First, surveys of local governments that have volunteers suggest that the approach enables them to provide services to the community that would otherwise lie beyond their means as well as to devote more detailed attention to clients (Brudney, 1990b; Duncombe, 1985). Second, through volunteering, citizens identify policy areas that they believe require greater attention, offer feedback to public administrators regarding community conditions, and expand agency capability to provide services and assistance in response to the needs identified. Third, many volunteers live in the communities where they donate their time and possess some familiarity with local resources and formal and informal helping networks. Using this knowledge, public organizations can engage more effectively in outreach and case-finding in the community, as well as tailor assistance to individual circumstances.

Organizational Benefits

Volunteers can prove to be an inventive asset to the operation and support of government agencies. Citizens' exposure to the public sector through volunteering appears to breed respect and approbation for government agencies, rather than contempt or ridicule. Despite the oft-noted apprehension and resistance of employees to their involvement, volunteers are effective advocates of agency interests who help to further organizational missions, achieve increased appropriations, and, thereby, preserve government budgets and paid positions (Marando, 1986). No evidence exists that volunteers are motivated by a desire to cut government budgets or staff. On the contrary, they are much more likely to press for increases in the policy domains where they have seen the need to give their own time and attention.

Not only are volunteers valuable to an agency in promoting community awareness and good public relations but they can also join external constituencies in crucial support activities, such as fund-raising and lobbying, from which government employees are normally precluded. Partly as a result of the independence and credibility that the public attributes to them, volunteers have earned the distinction of premier fund-raisers. They are equally adept at mobilizing popular support and petitioning centers of power. Lobbying campaigns by volunteers helped to shield the California public library system from the depredations of Proposition 13 (Walter, 1987) and the U.S. Small Business Administration from repeated attacks by President Reagan and his appointees (Brudney, 1990b).

Finally, because they are not tied to the standard organizational career and reward structure, volunteers enjoy relatively great latitude to envision and suggest departures and changes. As opposed to their paid counterparts, who labor under a very different set of incentives and constraints, volunteers need not see the environment or mission of the organization in the prescribed fashion. Thus, they may more frequently choose to bypass cumbersome agency routines, test bureaucratic procedures, act as advocates of client interests, raise conflicting points of view, and experiment with innovations. A seldom-recognized, intangible benefit of volunteers is that they present the organization with an internal constituency with fresh perspectives for evaluating existing practices and conceiving promising alternatives; this "insider" position can facilitate expression of those judgments. Not many bureaucracies can boast such an advantage.

In sum, the economic, responsiveness, and organizational benefits possible through the effective involvement of volunteers in government service delivery are persuasive. Their achievement cannot be taken for granted, however. To realize gains in these dimensions, public organizations and managers must comprehend and address a series of challenges inherent to the approach.

A Model of Government-Based Volunteer Programs

Volunteer programs sponsored by government agencies constitute prominent examples of "coproduction," or the active involvement of citizens with paid service agents in the design and especially the delivery of public goods and services (Ferris, 1984; Brudney and England, 1983; Parks et al., 1981). Citizen-government collaboration in service delivery is common and takes a variety of forms (see Sharp, 1980; Whitaker, 1980). In the type discussed in this chapter, labeled "collective coproduction" by Brudney and England (1983), citizen volunteers work directly with public employees to carry out the missions of government agencies in programs housed in and managed by these entities.

Figure 1 presents a heuristic model of this process. The model depicts and interrelates five principal challenges confronting government-based volunteer programs: (1) recruiting citizens for volunteer service, (2) gaining acceptance from paid employees, (3) maintaining accountability to the values and goals of the public sector, (4) providing a structure for effective management, and (5) evaluating program processes and results.

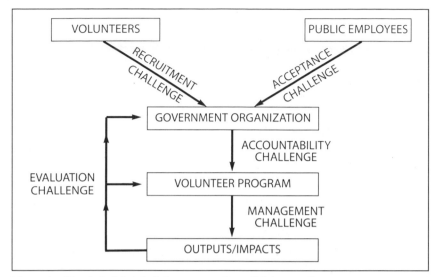

Figure 1   Heuristic Model of Government-Based Volunteer Programs

Recruitment Challenge

At its core, coproduction embodies a mixing of the productive labor and talents of citizens and paid personnel. For public organizations, the combining of effort raises two immediate challenges. The first is recruitment: Citizens must be enticed to volunteer in programs sponsored by government. Although this challenge is most crucial to the viability of the program, exhortations for greater volunteer involvement often presume the existence of a sufficient supply of citizens ready and motivated to lend their time to public agencies. Government is not the sole outlet for contributing one's time, however, and it must compete for volunteers with a huge variety of nonprofit, and even some for-profit, organizations. Program success starts with the availability of a pool of interested citizens, who must be persuaded to volunteer through jobs designed to render the public sector an attractive and worthwhile setting for service and through mechanisms aimed to make them aware of these opportunities.

Acceptance Challenge

Parallel to the recruitment of volunteers, the second challenge consists of winning the acceptance of paid staff for the active involvement of citizens in the delivery of services. Volunteer programs in government agencies constitute a partnership between employees and volunteers; they rest on the understanding that the labor and cooperation of both parties are essential to meeting agency objectives. Without the support of paid staff for the volunteer program, or at the least their tacit acquiescence, the gleaming promise of the approach loses much of its luster. Conflicts and antagonisms between paid and nonpaid staff sap the volunteer effort of vitality, impair organizational performance, and, ultimately, jeopardize client welfare. The means to overcome these difficulties must be built into the program.

Accountability Challenge

Popular conceptions portray government volunteers as fire fighters and police auxiliaries. As important as are these functions, public agencies entrust to volunteers a much broader array of responsibilities, tasks, and obligations in service domains spanning education and libraries, recreation and para-transit, judicial administration and advocacy, health care and counseling, homeless shelters and food distribution. With so many volunteers involved in so many areas, often with very thin lines of formal supervision and monitoring from paid personnel, maintaining accountability to the values and goals of the public sector can become problematic. If the volunteer program is independent or virtually independent of the agency it is meant to serve, as is the case in certain friends of the library, emergency medical service, and business assistance organizations, securing accountability is more tenuous.

Delegating public functions to these volunteer organizations is a form of what Donald F. Kettl (1988) calls "government by proxy," whereby governments grant authority (and often funding) to third parties, such as private businesses, nonprofit organizations, and volunteer groups and associations, to produce governmentally sanctioned goods and services. As with any government-by-proxy arrangement, the accountability challenge posed by the use of a volunteer corps is to ensure that the goals and effort of third-party service providers remain focused on and consistent with public values and purposes.

Management Challenge

No matter how constructive the intention, simply introducing volunteers into an agency without due consideration for the managerial task thus created will not solve, but rather exacerbate, the very problems citizen participation was sought to address. An effective volunteer program requires a sound management structure. Failure to attend to basic features of design leads to programs characterized by volunteers who are frustrated and uncertain about what little they are asked to do, on the one hand, and employees who are suspicious and apprehensive of the "true" reasons behind the volunteers' involvement, on the other. To avoid such problems, the volunteer program must be organized to screen citizens for relevant competencies and interests, and to place them in work assignments crucial to the agency that also allow them to meet some of their own needs (e.g., personal growth, esteem enhancement, career exploration, and community benefit). Performance on the job demands skills, so that training may have to be made available for volunteers as well as for the public employees expected to oversee and manage the citizen workforce. The management challenge consists of designing and implementing a program structure that develops, channels, and sustains volunteer talents and energies toward the achievement of organizational goals.

Evaluation Challenge

The evaluation challenge entails collecting systematic information on the processes and results of the volunteer program and applying these data toward program assessment and, hopefully, program improvement. Evaluation of the volunteer program should focus on its consequences for three target audiences: the clients or intended beneficiaries of the volunteer program; paid employees and other elements of the sponsoring agency; and the volunteers themselves. Ideally, a volunteer program should strive for positive results for all three constituencies. Evaluation is necessary to appraise both accomplishments and limitations of the program, and on this foundation, to proffer recommendations for changes and refinements.

Interrelationships among Challenges

The primary challenges to an effective volunteer program explicated by the model have consequences for one another. Perhaps the clearest connection is that between employee acceptance of volunteers and subsequent recruitment: Should paid staff prove unwilling to welcome or at least abide the involvement of citizens, the prospects of attracting volunteers to public agencies dim considerably. Another element crucial to the recruitment of volunteers is the availability of well-defined jobs that they might perform in service to government. The design of these positions, and consequent placement, are core management functions; the program must have a structure to match agency needs with citizen talents and backgrounds in suitable work assignments. Winning paid employees' acceptance of a volunteer program hinges on involving them in decisions on how to share the workplace with citizens, another management challenge. Employees need reassurance concerning not only respective job responsibilities but also the training and orientation to public sector roles extended by the program to citizen participants. In large measure, the degree of accountability realized by the program is contingent on the amount and quality of this knowledge imparted to volunteers. Finally, accountability and evaluation are closely intertwined: A goal in the evaluation of any program (volunteer or otherwise) is to generate information necessary to assess the degree to which authority and funding have been applied appropriately and effectively toward public purposes. Given these interrelationships, failure to address any of the challenges could have far-reaching implications for the success of the volunteer program.

Public Management: Meeting the Challenges of Volunteer Involvement

For volunteer involvement to yield the rich advantages it would seem to offer government agencies, public managers must confront the challenges it poses. Fortunately, proactive methods exist to surmount the difficulties.

Recruiting Volunteers

National surveys over the past decade (e.g., Hodgkinson et al., 1992) routinely show that approximately one-half of the American populace claim that they have volunteered in the past year (defined as "working in some way to help others for no monetary pay"). In light of these findings, observers might reasonably question whether the recruitment of citizens should be considered a challenge to the volunteer program.

Close examination of the surveys reveals, however, that with respect to the aims of building and sustaining these programs in government, the estimated rate of volunteering is markedly inflated: It includes all acts of volunteering, both formal (to an organization) and informal (outside of organizational auspices), regular (on a continuous basis) or sporadic (one-time only or episodic), and to all types of institutions (secular or religious). Correcting for these factors, Brudney (1990a) estimates that the effective pool of volunteers available to public agencies is likely only about one-third the size suggested by the national surveys. Moreover, this group is highly prized and sought not only by government but also by nonprofit organizations and an increasing number of private businesses. Given these factors, it should not be surprising that surveys of local governments with volunteer programs demonstrate that recruitment of citizens is the most serious obstacle (Brudney, 1993; Duncombe, 1985). Due to such factors as increased residential mobility and the growth of two-income families, some traditional sources of volunteering appear to be declining, particularly in rural communities. As one manifestation of the problem, a number of volunteer fire departments have moved toward incorporating a larger percentage of paid staff (Brudney and Duncombe, 1992).

A long-term strategy for recruiting volunteers to the public sector is the development of an organizational culture that welcomes and recognizes volunteers as full partners in attending to agency missions and clients. This process should begin with an explicit statement of the philosophy and goals underlying the volunteer program, agreed to by employees and their representatives and institutionalized in agency policy (see below). More immediate steps than the often painfully slow one of building a receptive organizational culture are open to public managers as well.

The most persuasive mechanism for recruitment is the availability of nonpaid positions that appeal to the multiplicity of needs of potential volunteers for challenge, stimulation, contribution to a cause, interesting work, personal growth, career exploration, or social interaction. Such an admonition can easily be misinterpreted to mean that every volunteer job must present close contact with clients, ample opportunity for self-expression, ready means for acquisition of job skills, avenues for leadership, and so on; that implication is incorrect. Because volunteers are richly diverse in the ends desired through this activity, public (and other) organizations will enjoy success in recruiting them to the degree that they can offer a range of jobs to appeal to a variety of motivations. An organization should no more allocate exclusively routine, repetitive tasks to volunteers than it should place them only in highly ambitious work assignments.

Public managers can turn to other practical methods to stimulate recruitment. Facilitation strategies include extending the opportunity to volunteer beyond traditional working hours (evenings and weekends); reimbursing all out-of-pocket expenses incurred by volunteers, including meals and child-care; providing nonpaid jobs that can be performed outside the agency (e.g., in the home or automobile); placing fixed terms on job assignments, subject to renewal by the volunteer and the agency (called "volunteer contracts"); and encouraging volunteer activity by groups (e.g., the family, church, or work unit or organization).

No matter how commendable the goals and processes of a volunteer program, public managers should not assume that citizens will take the initiative to learn about the effort and commit their time. According to the national Gallup surveys, only about one in five volunteers seeks out the activity on his or her own (Hodgkinson et al., 1992). Most volunteers are asked to become involved by someone participating in the program or benefiting from it. As a result, public managers must practice outreach. Agency officials (and volunteers) should make every effort to publicize the volunteer program and its opportunities for service at the workplace, school, church, synagogue, neighborhood group, civic association, and other institutions.

Gaining Employee Acceptance

No impediment looms as large or as obstinate to the successful inception and operation of a volunteer program as the often indifferent or antagonistic reception of paid staff. Unfortunately, insufficient attention to program implementation has in many cases given employees reason to be apprehensive. Some organizations have introduced volunteers without providing the proper foundation for collaboration, such as job protections for employees, adequate orientation and training for volunteers, clearly defined jobs for citizens, and a program structure that renders the use of nonpaid personnel simple and advantageous for paid staff.

The most productive method to surmount the acceptance challenge is to involve all parties—top-level organizational officials, paid staff members and/or their bargaining agents (unions), and, if they are already known to the agency, volunteers and their leadership—in planning the program and making crucial decisions regarding sharing the workplace (Brudney, 1990b). Top officials cannot unilaterally impose volunteer involvement successfully; they must earn the approbation and support of paid staff (Ellis, 1986). Paid personnel deserve input into decisions and changes that can so dramatically affect the workplace and the welfare of clients; they often harbor legitimate questions about the purpose and efficacy of a volunteer initiative. Employee participation in meetings intended to reach agreement on the goals underlying the program, the job tasks to be allocated to citizens and those to be retained, and the provisions and procedures to guide the effort help to build support for volunteers. This process should culminate in a formal agency policy and guidelines governing volunteer involvement.

Perhaps the most important facet of this agreement is the designation of job tasks to be assigned to volunteers. While no work assignment is inherently paid or nonpaid, tasks that are prime candidates for delegation to volunteers are those that (a) can be performed on a part-time basis; (b) do not require the specialized training or skills of paid personnel; (c) are not accommodated by present staff; and (d) can assist a position occupant in raising performance (Ellis, 1986, pp. 89–90). The respective job tasks should be codified in formal job descriptions for nonpaid and paid workers, with the express stipulation that neither group will hold the positions reserved for the other.

Implementation of a volunteer program can necessitate large-scale organizational changes. Legislation or rules and regulations may have to be introduced or amended to permit the use of nonpaid personnel; paid positions in volunteer administration may need to be created, posted, and bid; job descriptions may have to change to accommodate responsibilities for citizen participation; and resources must be committed to the program. To make these changes possible, and to demonstrate to volunteers and employees alike the agency's backing, program endorsement by top officials is essential.

To the degree that the volunteer program can facilitate the work of paid staff, employees are likely to accept it. The management challenge is to craft and implement a program structure that provides trained volunteers where they are needed. If this obligation founders, winning employee support becomes that much more difficult. In sum, public managers can work to meet the acceptance challenge by involving employees in volunteer program design, securing the support of agency leadership, and instituting a management structure that makes the work of paid staff easier and more rewarding. While public employee unions may still perceive a threat to their interests, programs formed in accordance with these recommendations that yield protections and advantages for the membership are much more difficult to resist.

Maintaining Accountability

Volunteers perform a great variety of important tasks for the public sector, ranging from *a,* accounting, in some jurisdictions, to *z,* zoo administration, in others. According to survey research (Morley, 1989), a minimum of one-tenth of a national sample of cities with a population over 4,500 use volunteers in the areas of culture and the arts (41 percent), food programs (37 percent), museum operations (34 percent), recreation (26 percent), homeless shelters (26 percent), programs for the elderly (25 percent), fire prevention and suppression (19 percent), emergency medical service (18 percent), ambulance service (17 percent), crime prevention/patrol (16 percent), libraries (13 percent), child welfare (11 percent), and drug/alcohol treatment (10 percent). Similarly, a national survey found that counties use volunteers in the delivery of a startling total of 133 of 135 services examined (National Association of Counties, 1990).

With such a broad delegation of functions to volunteers, establishing accountability for program processes and results emerges as a salient issue. Government managers must see that the application of citizen effort remains consistent with public norms, values, and goals. Two primary methods can help them to do so.

First, organizational leadership should establish a position that bears overall responsibility for management and representation of the volunteers. A paid volunteer director or coordinator position places accountability for the program squarely on the incumbent. This official is answerable for the performance of the program and, thereby, is given incentive to effectively oversee and supervise volunteer participation. The position offers further benefits to the organization. It presents a focal point for contact of all types with the volunteer operation (e.g., inquiries, requests, referrals, and complaints), and it provides a core structure for program administration. The coordinator works with department and other organizational officials to ascertain workloads and requirements for voluntary assistance and to arrange for any training that may be needed for either citizens or employees. As spokesperson for the volunteer program, the incumbent endeavors not only to express the perspectives and views of the volunteers but also to allay apprehensions of paid staff and to facilitate collaboration between these two groups.

Despite ample justification to create such a leadership position, relatively few public agencies appear to have done so. In a national survey of local governments, only about one-fifth of cities with volunteer programs had an official designated as head (21.9%); in many instances, the municipality had simply appended this obligation to an existing job description (Duncombe, 1985, p. 363). Similarly, a survey administered to all Georgia city and county governments found that just 12 percent of the jurisdictions that used volunteers in the delivery of services had a "volunteer coordinator or other official with recognized responsibility for volunteer programs" (Brudney and Brown, 1993). To increase accountability, public managers must dedicate resources to this position.

A second step toward greater accountability is to institute firm policies for orientation and training of citizen participants in government volunteer programs. In an attempt to secure an adequate supply of volunteers, public (and nonprofit) organizations can become overly concerned with recruitment at the expense of necessary requirements for screening, orientation, and training. The literature on volunteer administration repeatedly cautions against screening out volunteers, rather than recommending that positions be molded to their needs and interests; providing compact orientation and training sessions, rather than presenting a more comprehensive understanding of agency mission and functions; and exhausting all remedies other than termination, rather than simply releasing volunteers if circumstances warrant. Although, as explained above, recruitment offers a serious challenge, the primary focus of the organization and its volunteer program should not be to placate volunteers but to have an impact on agency clients and the external environment.

To achieve accountability with volunteer-based services, public agencies need to imbue citizens with appropriate norms and values regarding fair and equitable treatment, describe and clarify relevant rules and procedures, and provide training for often complex volunteer roles. The time and other demands of orientation and training will likely prove too steep for some citizen recruits, just as they do for some who seek paid positions. In both cases, the remedy is not to suspend legitimate requirements for orientation and training but to increase outreach and recruitment efforts to net a larger pool of contributing organizational members.

Managing the Program

An effective volunteer program rests on an organizational structure that channels and sustains citizen energies and skills toward the attainment of agency and individual objectives. The foundation for this structure has been discussed above: The volunteer program should begin with the establishment of a rationale or policy governing volunteer involvement. Paid staff should play a central role in this process as well as in designing the program and crafting guidelines for its operation. The program should offer a range of volunteer jobs to aid citizen recruitment. Establishment of a volunteer director or coordinator position and the provision of orientation and training activities enhance program accountability.

Program management entails these functions, as well as several others. To attract citizen participants, the agency must publicize and promote its volunteer effort. Officials must develop job descriptions for nonpaid positions and amend them as necessary. Prospective volunteers must be interviewed and screened to ascertain relevant competencies, background, experience, and aspirations. Successful placement or job assignment depends on matching these interests with the volunteer positions available in the agency. Once volunteers have been assigned to positions, the need for supervision arises. While paid employees typically provide direct oversight, program officials often monitor volunteer assignments and support them. Maintaining records on the volunteers; evaluating volunteer performance, as well as that of paid staff who work with them; and recognizing both parties to the relationship are also key management functions.

Lapses in any of these areas—publicity, recruitment, job design, screening, orientation, training, placement, supervision, recognition, and so forth—impair the viability of the volunteer effort. Although agency leadership may find the potential advantages offered by volunteers persuasive, they should not introduce citizens into the agency until a structure to maintain and direct their involvement has been put in place.

Several factors attest to the importance of fulfilling these functions and to the growing professionalization of volunteer administration. For example, proposed regulations by the Financial Accounting Standards Board (FASB), effective in 1995–96, would require organizations to make a full accounting of all donated labor, estimate its monetary value, treat these estimates as revenue, and report this information in a standardized format (see Harr, Godfrey, and Frank, 1992). In addition, a number of colleges and universities offer courses in volunteer management (some of them also have degree programs in nonprofit administration), which are supported by textbooks in the field (e.g., Fisher and Cole, 1993).

Evaluating Processes and Results

According to researchers, the evaluation function is carried out less often and less well than many of the other central elements of the volunteer program (Allen, 1987; Utterback and Heyman, 1984). In a national sample of cities with a population over 4,500 that enlisted volunteers in the delivery of services, only 11.6 percent had made an evaluation study (Duncombe, 1985, p. 363). Just 5 percent of a representative sample of Georgia cities and counties with volunteer programs had conducted an evaluation (Brudney and Brown, 1993). Organizations that rely on the assistance of volunteers may be reluctant to appear to question through evaluation the worth or impact of well-intentioned helping efforts. Officials may be apprehensive, too, about the effects of an evaluation policy on volunteer recruitment and retention and on public relations. Nevertheless, evaluation activities are essential to assess the results of the program, review its processes, and foster accountability. Three types of evaluation are useful.

First, volunteers should be subject to periodic evaluation. The fears of organizational leadership notwithstanding, this group has good reason to view performance appraisal in a favorable light. A powerful motivation for volunteering is to achieve worthwhile and credible results; evaluation can guide volunteers toward improvement in this dimension. Personnel evaluation is actually a form of compliment to the volunteer (Ellis, 1986, pp. 81–82). A sincere effort at appraisal indicates that the work merits review and that the individual has the capability and the will to do a better job. For many who contribute their time, volunteering offers an opportunity to acquire or hone desirable job skills or to build an attractive résumé for purposes of paid employment. To deny constructive feedback to those who give their time for organizational purposes and who could benefit from this knowledge—and often hope to do so—is a disservice to the volunteer.

Second, volunteer-based services normally require the participation of not only volunteers but also paid staff. If organizational officials are committed to having employees and volunteers work as partners, evaluation should apply to both members of the team. Although frequently neglected in job analysis, employees expected to work with volunteers should have the pertinent responsibilities written into formal job descriptions, and performance appraisal should assess the requisite skills in volunteer management. Just as demonstrated proficiency in this domain should be encouraged and rewarded, an employee's resistance to volunteers, or poor work record with them, should not be overlooked and thus implicitly condoned. The organization should support training for paid staff whose jobs require volunteer administration.

Third, agencies that mobilize volunteers for public purposes should periodically conduct an evaluation of the impact or progress toward goals registered by the program. Too often, what passes for "evaluation" is a compilation of the number of volunteers who have assisted the organization, the hours they have contributed, and the amount of client contacts they have made. Some agencies calculate the "equivalent dollar value" of the services provided by volunteers, based on the market price the organization would otherwise have to pay for these activities. While such statements routinely document tremendous levels of donated effort and monetary value across public (and nonprofit) institutions, they record the inputs or resources to a volunteer program rather than its results or accomplishments.

Accordingly, much as agency officials might be expected to do for any other organizational unit or program, they should at regular intervals assess the outcomes of the volunteer effort against its stated mission or goals. Officials need to review the aggregate achievement of the volunteers in assisting clients, addressing community problems, expediting agency operations, and meeting further objectives. Not only does the assessment yield information that can be used to monitor the program and improve its performance but it also reinforces the importance attached by the organization to the volunteer component.

In addition, agency officials should assess the processes undergirding the volunteer program. Evaluation should determine that procedures to meet essential program functions are in place and that they are operating effectively. In addition, evaluation helps to identify any areas requiring attention. Officials should attempt to gauge the satisfaction of volunteers and paid staff members with the program as well as their perceptions regarding its impact on clients and the external environment.

Conclusion

The involvement of volunteers in the delivery of services can offer substantial benefits to government organizations through increasing productivity and cost-effectiveness, enhancing responsiveness to clients and the community, and facilitating organizational operations and external support. This chapter elaborates an integrative model of the central challenges confronting volunteer programs in the public sector: recruiting citizen participants; gaining the acceptance of employees for volunteer workers; ensuring accountability to public values and goals; providing a management structure; and evaluating program processes and results. It describes appropriate managerial actions to surmount each challenge. The economic, responsiveness, and organizational advantages that can be realized through volunteer programs merit investment by public managers in these strategies.

References

Allen, N. J. 1987. "The Role of Social and Organizational Factors in the Evaluation of Volunteer Programs." *Evaluation and Program Planning* 10, no. 3: 257–262.

Barnes, K. 1994. "Counties Find Strength in Citizen Volunteers." *Leadership* (April–June): 26–28.

Brudney, J. L. 1990a. "The Availability of Volunteers: Implications for Local Governments." *Administration and Society* 21 (February): 413–424.

———. 1990b. *Fostering Volunteer Programs in the Public Sector: Planning, Initiating, and Managing Voluntary Activities.* San Francisco: Jossey-Bass.

———. 1993. "Volunteer Involvement in the Delivery of Public Services: Advantages and Disadvantages." *Public Productivity and Management Review* 16, no. 3: 283–297.

Brudney, J. L., and M. M. Brown. 1993. "Government-Based Volunteer Programs: Toward a More Caring Society." Paper presented at the Independent Sector Spring Research Forum, San Antonio, Tex., March 18–19.

Brudney, J. L., and W. D. Duncombe. 1992. "An Economic Evaluation of Paid, Volunteer, and Mixed Staffing Options for Public Services." *Public Administration Review* 52, no. 5: 474–481.

Brudney, J. L., and R. E. England. 1983. "Toward a Definition of the Coproduction Concept." *Public Administration Review* 43, no. 1: 59–65.

Clary, E. G. 1987. "Social Support as a Unifying Concept in Voluntary Action." *Journal of Voluntary Action Research* 16, no. 4: 58–68.

Duncombe, S. 1985. "Volunteers in City Government: Advantages, Disadvantages and Uses." *National Civic Review* 74, no. 9: 356–364.

Ellis, S. J. 1986. *From the Top Down: The Executive Role in Volunteer Program Success.* Philadelphia: Energize.

Ferris, J. M. 1984. "Coprovision: Citizen Time and Money Donations in Public Service Provision." *Public Administration Review* 44, no. 4: 324–333.

Fisher, J. C., and K. M. Cole. 1993. *Leadership and Management of Volunteer Programs: A Guide for Volunteer Administrators.* San Francisco: Jossey-Bass.

Gallup, Inc. 1986. *Americans Volunteer, 1985.* Princeton: Gallup Organization.

Harr, D. J., J. T. Godfrey, and R. H. Frank. 1992. *Accounting for Volunteer Services in a Charitable Organization.* Pittsburgh: Reese Brothers.

Hodgkinson, V. A., M. S. Weitzman, C. M. Toppe, and S. M. Noga. 1992. *Nonprofit Almanac, 1992–1993: Dimensions of the Independent Sector.* San Francisco: Jossey-Bass.

Kettl, D. F. 1988. *Government by Proxy: (Mis?) Managing Federal Programs.* Washington, D.C.: Congressional Quarterly Press.

Marando, V. L. 1986. "Local Service Delivery: Volunteers and Recreation Councils." *Journal of Volunteer Administration* 4, no. 4: 16–24.

Montjoy, R. S., and J. L. Brudney. 1991. "Volunteers in the Delivery of Public Services: Hidden Costs . . . and Benefits." *American Review of Public Administration* 21 (December): 327–344.

Morley, E. 1989. "Patterns in the Use of Alternative Service Delivery Approaches," in *Municipal Year Book, 1989.* Washington, D.C.: International City Management Association.

Naylor, H. H. 1985. "Beyond Managing Volunteers." *Journal of Voluntary Action Research* 14, nos. 2 and 3: 25–30.

National Association of Counties. 1990. *The Volunteer Toolbox: Visions for Improving the Service of America's Counties.* Washington, D.C.: National Association of Counties.

Parks, R. B., et al. 1981. "Consumers as Coproducers of Public Services: Some Economic and Institutional Considerations." *Policy Studies Review* 9, no. 7: 1001–1011.

Sharp, E. B. 1980. "Toward a New Understanding of Urban Services and Citizen Participation: The Coproduction Concept." *Midwest Review of Public Administration* 14, no. 2: 105–118.

Sundeen, R. A., and G. B. Siegel. 1986. "The Uses of Volunteers by Police." *Journal of Police Science and Administration* 14, no. 1: 49–61.

Utterback, J., and S. R. Heyman. 1984. "An Examination of Methods in the Evaluation of Volunteer Programs." *Evaluation and Program Planning* 7, no. 3: 229–235.

Walter, V. 1987. "Volunteers and Bureaucrats: Clarifying Roles and Creating Meaning." *Journal of Voluntary Action Research* 16, no. 3: 22–32.

Weisbrod, B. A. 1988. *The Nonprofit Economy.* Cambridge: Harvard University Press.

Whitaker, G. P. 1980. "Coproduction: Citizen Participation in Service Delivery." *Public Administration Review* 40, no. 3: 240–246.

10.

Leadership of a State Agency

Barbara Koremenos
and Laurence E. Lynn Jr.

During his relatively short tenure in office, Illinois Department on Aging (IDOA) Director Victor Wirth performed an apparent managerial miracle. Inheriting an agency ridden with internal conflicts and in bad repute with its contractors and constituencies, Wirth successfully refocused his department's operations on client service and on cooperation with contractors while complying with the governor's directive to cut the department's budget. This apparent demonstration that government can be better *and* cost less is a case of "reinventing government" that merits analysis.

Why do we believe that this is in fact a success story rather than another self-serving claim on behalf of a political executive? The testimony of agency officials and contractors at the end of Wirth's tenure was persuasive. They believed that his actions had led to better services for the state's older citizens, budget cuts notwithstanding, and that the compromises reached to cope with resource scarcity had been appropriate. Moreover, two years after Wirth's departure, based on evidence from an agency retreat, the department had apparently internalized his cooperative values. Pre-Wirth-era conflicts and dissatisfactions had not been revived; client service and cooperation with service providers, now expressed in the obscurantist vocabulary of "quality improvement," were the norms.

In this chapter, we analyze Wirth's success. Our objective is to produce insights into what constitutes "best managerial practice" in the "reinventing government" era. More than that, we explore the value of using game theoretic concepts to construct a heuristic model of IDOA operations which will generate nontrivial and nonobvious conjectures concerning how a public manager can transform an agency producing collective goods such as services for the aging.

Our choice of analytic approach is controversial in the field of public management. Thus, we begin with some observations on the study of public management practice and on the potential value of using a relatively formal heuristic model rather than relying on thick descriptions and practitioner reflections. Following these comments, we present a structured analysis of Wirth's direction of IDOA using our model. We conclude with an account of Wirth's success and with an assessment of the value of our analytic approach.

Studying Public Management

Students of public management practice display a considerable diversity of intellectual interests and a wide range of tastes for analytic methods. If there is a dominant approach, it is the retrospective (though often partially contemporary) analysis of particular cases involving featured actors, often including an agency head, in which the investigator depends rather heavily on the accounts and "theories in use" (as Chris Argyris [1976] uses the term) of key actors.

While reflecting life as managers experience it, this kind of approach raises a number of familiar methodological issues concerning the existence of selection bias, the absence of theory to structure inquiry, and the tendency to draw conclusions of questionable validity and generalizability. We do not defend the particular analysis we are about to present as always superior in principle to less structured case studies. Rather, our goal is to determine whether this kind of analysis "works" in the examination of a single, actor-centered case, that is, does it produce nontrivial, prescriptive insights of sufficient uniqueness and power to vindicate the effort?

We began with a predisposition to interpret Victor Wirth's success in theoretical terms, although we did not want to unduly sacrifice verisimilitude to the reductionist demands of theory and of orthodox protocols for testing it. These predispositions led to two questions: How might we construct a model that is adequately realistic, and how should we use it to structure empirical work on managerial practice? We considered a variety of potentially relevant theories. These included sociological models that view organizational behavior as ritualistic or as expressive of socially constructed realities; bounded rationality models; principal-agent models; models featuring power and information asymmetries; and, finally, public choice models involving more-or-less formal characterizations of behavior within and by hierarchies.[1]

Such a plethora of theories might lead one to prefer the kind of multiple frames approach employed by Allison (1971) in analyzing case material and by Bolman and Deal (1991) in analyzing a wide range of management issues. Lacking the resources to pursue such an intellectually ambitious agenda (developing a frame or lens requires considerable care), we decided to employ only one frame, albeit one of particular intuitive appeal to the authors. Elsewhere, Lynn (1993) has suggested the potential value of using game theory as a basis for analyzing the management of public agencies that administer social programs.[2] We decided to explore the value of game theory in this particular case for a variety of reasons.[3]

—Game theory is concerned with actors and their behavior under circumstances common in public agencies, that is, joint determination of consequences and the general infeasibility of binding commitments. Indeed, the "game" metaphor has long been thought to be useful for illuminating political and bureaucratic behavior.

—Game theory directs attention to intuitively meaningful empirical information: incentives, information states, alternative strategies, and criteria for choice.

—Game theory also directs attention to the role of administrative technologies and structures in shaping jointly determined outcomes. More specifically, game theory facilitates an understanding of the structural impediments to cooperation in large, complex organizations and, therefore, of reasons for policy and program failures. It thus helps identify actor strategies for promoting cooperation.

—To an extent that is not widely appreciated, game theory, especially in its more advanced versions involving repeated interactions, nesting, and coordinated strategies, establishes an analytic framework for evaluating the significance of the kinds of nonalgorithmic, intuitive, "soft" behaviors most of us believe are central to managerial practice. For example, the existence of multiple equilibria and "focal points" in repeated games; the consequences of communication and the manipulation of information states; the influence of social structures, multiple overlapping activities, and culture on strategic behavior; and the consequences of commitments, reputation effects and "trust," mutual visibility, small numbers, the intensity and frequency of contacts, and monitoring can readily be imagined to provide a conceptual vocabulary and logic for interpreting the most complex and intuitive managerial strategies in actual bureaucratic settings and for devising prescriptions likely to be useful in particular structural contexts.

—The concept of mixed strategies provides a way of interpreting the outcomes of repeated, simultaneous interactions such as those between service workers and clients or between contracting agencies and contractors.

—Game theory is consistent with intuitions that neither complete centralization nor complete decentralization will promote the kind of ideal bureaucratic state—cooperation throughout the hierarchy and with external actors in achieving a collectively endorsed objective—envisioned by administrative reformers.

Associated with these advantages, however, are important drawbacks.

—The theory is easily misapplied. "A good model in game theory has to be realistic in the sense that it provides a model for the *perception* of real life social phenomena. It should incorporate a description of the relevant factors involved, as perceived by the decision makers" (Rubinstein, 1991, p. 909). It may be difficult or impossible to identify the perceptions that would justify the application of the theory. This problem threatens the validity of the application; if it cannot be confirmed that actors behave in a self-consciously strategic way, we cannot claim to be observing games.

—Even if the use of game theory can be justified, observed behaviors and actor explanations are subject to various interpretations, especially if interaction is continuous. The probable existence of multiple equilibria and the likelihood that actors are pursuing mixed strategies, for example, make unambiguous interpretations of particular actions difficult.

—Equilibrium behavior may not be transparent (see appendix to this chapter). Indeed, the existence of a socializing equilibrium, in which actors explain or rationalize their actions as virtually inevitable or mandated, may obscure the very existence of strategic behavior.

—Although not unique to game theoretic applications, participants' accounts of what they did and why usually cannot be taken at face value. Sorting out the degree of subjectivity or deliberate misrepresentation in assessments of consequences or assertions of fact, especially in retrospect, will ordinarily be difficult. This is especially so when the search for evidence consistent with the kinds of abstract concepts employed in game theory induces the investigator to ask leading questions.

—Hierarchies are inevitably complex, maybe too complex to be modeled this way. No simple one-period, two-actor model is likely to get us very far. A variety of game structures may coexist, necessitating consideration of nesting, coordinated strategies, multiple equilibria, and the like. Such considerations place us well beyond theoretical, much less empirical, frontiers.

Nonetheless, we persist. In particular, we have chosen to model IDOA as comprising three nested, repeated games involving pairs of actors, each with a choice of two strategies, as shown in figure 1.[4] While this model structure is,

	Division Manager	
	C,c	C,nc
IDOA Director		
	NC,c	NC,nc
	Bureau Chief	
	C,c	C,nc
Division Manager		
	NC,c	NC,nc
	Case Manager	
	C,c	C,nc
Bureau Chief		
	NC,c	NC,nc

Figure 1

in a sense, arbitrary and simplistic, we believe it depicts the essential fault lines and interactions that affect the achievement of the bureaucratic ideal.

We have chosen to label the cooperative strategy as "C" and the noncooperative strategy as "NC". Further, we have designated Player 1 as hierarchically superior to Player 2; Player 1's strategies are in upper-case type, Player 2's in lower case. Thus, the pair C,c indicates mutual cooperation, NC,c indicates the superior is noncooperative while the subordinate cooperates, and so on.[5]

The bureaucratic ideal, or social optimum, is assumed to be achieved when the outcome of each game is C,c. An important question, to be addressed later, is whether the agency head, or any of the other actors, can be assumed to embrace what we label the "bureaucratic ideal" as a goal (Schwartz-Shea, 1991).

Victor Wirth and IDOA

One of IDOA's goals is to carry out mandates of the federal Older Americans Act (OAA) of 1965. The OAA authorizes funds for a number of programs, including a State and Community Grants Program, which stipulates that state agencies develop a comprehensive and coordinated service system for older persons at the local level to help them remain in their homes and out of institutions as long as they are able and wish to do so. Illinois meets these program requirements through its Community Care Program (CCP), a home-based service delivery program designed to prevent the premature institutionalization of the elderly by providing assistance with basic household personal tasks. Of IDOA's $100 million budget, two-thirds of it is consumed by CCP. In this analysis, we focus on the implementation of the Illinois CCP.

In 1991, when the State of Illinois was experiencing severe fiscal problems and, consequently, every department was under the gun to cut costs, IDOA was enjoying what could almost be called a revival. The director, Victor Wirth, was praised by interested parties ranging from case managers to the director of the Illinois Coalition on Aging. Attitudes improved, the department's emphasis was changed from paperwork compliance to service delivery, paperwork was reduced dramatically, and, perhaps most important, a sense of partnership began to replace the previously hostile relationships among the department, the case coordination units (CCUs), the service providers, and aging advocacy groups. In fact, although Wirth resigned for strictly personal reasons after only one year in office, many believe that the changes he brought about will endure well into the future.

At the same time that Wirth was earning the plaudits of his constituencies, he was complying with Governor Jim Edgar's edict that every program be a part of the state's fiscal solution by streamlining operations and taking budget cuts. The service caps Wirth implemented and his policy of prior approval for any service upgrades resulted in savings of $5.4 million for fiscal year 1991 and another $10 million for the following year.

Critical Assumptions

We assume that the most efficient way to serve older persons is through a coordinated approach in which the government, the CCUs, the service providers, and the aging network form a cooperative partnership. Additionally, within each of these organizations, cooperation must be forthcoming among its various levels. These assumptions are endorsed by every person interviewed for this project.

When using the term *implementation problem* or speaking of an improvement in policy implementation, we follow O'Toole's definition (1993). We assume that if the "policy implementers"—IDOA and CCUs—behave in expected ways, the effects on the clients will fulfill the intent of the OAA's winning coalition and the act will be considered successfully carried out. Thus, the implementation problem refers to an obstacle or factor that prohibits the carrying out of an act's intent. For example, collective action problems or opportunism stemming from an inability to monitor subordinate actions are implementation problems.

We focus on how a particular configuration of actor interests affects the quality of the outcome, measured by the extent of cooperation, and on how, given this configuration of interests, a better qualitative outcome is possible depending on the role a hierarchical leader chooses to take. We do not include in quality of outcome the adequacy of service levels or the appropriateness of the particular services provided by the agency.

Games in IDOA

The actors in our analysis are not only those within the formal hierarchy of IDOA but also the CCUs and service providers with whom IDOA enters into contracts. IDOA repeatedly contracts with the same contractors; for purposes of this analysis, those contractors will be incorporated into the IDOA hierarchy. The hierarchy is as follows: the governor (Jim Thompson and then Jim Edgar); the IDOA director (Otwell and Wirth)[6]; the division managers (of the Long-Term Care [LTC] Division and the Division of Administrative Compliance [DAC]; the bureau chiefs; head trainer; trainers; and, at the bottom, CCUs, including the case managers and service providers.[7]

We sought evidence for the presence (or absence) of common and conflicting interests, interdependence (the joint determination of outcomes), and strategic behavior.[8] Evidence is predominantly from interviews conducted during Wirth's tenure or while Nancy Nelson, his deputy, was acting director following his departure. In addition, Koremenos was a case manager during the tenure of the prior director, Janet Otwell, and we incorporate her recollections from that period.

Interviews with department employees, case managers, and network members indicate that the department was characterized by considerable conflict and an absence of trust prior to Wirth's appointment. According to Wirth, departmental management had evolved to a point "where basically the only thing they were interested in was compliance. They had put this huge instrument together to measure compliance. All it did was measure paperwork." For example, according to an employee, DAC once went through every piece of paper "just to see if all the blanks and lines were filled in and to check the dates. They did not look at all at the content."

This emphasis on formal compliance and the types of behavior it encouraged did not sit well either with members of the aging network, who wanted to insure that older persons were receiving quality service, or with the street-level workers, who were the ultimate targets of the emphasis on monitoring and control. These workers maintained that they could best serve the needs of their clients by being allowed greater autonomy in performing their jobs, but this preference put them into conflict with their compliance-minded superiors.

Interaction between Governor and Director. We have no firsthand information about the relationship between Governor Thompson and Director Otwell. There are indications, however, that Otwell's deputy actively created and sustained an environment of noncooperation. "Jan had a handicap. Her deputy was a political appointee who didn't know beans about aging." Apparently he kept the division managers away from her and nurtured competition among them.

Concerning Governor Edgar and Wirth, before accepting the appointment, Wirth told Edgar, "If you don't want an advocate, appoint somebody else." Wirth was willing to cooperate with the governor's commitment to resolve the state's fiscal problems as long as he could design and advocate what he considered to be the least harmful way of accomplishing budget reductions. Because Edgar apparently did not favor one way of cutting costs over another, Wirth was granted the autonomy he sought over programs and over hiring as well. He said, "I have not, from the time I've been in the department, had a call from the governor's office and been asked to accept one employee—which astounds me because I know what past practice has been." Moreover, before he took the job, he asked for Nelson as his deputy and got her.[9]

Interaction between Director and Division Managers. The director and division managers evidently behaved strategically, that is, they recognized that payoffs were jointly determined. For example, of one division manager Wirth said, "[She] had her own agenda and the way she worked her agenda was to limit information to you. When you wanted information, you got it so it told the story that she wanted to tell to you. Ultimately, what I had to do was put another person under her, that she fought me tooth and toenail on, that was really a computer whiz, to help her with information management. Then I started to get the full story."

As another example, IDOA had funded one of the universities to develop a model for quality assurance. The team leader went to Springfield to present the model to IDOA officials. Wirth said, "Before I ever saw a product, before I had a chance to sit and listen to the presentation, the Division of Compliance was telling me how bad it was, the Long-Term Care Division was telling me what problems there were with it. Quite frankly, what the University presented was right on track; focus on the client, how to look at client satisfaction."

Wirth believed that "you've got to have the freedom to communicate and communicate openly. And people can't feel threatened by that. And the division managers had to learn to have confidence that I would not use that against them. But that's how you learn about problems: from people who are dealing with other people." According to Wirth, "There were certain individuals who had their own agenda. [DM], who I highly regard, turned out to be a team player, but it was very difficult for him. He was the architect of the department's compliance program. And it was paper-driven. He was the first to tell you we never look into the home. We look for compliance to see that they have filled out their sheets of paper right. They'll go through every piece of paper, but only the paper. [DM's] agenda was to protect as much of what he had built as he could. I do have to say, though, that bringing [DM] in and sitting down with him, he was able to change some of his attitudes. But it's still very difficult for him."

Interaction between Division Managers and Bureau Chiefs. According to Wirth, his open-door policy (allowing divisional subordinates direct access to him) "was very threatening to division managers. In the beginning, if one of their staff would come talk to me, my God! that person, before they got 25 yards out of my office, was getting the third degree."

There apparently existed a "horrible, vicious feud between LTC and DAC that even manifested itself on a personal level." Perhaps partly because Director Otwell, or at least her deputy director, had operated in such a way that the division managers were constantly in competition for her ear, there was no cooperation or trust between the divisions, and in order to best compete with each other, both division managers exercised a great deal of control over their subordinates.

In an interview, one bureau chief revealed that she was forced to compromise herself when she was heading a task force. Her division manager did not like the task force recommendations and conclusions and asked the BC to change them. The BC did not want to make the changes but, in the end, she did because the DM was her superior and it behooved her to abide by her orders. This was a difficult situation for the BC because she believed that the original recommendations were in the clients' best interests.

Similar behavior was exhibited by one division manager who exercised a great deal of authority over her BC and even tried to restrict the BC's authority. The DM once sent the BC out to "do compliance, which is the worst job.

[BC's] staff should have been doing it. Because [BC] was sent out, [DM] was able to remove [BC] from two important task forces."

Interaction between Bureau Chiefs and Case Managers. A bureau chief's subordinate was talking to case managers about the way things were before the "Wirth-induced" changes. "Audits only catch those who don't know how to play the game, get around the rules. You all know how to do that: you could write a book on it. You won't have to do that anymore."

Case managers reveal the extent to which they are constrained by paper-work, rules, and efforts to restrict their autonomy. These constraints often pre-vent them from truly evaluating and serving the clients. For example, if they want to do a thorough evaluation of a client for service, they must often visit the client on the weekend or in the evening. Because rules prohibit such visits, if case managers want to appear to conform to the rules, they must either ne-glect certain clients and lie in their documentation or conceal the fact that the visits were done during off-hours. The majority of the case managers appeared to choose the latter option. One case manager said, "Overall, most CMs go way beyond their job descriptions on the clients' behalf. But there are repercussions because you get way behind on the paperwork. A lot of CMs will take their pa-perwork home [which is prohibited] but will deny it." Others said, "Among the little extras I do for my clients: shovel snow, pick up groceries—I'm afraid to document these things" and "If the doctor's statement comes a week later than 60 days, I set up services anyway. I'll bend that rule."

Choices

The evidence in the previous section is fully consistent with the preva-lence of strategic behavior among actors involved in carrying out the OAA. We believe that the essence of the strategic problem that these actors face can be captured by stipulating that they face two basic choices: cooperation (C) and noncooperation (NC). Although real-life choices contain nuances, this dichoto-mous choice is consistent with the way actors describe their situations.[10]

Across all levels, NC can be defined as emphasizing monitoring and con-trol or formal procedural compliance in behalf of narrowly defined operational goals. For those in hierarchically superior positions, this means retaining au-thority and enforcing formal compliance through the threat of imposing sanc-tions. For subordinates, NC means a willingness to conceal information and misrepresent the facts, although not necessarily outright defiance.

Also across all levels, C can be defined as behavior that is dedicated to fulfilling the organization's broad mission and that is characterized by openness, trust, and forthrightness. One could call such behavior risky because it exposes the actor to exploitation. For superiors, cooperation means delegating authority/autonomy to subordinates when appropriate. For subordinates, cooperation means using discretion in meeting the goals of the organization and accurately and fully reporting facts concerning services and decisions.

Evidence suggests that the actors in this case face this kind of choice. One case manager said that the most important goal or value of her office is "serving the client's need yet meeting IDOA standards. At times these conflict. When they do, too much time and energy is wasted on how to get around the conflict." One BC said of the Wirth changes that "we've relaxed somewhat on specifics. There's more flexibility on what can be accepted. This gives the case management level more discretion and autonomy. For social services, we were too rigid in the past. We're coming around to where there's a little more room. That's how it should be." He expressed hope for a "much better relationship" between IDOA and the CCUs.

After Wirth resigned, his deputy Nelson took over as acting director. In that capacity, she said the following: "Social service agencies will follow the rules and regulations, as a rule. We had been managing for the 2 percent that weren't going to follow the rules and not for the 98 percent that were. And we're really trying to make that shift." Nelson believes the focus should be more on technical assistance and training and less on files. "Now when we see a problem, we'll send [our team] to that problem and not make the assumption that just because there's a problem in one place that that problem exists all over."

Wirth's views echoed Nelson's.

These nonprofits, these social workers, these providers: they're in it for the right reasons. It's a small minority that isn't. But the whole measuring system was aimed at that minority rather than giving everyone the benefit of the doubt, involving them more. And the more ownership, and the more you would involve them, the more cooperation you get concerning the ultimate goal: the client. The system that was built was aimed at those very few vendors, that you're going to get in any business, that will trash you. We had one basic assumption: people were basically dishonest and they would try to falsify paperwork. This is not the case—99 percent. If you've ever spent time in the field, in nonprofits in the state, you'll find very, very dedicated people, very client-oriented people. Client advocacy really manifests itself at the provider level.

Payoffs

The quotes in the previous section have already suggested how participants rank outcomes. In this section we elaborate.

Game 1: Director and division managers. According to many of those interviewed, Wirth's predecessor, Otwell, was a client advocate and would have preferred to have had more cooperation and less conflict within the system (C,c > NC,nc). However, perhaps because of the influence of the deputy director appointed by Governor Thompson, exercising control over the department seems to have had a higher value to Otwell than high-quality client service achievable through mutual cooperation (NC,c > C,c). Unrequited cooperation with her subordinates (C,nc) would have been the worst outcome for Otwell. Thus Otwell's preferences are inferred to have been: NC,c > C,c > NC,nc > C,nc.[11]

Wirth appeared to rank outcomes differently. He preferred mutual cooperation to unilateral defection; he was committed to providing the highest quality services to Illinois' older residents and that, according to our assumptions, requires mutual cooperation. For example, he held numerous staff meetings during which he stressed the importance of cooperating with service providers. He told his staff that their raison d'être "was only one and that was to see that older people received the best services they could." Concerning case managers and providers, he added, "Our role is to help people who are out on the cutting edge, to make their task as easy as possible to serve older people." Wirth also supported the university study mentioned above. "In their study, they went out and talked to a lot of vendors. They focused on the fact that it was a team effort and that we had a lot of different levels of this team. But there's one focus: the person in the home and how we can best get the appropriate service to them." Thus, Wirth's ranking was: C,c > NC,c > NC,nc > C,nc.

Wirth's division managers cared enough about the department's customers to prefer mutual cooperation to mutual defection: C,c > NC,nc. However, because, under Otwell, the deputy director promoted competition among them for the director's ear, and because they increased their utility by self-serving reports and pro forma compliance, they preferred unilateral defection to mutual cooperation: C,nc > C,c. For their part, therefore, Wirth's division managers appeared to rank outcomes as follows: C,nc > C,c > NC,nc > NC,c.

Game 2: Division managers and bureau chiefs. The head of the compliance division, who had invented the system, naturally preferred it over the alternative of granting autonomy to subordinates (NC,c > C,c). Of the head of the long-term care division, one bureau chief said: "The exercise of authority and control are very important to her." Also, one of the division managers "killed the Home Health Care component of CCP because she wanted hourly rates from vendors and they will only give day rates. Because it couldn't be exactly the way she wanted it, she killed it completely" over the strong objections of the bureau chiefs. The preferences of DMs were for not emphasizing discretion and trust more broadly. According to one, case managers, when confronted with a paperwork discrepancy, say, "You've never seen the client. You don't know what it's like to live here from day to day, trying to see all these clients. You don't appreciate me, and I feel like I ought to quit and go be a bartender." Also, "[DM] constantly wanted to hold a club over the vendors rather than become partners with them. He's willing to change that style, but it's difficult." In this game, division managers ranked outcomes as follows: NC,c > C,c > NC,nc > C,nc.

Serving older persons is of a higher value to bureau chiefs than exercising control, and older persons can best be served, in their view, by cooperation throughout the organization. This commitment of the bureau chiefs and their staffs is acknowledged by many others in the organization. It also came through in the interviews with the bureau chiefs. For example, one offered advice to a potential policy maker: "Remember the people at the end." Moreover, one of the bureau chiefs was a homemaker—a service provider—before she joined the department. The bureau chiefs appeared to rank outcomes as follows: C,c > NC,c > NC,nc > C,nc.

Game 3: Bureau chiefs and case managers/CCUs. If Game 3 were played in isolation, the preferences of the bureau chiefs would be: C,c > NC,c > NC,nc > C,nc. In other words, their preferences in Game 3 are the same as those in Game 2. The following quote by a bureau chief's subordinate about case managers and workers is evidence of the first (and true or latent) payoff ranking: "They can write a good care plan because they *do* care." However, as we will explain later, Game 3 is "nested" in Game 2, that is, the BCs' strategic choices in Game 3 are influenced by how they play Game 2.[12] This phenomenon of nesting can be shown in two ways. One way is by giving the bureau chiefs a new preference ordering that reflects the influence of play in Game 2: NC,c > C,c > NC,nc > C,nc.

Case managers give highest priority to serving clients and seem to prefer that this be accomplished in a spirit of cooperation; they wish to be trusted and given discretion in serving their clients. As one case manager said, "At times, the clients fall between the cracks with the points; it's not always black and white." Said another, "The most important reason I work here is making a difference with the client's life." At the unveiling of the new "Wirth/Nelson approach" at a local hotel, many CCU employees actually complained about the amount spent by the department taking them to lunch, preferring to have paid

	Division Manager		
		c	nc
Director Otwell C		3,3	1,4
NC		4,1	2,2

Figure 2

for their own meals. Thus, the preferences of the case managers/CCUs are: C,c > C,nc > NC,nc > NC,c.

Outcomes

The preference orderings just described can be translated into game structures and outcomes that describe the situation under Otwell. Game 1, between the director and division managers, is structured as in figure 2.[13] Game 1 is thus a Prisoners' Dilemma, with noncooperation being the dominant strategy for both players leading to a Pareto-inefficient but stable equilibrium: NC,nc.

Game 2 between division managers and bureau chiefs has the structure in figure 3. In this game, the bureau chief has no dominant strategy but the division manager does: noncooperation. Knowing this—and the evidence from our interviews strongly indicates that participants at one level are well aware of the preferences of other levels—the bureau chief will play a noncooperation strategy as well. Again, the outcome is a stable, Pareto-inefficient equilibrium. Formally, iterated deletion of strictly dominated strategies yields the outcome: NC,nc.

As noted above, this outcome in Game 2 greatly influences Game 3. Because the bureau chiefs participate in both games, their noncooperation strategy in Game 2 conditions their play of Game 3. If it is rational for the bureau chiefs to report only what is required to comply with departmental rules, then it is reasonable for them to prefer a compliance strategy in Game 3, which is structured as in figure 4. The bureau chiefs have a dominant strategy: noncooperation. Although the case managers do not have a dominant strategy, they know that the bureau chiefs do, so they, too, will choose noncooperation. Again, iterated deletion of strictly dominated strategies yields the outcome: NC,nc.

Bureau Chief		
	c	nc
C	3,4	1,3
NC	4,1	2,2

Division Manager

Figure 3

Case Manager		
	c	nc
C	3,4	1,3
NC	4,1	2,2

Bureau Chief

Figure 4

Had Game 3 been uninfluenced by Game 2, the game would be structured in accordance with the alternative preference ordering described above and would look as in figure 5. Neither participant in this game has a dominant strategy. Both players might play a mixed strategy or more likely use signaling/coordination procedures to arrange mutual cooperation. (Formally, there are two pure strategy Nash equilibria in this stage game of the repeated game: C,c and NC,nc.)[14]

Interdependent Outcomes

The interdependence, or nesting, of hierarchical games deserves further discussion.

Because case managers interact repeatedly with their bureau chiefs, they become well aware of their superiors' preferences in both their own game and in the higher-level game. They also know the preferences of the division managers. They come to know, for example, that the bureau chiefs choose noncooperation in their relationships with the division managers. Indeed, the bureau

	Case Manager		
		c	nc
Bureau Chief	C	4,4	1,3
	NC	3,1	2,2

Figure 5

chiefs often signal their true preferences along with the fact that their strategy in Game 3 is necessarily governed by their interests in Game 2. According to one bureau chief, when she is truly committed to a policy, she tries "to explain why the policy is called for, in other words, the 'why' and not just the 'what' and how the policy is in the client's best interest." When it is a policy with which she does not agree, she will say something like, "This is the department's position, and this what we are going to do." Additionally, case managers are often encouraged by bureau chiefs and their subordinates to "cover their butts." As one case manager put it about a division manager, "She thinks we like and trust her, but we don't."

Wirth seemed well aware that the Prisoners' Dilemma under Otwell meant that a Pareto-efficient change in departmental direction was possible. Since it was in no one's interest to deviate unilaterally from the noncooperative strategy, however, Wirth faced a significant management challenge if he was to improve client service through cooperation with service providers. The game between Wirth and his division managers was as shown in figure 6. The division managers were resistant to being led out of the dilemma. Wirth knew that this would take time (because, in our terms, binding commitments—and, therefore, effective contracts—were unfeasible). He also was well aware of the preference orderings of bureau chiefs and case managers and the nesting of Games 2 and 3. So that cooperation in Game 3 would not have to wait for division managers to come around, Wirth in effect "de-nested" Game 3 from Game 2. In the meantime, Wirth went to work on his division managers.

Axelrod (1984) has pointed out that a small cluster of cooperators with only a small fraction of their interactions with each other can invade a population of "meanies." Wirth's style of leadership was consistent with this proposition. He did not bypass the DMs; he repeatedly sought to instill the value of

	Division Manager		
		c	nc
	C	4,3	1,4
Director Wirth			
	NC	3,1	2,2

Figure 6

cooperation in them. Their resistance was not fatal to cooperation, however, because he also communicated around them to subordinate levels. A member of Wirth's top management team said, "We haven't had a strong leader at the top for many, many years. We've had client advocates at the top, but they weren't administrative leaders." He added, "Vic has something about him. He would go down to the smoking room, meet people, talk to people, feel them out, listen to their problems." One of the bureau chiefs said, "Vic was very personable, liked to manage by roaming; it wasn't unusual to see him on the various floors talking to staff. He talked to the janitors as well as he'd talk to his deputy director." Wirth also began to make the rounds to case managers. As one employee of a CCU remarked, "It was the first time a director had ever been here. We were so impressed with what he actually knew. We could exchange thoughts about the details of the program. He was very open, easy to talk to, and we were very excited about being able to work with someone who would bring that level of understanding and commitment to the job." During his CCU visits, he would say to case managers, "I want you to tell me how we can help you do a better job," and they would unload on him.

   Apparently, the preferences of the division managers were common knowledge both within the department and throughout much of the network. Many believed that the noncooperative outcome originated at that level. Thus, when Wirth was appointed director of IDOA, he was "besieged with calls" from network members asking him if he was going to get rid of [DM]. However, Wirth does not work that way. He was confident that by creating an expectation of mutual cooperation and by making it clear that he would not tolerate unilateral defection, the division managers would begin to cooperate. As director, Wirth was able to operationalize a trigger strategy. He said at the time, "Over the next couple of years, what you're going to find is that the people who can really blend into that management style are really going to enjoy working; it'll be a really good work environment. The people who can't will leave. They will find something else." In short, Wirth gave the division managers a choice: cooperate or leave. In that way he shifted the focal equilibrium from NC,nc to C,c.[15]

The following is an actual example of a changed strategy at the DM level: from NC to C. A client was assigned to an adult day care center with a superb reputation, and she showed immense improvement. At the formal case re-evaluation, however, her scores indicated that she should receive only three days of service, not the five days she had been receiving based on her old evaluation. The case manager, however, knew that the client's condition would deteriorate with less than five days of service. Under Wirth, the case managers were expected to notify the department with an explanation in the event of deviation from the authorized care plan. Despite the deviation, the DM approved the extra service. This same DM has been instrumental in refining and implementing Wirth's cooperative regime.[16]

Conclusions

Our model generates a repertoire of actions that principals such as Wirth can take to promote cooperative outcomes. We first inventory the primary actions and then interpret Wirth's strategy in their light.

The Manager's Repertoire

Miller (1992) emphasizes the importance in repeated games of a leader selecting or identifying a focal equilibrium and solving the coordination problems necessary for it to be *the* equilibrium strategy chosen by participants. Ideally this focal equilibrium will involve substantial mutual cooperation and a sharing of the gains, but this result is not inevitable; focal equilibria may range from cooperative to noncooperative, and the distribution of gains may be exploitative.

Miller also emphasizes the importance of creating and sustaining a reputation for rewarding cooperation and punishing defection. Bianco and Bates (1990) add the important qualifications that leaders who can monitor only output and not subordinate actions and who cannot target sanctions on defectors will be unable to fulfill Miller's expectations. They also highlight the importance of the leader's own reward structure and of the leader's skill in establishing a reputation for effective monitoring and for delivering rewards and sanctions.

Thus, assuming incomplete information (i.e., subordinate uncertainty concerning the leader's payoffs), a leader who can identify defectors may be able to initiate cooperation by promising to reward cooperation and punish defection; uncertainty will work in the leader's favor, but only if the leader establishes his or her credibility rather quickly.

A leader may also increase his or her influence over departmental performance by using intermediate levels of the hierarchy to reduce the likelihood of free riding by service workers and contractors. By establishing performance criteria for intermediate managers, monitoring them, and effectively targeting rewards and sanctions, a leader may be able to reduce the large numbers problem inherent in decentralized program operations. Cooperation may also be enhanced by strengthening solidarity in the lower-level, local games, thus gaining the advantages of self-regulation in decentralized operations (unless, of course, local and global goals conflict or there are attractive possibilities for local collusion in free riding).

Wirth's Repertoire

Wirth emphasized communicating with employees and involving them in decision making. For example, Wirth communicated his conviction that the role of the department is to make the task of the street-level workers, which is to serve older persons, as easy as possible. One way to do this was to reduce their paperwork. In its symbolism, paperwork reduction also furthered Wirth's objective of reducing the emphasis on compliance.

While all state agencies were attempting to reduce paperwork, Wirth's approach was unique in that he drew primarily on the CCUs and the service providers to devise his approach. He formed a task force and asked members for two months of volunteer time to review every piece of paper required by the CCP and by other department mandates. The result was a list of recommendations, and "a hunk of them were implemented" according to one participant. Wirth claimed, "I accepted about 98 percent of them. The ones that could be done without rule changes were done immediately; the ones that required rule changes are in the process." According to the head trainer for the Bureau of Field Operations, paperwork required for new care plans was reduced by 60 to 70 percent.

Case managers and service providers say they are pleased with these changes. From Wirth's point of view, the benefit was increased cooperation. The task force, he said, "helped tremendously in drawing the group together because it's the first time the department had ever really come to them and said, 'Would you be our partners?' and, after all, it is a partnership."

A spirit of partnership was furthered by another of Wirth's changes. When he became director, there were two advisory committees on which workers from the CCUs, service providers, and members of the network served: the Policy Advisory Committee (PAC) and the Rate Advisory Committee (TRAC). Departmental employees were in charge of the agenda and the meetings. Wirth combined PAC and TRAC so that both issues and rates could be addressed concurrently, thus increasing the likelihood that his cost containment measures would be understood. He also insisted that someone from outside the department run the meetings. The department would work with the outside chair, but the chair would have the final responsibility. As Wirth put it, "Any issue that folks in the field feel should be discussed, it's going to be on that agenda; it's going to be discussed in the meeting."

Nelson, Wirth's deputy, said that her top management team often uses outside associations. She encourages subordinate levels to come to the department with three or four recommendations. "As an association, they'll monitor each other and come up with some very strong recommendations and collectively much better than we can come up with here because they know the program." Thus, the top level encourages associations; it doesn't feel threatened by them or fear a loss of control. Nelson adds that sometimes the top level "lets them know they've gone too far, but they *are* advocates."

Lest this seem naive, Wirth's associate director said:

> We're going to send administrative compliance out to those CCUs that we feel are inflating the care plan. But we'll approach it more as technical assistance than as a sanction. But if they're really doing it and continue to do it, then we'll look at some sanctions because we have to get control of the program. But being a program person, I believe you have to work with the people in the network to get them to improve and to bring them along rather than just go in and impose sanctions. But then I think as you move along and are able to work together, it really does become a team. Even with the costs, we've only had one or two that have really, really fought us. The department has involved the network in the cost containment process. It has, on numerous occasions, asked for recommendations.

Wirth's personal style and the fact that he knew the network both formally and informally helped him tremendously in identifying a focal equilibrium and solving the coordination problems which would prevent it from becoming the equilibrium of the game. He explained, "I have one rule in my life for the people I deal with. I don't like surprises, and I don't want others to deal with surprises. I have only one way to deal with this: all the cards on the table, total honesty. When this whole thing started, I made some calls to every one of the agencies. I said, 'I want you to know we're really under the gun from the [Budget] Bureau, and we're going to need to make some changes in the program. We're going to come up with the least painful set of changes. When we get these together, we'll talk with you.'" And Wirth followed through. No one in the network had any reason to doubt him.

Additionally, one of Wirth's personal rewards came from outside the state: the maintenance of his reputation among allies in the aging network. The network oversees Wirth's department, and Wirth could at some point want to return formally to the network.[17] Such rewards reinforced Wirth's natural inclinations.

Wirth's associate director notes the following about Wirth: "People had a lot of confidence in his ability to bring the network together; they had a lot of trust in him which allowed him to do just that. He was upfront with plans and the network gave him patience and support in turn." In other words, the network gave him the benefit of the doubt in the form of time and a chance to try to implement his changes. Describing the top management team's conversations with the directors of the agencies running CCUs, the associate director said, "We would go in and sit down and talk to them about what we planned to do. As advocates, they still have a job to do as far as the legislature is concerned. There's a basic understanding."

It is important to note that the client-oriented premises that Wirth sought to introduce into departmental operations were not unique to him. His predecessor, Jan Otwell, was a client advocate as well and, we often heard, shared many of Wirth's views. She was unable to implement these beliefs, however. She proved unable to promote trust and open communication, even though she preferred mutual cooperation to an emphasis on top-down control and the strategic conflict it engendered. About Otwell, one bureau chief said, "She was a very nice person, but didn't know how to get things done. She was quiet, soft-spoken, willing to stay in the background. Vic is a strong leader but willing to share ownership with other people, realizing that that's going to make it stronger; Jan didn't know how to do that." Said another, "Jan didn't really go out on the floor and get to know the staff."[18]

Does Game Theory "Work"?

Applying our rather complex model to the Victor Wirth case forced several questions on us.

— Do bureaucratic actors believe they have choices in how they perform? What are these choices? In other words, what is the extent of autonomy within the agency, and how can actors use their autonomy?

— In what terms do actors evaluate payoffs or utilities? That is, what is in it for them to do one thing rather than another?

— How do actors rank outcomes? Do they believe that payoffs are affected by the behavior of other actors with whom they interact? In other words, what is the extent of self-conscious strategic behavior among actors involved in public policy implementation, and what are the incentives that influence actor behavior?

— How attractive is defection relative to cooperation? That is, how costly will it be to induce a noncooperative actor to cooperate? Redefining the lowest-level game in figure 1 shows the issue here. Suppose participants in that game are individual service workers and, further, that "cooperation" means adopting a new technology favored by management. If the technology is threatening to service workers, they may strongly prefer unilateral defection, that is, their interests may favor stubborn resistance to management.[19] The costs of overcoming their resistance may be exceedingly high.

— What are the information structures of the games? What do actors know, and what can they observe? Are there information asymmetries? How does information structure affect outcomes? In other words, to what extent is the agency's performance affected by ambiguity, ignorance, misinformation, and uncertainty? How can managers use information structures, that is, uncertainty as to their own payoffs, to achieve their goals?

— Are actor strategies equilibrium strategies? Are they Nash equilibria? In other words, to what extent are actors at a particular level "dug in"? Are they "dug in" because of choices, structurally induced incentives, or information asymmetries, etc.?

— How does the outcome of a game at one hierarchical level affect games occurring at other levels? Does it alter preference orderings or values? Does it induce the coordination of strategies? Does it affect the selection of a focal point in repeated interactions? Does it affect "trust" or "reputation"? In other words, how do decisions at one level affect behavior at other levels? In particular, in what specific ways are the effects of executive actions transmitted downward in an agency? What are the structural obstacles to executive effectiveness? What kinds of rewards and sanctions would actors regard as influential, how might these rewards and sanctions be targeted on particular actors? What are the obstacles to monitoring, and what forms of monitoring would be effective?

Addressing such questions leads to insights of considerable practical value. Many otherwise well-researched case studies seem shallow, unconvincing, or incomplete because they have failed to conceptualize the underlying dynamics of bureaucratic behavior, policy implementation processes, and executive effectiveness. Employing a model such as ours to structure empirical work forces a set of relevant questions on an investigator without necessarily restricting the focus or richness of a study. It gives an investigator tools to penetrate veils of vocabulary, claims, and rationalizations that serve only to obscure the facts of a case. For example, we believe we know more about Wirth's effectiveness because we asked such questions and were able to identify the dynamics of the transformation he brought about.

We also think that employing such a model increases the likelihood that conclusions and prescriptions will be contingent and robust rather than didactic, unqualified, and trivial. Wirth believed, for example, in emphasizing the needs and well-being of the client, and since his departure the department has adopted the vocabulary of the so-called quality improvement approach to express its management objectives. "Best practice" researchers might say that Wirth transformed his agency by emphasizing customer satisfaction. We regard this as a trivial point. His predecessor had the same emphasis but could not make it operative.[20] Other "best practice" researchers might argue that, unlike his predecessor, Wirth had a specific goal, and he managed by walking around and reiterating his goal. But is having a goal and walking around all there is to transforming an agency? Knowing this about Wirth really does not tell us much about why he succeeded or how other managers might succeed in their particular circumstances.

It is more useful to view Wirth's management in the light of the strategic structure of IDOA. Using our analytic framework, we can say that Wirth's problem was noncooperation originating at the top of the agency and institutionalized primarily at the division manager level, from where it was transmitted downward to the field. At lower levels, Wirth had ideological allies whom he could easily mobilize to squeeze the division managers into line. This is not a universal principle of public management, however. In a social service agency where noncooperation originates at lower levels, Wirth's walking around nattering about goals might well fail. A better strategy in such an agency might be the opposite of Wirth's: to recruit middle management to monitor the field and deliver rewards and sanctions sufficient to overcome resistance to change. What works, therefore, will depend on the internal dynamics of the agency.

To document obvious managerial behaviors and demonstrable successful outcomes and assume that the former caused the latter, as so many studies of managerial practice do, teaches us little about management. We want to know why particular managerial strategies worked in a given context and why these same strategies might not work in others. We want to identify the questions a manager should ask before choosing a strategy. For this, we need theory.

Appendix

This appendix describes procedures used to order the preferences of the various actors and discusses some of the limitations of these procedures, drawing in particular on the work of Snidal (1986).

Preference orderings are based on information obtained from personal interviews and observation. Most of the interviews were conducted by Koremenos for a project that preceded the introduction of a game theoretic framework into the research. Moreover, subsequent interviews were unencumbered by preconceptions concerning a particular game structure or hypothesized preference ordering.

There are, nonetheless, obvious dangers in this approach. As Snidal notes, "*What* has happened cannot serve as an explanation of *why* it happened" (1986, p. 40). The "revealed preference" approach can be circular. Moreover, such an inductive approach supplies information for only one of the four cells in the already simplified 2 x 2 game. Ideally, we should provide a theoretical specification of actors' preferences in order to exploit the deductive power of game theory. Only then would the exercise become more than a "redescription of the issue in more formal language" (p. 41); it would become an analysis generating falsifiable predictions.

Unfortunately, such a theoretical specification may not be entirely convincing in an application such as the one in this chapter. Are all division managers alike? More to the point, do the preference orderings of division managers transcend specific agencies and states? Perhaps in the case of street-level workers, powerful norms operate across agencies and states and produce consistent preference orderings. For other actors, we must be content with preference orderings derived from ex post data.

The interviews, all of which were one-on-one, included numerous open-ended questions. In interviews conducted subsequent to the decision to use a game theoretic model, questions were designed to elicit information for all four cells of the 2 x 2 matrix. Gathering such data is particularly problematic in cases such as this one which are characterized by stable equilibria. Actors may have suppressed their awareness of having once made strategic choices and now interpret their actions as inevitable. To circumvent this problem, actors were often asked questions of the form, "Can you imagine doing something differently?" or "Under what circumstances would you act differently?" Through devices such as these, plausible preference orders were obtained. In addition, Koremenos was a participant observer of the agency from 1987 to 1989.[21]

Two important contributions result from this inductive approach to deriving preference orderings. First, formalization is itself useful. The game theory framework directed attention to an apparently stable equilibrium that existed prior to Wirth's assuming office (and the transmission of the noncooperative equilibrium from the top-level game down through the organization), the transition to a Pareto cooperative equilibrium during Wirth, and the stability of the cooperative equilibrium after Wirth. Further, falsifiable predictions were generated. In the summer of 1993, following an eighteen-month hiatus in contacts with IDOA, Koremenos attended a department conference in Chicago and conducted additional interviews in the following month. Two major predictions seemed to be confirmed: (1) the Pareto equilibrium induced by Wirth appeared stable, that is, virtually institutionalized as a new norm of cooperation; and (2) one of the recalcitrant division managers had left the agency rather than continue to play, and the other had changed strategies, choosing cooperation over defection.

Notes

1. This list is hardly exhaustive. We ignore those "theories" that are primarily taxonomic and lead to descriptive rather than analytic findings.

2. On the appropriateness of using game theory to model "reality," see Rubinstein (1991).

3. There are a number of more-or-less formal approaches to analyzing the dynamics of hierarchies. These include Bendor and Mookherjee (1987, pp. 140–144), Bianco and Bates (1990), Dunleavy (1985, 1991), Gauthier (1990), Miller (1990, 1992), Schwartz-Shea (1991), and Williamson (1975).

4. In this chapter, we present a static formal model and consider the dynamic aspects informally. For a complete formal presentation of the dynamic game, see Koremenos (1994).

5. The hierarchically superior actor might be labeled the Principal and the subor-

dinate labeled the Agent. Although it is strongly tempting to integrate agency theory and game theory in analyzing the management of hierarchies, we do not do so for two reasons. First, as Radner (1991) observes, there has been no "significant progress on more comprehensive models of organization that combine these two sub-models in a systematic way" (p. 218). Second, the kinds of managerial tools suggested by agency theory—binding commitments and incentive contracts—are less useful to public executives than the kinds of measures for overcoming noncooperation associated with game theory.

6. Throughout this chapter, we treat IDOA Director Wirth as synonymous with the top management team of the department. In fact, Wirth's team included Deputy Director Nancy Nelson and Associate Director Mike Phelps, and there is considerable evidence of sustained teamwork. Said Phelps: "We went round and round sometimes. We could say anything at the table, very candid. But decisions were team decisions." Said Wirth: "I make no decisions totally by myself. . . . I put the deputy in charge of all the division managers, nuts and bolts, day to day. The role of the associate director is to troubleshoot for me in every division, to go through and make sure the divisions are really carrying out the concepts that we want them to."

7. CCUs are organizations, staffed primarily by case managers, responsible for evaluating clients for the CCP program and for determining how much and what kind of service each client needs. Once a client is determined to be eligible for services and a service plan is completed, the case managers contact the service providers (who have separate contracts with IDOA) to implement the service plan. In this analysis, the CCUs and service providers are modeled as one level: the case management level.

8. If an interaction is not characterized by common and conflicting interests, interdependence, and strategic behavior, it will not be modeled as a game in later analysis. If, for example, two levels of a hierarchy have identical interests, in game theoretic terms harmony prevails and cooperation is not problematic for the realization of mutual goals.

9. The game between the governor and the director will not be modeled. No information is available for the game while Otwell was director. Regarding Edgar and Wirth, Edgar wanted to appoint a client advocate and he did; however, he gave Wirth free rein in terms of operations as long as Wirth achieved budget cuts. Hence, Edgar's self-interest did not affect implementation once Wirth was appointed. In game theoretic terms, we are assuming Edgar had no preferences among the possible outcomes.

10. We do not attempt to model games that might exist inside the bureaus or inside the CCUs. We assume, plausibly, that harmony prevails inside these units and that they can be treated as unitary actors for the purpose of analyzing Wirth's impact. Information obtained in interviews supports this assumption for within-bureau interactions.

11. An alternative view of Otwell's situation, supported by some of the interviews, is that she viewed the compliance system as a means of avoiding the kinds of criticisms lavished on other social service agencies in Illinois. In this view, compliance protects the agency from lawsuits, bad press, loss of morale, and budget reductions.

12. Analytically separable games may become linked or nested when they have a common participant with interdependent interests who seeks to maximize joint gains. See, for example, Tsebelis (1990), Mayer (1991), and Schwartz-Shea (1991).

13. In this and subsequent game matrices, outcomes are ordinal rankings: $4 > 3 > 2 > 1$.

14. Another way nesting can be represented is with the true payoff rankings but with the bureau chiefs playing NC repeatedly, which appears to be an irrational strategy when taken in isolation.

15. Note that C,c is only a Nash equilibrium in the dynamic game. Koremenos (1994) describes the formal conditions necessary to support cooperation as an equilibrium of the dynamic game.

16. An alternative view, suggested by interviewees, is that this DM preferred the cooperative outcome but was constrained by the situation under Otwell to emphasize compliance and control. As one source said, "Under Jan, everything became a turf issue between the divisions and [DM] felt more or less trapped."

17. In fact, that is what he eventually did.

18. Given the repetitive nature of the game between Otwell and her subordinates, the question arises as to why a cooperative move by Otwell did not initiate a sequence of moves leading toward mutual cooperation. The answer probably lies in the absolute magnitude of the differences in the payoffs for cooperation and defection. The gains to subordinates from unilateral defection were presumably high enough to discourage any attempt at cooperation. In other words, unlike Wirth, Otwell was unable to establish a sufficiently high relative reward for cooperation.

19. This has been called a "layered Prisoners' Dilemma" by, for example, Schwartz-Shea (1991).

20. Given the new, institutionalized equilibrium, moreover, successors might abandon the rhetoric of customer satisfaction without in any way changing the department's emphasis on client-oriented service.

21. Koremenos's experience as a social worker in the aging field enhanced her credibility with interview subjects and enabled her to garner information from subtle, indirect communications.

References

Allison, Graham T. 1971. *Essence of Decision: Explaining the Cuban Missile Crisis.* Boston: Little, Brown.

Argyris, Chris. 1976. "Leadership, Learning, and the Status Quo." *Organizational Dynamics* 4, no. 33: 29–43.

Axelrod, Robert. 1984. *The Evolution of Cooperation.* New York: Basic Books.

Bendor, Jonathan, and Dilip Mookherjee. 1987. "Institutional Structure and the Logic of Ongoing Collective Action." *American Political Science Review* 81, no. 1: 129–154.

Bianco, William T., and Robert H. Bates. 1990. "Cooperation by Design: Leadership, Structure, and Collective Dilemmas." *American Political Science Review* 84, no. 1: 133–147.

Bolman, Lee G., and Terrence E. Deal. 1991. *Reframing Organizations: Artistry, Choice, and Leadership.* San Francisco: Jossey-Bass.

Dunleavy, Patrick. 1985. "Bureaucrats, Budgets, and the Growth of the State: Reconstructing an Instrumental Model." *British Journal of Political Science* 18, no. 1: 21–49.

———. 1991. *Democracy, Bureaucracy and Public Choice.* New York: Prentice-Hall.

Gauthier, Bernard. 1990. "Hierarchies and Delegation: Sequential Production Process in an Organizational Setting." St. Louis, Mo.: Washington University, Political Economy Working Paper, 138.

Koremenos, Barbara. 1994. "A Dynamic Game-Theoretic Model of Administrative Leadership and Bureaucratic Interaction: The Folk Theorem and Real Folks." Manuscript.

Lynn, Laurence E., Jr. 1993. "Policy Achievement as a Collective Good: A Strategic Perspective on Managing Social Programs," in Barry Bozeman, ed., *Public Management: The State of the Art,* pp. 108–133. San Franciso: Jossey-Bass.

Mayer, Frederick W. 1991. "Domestic Politics and the Strategy of International Trade." *Journal of Policy Analysis and Management* 10, no. 2: 222–246.

Miller, Gary J. 1990. "Managerial Dilemmas: Political Leadership in Hierarchies," in Karen Schweers Cook and Margaret Levi, eds., *The Limits of Rationality,* pp. 324–348. Chicago: University of Chicago Press.

———. 1992. *Managerial Dilemmas: The Political Economy of Hierarchy.* Cambridge: Cambridge University Press.

O'Toole, Laurence J., Jr. 1993. "Multiorganizational Policy Implementation: Some Limitations and Possibilities for Rational Choice Contributions," in Fritz W. Scharpf, ed., *Games in Hierarchies and Networks,* pp. 1–39. London: Westview.

Radner, Roy. 1991. "Dynamic Games in Organization Theory." *Journal of Economic Behavior and Organization* 16: 217–260.

Rubinstein, Ariel. 1991. "Comments on the Interpretation of Game Theory." *Econometrica* 59, no. 4: 909–924.

Schwartz-Shea, Peregrine. 1991. "Understanding Subgroup Optimization: Experimental Evidence on Individual Choice and Group Processes." *Journal of Public Administration Research and Theory* 1: 49–73.

Snidal, Duncan. 1986. "The Game *Theory* of International Politics," in Kenneth A. Oye, ed., *Cooperation under Anarchy.* Princeton: Princeton University Press.

Tsebelis, George. 1990. *Nested Games: Rational Choice in Comparative Politics.* Berkeley: University of California Press.

Williamson, Oliver E. 1975. *Markets and Hierarchies: Analysis and Antitrust Implications.* New York: Free Press.

11.

Rational Choice and the Public Management of Interorganizational Networks

Laurence J. O'Toole Jr.

Policy implementation refers to the connection between the expression of governmental intention and the achievement of results in the world of action. While implementation is sometimes accomplished through the efforts of a single administrative agency, increasingly, success may require multiple organizational units to achieve policy goals. The importance of intergovernmental grant programs and regulatory mechanisms, the prominence of public-private partnerships, and the emergence of salient policy problems cutting across administrative jurisdictions on issues ranging from health care to homelessness to economic growth all testify to the centrality of interorganizational arrangements for dealing with today's implementation challenges.

This chapter focuses on understanding and managing implementation in these interorganizational settings: the numerous cases in which two or more organizations (or, more precisely, parts of two or more organizations), sometimes even complex networks of interdependent actors, are required to cooperate and perhaps coordinate for policy success. Even if implementation in and through networked settings is practically important, the processes are not as

A preliminary version of these ideas was presented at the Workshop on Management in Interorganisational Networks of the European Consortium for Political Research, Limerick, Ireland, March 30–April 4, 1992. This chapter appears in slightly different form in the *American Review of Public Administration,* which has given permission for its inclusion in this volume.

well understood as the more familiar public management challenges arising within lone administrative units. Interunit implementation may face special challenges from the lack of authoritative and efficient channels for joint decision and action, the complications of multilateral bargaining, and the diverse interests often represented through multiple organizations. As a consequence, successful implementation can be especially daunting.

Despite its widely recognized importance, and despite its having been investigated with considerable intensity for several years now, the study of interorganizational policy implementation stands in need of much more development. Many improvements in empirical methods have been introduced since the initial case studies (e.g., Pressman and Wildavsky, 1984). Still, there is as yet little agreement on a theory of interorganizational implementation (for a documentation and analysis of this state of affairs, see Goggin et al., 1990; O'Toole, 1986; and Palumbo and Calista, 1990). It is quite clear that further efforts at theory building are necessary, both to advance the scholarly study of the subject and to encourage better public management practice.

This chapter addresses the question of how one category of theory development might provide assistance for managing implementation in network settings. The argument here examines formal, especially rational choice, approaches such as game theory. I explore the idea of modeling interorganizational implementation via a rational choice approach. The first conclusion is that serious limitations constrain what may be possible through the formal rational choice representation and analysis of many such settings. The second conclusion, however, is that these limitations for theorists do not mean that practical implementation success is itself problematic. In fact, an exploration of the limitations of formal approaches actually reveals the ways that practicing managers may be able to induce success under challenging network conditions: The *modeling* problems themselves point systematically to the practical *management* possibilities. The overall argument is developed largely in the languages of implementation theory and game theory; but no detailed knowledge of the latter specialty is required, and no formal analysis is undertaken.

Implementation, as used in this chapter, refers to the set of actions induced among those who are required by a public policy to cooperate and perhaps coordinate toward the achievement of a mandate. The investigation here focuses on the important class of implementation cases involving interorganizational, or "networked," arrangements.

A few clarifying comments are in order. First, the *explanandum* is the behavior of various actors (or the interunit network as a whole). Second, the conceptualization is purposely broad on the notion of "require." In the present analysis, both technical and political necessity are consciously included. A result is that the interorganizational implementation network subject to investigation may be expected to include a complex and disparate set of organizational actors. Finally, the subject of this chapter embraces "management" of interorganizational networks (see Gage and Mandell, 1990), a function involving the task of developing and maintaining cooperative links—and possibly of achieving some generally appreciated objectives—in and through the interorganizational pattern. The meaning, then, is close to the "reticulist" function of Friend, Power, and Yewlett (1974), as well as the notions of "fixing" (Bardach, 1977) policy implementation, or engaging in multilateral brokerage (Mandell, 1984) and policy entrepreneurship (e.g., Kingdon, 1984).

There has been general recognition of the potential importance of the linking, mediating, and coordinating function often observed in networks, even if there is little agreement regarding the precise activities being embraced or the requisites for their successful fulfillment. For purposes of this chapter, the term *management* refers to this coordinative function, which may be crucial for implementation success.

Rational Choice and Interorganizational Implementation: The Present Limited State of the Field

Although additional theoretical approaches to the question of interorganizational implementation are needed, and although there is little agreement on the directions in which such development should proceed, a notable feature of the research conducted thus far on this subject is that its orientation is very heavily inductive (see Mazmanian and Sabatier, 1989, for a similar characterization).[1] To the extent that deductive approaches have been offered in the study of policy implementation, these typically either have focused on single organizations or have been characterized by a top-down, compliance orientation. Lynn's work with Koremenos in the present volume (chap. 10) constitutes a partial exception; yet even there the setting modeled is formally hierarchical (see also Lynn, 1993).

Network theory and formal exchange models have received considerable attention among social scientists in recent years. However, the literature of interorganizational implementation and its management has tended to utilize the notions of network and exchange in metaphorical rather than carefully analytical ways. It might be expected that formal approaches would have been examined in efforts to improve at least the precision and clarity of scholarly dialogue on the subject. Some attempts have been made to apply such approaches to other aspects of policy settings (note, especially, Scharpf 1993). And Stoker (1991) has sketched a suggestive intergovernmental implementation analysis involving an informal application of game theory (see also Kettl, 1993, on contracting relationships). Yet at this point the interorganizational/network implementation setting has been all but ignored by formal theorists.

Some rational choice modeling of implementation arrangements has been conducted. Nevertheless, these efforts are clearly unsatisfactory in their present forms, since they typically fit into one of two categories: formal representations of bureaucratic agents within a single administrative unit (see Bendor, 1990; Noll and Weingast, 1991) or models that attempt to capture interunit processes through a variant of principal-agent theory (see, e.g., Chubb, 1985, who models multiple principals in an intergovernmental network). Both types are vulnerable to the criticisms advanced against top-down implementation theory; and, if the framing comments discussed earlier in this chapter are valid, these efforts are inadequate to deal with modeling cooperation in broader networked contexts.

Still, examining the potential applicability of rational choice approaches may be useful in addressing two general questions. First, does such a perspective hold potential for significantly advancing theory about interunit implementation? Given the potential power, rigor, and generality of carefully constructed deductive approaches, as well as the lack of a currently accepted general approach to the subject under investigation, this issue is one worth consideration in the study of implementation networks. The answer offered here is that serious difficulties constrain what is possible through such approaches.[2] Second, even if rational choice analysis is limited in its direct theory-building applicability, can it serve a purpose by alerting analysts to matters of practical moment for those interested in network management? This more circumscribed albeit pragmatic objective receives attention in this chapter, and on this latter score the review draws a cautiously optimistic conclusion—one different from but not necessarily inconsistent with the main theme of Lynn's chapter in this book (chap. 2). The very features of interorganizational implementation that preclude successful modeling are the elements that are the most promising objects of managers' attention. And understanding why rational choice theoretical approaches face substantial impediments in turn points to the ways in which managers can enhance chances for practical implementation success.

Interorganizational Implementation: An Analysis

Interorganizational implementation,[3] the action of two or more units on behalf of a public policy, can be conceptualized as a problem of cooperation, and possibly of coordination.[4] If the literature on organization and interorganization theory documents anything, it is that such cooperation across units is unlikely to arise spontaneously. This is not to say that stable interunit ties cannot develop; in fact, examples like iron triangles and more complex, networked policy settings suggest that patterns of cooperation can be built over time and endure. The point, rather, is that the existence of such cases must be explained rather than assumed. The following discussion telescopes an argument that could be developed at considerably more length. Here, however, it is necessary only to sketch the basic logic. The point is to identify some features of the interorganizational network setting that are especially important for rational choice theoretical efforts.

Two broad reasons interorganizational action is often more difficult than the intraunit variety are: (1) the use of mechanisms of coordination within single organizations can itself render interorganizational coordination more problematic; and (2) the forms of inducement to interunit cooperation are typically weaker than those available within simpler structures.

Intraorganizational coordinating mechanisms—routines, for instance— work to simplify the search for optimum equilibria among individuals within organizational units. In so doing, however, these complicate searches for solutions *across* structures. Even for problems of pure coordination (in game theoretic terms, so-called assurance games), within-unit settlements enacted prior to interunit coordinative efforts reduce the set of possible solutions.

Given this set of circumstances, interorganizational implementation must be induced. Yet the availability of inducements is often constrained by characteristics of the standard interunit network setting. In a number of instances, the challenge of networked cooperation is met, at least in part, by the existence or development of norms that embrace shared meaning among participants and that influence implementation action. Absent substantial quantities of either authority or common interest (including common perspectives, such as norms) across the parties, and given the complications of collective action problems even where there are significant shared interests in cooperation (see Hardin, 1968; Ostrom, 1990), exchange may have the most potential. Yet even from a rational choice perspective, successful exchange is by no means assured in interorganizational/network settings. The complexity of multiunit settings and, often, the difficulty of negotiating exchanges themselves can pose substantial impediments. Stable bargaining solutions may thus be possible in principle, but exchanges face challenges stemming from information problems and the introduction or reintroduction of uncertainty in the network setting.

These conclusions regarding the limited reach of authority and common interest in inducing interunit implementation can be put in a somewhat different way to highlight implications for modeling implementation. This argument suggests that cases of interorganizational implementation cannot be treated as pure instances of self-forming networks, nor as straightforward cases of principals and agents. To the extent that top-down approaches have been theoretically explicit, these have tended to minimize the former aspects of implementation networks; bottom-up researchers can likewise be faulted for omitting aspects of agency often considered important by the participants themselves. Interorganizational networks for implementation contain some properties found in self-forming networks—including the absence of formal hierarchy and the presence of some self-selection—and some characteristics of externally or centrally directed chains of agency.

A similar way of establishing this point has been offered quite recently by Sabel: "The combination of elements of horizontal coordination by market and vertical coordination by hierarchy in a single governance structure . . . transforms the operation of both and produces an irreducibly distinct pattern of adjustment to environmental changes" (1993, p. 79).

Needless to say, rational choice perspectives have not produced such a synthesis. Caution should thus be exercised in deriving management implications from either self-forming or principal-agent models of the implementation process. This kind of complication, in both theory and practice, can be expected when official actors are putatively authoritative but must typically rely on multilateral persuasion and exchange.

The argument outlined thus far suggests that exchange in networks to facilitate policy implementation is possible but often not straightforward. Of course, interdependent choice among strategic actors is precisely what rational actor approaches seek to model. More synthetic rational choice models would be necessary to capture the important elements of the networked implementation setting, and these models have thus far not been developed. However, more fundamental constraints actually impose significant limitations on what may be possible in principle from this perspective, even with further developments in formal theory.

Two general complications are sketched here: difficulties stemming from the introduction or reintroduction of uncertainty in the network setting, and, relatedly, challenges to institutional analysis in cases of interorganizational implementation. The following two subsections emphasize some serious limitations that affect efforts to conduct rigorous modeling of the interunit context. Neither can be expected to be overcome by theoretical advances in the tradition of rational choice.

Problems of Uncertainty

As implementers seek to give practical meaning to policy, they can be challenged by uncertainty arising from and regarding the setting in which they try to act. High levels of uncertainty in turn create complications for rational choice modeling. A consideration of implementation in network settings suggests that the number of sources of uncertainty in such cases, especially at the early stages of implementation, creates inherent limitations restricting the ability of formal approaches to model the most important elements of empirical cases.

Numerous aspects of the topic of uncertainty—for example, the possibility of its backward induction into a multiunit interaction—have been intensively analyzed in literatures on game theory. This chapter is not the place for even an overview of the important issues. However, it is appropriate to summarize some of the complications for modeling. These complications carry ramifications for practice.

First, uncertainty is often present for participants in interunit settings for implementation because of lack of knowledge of other actors' true preferences. Second, the sheer number of units involved in the interorganizational effort, when coupled with the number of strategies potentially available to each, may be sufficiently large so as to provide another source of uncertainty. The network in many actual cases may be too large for fully specified modeling.

Third, the structure of interdependence among the units may be sufficiently complex that the arrangement of the overall network becomes a complication in the strategic interactions. The point is this: For any number of reasons there may be uncertainties among actors as well as analysts regarding the structure of interdependence itself. If the actors are linked reciprocally, the complexity of network structure itself may magnify the uncertainties stemming from the other sources already outlined.

A fourth point, much more well known than the preceding one, is that problems of monitoring and enforcement can be substantial in interunit implementation networks. Second-order collective action difficulties may reduce or eliminate monitoring or sanctioning altogether: It may be in all participants' interest to monitor compliance with the terms of an agreement among several organizations on an innovative social services program, for instance, but each may find the task too burdensome to handle alone and thus all may suffer from inadequate oversight. Yet, even disregarding this possibility, well-studied issues like the problem of moral hazard in principal-agent relations threaten to vitiate the mechanism. Once again, issues for modeling (and also for action) present themselves.

Another interesting source of uncertainty has to do with the connectedness of strategic interactions in the network. First, the good news: The theory of connected or nested games as developed in recent years offers suggestive ways of modeling important aspects of interorganizational implementation as well as other types of network settings (see, e.g., Alt and Eichengreen, 1987; Alt, Putnam, and Shepsle, 1988; Tsebelis, 1990). Furthermore, analysts have offered interesting arguments regarding how actors in such settings may buffer against the uncertainties stemming from such connectedness by segmenting their "games" and playing them separately (see Scharpf, 1990).

Now, however, the bad news (bad, that is, from the standpoint of those who hope to use rational choice approaches to model such interunit settings): Another source of uncertainty here is second-order strategic behavior regarding the nature of the links that bind the actors into their circumstances of interdependence. Even as some actors seek segmentation of the games and therefore a simplification of the layering phenomenon, others may be advantaged by continuing to tie the games together. Complications for implementation practice can ensue when, for instance, a business firm insists on linking tax abatement decisions and city budget allocations to its "game" of negotiating with a local public agency on the terms of a public-private partnership. The essential point, however, is that the tendency of networked actors to engage in such strategic linking behavior makes the task of formalizing interunit bargaining exceedingly daunting. There may be virtually no end to the "moves" available in interorganizational negotiations, and models simply cannot capture the full array of options.

Uncertainty, in short, poses challenges from a number of directions to the potentially powerful idea of rational choice analyses of implementation networks. It can sometimes also vitiate implementation practice.

Implementation Networks and Institutional Dynamics

A great deal of attention has been devoted in recent years to the "new institutionalism" in the social sciences. Rational choice approaches themselves have often been crafted to model the impact of basic institutional features in politically important settings such as elections, legislatures, and bureaucracies. The notion of institution as used in this discussion is meant to include not merely formal or officially adopted structures but all understandings regarding regularized action in social settings; Ostrom's idea of institutions as sets or clusters of working rules is apropos (1986a, 1986b, 1990).

The issue of institutions is central in the current analysis because formal modeling (especially rational choice modeling, even through complex approaches like connected games) must *assume* considerable institutionalization in the relevant setting, and yet many networks for implementation are not highly institutionalized—especially in the important early stages of implementation action. A lack of institutionalization at the outset of multiunit implementation means that formal models inherently cannot capture the key elements of the social setting and develop robust predictions. Ex post facto explanation is the most that can be expected.

Some rational choice approaches have addressed the question of how to model, or at least explore systematically, issues of institutional change (Tsebelis, 1990). However, even under the most optimistic conditions, such approaches must assume a base institution from which possible departures can be examined. When implementation develops across institutions, among units or groups that do not have at least the outlines of an interunit-institutional starting point, rational choice explanations become much less useful.

The point here goes to the question of theory development rather than the matter of management. The critique of rational choice approaches sketched above implies inherent and serious limitations on what formal approaches can offer: Models cannot provide much information regarding what is likely to happen in a given interorganizational implementation setting.[5] But one cannot conclude from this discussion that cooperation itself (implementation success) is unlikely. Indeed, such a point would be a manifest absurdity. The literature of interorganizational implementation has now documented large numbers of "successful" implementation cases. Rather, the claim is that rational choice approaches are not particularly helpful in the careful predictive modeling of such emergent processes.

So implementation in networks can be successful, even if its emergence often cannot be formally modeled. How? Here, paradoxically, is where the preceding analysis carries a more optimistic implication. Modeling attempts and practical implementation efforts are distinct, but they are linked by the important point that uncertainty and a lack of institutionalization pose potential threats to the success of each. The limitations for modelers, however, point in turn to the sites of most potent leverage for implementation managers. The review of *impediments to modeling* presented above—principally deriving from uncertainty and lack of institutionalization in the implementation setting—points directly to the most important *opportunities for management* intervention. Understanding the limitations on modeling efforts highlights simultaneously the important targets and methods of implementation management in practice: Implementation managers in network settings can be successful by intervening at several points implied above to reduce uncertainty and institutionalize cooperation. These broad approaches include several more specific moves, which are identified below.

Implications for Managing Implementation in Networks

The subject of interorganizational management has been of increasing interest in the field of public administration (see, e.g., Agranoff, 1991; Gage and Mandell, 1990; Hanf, 1992; Hanf and O'Toole, 1992; O'Toole, 1983, 1988, 1989). The foregoing analysis can be used to identify and analyze the multiple possibilities for management in practice of networked implementation settings. The next sections explore modes of altering multiactor network settings to encourage cooperative solutions to implementation problems.

The reason why disappointing conclusions for modelers may nevertheless point toward helpful ideas for managers turns on the very different meanings of the concept of "solution" in game theory and in network management. Game theorists use this label to designate the predicted outcome of strategic choice (thus, a mathematical solution), including noncooperative outcomes. The paradigmatic example is the dominance of defection as the solution to the prisoners' dilemma game. The argument earlier in this chapter is that uncertainty precludes predictive game theoretic solutions—cooperative or not—to many instances of interunit implementation. However, the notion of "solution" carries a different meaning to managers: problem solving. For public actors managing programs through networks, looking for solutions means searching for options sufficiently cooperative to encourage or permit programs to work. *This* type of success is not necessarily reliant on predictive game theoretic solutions. Indeed, the multiple uncertainties that preclude game theoretic solutions are themselves potential objects of influence by network managers as they seek their own variety of "solution."

Game Theory and the Implementation "Game"

The argument of this chapter suggests that formal rational actor analytic approaches cannot be expected to provide a theoretic resolution of interorganizational implementation cases. Approaches like game theory require more clarity and resolution of uncertainty than can be expected in the early stages of most real cases. Nevertheless, the terms of reference of game theoretic approaches, and the specific complications that can be expected in empirical settings, provide a practically useful template that can be used to identify and distinguish the types of managerial moves available for improving the odds of success in actual implementation "games." The following discussion, then, uses the organizing perspective of the game—in the sense of interdependent, strategic choice—to analyze the managerial options for enhancing implementation.

One important channel for influencing the likelihood of implementation success in network contexts reaches beyond the realm of "management," narrowly construed. It is the very content of policy, which can be of significant assistance or hindrance to cooperative efforts in an implementation context. (For coverage of how the design of policy can influence the likelihood of interorganizational cooperation, see O'Toole, 1988.) Policies set the implementation game in motion; they constitute the initial important step in determining the ways in which uncertainty may be reduced and institutionalization facilitated in the interests of policy objectives.

Policies alone cannot design full-blown cooperative institutions; but they are consequential in the setting where institutionalization may take place, and they sometimes stipulate or encourage the use of certain technologies that themselves constitute a kind of "fix," or specification, of elements in the implementation game. To the extent that policies mandate behavior unacceptable to the actors in a particular setting, of course, they are unlikely to accomplish much. Yet, they can establish certain features of the context and perhaps signal appropriate modes or points of coordination (e.g., in settings allowing assurance games). Such can be the function of policies designating lead agencies or procedural matters like requirements for hearings, scheduling stipulations, or deadlines. In more complex cases, they can increase or decrease actors' ability to reach Pareto-efficient equilibria (see Stoker, 1991). They also determine or affect payoffs in at least some of the sets of games in an interorganizational matrix through budgets, mandates, and a host of additional provisions. Furthermore, they influence the relevant structures of interdependence, as discussed earlier. Nevertheless, there has been surprisingly little research on how the attributes of policy are likely to influence the possibilities for cooperative solutions in implementation networks. Rational choice approaches point clearly to policy characteristics as key variables, and such perspectives also provide clues to the ways in which policy might matter. Recent attention being devoted to policy design may signal an emerging interest in this subject.

One final point regarding the issue of policy may be mentioned. Findings from a systematic investigation of the importance of policy content as an external influence on the interunit implementation setting can be quite important for management. However, implementers themselves, including managers in the network, are not typically the same actors who craft the official policy. Therefore, their potential modes of influence over it, or over its redesign, are likely to be indirect and more subtle. It is not, then, a simple matter of managers' putting such knowledge to use. They more typically need to persuade at least some others. This point, in turn, suggests another wrinkle: The network for policy formulation or reformulation overlaps that for implementation. The latter is interdependent with the former, and managing successfully in one may require understanding how various moves made at the intersection of the networks affect each set of games. Furthermore, applying a rational choice perspective, at least in general terms, to questions of institutional design for policy making may be of utility in assisting managers of implementation in network settings.[6]

Network Management Options:
Playing, Linking, and Altering the Implementation Game

Many times the implementation game cannot be fixed or arranged from the start by the careful design of policy. And in any event, managers in implementation networks may have to seek additional points of leverage over complex implementation processes. The analysis in the first part of this chapter shows that formal analysis cannot "solve" emergent implementation puzzles in modeling terms. However, the sources of complication for formal analysis—principally, uncertainty and underinstitutionalization of the nascent implementation setting—point directly to the points of leverage for managers. Those in implementation networks can affect the outcome of the implementation "game" by moving in a number of ways, and at a number of levels, to reduce uncertainty and institutionalize cooperative arrangements in the interests of policy success.

By pointing to the problems (for modelers) of uncertainty and lack of institutional predictability at the outset of implementation processes, a consideration of formal analysis thus identifies (for practice) the strategic sites for management intervention. Therefore, rational choice analysis suggests a conclusion broadly consistent with that reached in much of the more inductively generated implementation literature: the presence of an active and skillful multilateral broker (or network manager) at key points in the interunit structure can be crucial for the emergence and stability of cooperative solutions.

Approaching such implementation settings from the standpoint of formal approaches, and with an appreciation for the range and importance of the barriers to interunit cooperation, can highlight the key role of managers in handling a wide variety of threats to cooperative action. Some of these are explored briefly here, in order of increasingly significant alterations to the implementation "game"—a term used, once again, in the game theoretic sense of interdependent strategic choice.

Assisting the Play of the Game

Managers may be active, first of all, in the initiation of certain moves that do not alter the game theoretic structure of the strategic situation, such as signaling (e.g., letting units know of each other's involvement and interest, or identifying possible points of cooperation), commitment, and iteration (predictable repetition of the interdependent action). When the coincidence of interests among implementation participants is relatively close, managers in networks may make all the difference by facilitating the strategic moves of the units involved rather than by seeking to change the pattern of interdependence.

Linking Games

Formal analysis points to the possibility that more forceful managerial moves may be necessary under more complex conditions of uncertainty, and/or "games" involving circumstances of mixed but not completely opposed interests across participants (say, chicken games). Here, success may be encouraged by managers' proposing appropriate or potentially acceptable coordination points, that is, Pareto-efficient equilibria. Interestingly, in the typically more complex interunit setting, such managerial actors can ease both the identification and the stabilization of equilibria by proposing enforceable modes of linking games among interdependent actors (e.g., alternating the adopted equilibria in paired chicken games within an interunit setting so as to rotate the advantage across all parties). An illustration here would be suggesting that a donor unit accede to the needs or demands of a recipient agency in an intergovernmental grant program in exchange for the latter's deference to the former on a matter of mutual concern in a different program administered by both units—the implementation management equivalent to legislative-style logrolling in the interest of coalition building. In this fashion, network managers may take the complexity and potential uncertainty often present in the network setting—a condition that can easily lead to destabilization via cascading uncertainty—and utilize the potential connectedness of mixed-motive games to build stable agreements on a range of related issues. Even the formal examination of some of these games after the fact, including the identification of observed bargaining ranges, might be useful in explicating challenges and potential solutions to implementation management.

Another insight derived from rational choice analysis refers to potential links between "levels" of games in the implementation context. Managers may be able to play key roles in solving or mitigating the second-order collective action problem in implementation settings. Even if all necessary parties agree on the advisability of cooperation to resolve a situation of interdependent choice, such an agreement may require monitoring and enforcement to prevent unraveling. And yet although all parties may be advantaged by the agreement, in many cases no single party will have an interest in devoting the energy, time, and resources needed to monitor and enforce. However, a manager—either centrally designated or decentrally recognized—may be an ideal party. (The self-interest of all parties may be served by contributing resources to the management function in the interests of dependable monitoring of the primary cooperative arrangement.)

The first part of this chapter, thus, shows that formal theory does not yield straightforward solutions to emergent network implementation challenges, in part because of the ability of actors to link games strategically and in complex ways on behalf of their own interests. In considering implications for practice, however, this modeling limitation becomes a managerial opportunity: Implementation managers, too, can act strategically by linking games of interdependent choice among the participants in an implementation effort, and they can do so with the aim of *enhancing* chances for practical success.

Changing the Game: Active Implementation Management

Managers may increase the likelihood of implementation by facilitating the play of the strategic game when interests are closely aligned but coordination is needed. They may improve the odds of success in more complicated circumstances—games with high uncertainty and/or games with conflicting interests among the parties—by explicitly connecting the implementation game to other parallel games or to a second-order monitoring or enforcement game. Sometimes, however, these options are either unavailable or insufficient. Circumstances requiring the greatest managerial creativity and effort, therefore, are likely to arise when the game is unplayable, that is, when the only "solutions" in a game theoretic sense are choices that vitiate the intent of the policy.

A number of options for altering the implementation game can be identified by considering the ways in which managers might shift the character of the strategic game itself. Formal analyses of interdependent choice define "games" in terms of the preferences of participants and the structure of their interdependence. Similarly, then, managers can consider trying to change the implementation game to reduce uncertainty and institutionalize cooperative action by influencing preferences of those in the network or shifting the structure of interdependence among those in the interunit array. Each of these possibilities is thus identified with the aid of formal theory, although technically such moves lie outside the bounds of formal analysis (each involves changing the game rather than solving it in formal terms). The following discussion, then, illustrates how rational choice perspectives can assist in the analysis of active forms of implementation management, even if such approaches cannot usually produce formal, deductive "solutions" to problems of cooperation.

Influencing Preferences. Managers may employ persuasion to increase perceived common interest as well as to catalyze agreement during negotiations. Formal theory operates by analyzing given preferences among interdependent actors (individuals or organizations), not by considering possibilities for shifts in these preferences. Yet, practical implementation management may be assisted by encouraging changes that would increase the prospects for cooperative solutions.

Persuasion can work at several levels if actors are intendedly yet limitedly rational. Participants in a network may be influenced in their evaluations of specific expected consequences by their counterparts in other units and, certainly, by a network manager. Managers may find chances to alter payoffs (or the perception of payoffs, which is actually the crucial consideration) for the players for various options—perhaps with the assent of all parties—and thus encourage cooperative outcomes. Further, since transaction costs may be considerable, managers in complex settings can facilitate cooperation by working to develop generally accepted understandings of "exchange rates" across resource types and perhaps building an institutional memory for some of the important if intangible debits and credits across units in the network (this task assists exchange and also monitoring).

Persuasion can influence choice at another level by convincing actors of the advantages of stable cooperation more generally among the units, even if the short-run or narrowly prudential calculation for the immediate task seems to argue against it. And persuasion can be consequential not only for actors' evaluations of alternatives and consequences but also for their basic interpretation of complicated signals from elsewhere (see, e.g., Kahneman and Tversky, 1984).

Implementation managers can also use persuasion in a network to encourage the development of "appropriate" norms: norms of cooperation and others, including professional norms (see Provan and Milward, 1991), that enhance predictability in a setting of nascent institutionalization. Norms are important parts of the institutional setting—even if they are sometimes unnecessarily neglected in rational choice formulations (see Elster, 1989, for a provocative exception). Furthermore, and in a fashion related to the reduction of second-order collective action problems discussed above, network managers can call attention to violations of such norms, either privately or across broader parts of the network setting, thus monitoring and enforcing patterns of cooperation.

By so doing, and by encouraging the development of norms of reciprocity, civility, and mutual respect, two important consequences may follow. First, of course, norms such as these begin a process of network institutionalization that itself helps to reduce uncertainty and increase the ability and incentive of the various actors to seek cooperative solutions. Second, the development of such norms stimulates the beginnings of a climate of trust among the units, thus also reducing uncertainty and encouraging longer-term cooperation in a more subtle fashion. This conclusion follows from the impact of trust itself on the temporal perspectives of rational actors. Formal as well as experimental research has shown that trust in those with whom one has to make interdependent decisions means that the relevant actors are less likely to discount steeply their cooperative investments in the future (see, e.g., Axelrod, 1984; Stoker, 1991).

There are likely to be multiple opportunities for network managers to encourage the development of trust. Indeed, the mere presence of an individual or unit with recognized responsibilities for the interunit venture increases the likelihood of trust, since other actors may begin to assume the presence of some monitoring and enforcement. Additional modes of developing trust are numerous. Indeed, in his analysis of the importance of trust over opportunism in many interunit settings, Sabel notes that "the connection between situation and outcome as observable by an outsider is . . . quite loose. . . . The outcome . . . can only be explained by reference to the history of a (perhaps changing) bundle of local conditions, including of course the participants' changing views about the advantages and feasibility of cooperation" (1993, p. 85; see also Ostrom, 1990). These conditions, of course, are subject to some influence by network managers (Sabel's "superintendents"). Two illustrations can indicate once again how the form of analysis used here is likely to point to possibilities. One is for network managers to be guided in directing information flows and timing within the network not only by the technical requisites of the policy but also by the need to respect confidences and avoid embarrassments on the part of organizational units whose mutual trust may be essential for long-term success. A second implication of formal analysis is that managers may be advantaged by seeking to engage the various units initially in relatively low-risk cooperative ventures with each other. Success (that is, cooperation) at ostensibly unimportant interorganizational matters may breed success at larger enterprises.

Shifting the Structure. Network managers can also take advantage of opportunities to alter the interunit structure itself to encourage cooperation. There can be many possibilities, and network managers themselves are best situated to evaluate their potential in a specific policy context. One fashion in which this issue has already been raised is the discussion of managers' working strategically to separate or link potentially distinguishable games, since the process of connecting two or more games itself constitutes a shift in the structure of interunit interdependence.

Another possibility, interestingly enough, works in the opposite direction: to reduce interdependence by employing buffering devices rather than to link games to encourage cooperation. Scholars using rational choice approaches have analyzed ways of buffering networks, or portions of networks, from such sources of uncertainty as channels for backward induction. One type of buffering sometimes observable in interorganizational settings is the conscious reduction of requirements for joint decision making to those necessary for serving the interests of both (all) parties. This mode, called "negative coordination" by Mayntz and Scharpf (1975), was first described in German administrative settings and can simplify at least some of the complexity in network arrangements (see also Scharpf, 1978). Managers, in turn, can look for ways of decoupling portions of the joint decision-making activities if these are not actually called for by the task. This point should not be taken to mean that some simplified public choice logic is appropriate. There may be many reasons why negative coordination is unacceptable.

An overall implication of this analysis of structural change for those interested in practical interunit management is that it is the *overall* structure, not simply the discrete and directly observable, often-dyadic interactions, that is most significant in the implementation setting. The overall structure heavily influences the answers to such central questions as who can make relatively autonomous moves; as well as who is strategically advantaged, in terms of the range and distribution of payoffs, in games where interests do not clearly mesh. The ability to analyze and compare network structures systematically has advanced considerably in recent years. Consequently, it may be important for those who seek improvement in managers' ability to effect interunit cooperation to encourage the use and further refinement of network analysis. Rational choice approaches have shown deductively that ostensibly small adjustments in interunit structure can be expected to make for large alterations in outcomes. An analogous point is that it may be important for those concerned with managing implementation in interorganizational patterns to encourage a more systematic examination of structural options.

One example is apropos. Despite the great political interest in privatization in numerous Western national contexts during the 1980s and 1990s, and despite the current ferment and dynamism in Eastern Europe on this issue, the privatization phenomenon constitutes a host of quite different strategies, and these approaches in turn rely on quite different structural arrangements. How these can be understood, and whether and how managers can encourage appropriate cooperative efforts in circumstances of complex public-private interdependence, are issues that analysts have hardly begun to explore. It is obvious, therefore, that more rigorous examination of a wider variety of structural arrangements is sensible for both practical and scholarly ends.

There are, of course, many additional fashions in which interorganizational managers might be able to induce or influence structural change in the direction of cooperative arrangements. Indeed, the point made earlier regarding the lack of institutionalization in the nascent network setting may here be seen as an opportunity. Although rational choice modeling is rendered all but impossible in implementation settings at a pre- or proto-institutional stage, still the lack of poorly designed structure (for the purpose at hand) can be counted as a practical advantage that may be exploited by skillful managers.

And even if it is not typically possible to *design* the interunit structure comprehensively, from the point of view of the network manager, there may be multiple opportunities to alter the arrangement. To the extent that institutionalized arrangements do not favor cooperative solutions to problems of interdependence, managers may be able to take advantage of ad hoc situations to encourage a shift, even if only an incremental adjustment, when the episodic salience of an issue peaks. Examples might include establishing a lead agency, agreeing to stable funding for an interunit coordinating group, or decentralizing program decisions to organizations that have the most to gain from implementation success. Indeed, even modest structural adjustments may have considerable impact on the outcomes of multiunit games.

Conclusion

Rational choice approaches may seem to be attractive for the analysis of issues of interorganizational implementation. Perspectives like game theory offer several advantages, including the rigor of deductive theory; the potential to unite strengths of both top-down and bottom-up perspectives by treating all relevant actors as strategic players; and ideas about conceptualizing interdependence across "games" as well as across actors (organizations) and decisions. Still, actual implementation networks contain complications that modeling can appropriately neither ignore nor address. The obstacles to rational choice efforts are well-illustrated by, albeit not limited to, the issues of uncertainty and institutionalization.

Nevertheless, considering interorganizational implementation from the perspective of rational choice is not futile. Rather, less formal analyses offer potential utility, especially in terms of management practice. Although it is not possible in most interesting cases to deduce rigorously modeled predictions regarding actual implementation settings, the concepts of rational choice provide leverage to scholars of network management as well as to managers themselves. The limitations of such approaches point to ways in which managers can increase the odds of cooperation in the direction of policy success among diverse organizational units. While the analysis here is far less than a practical manual for implementers, its coverage of the differentiated landscape of interorganizational implementation may provide some candidate approaches to which implementers might turn.

Considering the implementation setting via approaches like game theory focuses attention on issues of broad significance. Examples from the analysis presented here include the central role of exchange and persuasion in implementation, the importance of uncertainty (and its diverse sources) as a potential barrier, and the numerous analytically coherent even if empirically disparate ways in which the interunit manager can influence interdependent action in the direction of cooperative outcomes. For improving the management of networked implementation, more comprehensive exploration of these issues is essential.

Notes

1. This section and the one following contain brief summaries of material from recent articles exploring the limitations and opportunities for rational choice contributions to the theoretical literature (e.g., O'Toole, 1993a, 1993b). An earlier version of that argument was presented at the workshop on Games in Hierarchies and Networks, Max-Planck-Institut für Gesellschaftsforschung, Cologne, Germany, September 1991. The present chapter extends the analysis to examine the issue of interorganizational/network management.

2. An unexamined assumption in the present context is that implementation can be appropriately interpreted in instrumental terms. Some analysts (e.g., Eckstein, 1991) offer critiques of the idea of intendedly rational human action, at least under certain circumstances, whereas others (e.g., Nakamura, 1990) point out the symbolic content in some implementation efforts. However, several features of the implementation context suggest that it is sensible to treat implementation action as largely oriented toward consequences—even if these are not always manifestly stated nor unanimously held among the actors.

3. The argument in this section is based on, and developed more completely in, O'Toole, 1993a, 1993b.

4. This last point can be clarified. Coordination—actors' treating the moves of other interdependent parties as contingencies for their own—may be a part of interunit implementation. The determining factor is what *type* of interdependence is required. In James Thompson's terms, reciprocal interdependence, but not the pooled or sequential varieties, demands conscious coordination, or strategic interaction (1967). Therefore, strategic varieties of rational choice theory fit only those cases in which coordination matters (see on this point O'Toole, 1993b; Scharpf, 1990).

5. There may nevertheless be some value to a more limited application of the rational choice approach by students of policy implementation. One option, for instance, is to investigate carefully when and how simplifying assumptions in network settings *can* legitimately be used to allow the application of game theory or similar approaches (see, e.g., the research program initiated by Scharpf, 1990, 1991). Some complementary strategies (discussed more carefully in O'Toole, 1993a, 1993b) include the following: (1) modeling cases of observed "success" in policy implementation; (2) modeling cases in which success might have been expected but which produced disappointing results in practice; (3) examining structurally "easy" settings, interunit implementation cases in which substantial institutionalization allows for a more readily interpretable modeling effort; and (4) explicating discrete, identifiable, recurring, and potentially significant portions of a larger and more complicated interorganizational setting. Further, to the extent that these research approaches yield insights into the world of interorganizational implementation, they may also generate implications for management.

6. Ostrom's terminology (1990) may be helpful here: the meta-questions of institutions for policy making—"constitutional" questions—may be addressable in part via rational choice approaches; and may in turn carry fairly direct implications for managers of implementation.

References

Agranoff, Robert. 1991. "Human Services Integration: Past and Present Challenges in Public Administration." *Public Administration Review* 51:533–542.

Alt, James E., and Barry Eichengreen. 1987. "Overlapping and Simultaneous Games: Theory and Applications." Paper presented at the NBER Conference on the Political Economy of International Macroeconomic Policy Coordination, Andover, Mass.

Alt, James E., Robert D. Putnam, and Kenneth A. Shepsle. 1988. "The Architecture of Linkage." Paper presented at the Workshop on Connected Games: Theory, Methodology, and Applications, Max-Planck-Institut für Gesellschaftsforschung, Cologne.

Axelrod, Robert M. 1984. *The Evolution of Cooperation.* New York: Basic Books.

Bardach, Eugene. 1977. *The Implementation Game.* Cambridge: MIT Press.

Bendor, Jonathan. 1990. "Formal Models of Bureaucracy: A Review," in Naomi Lynn and Aaron Wildavsky, eds., *Public Administration: The State of the Discipline.* Chatham, N.J.: Chatham House.

Chubb, John. 1985. "The Political Economy of Federalism." *American Political Science Review* 79:994–1015.

Eckstein, Harry. 1991. "Rationality and Frustration in Political Behavior," in K. R. Moore, ed., *The Economic Approach to Politics: A Critical Reassessment of the Theory of Rational Action.* New York: Harper Collins.

Elster, Jon. 1989. *The Cement of Society: A Study of Social Order.* New York: Cambridge University Press.

Friend, John K., J. M. Power, and Chris J. L. Yewlett. 1974. *Public Planning: The Inter-Corporate Dimension.* London: Tavistock.

Gage, Robert W., and Myrna P. Mandell, eds. 1990. *Strategies for Managing Intergovernmental Policies and Networks.* New York: Praeger.

Goggin, Malcolm L., Ann O'M. Bowman, James P. Lester, and Laurence J. O'Toole Jr. 1990. *Policy Implementation: Toward a Third Generation.* Glenview, Ill.: Scott Foresman/Little, Brown.

Hanf, Kenneth I. 1992. "Networks as Purposeful Instruments of Policy Management." Paper presented at the Workshop on Management of Interorganisational Networks, European Consortium for Political Research, Limerick, Ireland, March 30–April 4.

Hanf, Kenneth I., and Laurence J. O'Toole Jr. 1992. "Revisiting Old Friends: Networks, Implementation Structures, and the Management of Inter-organizational Relations." *European Journal of Political Research* 21:163–180.

Hardin, Garrett. 1968. "The Tragedy of the Commons." *Science* 162:1243–1248.

Kahneman, Daniel, and Amos Tversky. 1984. "Choices, Values, and Frames." *American Psychologist* 39:341–350.

Kettl, Donald F. 1993. *Sharing Power: Public Governance and Private Markets.* Washington, D.C.: Brookings Institution.

Kingdon, John W. 1984. *Agendas, Alternatives, and Public Policy.* Boston: Little, Brown.

Lynn, Laurence E., Jr. 1993. "Policy Achievement as a Collective Good: A Strategic

Perspective on Managing Social Programs," in Barry Bozeman, ed., *Public Management: The State of the Art,* pp. 108–133. San Francisco: Jossey-Bass.

Mandell, Myrna. 1984. "Application of Network Analysis to the Implementation of a Complex Project." *Human Relations* 37:659–679.

Mayntz, Renate, and Fritz W. Scharpf. 1975. *Policy Making in German Federal Bureaucracy.* Amsterdam: Elsevier.

Mazmanian, Daniel A., and Paul A. Sabatier. 1989. *Implementation and Public Policy,* rev. ed. Latham, Md.: University Press of America.

Nakamura, Robert T. 1990. "The Japan External Trade Organization and Import Promotion: A Case Study in the Implementation of Symbolic Policy Goals," in Dennis J. Palumbo and Donald J. Calista, eds., *Implementation and the Policy Process: Opening Up the Black Box,* pp. 67–86. Westport, Conn.: Greenwood Press.

Noll, Roger, and Barry Weingast. 1991. "Rational Actor Theory, Social Norms, and Policy Implementation: Applications to Administrative Processes and Bureaucratic Culture," in K. R. Moore, ed., *The Economic Approach to Politics: A Critical Reassessment of the Theory of Rational Action.* New York: Harper Collins.

Ostrom, Elinor. 1986a. "An Agenda for the Study of Institutions." *Public Choice* 48:3–25.

———. 1986b. "A Method of Institutional Analysis," in Franz-Xaver Kaufmann, Giandomenico Majone, and Vincent Ostrom, eds., *Guidance, Control, and Evaluation in the Public Sector.* New York: Walter de Gruyter.

———. 1990. *Governing the Commons.* Cambridge: Cambridge University Press.

O'Toole, Laurence J., Jr. 1983. "Interorganizational Cooperation and the Implementation of Labour Market Training Policies: Sweden and the Federal Republic of Germany." *Organization Studies* 4:129–150.

———. 1986. "Policy Recommendations for Multi-Actor Implementation: An Assessment of the Field." *Journal of Public Policy* 6:181–210.

———. 1988. "Strategies for Intergovernmental Management: Implementing Programs in Interorganizational Networks." *International Journal of Public Administration* 11:417–441.

———. 1989. "Goal Multiplicity in the Implementation Setting: Subtle Impacts and the Case of Wastewater Treatment Privatization." *Policy Studies Journal* 18:3–22.

———. 1993a. "Applying Rational Choice Contributions to Multiorganizational Policy Implementation," in James L. Perry, ed., *Research in Public Administration,* 2:79–119. Greenwich, Conn.: JAI Press.

———. 1993b. "Multiorganizational Policy Implementation: Some Limitations and Possibilities for Rational Choice Contributions," in Fritz W. Scharpf, ed., *Games in Hierarchies and Networks,* pp. 1–39. London: Westview.

Palumbo, Dennis J., and Donald J. Calista, eds. 1990. *Implementation and the Policy Process: Opening up the Black Box.* Westport, Conn.: Greenwood Press.

Pressman, Jeffrey, and Aaron Wildavsky. 1984. *Implementation,* 3d ed. Berkeley: University of California Press.

Provan, Keith G., and H. Brinton Milward. 1991. "Institutional-Level Norms and Organizational Involvement in a Service-Implementation Network." *Journal of Public Administration Research and Theory* 1:391–417.

Sabel, Charles F. 1993. "Constitutional Ordering in Historical Context," in Fritz W. Scharpf, ed., *Games in Hierarchies and Networks,* pp. 65–123. London: Westview.

Scharpf, Fritz W. 1978. "Interorganizational Policy Studies: Issues, Concepts, and Perspectives," in Kenneth I. Hanf and Scharpf, eds., *Interorganizational Policy Making.* London: Sage.

———. 1990. "Games Real Actors Could Play: The Problem of Connectedness." Manuscript, Max-Planck-Institut für Gesellschaftsforschung, Cologne.

———. 1991. "Games Real Actors Could Play: The Challenge of Complexity." *Journal of Theoretical Politics* 3:277–304.

———, ed. 1993. *Games in Hierarchies and Networks.* London: Westview.

Stoker, Robert B. 1991. *Reluctant Partners: Implementing Federal Policy.* Pittsburgh: University of Pittsburgh Press.

Thompson, James D. 1967. *Organizations in Action.* New York: McGraw-Hill.

Tsebelis, George. 1990. *Nested Games.* Berkeley and Los Angeles: University of California Press.

IV.

Bringing Theory and Practice Together

12.

Critical Incidents and Emergent Issues in Managing Large-scale Change

**John M. Bryson, Fran Ackerman,
Colin Eden, and Charles B. Finn**

History is one damn thing after another.
—Robert Sherrill

If we don't succeed, we run the risk of failure.
—Dan Quayle, former vice president of the United States

We didn't know where we were 'til we got there.
— John Dankworth, British jazz musician and conductor

The public sector has been subject to persistent calls for change. The latest round in the United States includes exhortations, among other things, to "reinvent government" (Osborne and Gaebler, 1992; Thompson and Jones, 1994), "break through bureaucracy" (Barzelay, 1992), and innovate in various ways (National Commission on the Public Service, 1989; National Commission on the State and Local Public Service, 1993). In the United Kingdom, the "Thatcher Revolution" has brought enormous and rapid changes to the public sector, with more change on the agenda no matter which party wins the next election. What remains relatively unexplored is exactly how the leaders, managers, and other stakeholders involved are to manage the transitions from one state to another with minimum pain and maximum benefit.

This chapter seeks to make a small contribution toward rectifying that shortcoming. The chapter presents an analysis of "critical incidents" in the management of two large-scale public sector change efforts, one in the United States involving a large public school district, and one in the United Kingdom involving a major part of the British prison system. Based on the analysis, we argue that there are a number of "emergent issues" that must be managed effectively if change efforts—particularly those involving outside consultants and facilitators—are to be successful.

There are books and articles that highlight all or most of the issues identified in this research (see Benveniste, 1989, and Pettigrew, Ferlie, and McKee, 1992, for two excellent examples). What these works generally do not do is clarify the systemic nature of the interconnections among the issues, nor do they point out how the issues are connected to, and flow out of, underlying critical incidents, or instantiations, of the issues. As a result, most works provide neither the systemic overview nor the underlying detail to help researchers or practitioners understand adequately the management of change. We offer at least one way of looking at the management of change that articulates the issues that are likely to emerge in a change process, their interconnections, and their origins in an underlying series of critical incidents.

We suggest that those in charge of managing change, as well as consultants and facilitators, recognize and manage an agenda of emergent issues, each consisting of a set of potential critical incidents that are related to the content, context, process, and outcomes of change efforts. Further, we argue that if adequate attention is paid to managing these "portfolios" of incidents, the chances of the change effort succeeding are enhanced. On the other hand, while we regard successful management of these issues as a necessary condition for success, doing so is not sufficient to guarantee a successful overall result. Too much either cannot or should not be controlled to allow for such guarantees.

Methodology

Two parallel research projects focused on the identification of critical incidents in a major change effort. The first effort involved the planned change of a large suburban school district in the United States. Bryson and Finn acted as consultants and facilitators to the district board and administration over the course of the process. In the United Kingdom, the effort involved a major part of the British prison system. Eden and Ackerman acted as consultants and facilitators to the senior management in charge of that effort. The consultants helped design and provide a kind of "group decision support" (Eden and Radford, 1990) to the actors who had major responsibility for the change effort.

Each project used a combination of the methodology developed by John

Bryson for strategic planning in public and nonprofit organizations (Bryson, 1988 [1995], 1994; Bryson and Roering, 1988) and the methodology developed in the United Kingdom by Colin Eden, Fran Ackerman, and others known as Strategic Options Development and Analysis (SODA) (Eden and Huxham, 1986; Eden, 1989; Eden, Ackermann, and Cropper, 1992). The efforts involved fairly broad participation by decision makers and various stakeholder representatives. Shared group "strategy maps" were developed that consisted of goals, strategic issues, and options for addressing the issues. The maps served as "facilitative devices" (Eden, 1989; Bryson and Finn, 1995) that focused group attention on what they thought should be done and why, over the course of the change efforts. The projects were undertaken after all of the authors had satisfied themselves that they had relatively similar ways of working and relatively similar "worlds-taken-for-granted" about consultation and facilitation practice.

The study employed a "grounded theory" approach to research (Glaser and Strauss, 1967). The authors decided that each team of researchers would keep a careful log of events that occurred over the course of their respective change efforts. In particular, each team would search for what appeared to be critical incidents. The authors then agreed to search for any patterning to the critical incidents across the two change efforts and whether there appeared to be a set of change management issues that emerged from the incidents.

Mapping Critical Incidents

Critical incidents methodology has a long history. It has been used extensively and effectively to isolate key dimensions of roles, jobs, and activities within organizations. More recently, it has been used to gather and analyze information about ethics, attitudes, and other topics (Clawson, 1992). The two classic sources on the use of the method are Flanagan (1954) and Campbell et al. (1970).

Critical incidents are events that are particularly consequential. For our purposes, we used a "rough and ready" guide to what might constitute candidate critical incidents. In particular, we were intested in events that had one or more of several characteristics. An event could be termed a critical incident if it were

—a turning point, or "flip-flop";

—a particularly memorable episode or distinct piece of action that stood out from the flow, for example, one that was talked about by many people as being "critical";

—a "fan" or "junction point" offering multiple possible choices in which a decision about which choice to make was made deliberately;

—a point at which alternative futures became apparent;

—a point at which something "fundamental" happened, or an important milestone was reached;

—an event that provided participants with a particularly important, and often unexpected, insight into the nature of their situation or the methods they were using;

—something that stopped the participants or the consultants "in their tracks";

—something the participants or consultants were glad we got "right," or were "spot on"; or something they or we were really glad we did not get wrong; or

—something the participants or consultants were distressed to find we had "screwed up" or gotten "wrong."

The benefits of cataloging events that have one or more of the above characteristics are several:

—There is an emphasis on observable behaviors.

—Data are collected from the actors' perspectives—including those of the researchers, who were also active participants in the change efforts.

—The approach generates rich qualitative data.

—The incidents are helpful for constructing grounded theory, that is, for developing a theoretical model from the data.

—The incidents are particularly helpful for highlighting what are likely to be situationally specific aspects of the change efforts.

—The catalog of events helps researchers develop a comprehensive picture of both change and stability.

—The method can assist with the discovery of more universal as well as more contingent behaviors.

—The critical incidents method has a proven track record.

In spite of the many benefits of the critical incidents method, there are several difficulties inherent in its use. First, participants may not realize the consequential nature of events as they occur. However, since we had an opportunity to review our logs in the light of subsequent experience with each change effort, we have some confidence that a major portion of the critical incidents was captured. On the other hand, since each team acted as outside consultants and facilitators, we were not privy to everything that happened in each case.

While we remained in frequent contact with our sources inside each organization, the chances are high that we missed at least some of the critical incidents.

Second, the method relies to a considerable degree on the subjective impressions of the participants and ourselves. They and we have perceptual filters that may blind us to what actually occurred, in contrast to our interpretations of what happened. On the other hand, the collection of a large number of incidents and the discipline of having frequent conversations about them within each team and between teams reduces some of this risk.

Third, the method generates good qualitative data but little quantitative data. A typical way of countering this problem is to use critical incidents studies as a means of developing more quantitative rating scales, such as behaviorally anchored rating scales (BARS) or behavior observation scales (BOS). We view this research as essentially exploratory, and thus are not seeking to develop such scales at present. On the other hand, a possible aim of future research might be the development of such scales.

Finally, a large sample of critical incidents may be needed to conduct a valid study. Each of our projects resulted in scores of incidents, but whether there is some "correct" number of incidents, whether we got the "right" ones, and whether they are all "critical" remain open questions. We view this study as the first of several that we hope will result in greater assurance that we have the appropriate means of identifying critical issues and that we have a reasonably valid grasp on the emergent change management issues they represent.

Mapping Emergent Issues

As the critical incidents were identified, they were tracked and mapped to record their relationship to one another within and across projects. In exploring the critical incidents, we searched for common themes that "held" sets of incidents together. The mapping process, and the reflection which it represented, gradually resulted in the identification of eight "emergent" clusters of incidents (Eden, 1989; Eden, Ackerman, and Cropper, 1992). These issues are discussed in the next section. Also discussed are the change management goals toward which effective management of the issues is presumed to lead.

The emergent issues that arose out of the critical incidents signal one or more of three kinds of themes. First, they can represent an area of change management in which particular attention must be devoted to the design, implementation, or monitoring and review of the change process. Second, they may highlight an area that requires concentrated attention that goes far beyond what is commonly recognized in the literature. And third, they may point to the importance of being able to manage the flow of otherwise noncritical events. In other words, disruptions in the flow of more "normal" events could severely threaten the success of the project, resulting in a "crisis" (Bryson, 1981), "accident" (Perrow, 1984), or "chaos" (Kiel, 1994).

Results

In this section, we present the results of our analyses in the form of a series of maps. While the maps were constructed from the "bottom up" (from critical incidents to emergent issues to purposes to be served by effective management of the issues), it is easier to understand them if they are presented first from the "top down" (that is, by starting with purposes, discussing the change management issues, and then presenting illustrations of critical incidents represented by the issues). Figure 1 presents the extreme "top end" of the map, along with the eight emergent issues. The purpose of attention to the emergent issues (which are presented in more detail in subsequent maps) is to allow change managers to pay careful, perhaps even meticulous, attention to selected aspects of *process design, implementation,* and *monitoring and review.* We argue that by doing so they will be in a better position to ensure continual *value-added* to the change effort through attention to the systemic interaction of process, content, context, and outcomes. By value-added, we mean better intermediate and final change effort outcomes than otherwise would be the case.

Figure 1 also indicates how the emergent issues contribute to these larger themes and the overall purpose of achieving continual value-added to the change effort. As noted, there are eight emergent issues arrayed around, and contributing to, the themes. In all of the figures, "arrows in" indicate what it would take to achieve something, while "arrows out" indicate the likely consequences of having done something. The set of arrows in and out represent the "meaning" of a construct (Eden, Ackerman, and Cropper, 1992). The emergent issues are as follows:

—Gain the commitment and trust of internal stakeholders to one another and to the consultants (EI1).

—Carefully manage the partnership development between the primary client, "partners," and consultants (EI6).

—Specifically tailor tools and techniques, agendas, and stage management to specific situations (EI7).

—Gain both emotional and reasoned commitment to specific actions (EI8).

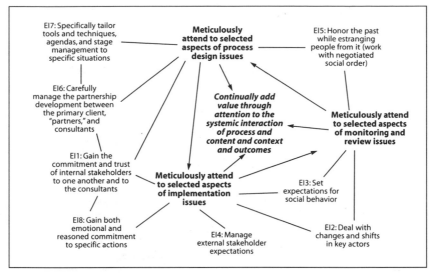

Figure 1   Change Management Goals and Emergent Issues

—Manage external stakeholder expectations (EI4).

—Set expectations for social behavior (EI3).

—Deal with changes and shifts in key actors (EI2).

—Honor the past while estranging people from it (EI5).

These eight issues appear to be linked in a fairly straightforward way to the larger themes. Meticulously attending to selected aspects of *process design* depends primarily on tailoring tools and techniques and other aspects of the process to the situation, carefully managing the partnership between insiders and outsiders, gaining the trust and commitment of internal stakeholders to one another and to the consultants, and honoring the past while estranging people from it. Meticulously attending to *implementation* relies on gaining the commitment and trust of internal stakeholders, and it also depends on gaining both an emotional and reasoned commitment to specific actions, managing external stakeholder expectations, setting expections for social behavior, and dealing with changes and shifts in key actors. Meticulously attending to *monitoring and review* issues depends on setting expectations for social behavior and dealing with changes and shifts in key actors, and, in addition, on honoring the past while estranging people from it. We now move to discussing the emergent issues in more detail, in particular, by elaborating on a sample of the critical incidents that constitute each issue.

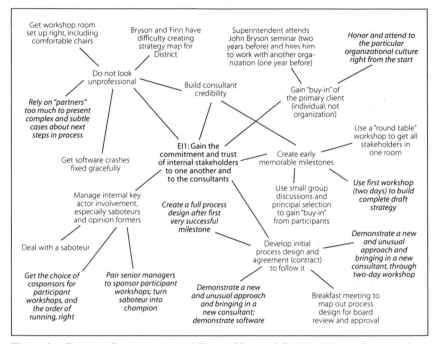

Figure 2   Gain the Commitment and Trust of Internal Stakeholders to One Another and to the Consultants

Gain the Commitment and Trust of Internal Stakeholders to One Another and to the Consultants

Gaining the commitment and trust of internal stakeholders appears to be the most complex emergent issue, as it consists of six subissues (see fig. 2). Gaining the commitment and trust of internal stakeholders appears to depend on gaining "buy-in" of the primary client (an individual, not the organization); building consultant credibility; developing an initial process design and agreement (in our cases, contracts); creating early memorable milestones; the consultants' *not* appearing unprofessional; and managing the involvement of internal key actors, especially that of opinion leaders and saboteurs.

Representative critical incidents from the two change efforts have been arrayed around these subthemes. Gaining buy-in of the primary client followed different routes in the two efforts. In the school district case, the superintendent (the primary client) had attended a two-day strategic planning training session led by Bryson two years before the project began. That initial contact led to a series of discussions that ultimately resulted in a contract. In the prisons case, initial contact with Eden and Ackermann was through staff, which later led to meeting with the chief executive (the primary client).

Building consultant credibility was a result both of creating early memorable milestones and of *not* appearing to be unprofessional. In the school district case, an important early milestone was the creation of a "community roundtable." Representatives of all key stakeholder groups participated, and the meeting resulted in recognition of the need for a major change effort, as well as general agreement on the basic goals of such an effort. In the prisons case, a parallel event was a two-day workshop involving high-level stakeholders that resulted in an agreed-upon basic strategy outline.

Not appearing unprofessional was a subtheme with an embarrassing number of critical incidents around it. In the school district case, Bryson and Finn found they had difficulty creating a strategy map for the district, a requirement of the SODA method. In addition, a computerized mapping program they needed crashed on them in the midst of a school board retreat they were facilitating. They had to scramble to figure out how to fix the computer before they risked being written off as incompetent. In the prisons case, Eden and Ackermann had to find a way of fixing the damage done when their internal partners presented too simplistic and naive an account of the change process to key stakeholders at a major meeting. Eden and Ackermann had to do so diplomatically to avoid embarrassing their partners, but they also had to present a more realistic view or their credibility as consultants would be damaged.

Managing internal key actor involvement, especially saboteurs and opinion leaders, also was important to gaining the commitment of trust of internal actors. In the schools case, one critical incident occurred when the superintendent confronted the district's personnel director, who was leaking information about the board's and superintendent's strategies to the teachers' union. The leaks stopped, and ultimately the personnel director became a supporter of the change effort. In the prisons case, the careful pairing of a potential saboteur with a supporter of the change effort resulted in the former becoming a strong supporter of the change effort.

Developing an initial process design and agreement to follow it is the final subtheme contributing to gaining commitment and trust. In the school district case, one critical incident was roughing out a possible process design during a breakfast meeting with the superintendent and assistant superintendent. The design became the basis for discussions with the school board and, ultimately, with minor modifications, became the process that was followed.

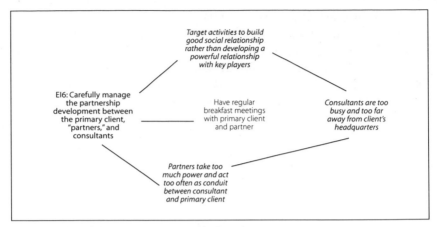

Figure 3   Carefully Manage Partnership Development

In the prisons case, an extended process design was formulated after the first very successful milestone, a workshop that the consultants presumed would be a "one-off," or one-time, affair, but actually led to several more.

Carefully Manage the Partnership Development between the Primary Client, "Partners," and Consultants

A consultant-assisted and facilitated change process typically is based in part on a sound relationship between key organizational actors and the consultants (Schein, 1988; Bellman, 1990). We have found it useful to distinguish between "sponsors" and "champions" (Bryson and Roering, 1988); or alternatively, "primary clients" and "partners." The sponsors, or primary clients, are those people in a position of power and authority who legitimize and protect the process and expect that it will happen, but who do not necessarily do the day-to-day work of making it happen. That task falls to the champions, or partners. In the school district case, the sponsors were the board and superintendent, and particularly the superintendent. The superintendent also was a champion at times, but the prime champion was the assistant superintendent. In the prisons case, the primary client was the chief executive of the system, while the champions, or partners, were two staff officials.

In the school district case, the relationship was managed primarily through a series of regular breakfast meetings that typically lasted two to three hours (see fig. 3). Many of these ranked as critical incidents because of the understandings, strategies, and tactics developed there. In the prisons case, there was

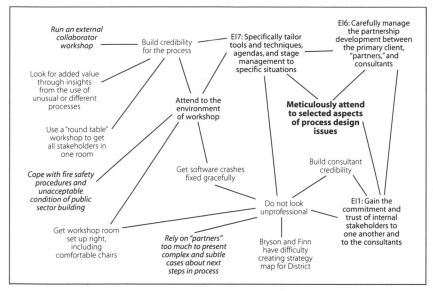

Figure 4   Specifically Tailor Tools and Techniques, Agendas, and Stage Management

less attention to management of the relationship. As a result, the partners in the prisons case may have assumed too much power and too often served as a conduit, or undesirable filter, between the consultants and the primary client. The consultants thus were often "out of the loop" and less effective than they otherwise might have been.

Specifically Tailor Tools and Techniques, Agendas, and Stage Management to Specific Situations

Tailoring the tools and techniques, agendas, and stage management to specific situations is a basic part of the facilitator's kit bag. Figure 4 highlights how intimately this set of requirements and skills is connected to other emergent issues and subissues, such as gaining the commitment and trust of internal stakeholders and carefully managing the partnership development, building consultant credibility, and not appearing unprofessional. In the school district case, the use of the community round table and strategy mapping (a new approach for the participants) provided important critical incidents that highlighted the importance of carefully tailoring interventions. In the prisons case, representative critical incidents involved dealing with a badly designed meeting space and getting workshop rooms set up properly.

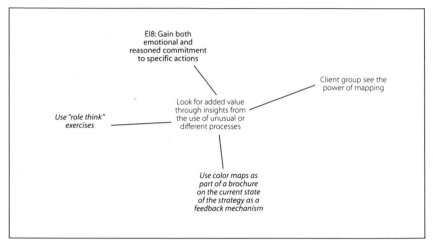

Figure 5   Gain Both Emotional and Reasoned Commitment to Specific Actions

Gain Both Emotional and
Reasoned Commitment to Specific Actions

The primary route to gaining both emotional and reasoned commitment to specific actions was through the use of unusual processes, or processes different from most change efforts (see fig. 5). For example, in the school district case, the SODA method and a software specifically designed to support it (GC COPE) was used to help the board, superintendent, and cabinet alter their view of the world and reach specific commitments about what the district's mission and goals should be and about what strategic issues should be addressed as part of their change process. The workshop at which the draft map was first presented and then refined was an emotional "high" for those involved, and in large measure they followed through on the commitments made there. Similarly, the mapping exercises that were part of the workshops used in the prisons case also led to reasoned insights, commitments, and emotional satisfaction with the strategic plan that resulted. Such participatory methods were quite outside the participants' ordinary practice.

Manage External Stakeholder Expectations

A number of critical incidents were concerned with the management of external stakeholder expectations (see fig. 6). In the case of the school district, three in particular stand out. One was the community round table already discussed. Another was the hiring of a new principal at a high school. The way

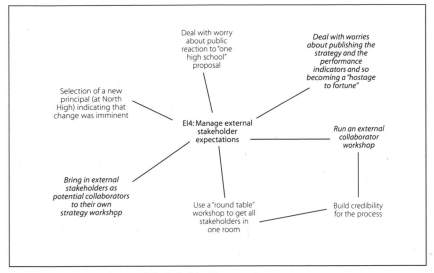

Figure 6   Manage External Stakeholder Expectations

the job description was developed based on community input, and the way the process was managed so that someone from outside the community was hired, indicated that change was imminent. Finally, there was the substantial public relations campaign that was undertaken to deal with public reaction to the board's first plan (subsequently changed) to merge the district's two high schools into a single, quite large high school.

The prisons case also had critical incidents related to this issue. The first was the running of a workshop for "external collaborators" of the prison system, such as prisoners' families. This was a "first," and indicated that major changes might be possible. Another incident focused on a decision about whether to publish strategy performance indicators in the system's strategic plan, because doing so might make the system a "hostage to fortune." The client decided not to publish the indicators.

Set Expectations for Social Behavior

Expectations for social behavior were set in several ways (see fig. 7). For example, in the school district case, a special event was designed to initiate the work of the task forces used to explore strategic issues. The event was used specifically to set expectations for the task forces. In the prison case, known skeptics were recruited to start workshops and set expectations, based on the

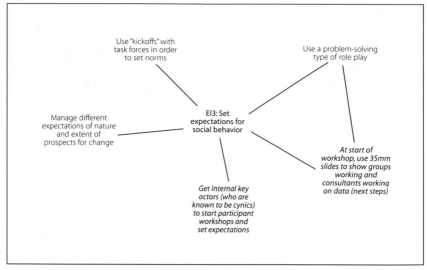

Figure 7   Set Expectations for Social Behavior

belief that their own expectations probably would be altered as well. In addition, people inexperienced with some of the unusual change management tools and techniques were shown 35-millimeter slides of how other groups used the techniques so that they could imagine themselves using them.

Deal with Changes and Shifts in Key Actors

Changes in key actors affected both efforts significantly (see fig. 8). In the school district, the president of the school board lost his seat on the board in a districtwide election, in large part because of his outspoken support for the need to change the teacher contract. The hiring of a new principal for one of the high schools was another change that altered district politics. In the prisons case, the primary client was promoted to another job and, as a result, new actors came on the scene who were less keen on change.

Honor the Past while Estranging People from It

Getting people to break with the past was a major focus of several critical incidents (see fig. 9). In the case of the school district, it was important that the board be assured that previous work they had done on goal-setting would not be lost. In the prisons case, participants needed to have their particular "cul-

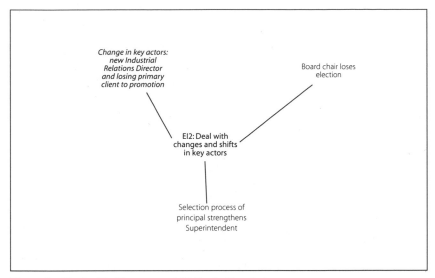

Figure 8   Deal with Changes and Shifts in Key Actors

ture" honored before they were willing to embrace any changes. Further, while the chief executive was open to major ("clean sheet") changes, it was important that the changes emerge organically from the process and from what the prison service was already doing.

Outcomes

In both change efforts, significant outcomes were achieved, although the record was mixed. In the school district case, most of the actions outlined in the district's strategic plan have been taken or are under way. The district is moving toward site-based management of its schools, the teachers' contract has been altered, curriculum reforms are under way, efforts are being made to increase the use of technology in the schools, and so on. In addition, after two bond referenda failed, a third one was passed that allows a new high school to be built on the site of an old high school, which will be mostly demolished. The strategic plan the board adopted thus is well on its way to full implementation. On the other hand, the board has been altered significantly in several elections, in part as a consequence of the dissatisfaction of various stakeholder groups with the change effort. Nonetheless, the change effort overall must be viewed as a "big win" (Bryson and Crosby, 1992, pp. 228–233).

In the prisons case, the management team began to work as a team for the

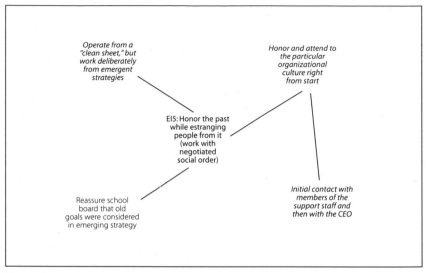

Figure 9   Honor the Past while Estranging People from It

first time, and a potential saboteur of the change effort became one of its greatest supporters. Media relations were dramatically improved, at least until a change in ministers led to a worsening of media relations. A number of collaborative strategies were undertaken with stakeholders, such as trade unions, who traditionally had been ignored or treated as adversaries. And prison "regimes" were altered. Many of the gains were lost, however, when the system's chief executive, or primary client, was promoted. Nonetheless, the plan that was developed as part of the process still provides the starting point for considering any changes in the system, so all was not completely lost.

The outcomes in both cases seem to be related to the management of the critical incidents that occured throughout the change efforts. These incidents often were clear turning points that resulted in desirable or undesirable intermediate outcomes and which led to either enhanced or diminished chances of overall success. Sometimes these incidents were managed well, sometimes not, and sometimes they could not be managed at all.

Conclusions

One thing that is clear from the analysis is how complex a major public sector change effort is likely to be. The mélange of critical incidents—and the emergent issues they represent—are likely to tax the attention, intelligence, powers, and will of anyone or any group interested in initiating and managing such a change effort. There are simply so many ways for things to fall apart, or to *not* come together, that perhaps we should *expect* failure, as Pressman and Wildavsky (1973) warned us long ago. Alternatively, success in change efforts may be more a matter of chance than good management, since public sector settings might well be characterized as "garbage cans" or "organized anarchies" (Cohen, March, and Olsen, 1972; Kingdon, 1995).

On the other hand, the identification of an "emergent" structure of issues based on the critical incidents is a reason for hope. The emergent issues may be thought of as a change agenda to be managed effectively if the chances of overall success are to be increased.

Viewing change management as the management of a set of emergent issues is different from more typical, phase-based approaches to change (Van de Ven, 1980). Instead of thinking in terms of a set sequence of phases to be followed as part of any change effort, it is probably more useful to think of the emergent issues as a set of eight parallel "tracks" consisting of critical incidents that must be managed effectively if the overall change effort is to be successful. A cumulation of successfully managed critical incidents across tracks is more likely to result in success than a cumulation of unsuccessfully managed incidents. This is not to say that phases are unimportant, only that rigid sequences of phases are unlikely to be found unless they are legislated; and, even then, circular flows of activity involving many of the tracks are probably more likely than set sequences of activity that occur in lockstep fashion across the tracks (Van de Ven, Angle, and Poole, 1989).

Viewing change in this way highlights the complex nature of leadership and the many other roles that are present in change efforts. Positional and nonpositional leaders, sponsors, champions, and various stakeholder groups all have a part to play. Only a kind of collective leadership is likely to result in successful change efforts (Bryson and Crosby, 1992). Certainly, more work is needed to clarify the ways in which various actors are necessary for successful change to occur, or to clarify the ways in which change can be stymied.

Finally, the change efforts highlight the fact that those interested in, and charged with, major public sector change efforts probably need some kind of group decision and action support system (Rosenhead, 1989; Bostrom et al., 1992). There is simply too much information to be processed, there are too many roles to be played, and there are too many decisions and actions to be taken for change managers not to wish for adequate supports. The development of public sector group decision support systems is likely to be an important area of work in the coming years.

In summary, by now the reasons for our choice of epigrams at the beginning of this chapter should be clear. The list of critical incidents often made them seem like "one damn thing after another." Nevertheless, unless these various critical incidents could be managed successfully, an overall failure of the change efforts clearly was possible. And finally, in mapping the incidents, we had no clear idea where we were headed until we got there. We hope the readers have found the journey useful, and, in particular, will find the mapping of critical incidents, the management of emergent issues, and the tracks idea worthy of pursuit.

References

Barzelay, M. 1992. *Breaking through Bureaucracy.* Berkeley: University of California Press.

Bellman, G. 1990. *The Consultant's Calling.* San Francisco: Jossey-Bass.

Benveniste, G. 1989. *Mastering the Politics of Planning.* San Francisco: Jossey-Bass.

Bostrom, R., R. Watson, and S. Kinney. 1992. *Computer Augmented Teamwork: A Guided Tour.* New York: Van Nostrand Reinhold.

Bryson, J. 1981. "A Perspective on Planning and Crises in the Public Sector." *Strategic Management Journal* 2:181–196.

———. 1988, rev. ed. 1995. *Strategic Management for Public and Nonprofit Organizations.* San Francisco: Jossey-Bass.

———. 1994. "Strategic Planning and Action Planning for Nonprofit Organizations," in R. Herman, ed., *The Jossey-Bass Handbook of Nonprofit Leadership and Management.* San Francisco: Jossey-Bass.

Bryson, J., and B. Crosby. 1992. *Public Leadership, Tackling Public Problems in a Shared-Power World.* San Francisco: Jossey-Bass.

Bryson, J., and C. Finn. 1995. "Development and Use of Strategy Maps to Enhance Organizational Performance," in A. Halachmi and G. Bouckaert, eds., *The Challenge of Management in a Changing World.* San Francisco: Jossey-Bass.

Bryson, J., and W. Roering. 1988. "Initiation of Strategic Planning by Governments." *Public Administration Review* 48, no. 6: 995–1004.

Campbell, J., M. Dunnette, E. Lawler, and K. Weick. 1970. *Managerial Behavior, Performance, and Effectiveness.* New York: McGraw-Hill.

Clawson, V. 1992. "The Role of the Facilitator in Computer-Assisted Environments: A Critical Incidents Study." Ph.D. diss., Walden University.

Cohen, M., J. March, and J. Olsen. 1972. "A Garbage Can Model of Organization and Choice." *Administrative Science Quarterly* 17:1–25.

Eden, C. 1989. "Strategic Options Development and Analysis—SODA)," in J. Rosenhead, ed., *Rational Analysis for a Problematic World.* New York: Wiley.

Eden, C., F. Ackerman, and S. Cropper. 1992. "The Analysis of Cause Maps." *Journal of Management Studies* 29, no. 3: 309–324.

Eden, C., and C. Huxham. 1986. "Action-Oriented Strategic Management." *Journal of the Operational Research Society* 39, no. 10: 889–899.

Eden, C., and J. Radford. 1990. *Tackling Strategic Problems: The Role of Group Decision Support.* Newbury Park, Calif.: Sage.

Flanagan, J. 1954. "The Critical Incident Technique." *Psychological Bulletin* 51, no. 4: 327–358.

Glaser, B., and A. Strauss. 1967. *The Discovery of Grounded Theory.* Chicago: Aldine-Atherton.

Kiel, L. D. 1994. *Managing Chaos and Complexity in Government.* San Francisco: Jossey-Bass.

Kingdon, J. 1995. *Agendas, Alternatives, and Public Policies,* rev. ed. Boston: Little, Brown.

National Commission on the Public Service. 1989. *Leadership for America, Rebuilding the Public Service.* Lexington, Mass.: Lexington Books.

National Commission on the State and Local Public Service. 1993. *Hard Truths/Tough Choices: An Agenda for State and Local Reform.* Albany, N.Y.: The Nelson A. Rockefeller Institute of Government.

Osborne, D., and T. Gaebler. 1992. *Reinventing Government.* Reading, Mass.: Addison-Wesley.

Perrow, C. 1984. *Normal Accidents.* New York: Basic Books.

Pettigrew, A., E. Ferlie, and L. McKee. 1992. *Shaping Strategic Change.* Newbury Park, Calif.: Sage.

Pressman, J., and A. Wildavsky. 1973. *Implementation.* Berkeley: University of California Press.

Rosenhead, J. 1989. *Rational Analysis for a Problematic World.* New York: Wiley.

Schein, E. 1988. *Process Consultation: Its Role in Organizational Development,* 2d ed. Reading, Mass.: Addison-Wesley.

Thompson, F., and L. Jones. 1994. *Reinventing the Pentagon.* San Francisco: Jossey-Bass.

Van de Ven, A. 1980. "Problem Solving, Planning, and Innovation. Part 1, Test of the Program Planning Model." *Human Relations* 33:711–740.

Van de Ven, A., H. Angle, and M. S. Poole. 1989. *Research on the Management of Innovation.* New York: HarperCollins.

13.

Organizational Redesign in the Public Sector

James R. Thompson
and Patricia W. Ingraham

The conviction that public organizations should be made to operate more like private organizations has been the foundation of many public sector management reforms. President Clinton's effort to reinvent government is no exception. Although the introduction to Clinton's reinvention manifesto, the *Report of the National Performance Review,* questions the extent to which private sector models of organizational change are applicable to government, many of the actual recommendations in the report flow directly from private sector principles and presumed successes. The introduction to the report states, for example, that "our approach has much in common with other management philosophies, such as quality management and business process reengineering. But these management disciplines were developed for the private sector, where conditions are quite different . . . private sector management doctrines tend to overlook some central problems of government: its monopolies, its lack of a bottom line, its obsession with process rather than results" (U.S. National Performance Review 1993a, p. 8).

Despite this qualification, most of the *Report of the National Performance Review* relies heavily on private sector models. Chapter 2, entitled "Putting Customers First," includes the following subheadings: "Giving Customers a Voice—and a Choice," "Making Service Organizations Compete," "Creating Market Dynamics," and "Using Market Mechanisms to Solve Problems." Clearly, the private sector influence is very strong.

The success of the National Performance Review will depend to a very large extent on whether private sector models of organizational change are applicable to government. This chapter examines the application of a leading private sector model, business process reengineering, to one of the larger federal agencies, the Internal Revenue Service (IRS). Key components of the process reengineering model are reviewed, and the experience of the IRS in implementing the model is analyzed. The intent is to determine the ease of the "fit" between the private sector model and the public organization's reality.

Business Process Reengineering

Michael Hammer and James Champy popularized the technique of business process reengineering with their book, *Reengineering the Corporation* (1993). Hammer and Champy argue that the functional structures around which traditional organizations are organized create fragmented processes. In such organizations, each process requires numerous "hand-offs" between functional units which impede coordination and increase the incidence of errors. They take the position that a process orientation facilitates coordination between units and keeps the focus on the customer and what the customer values.

Hammer and Champy draw a distinction between business reengineering and other approaches to organizational change including quality management. They emphasize the radical nature of the change engendered by reengineering: "Business Reengineering means starting all over, starting from scratch" (1993, p. 2). They state that "quality programs work within the framework of a company's existing processes and seek to enhance them by means of . . . continuous incremental improvement" whereas reengineering "seeks breakthroughs, not by enhancing existing processes, but by discarding them and replacing them with entirely new ones" (1993, p. 49).

Elements of the model that Hammer and Champy develop include the use of case manager positions that combine functions and provide a single point of contact for the customer; the use of cross-functional teams to facilitate communication and coordination; and the reduction of checks and controls that add to costs, prolong processing, and do not add value for the customer.

The use of information technology is key to restructuring processes. Examples of "disruptive" technologies that provide an ability to "break the rules" of previous organizational practice include shared databases, expert systems, telecommunications networks, wireless data communication, and portable computers (1993, chap. 4).

Hammer and Champy provide some guidelines and cautions about redesigning organizations based on processes. They list common reasons for failure: (1) not changing other organizational systems, such as reward systems, to make them congruent with the new organization structure; (2) a tendency to "dissipate energy across many reengineering projects"; (3) the failure "to distinguish reengineering from other business improvement programs"; and (4) trying to "make reengineering happen without making anybody unhappy" (1993, chap. 14).

The business process redesign model used as a basis for the changes at IRS was developed at the Management Development Center at the University of Tennessee; it is summarized in a book edited by Michael Stahl and Gregory Bounds entitled *Competing Globally through Customer Value* (1992). Stahl and Bounds use the term "strategic suprasystems" to describe business processes that cross functional units: "These systems are large, complex, and run horizontally across the organization" (Kirby, 1992, p. 219).

The IRS also used the Juran Institute to assist in redesigning the organization. In contrast to Hammer and Champy, Juran's approach, as set forth in *Juran on Leadership for Quality* (1989), regards process redesign as entirely compatible with quality improvement programs. Juran's approach to quality management includes three elements: quality planning, quality control, and quality improvement. These correspond to reengineering, operation, and improvement. Juran urges companies to start with quality improvement efforts that are incremental in nature. These teams must provide opportunities for employee involvement in specific projects; they must also provide early and measurable returns on investment in quality management.

In contrast to quality improvement, quality planning requires companies to review "macroprocesses" that cross functional units and to focus on who the customers are, what their needs are, and how processes can be changed so that products include features that respond to those needs (Juran, 1989).

Juran emphasizes the importance of assigning "ownership" of each process to an individual manager. The owner is responsible for "defining the subprocesses," "identifying critical success factors and key dependencies," and "resolving or escalating cross-functional issues" (1989, p. 223).

Although each of the three models described above takes a slightly different approach to change, they are all centered on restructuring the organization around business processes. The IRS has developed a composite model by extracting elements from each of those described, as well as on the basis of advice from consultants and on lessons learned from various companies that have reengineered.

Reengineering the Internal Revenue Service

The Internal Revenue Service is in the relatively early stages of this major effort to change from a functionally based to a process-based organization. Information on both the intent of the change and actual experience to date was obtained through two sets of interviews with senior IRS personnel in September 1993 and September 1994 and from various documents describing the project.

The Impetus: Tax Systems Modernization

According to those interviewed, the magnitude of the present change had not been anticipated when a project to upgrade computer systems began in the late 1980s. The computer upgrading, called Tax Systems Modernization (TSM), is the third attempt in the last two decades to modernize the systems being used to process tax returns. The first two attempts, one during the 1970s and one from 1982 to 1986, faltered. The problems encountered were partly the result of concerns about the implications of equipment changes for privacy related issues and partly related to technical problems. As a result of these failures, the hardware and software being used by the IRS is extremely antiquated.

The dimensions of the problem were dramatically described by the director of the Systems Design Division, who observed that some of the machines now being used by the IRS will literally fall apart if not replaced within the decade, that the IRS has had to build its own parts shop to manufacture parts for computers that are no longer available on the market, that some of the "code" now being used dates from 1959, and that maintenance of both the code and the equipment is extremely costly to the Service.

These and other problems provided the impetus for reexamining agency structure. Initially, the modernization program was directed toward automating existing tasks and procedures. Reviews by two powerful outside agencies, however, forced the IRS to examine the option of restructuring the organization to take full advantage of the investment in modernizing the computer systems. The arguments presented in reviews by the General Accounting Office (GAO) and the National Academy of Sciences (NAS) were that by merely automating existing processes, the IRS would get only 10 percent of the potential benefit of systems modernization and would, in effect, waste time and money.

In testimony before the House Government Operations Subcommittee on Commerce, Consumer, and Monetary Affairs in July 1991, a representative of the GAO stated that the IRS *Design Master Plan for TSM* "does not provide a corresponding vision of how the new technology could enable the agency to transform its future organizational structures and business operations. . . . We think that the modernization effort should prompt IRS to engage in a comprehensive and thorough reexamination of not only its organizational structure but of its work processes and program strategies—in short, the way it does business across the entire agency" (U.S. General Accounting Office, 1991, pp. 1–2, 7).

Organizing around Core Business Systems

As a result of this external prodding, the IRS developed a "Business Vision" that calls for "fundamental changes in the way we do business, supported by Tax Systems Modernization and the introduction of new technology" (Philcox, 1992, p. 1). The plan includes three key elements: (1) dramatically reducing the burden on taxpayers; (2) generating substantial additional revenue through improved voluntary compliance; and (3) achieving significant quality-driven productivity gains throughout the IRS (1992, pp. 1–2).

Using business process reengineering concepts, IRS leadership decided to shift from a hierarchy that included a senior deputy commissioner, two deputy commissioners, and ten assistant commissioners, to a process-based organization headed by a deputy commissioner and six "business system owners." Functionally based units such as Collection, Examination, and Taxpayer Service and Returns Processing have been reorganized into the following business systems: Value Tracking, Informing and Educating, Managing Accounts, Ensuring Compliance, Resourcing, and Developing and Maintaining Systems. The number of layers of management are to be reduced from seven to five.

Extensive changes in organizational processes will be based on two studies that were commissioned by the agency leadership. Each study was conducted by a carefully selected task force comprised of agency employees regarded as "the most creative and progressive thinkers" in the organization. The District Organization Study (DOS) "defines a completely new District environment in which functionalism is virtually eliminated for activities involving face-to-face contact with our customers. Highly trained, multi-disciplined professional employees, supported by modern technology, will work in a substantially less hierarchical organization" (U.S. Internal Revenue Service, 1993a, p. 6). Perhaps the most radical change envisioned in the report, the creation of a position of "field service representative" to combine the positions of revenue agent, revenue officer, tax auditor, taxpayer service representative, and taxpayer service specialist, was not accepted by the IRS Executive Committee, although a "blended group" concept is being given consideration in its place. Also, although the report suggested cutting the number of district offices from sixty-three to as few as thirty-two, the executive committee decided that no district offices would be closed.

The Service Center Organization Study (SCOS) Task Force was given two constraints: lay off no current employees and maintain some level of employment at all ten service centers. The SCOS envisions a number of significant changes in IRS work processes that take advantage of the new technologies to be made available through TSM. Taxpayers would be able to make payments, enter into installment agreements, amend tax returns, and perform other transactions directly over the phone through use of voice response unit (VRU) technologies without using forms or having to deal directly with IRS employees. Customer service representatives would be trained to handle issues not resolvable through the VRU so that 95 percent of all inquiries are resolved in the first contact (U.S. Internal Revenue Service, 1993b).

A major emphasis would be placed on the electronic filing of tax returns. The report includes a recommendation that Congress pass legislation requiring electronic filing of all returns by preparers who file one hundred or more returns per year. Paper tax returns would be scanned using imaging technologies; tax refunds and payments would be made through the electronic transfer of funds; and returns processing would take place at only five of the ten sites currently used. Customer service sites would be reduced from forty-four to twenty-three (ibid.).

The changes now under way will take eight to nine years to fully implement. Tax systems modernization will cost a total of about $23 billion, $7.5 billion more than the cost of maintaining the present systems. The IRS sought and has received union cooperation in the changes in return for the issuance of a policy statement that no layoffs would result. The changes will allow dramatic improvements in productivity that could permit a reduction in the current workforce of 115,000 by as many as 20,000 positions. However, instead of downsizing, it is anticipated that many employees will be shifted into compliance activities where, it is claimed, there is a five-to-one payoff in increased returns and penalties for each dollar invested.

Communicating with Employees

An elaborate communications strategy has been developed to explain the changes to employees and to minimize resistance. The strategy includes preparation of an "IRS Managers' Communications Toolkit," which explains the changes in a question-and-answer format suitable for managers in conducting a dialogue with employees, a newsletter entitled *IRS Transitions,* and a "voice response system" that IRS employees can dial up on the telephone.

The Political Realities

Top officials at the IRS perceive the situation faced by the agency as a crisis. They express concern that absent the changes, the agency will not survive in its present form. They see threats both from the possible privatization of significant portions of the workload and from the potential transfer of tax collection to other agencies or to other levels of government.

One official presented several scenarios that could result from congressional dissatisfaction with the ineffectiveness of the present tax collection system. Alternatives that could be considered by Congress include the substitution of a value-added tax collected through the Federal Reserve banks for the income tax, contracting with state tax agencies for federal tax collection, and the transfer of some IRS functions to other agencies. All of these alternatives, of course, have significant implications for both the structure and the functions of the IRS.

An important consideration for IRS leaders is a perception that the fiscal environment will not allow continued increases in expenses. One official noted that between 1988 and 1993 the agency's budget increased from $5.8 billion to $7.5 billion and the number of employees increased from 85,000 to 115,000. His perception was that neither Congress nor the administration would continue to authorize such increases. The agency's former chief financial officer pointed out that it simply did not make sense for him to "draw down front-line people" in order to meet budget goals while maintaining large numbers of upper- and middle-level managers.

A document entitled "Reinventing the IRS," which is being distributed to employees, cites the following "troubling trends" in the five years prior to 1993:

—The delinquent accounts inventory has almost doubled to a likely-to-be-collected level of $27 billion.

—Although overall compliance rates are constant at 82.7 percent, the overall tax gap between income taxes due and paid has increased from a range between $82 billion and $94 billion to $110 billion and $127 billion.

—The nonfiler population has increased to about 10 million.

—Examination coverage is down from 1.1 percent to 0.95 percent.

—The percentage of callers getting through to an IRS assistor on the first try has fallen from around 80 percent to about 60 percent.

—Labor costs have increased by 37 percent (U.S. Internal Revenue Service, 1993c, p. 5).

Privately, top officials are passionate about the need for change. They express fear that as a perception of widespread noncompliance spreads, voluntary compliance rates will dip dramatically. They talk about the implications of efficient tax administration for the federal government's fiscal situation and for funding basic programs. They see very high stakes for the nation itself.

Centralization of Power

The restructuring will clearly result in a centralization of power within the agency. In addition to the reordering at the top and the replacement of the deputy commissioners and assistant commissioners by the business system owners, there will be a shift in power from the seven regional commissioners to the national office. During the agency's last major reorganization in the late 1940s, the regional offices were given considerable authority over policy issues. In the new structure, the number of regional offices will be reduced from seven to five and the size of each office will be cut from about 375 employees to about 100 employees. Major responsibilities of the regional commissioners will be transferred to the business system owners at the national office.

Timing

The target date for full implementation of the changes is 2001 (although this may be delayed by budget cuts). By 1996, the agency planned to have prototype sites available to test the new technologies.

Applying Private Sector Models of Change in the Public Sector

The IRS has chosen to implement these changes based largely on models developed in the private sector. The effort raises important questions and issues. First, to what extent are private sector models of organizational change, in this case business process reengineering, applicable in the public sector? Second, how do the peculiarities of the public sector environment affect implementation of this model? And third, what can we learn from the IRS experience that will be of use to other public organizations?

We examine these questions in the context of Rainey's list of distinctive characteristics of public management and public organizations (Rainey 1991).

Excerpts from that list are followed by a discussion of how each item relates to the IRS change process.

Oversight Agencies/Regulations
Distinctive Characteristics of Public Organizations. . . .
I.2   Presence of particularly elaborate and intensive formal legal constraints as a result of oversight by legislative branch, executive branch hierarchy and oversight agencies, and courts.

      a.   *More constraints on domains of operation and on procedures (less autonomy of managers in making such choices).*

      b.   *Greater tendency to proliferation of formal administrative controls.*

      c.   *Larger number of external sources of formal authority and influence, with greater fragmentation among them. . . .*

III.3.a. Public managers have less decision-making autonomy and flexibility because of elaborate institutional constraints and external political influences. More external interventions, interruptions, and constraints. . . .

III.6.a. Numerous studies show that public managers and employees perceive greater administrative constraints on administration of extrinsic incentives such as pay, promotion, and disciplinary action than do their counterparts in private organizations. (1991, pp. 33–34)

Oversight agencies have affected the changes at the IRS in fundamental ways. The GAO provided a critical impetus by forcing the IRS to confront the issue of organizational redesign in order to gain full advantage of its investment in technological improvements. Other oversight agencies have also cooperated with the changes. The National Academy of Sciences was brought in by the IRS to alleviate congressional concerns about its ability to manage the technological improvements. A special panel convened under the auspices of the National Research Council strongly reinforced the GAO recommendation for a radical restructuring. The Office of Management and Budget (OMB) also cooperated by "fencing" the money for TSM to make sure that it was not spent on other agency requirements.

Although the GAO played a role in fostering the change, it also created problems that may inhibit implementation. The IRS has been extremely cautious about discussing implications of the changes for specific units because change leaders feared that the GAO would provide this information to Congress, thus stimulating premature political intervention. As one official put it, they have to be careful because "the whole damn process can come down around one or two powerful Congresspeople." The withholding of information has heightened tensions among employees and will obviously complicate implementation.

Other institutional constraints have affected the IRS. Procurement regulations greatly prolonged and complicated the purchase of the new computer systems. Personnel regulations had an even greater impact. All the private sector models cited above emphasize the importance of changing personnel processes and systems to correspond to the business changes. Hammer and Champy envision dramatic changes in the work environment: "Work units change—from functional departments to process teams"; "Jobs change—from simple tasks to multidimensional work"; "People's roles change—from controlled to empowered"; "Job preparation changes—from training to education"; "Focus of performance measures and compensation shifts—from activity to results"; "Advancement criteria change—from performance to results" (1993, chap. 4).

Carothers, Bounds, and Stahl also emphasize the importance of using collateral systems to reinforce the changes. "The managerial leaders must ensure congruence of rewards, appreciation systems, promotional criteria, information systems, performance evaluation, and reporting systems with the definition of the managerial jobs" (1992, p. 90). Many of these features are included in the IRS plans.

Like other federal agencies, the IRS is subject to federal civil service law (USC §5) as well as to regulations promulgated by the Office of Personnel Management (OPM). As a result, the IRS has limited ability to significantly alter personnel processes as a means of changing employee behavior. One top official lamented that he would like to "outplace" people "who don't fit the style and type of executive we'd like to see in the future" but that he was prevented from doing so by the civil service process. He noted that it would be better to eliminate some executive positions than to take people off the front lines, but that "these kinds of things" have to go through the Department of Treasury, OPM, and congressional oversight panels.

Although civil service law and personnel regulations will impede implementation, in the final analysis, the IRS does not believe that the requirements they impose will seriously threaten the restructuring. The director of the Human Resources Division noted that the OPM indicated a willingness to cooperate by allowing the waiver of restrictions such as that prohibiting the involuntary transfer of employees. That waiver is important to the success of the restructuring in light of the pledge to avoid layoffs. She and others interviewed commented that the National Performance Review has made it much easier for agencies to challenge these types of restrictions. She concluded that the net effect of constraints presented by personnel regulations was simply that "you can't do things as quickly."

Congress

Several of the officials interviewed perceive the fickleness of Congress as the greatest threat to the restructuring. One official observed that every private sector agency that has gone through this kind of change has asked the shareholders to bear with them while they "bottomed out." Students of private sector change have confirmed this. At the National Performance Review's "Reinventing Government Summit" in June 1993, Rosabeth Kantor of the Harvard Business School commented, "One of my basic truths of management and politics, if not of life, is that everything looks like a failure in the middle" (U.S. National Performance Review, 1993b, p. 31). IRS officials are aware that if their restructuring "looks like a failure in the middle," Congress may well pull the plug on funding. They have little margin for error in managing the change. Several referred to the "disastrous" experience during the 1985 filing season when problems in implementing new computer software resulted in delays in issuing refunds and increased interest expenses for the government. This incident attracted much media interest and, as a result, became a focus of additional congressional oversight and other activity.

Another concern is whether the agency can sustain congressional commitment to the project under conditions of severe budgetary restraint. In fiscal year 1995, Congress made substantial cuts in TSM funding. Both IRS officials and congressional staff members indicated that the cuts were primarily a result of the very stringent constraints on discretionary funding imposed by the Budget Enforcement Act of 1993. The 1995 cuts will set TSM back by as much as eighteen months, according to IRS officials. If additional cuts are imposed in future years, the final implementation date could be delayed substantially beyond the 2001 target date.

Managing Stakeholders
Distinctive Characteristics of Public Organizations. . . .
I.3 Presence of more intensive external political influence.
>   *a. Greater diversity and intensity of external informal political influences*
>   *on decisions (political bargaining and lobbying, public opinion, interest*
>   *group, and client and constituent pressures).*
>   *b. Greater need for political support from client groups, constituencies, for-*

*mal authorities, in order to attain appropriations and authorization for
actions.* (Rainey, 1991, pp. 33–34)

As part of the reorganization, the IRS announced plans to reduce the number of customer service sites from forty-four to twenty-three and to reduce the number of district offices from sixty-three to thirty-three at a savings of $1 million per office. The agency anticipated considerable resistance to the announcement, and it developed a tightly coordinated effort to explain the rationale behind the closings to key stakeholders, including union officials and members of Congress, prior to its public release. The strategy appears to have been successful because several officials commented that the reaction from Congress was muted.

The cooperation of the National Treasury Employees' Union in the overall effort explains the lack of strong reaction by Congress. The decision by agency leadership to coopt union support for the restructuring was intended partly to mitigate opposition from Congress and partly to minimize internal resistance. There is an awareness, however, that the agreement presents a dilemma. On the one hand, union acquiescence in the changes may greatly facilitate their implementation. On the other hand, members of Congress and the administration may demand that a significant downsizing accompany the investment in new technology and the subsequent productivity improvements. In the case of a downsizing, the union would almost certainly change its position and oppose the restructuring.

The issue surfaced during a 1993 hearing before the House Government Operations Subcommittee on Commerce, Consumer, and Monetary Affairs. Members of the subcommittee argued against the no-layoffs policy and for reducing the total number of agency employees (U.S. House of Representatives, 1993, p. 64). It is very likely to be raised again, perhaps in other contexts. One member of the agency's executive committee, for example, sees union opposition as inevitable, not necessarily because of demands to downsize but because as the changes are implemented, grassroots employee opposition will be sufficiently intense to force union leadership to change its stance.

Reducing Checks and Controls

The reduced costs and expedited processes that are the objectives of reengineering result in large part from a reduction in checks and controls. Hammer and Champy make the case as follows:

> Conventional processes are replete with checking and control steps, which add
> no value but are included to ensure that people aren't abusing the process. . . .
> Reengineered processes exhibit a more balanced approach. Instead of tightly
> checking work as it is performed, reengineered processes often have aggregate
> or deferred controls. These control systems will, by design, tolerate modest and
> limited abuse, by delaying the point at which abuse is detected or by examining
> aggregate patterns rather than individual instances. (1993, p. 58)

A problem this model presents for public sector applications is the very high premium put by politicians on avoiding abuse in government programs. As the *Report of the National Performance Review* states, "In Washington's highly politicized world, the greatest risk is not that a program will perform poorly, but that a scandal will erupt. Scandals are front-page news while routine failure is ignored" (U.S. National Performance Review, 1993a, p. 3).

The same dynamic may inhibit implementation of another key element of the model, the empowerment of employees. By definition, empowered employees are allowed more discretion in the conduct of their duties, are less subject to checks and controls, and, therefore, create a greater threat of error and abuse. A recent incident highlights the threat that empowerment presents to the organizational changes. In August 1993, the GAO revealed that 370 IRS employees in the Southeast Region were disciplined for using government computers to gain improper access to taxpayer data. Some employees got "kickbacks" from bogus refund checks that were issued. The incident generated a letter from Senator John Glenn stating that the agency "cannot permit any perception to exist that employees who may have breached Americans' trust in the confidentiality of their tax information will go undetected and, if guilty, unpunished" (Barr, 1993, p. A4). This dynamic may thwart the elimination of checks and controls in IRS systems, thereby mitigating the benefits of key aspects of the model.

The Public

A critical question for the IRS is whether and to what extent the broader public can be made to understand and support the changes. One official commented that most members of the public currently have limited contact with the IRS; they send in their tax form once a year and receive a refund check four to six weeks later. As part of the restructuring, the IRS is actively engaged in trying to determine what the public wants from the tax collection system. One official said that their surveys have shown that people place much greater importance on simplifying the tax law than on getting their refund a few days earlier. Those changes that would do the most to achieve public support are therefore beyond the agency's control.

Privacy

Distinctive Characteristics of Public Organizations. . . .

II.3   Government activities often have a broader impact and greater symbolic significance. There is a broader scope of concern, such as for general public interest criteria. . . .

II.4   There is greater public scrutiny of public managers. . . .

II.5   There are unique public expectations for fairness, responsiveness, honesty, openness, and accountability. (Rainey, 1991, pp. 33–34)

The privacy issue has been central to discussions about the IRS reorganization. Agency officials are extremely sensitive to claims that enhanced computer capabilities will compromise the protection of private tax data. Privacy concerns helped derail both previous attempts at systems modernization. This time, the agency has taken additional measures to address these concerns, including the hiring of a "privacy advocate" to ensure that features to protect privacy are built into the new systems. A "Policy Statement on Taxpayer Privacy Rights" issued by the IRS states that "among the most basic of a taxpayer's privacy rights is an expectation that the Service will keep personal and financial information confidential. Taxpayers also have the right to expect that the Service will collect, maintain, use, and disseminate personally identifiable information and data only as authorized by law and as necessary to carry out agency responsibilities" (Richardson, 1993, p. 2).

Despite these efforts, there is still a concern that TSM could be derailed by privacy concerns, as have previous efforts at systems modernization. Agency officials have met with outside privacy advocates, but as one official noted, these advocates do not believe enhanced data retrieval systems are compatible with privacy and will oppose the changes regardless of the protections that are built into the systems. In this case, the official noted, it really comes down to a matter of philosophy and whether opponents are able to convince Congress that the changes constitute a significant threat to the privacy of tax records. The officials interviewed acknowledge the problem, but they concur that the case for TSM is sufficiently compelling that Congress will not allow privacy considerations to prevent the changes.

Serving the "Customer"

Distinctive Characteristics of Public Organizations. . . .

*III.1.a   Greater vagueness, intangibility, or difficulty in measuring goals and per-
           formance criteria; the goals are more debatable and value-laden. . . .*
*III.1.b   Greater multiplicity of the goals and criteria (efficiency, public account-
           ability and openness, political responsiveness, fairness and due process,
           social equity and distributional criteria, moral correctness of behavior).*
III.1.c   Greater tendency of the goals to be conflicting, to involve more trade-offs.
           (Rainey, 1991, pp. 33–34)

The prior discussion highlights the problem with the multiplicity of goals
in government which are described by Rainey. Consistent with the private sector basis of the model, IRS officials have sought to base the reengineering effort
on improving services that their "customers" value. They have determined that
"the compliant taxpayer" is their ultimate customer. A separate "Value Tracking" core business system was established for the express purpose of ascertain-
ing taxpayer preferences. A series of focus groups and formal surveys have been
used in this context. A "Customer Satisfaction Survey" is conducted each spring
to measure taxpayer attitudes toward the Service. The 1993 survey showed a decline in customer satisfaction on such key questions as, "Does the IRS accurately
answer questions about taxes?" and "Does the IRS have employees who are
available to respond to people's requests?" In response, the agency commented,
"Our reorganization . . . is designed to improve exactly those things taxpayers
tell us we need to improve" (U.S. General Accounting Office, 1994, p. 61).

DiIulio, Garvey, and Kettl identify some of the competing values that surface in government by seeking to serve the "customer" (1993, p. 48). They identify four "competing approaches" that "drive the government in four different
directions in seeking to serve the customer": "citizens as service recipients,"
"partners in service provision," "overseers of performance," and "citizens as
taxpayers." The four approaches correspond to the objectives of responsiveness, effectiveness, accountability, and efficiency. The problem occurs when
these values are transmitted, and sometimes distorted, by the political process.
As the authors point out, there is no guarantee that the perspective of the "overseers" will coincide with that of the "citizens as customers" (1993, p. 50).

Measuring what customers value is of limited worth when the findings
must be constantly filtered politically. A *USA Today* / CNN poll found that 68
percent of the public "support federal spending cuts, even if programs in their
congressional districts are cut" (Baumann, 1993, p. A11). Clearly, the public
would endorse the closure of unneeded and superfluous IRS offices that IRS
officials will keep open because of political considerations. The value of a customer-oriented model in these circumstances is substantially diluted.

Involving Employees
Distinctive Characteristics of Public Organizations. . . .
III.3.b   Public managers have weaker authority over subordinates and lower levels
as a result of institutional constraints. (Rainey, 1991, pp. 33–34)

Bounds and Dewhirst argue that "it is well established that people are more likely to accept, support, and participate in innovation and to change if they perceive that a crisis exists" (1992, p. 320). IRS leadership acknowledges that many employees, even at very high levels in the organization, are not convinced that there is a crisis or a need for change. Unlike private sector agencies, the IRS does not face the prospect of extinction due to an inability to compete in private markets. Employees are afforded substantial protection from job loss by the civil service system and by political considerations that mitigate against layoffs. Although the agency is using an elaborate communications strategy to convince employees of the need for change, overt or covert resistance from within the agency presents a real threat to implementation. Further, even though employees have been told that no one will be laid off, many are still faced with the disruption and trauma of extensive retraining and the necessity to move. Changes in traditional career ladders within the agency are a cause for anxiety for many employees. Several officials see employee resistance as a threat to the reorganization. One official mentioned the possibility of absenteeism, discipline problems, leaks, and sabotage on the part of individual employees. Her conclusion was that unless the agency could convince employees it is working in their best interests, rearguard actions to dampen the effect of employee opposition will be required.

Leadership and Organizational Change
Distinctive Characteristics of Public Organizations. . . .
III.3.d   More frequent turnover of top leaders due to elections and political appointments causes more difficulty in implementing plans and innovations.
(Rainey, 1991, pp. 33–34)

The IRS is one of the least political federal agencies in terms of political appointees. Only two of the top positions are political: the commissioner and the chief counsel. The deputy commissioner and all the business system owners are members of the career civil service. This provides the agency with an unusual degree of leadership continuity. Still, the 1993 change in commissioners caused considerable anxiety among agency leadership. One of the new business system owners described her concern about the new commissioner—"Is she going to buy in to all this?"—and her relief when the new commissioner did "buy in." The same individual commented, however, that the IRS could not proceed with changes of this magnitude if all the top positions were political, as they are in most other agencies. She said that every time a new administration comes in, "the focus changes dramatically."

The issue of leadership is central to the process of organizational change. In the case of the IRS, the leadership necessary to bring about the changes now under way came about through a symbiotic relationship between political and career officials. The chief information officer (a career official) gave credit to former IRS Commissioner Fred Goldberg for recognizing the need for the IRS to change and for bringing in change-minded members of the career service to provide the necessary leadership. This official commented that Goldberg stimulated a "change in thinking among career personnel" and "provided a spark" that started them off in a "whole new strategic direction." The balance between the political and career leadership appears to have been optimal in fostering the changes at IRS; a political official recognizing the need for change was able to put into place career officials who were in a position to see the change process through.

Conclusions

Our analysis highlights several critical components of the IRS reengineering effort that question the guidance and heuristic power of the private sector model. First, the role of the external political environment, particularly the role of Congress, in allocating agency resources and in overseeing their expenditure is central to the process at IRS. Second, the discontinuity of leadership in public agencies is demonstrated by the change in political leadership early in the change activity. The problems experienced by the IRS would be exacerbated in agencies with more political executives. Third, the cumulative effect of multiple public sector procedural constraints in prolonging implementation has added enormous complexity to the IRS effort.

The Role of Congress in Resource Allocation

The process reengineering models developed in the private sector rely on the concept of customer value. Each task and each process is evaluated based on its contribution to customer value. That measure of value is directly related to the amount of resources allocated to a private corporation by the decision of each customer to purchase—or not purchase—a product or service.

Customer preferences as measured by the IRS, and as built into TSM, are not necessarily reflected in the allocation decisions made by Congress. Congressional actions with regard to TSM suggest that fiscal considerations, that is, the capacity of the agency to collect the maximum amount of revenue at the least possible cost, far outweigh service considerations. At the same time that $340 million was being cut from TSM in the fiscal year 1995 budget, Congress authorized $426 million for an additional five thousand positions in the compliance function when the IRS promised a five-to-one payback for each dollar invested.

Tax systems modernization appears to have received Congressional support to date for two reasons: a pledge by the IRS that it would pay for itself in productivity improvements and the promise that TSM holds for improving revenue collections without having to legislate a tax increase. Quality of service considerations do not appear to carry much weight with legislators. A top IRS official commented that "if the IRS weren't revenue producing, we wouldn't be to first base" with the modernization effort.

Discontinuity of Leadership

Top IRS officials acknowledge that it would not be possible to undertake a change effort of the magnitude of TSM where, as in most federal agencies, continuity of leadership is lacking because of high rates of turnover among political appointees. One aspect of the problem relates to the time horizons of the two categories of officials. B. Guy Peters comments:

> Career civil servants, by virtue of their permanence, longer time perspective, and functional expertise, take a different view of policymaking from that held by the political executive. The political executive in most governments is only in office for a short period of time and must accomplish something in that time—if only so that he or she can hold another office sometime in the future. Political executives therefore cannot afford to advocate policies which take a long time to come to fruition although they may be technically superior. (1988, p. 147)

The IRS had three different commissioners between 1991 and 1994. The *Report of the National Performance Review* states that "in a large corporation, transformation takes 6–8 years at best" (1993a, p. 9). The IRS changes will not be implemented fully until 2001 at the earliest. Even at the IRS, where a critical mass of top-ranking career officials is available to provide ongoing leadership, the restructuring is under the constant threat of changing priorities with each new administration, commissioner, or session of Congress.

Time and Complexity

The issue of the time necessary to wade through complex issues and pro-
mulgate change is the third key point of distinction between public and private
change efforts. Many of the peculiarities of the public sector environment, such
as elaborate procurement regulations or the civil service system, could be regarded as differing from the private sector only, as Laurence Lynn has observed,
"as a matter of degree" (1981, p. 136). The cumulative effect of multiple constraints, however, particularly with regard to the time frame needed to create
significant change, constitutes "a difference in kind."

A number of observers of private sector change efforts have emphasized
the need to act quickly. Hammer and Champy, for example, comment that
"reengineering is stressful for everyone in a company, and stretching it over a
long time period extends the discomfort" (1993, p. 212). Although the IRS effort will not be complete until 2001, IRS officials already express concern about
a loss of patience and commitment to the project on the part of Congress.

An additional threat is that some of the top career officials who initiated
the change effort will themselves leave the agency and that their replacements
will be less committed to the project. A change in union leadership would also
present complications. Of course, the highly dynamic and unpredictable political environment at the federal level could result in a drastic rearrangement of
priorities with each election.

In highlighting these three points at which the application of private sector change models to the public sector appear particularly problematic, it is
important to consider factors peculiar to TSM and to the IRS itself. As noted,
the IRS leadership structure allows more continuity than is possible in most
federal agencies and may therefore be more conducive to the implementation
of dramatic change. Further, the centrality of the IRS function to the operation
of government has given it a "cushion" of consensus in the political environment that tolerates a broader range of action than sometimes is found in public organizations.

On the other hand, the magnitude of the tax collection operation, the processing of 200 million tax returns per year, adds both another dimension of
complexity to the change effort at the IRS and increases demands for the change
to be successful. The $7.5 billion cost of the TSM project adds to this dynamic.
On the one hand, the project has received a fair amount of attention in Congress and has even developed its own constituency there. However, it also becomes an easy target for budget cuts because it is such a large item and because
there is no immediate adverse impact on services.

The TSM project, although idiosyncratic in some respects, is nevertheless useful in highlighting key issues that surface in applying private sector change models to public sector organizations. The issues raised here—leadership, political support, and the time frame for change—all have a particular public dimension that is different from most private organizations. They must be an integral part of any model that purports to guide or direct change efforts in the public sector. Further, the lessons learned from experiences of *public* organizations must be as significant as private models in the design of change and change implementation models. Major public sector change efforts will benefit from careful evaluation of the kinds of issues we have analyzed.

References

Barr, Stephen. 1993. "Glenn Calls IRS Lax on 'Browsing.'" *Washington Post,* August 4, p. A4.

Baumann, Marty. 1993. "Most Want Reform, Doubt Success." *USA Today,* September 16, p. A11.

Bounds, Gregory M., and H. Dudley Dewhirst. 1992. "Assessing Progress in Managing for Customer Value," in Michael Stahl and Gregory Bounds, eds., *Competing Globally through Customer Value.* New York: Quorum.

Carothers, G. Harlan, Jr., Gregory M. Bounds, and Michael J. Stahl. 1992. "Managerial Leadership," in Michael Stahl and Gregory Bounds, eds., *Competing Globally through Customer Value.* New York: Quorum.

DiIulio, John J., Jr., Gerald Garvey, and Donald F. Kettl. 1993. *Improving Government Performance: An Owner's Manual.* Washington, D.C.: Brookings Institution.

Hammer, Michael, and James Champy. 1993. *Reengineering the Corporation: A Manifesto for Business Revolution.* New York: HarperBusiness.

Juran, Joseph. 1989. *Juran on Leadership for Quality: An Executive Handbook.* New York: Free Press.

Kirby, Kenneth. 1992. "Organizational Change: The Systems Approach," in Michael Stahl and Gregory Bounds, eds., *Competing Globally through Customer Value.* New York: Quorum.

Lynn, Laurence E., Jr. 1981. *Managing the Public's Business: The Job of the Government Executive.* New York: Basic Books.

Peters, B. Guy. 1988. *Comparing Public Bureaucracies.* Tuscaloosa: University of Alabama Press.

Philcox, Henry (Chief Information Officer of the IRS). 1992. Speech at the Harvard Institute for International Development.

Rainey, Hal G. 1991. *Understanding and Managing Public Organizations.* San Francisco: Jossey-Bass.

Richardson, Margaret (Commissioner of the Internal Revenue Service). 1993. Memo-
    randum from the Commissioner of the Internal Revenue to All Employees, Octo-
    ber 20.
Stahl, Michael, and Gregory Bounds, eds. 1992. *Competing Globally through Customer
    Value.* New York: Quorum.
U.S. General Accounting Office. 1991. *Identifying Options for Organizational and Busi-
    ness Changes at IRS.* Washington, D.C.: General Accounting Office.
————. 1994. *Financial Audit: Examination of IRS' Fiscal Year 1993 Financial State-
    ments.* Washington, D.C.: General Accounting Office.
U.S. House of Representatives. 1993. *Reorganization of the Internal Revenue Service.*
    Hearing before the Commerce, Consumer and Monetary Affairs Subcommittee of
    the Committee on Government Operations, November.
U.S. Internal Revenue Service. 1993a. *Final Recommendations of the District Organi-
    zation Study.* Washington, D.C.: Internal Revenue Service.
————. 1993b. *Final Recommendations of the Service Center Organization Study.* Wash-
    ington, D.C.: Internal Revenue Service.
————. 1993c. *Reinventing the IRS.* Washington, D.C.: Internal Revenue Service.
U.S. National Performance Review. 1993a. *From Red Tape to Results, Creating a Gov-
    ernment that Works Better and Costs Less: Report of the National Performance Re-
    view.* Washington, D.C.: National Performance Review.
————. 1993b. *Reinventing Government Summit: Proceedings.* Washington, D.C.: Na-
    tional Performance Review.

Conclusion:
What Is Public Management?

H. Brinton Milward

The chapters in this volume share the underlying assumption that public management theory is relevant to the world of practice. Most share another assumption: Public management is linked and should be linked, either tightly or loosely, to social science theory.

This is a major change from the first National Public Management Conference held at the Maxwell School at Syracuse University in 1991. The volume that came out of that conference concluded that public management theory was often hollow at its core; too quick to prescribe from the lessons of a single case or the idiosyncratic experience of one individual (Bozeman, 1993, p. 362). Barry Bozeman, the organizer of that conference, bluntly stated that public management theory "falters chiefly when it evinces too much concern with prescription and too little with theory. . . . In my view public management is at its best when it concerns itself with theoretically informed, experience-based prescription" (ibid.). Laurence Lynn's paper in that volume issued the clearest call of the dangers of public management theory that is divorced from social science theory.

The chapters in this book, selected from presentations at the second National Public Management Conference, have a more confident tone. The tentative nature of the link between public management and theory is much more explicit here. These authors present a compelling case against the view of public management as a field based in the experience of successful practitioners, which Lynn (1994) characterized as devoted to pursuing case study research strategies aimed at articulating, refining, and circumscribing the knowledge about management that wise and experienced managers already have, where the institutional context is a given.

The work of those who look for guidance in the work of excellent managers is not wrong (Behn, 1991, 1988). It is extremely useful as a source of hypotheses that can be compared to systematic findings about the way public organizations and networks behave. The problem with the "best practice" research is that it is limited to situations managers have faced before. What happens in new situations? As we reinvent government or move to a "hollow state," where do we look for guidance when we have, in Donald Kettl's phrase, "gone off the map"?

Best practice researchers have ignored institutional context. In many ways, they are like the organization theorist who assumes that history, context, and institutional ownership do not matter as variables that explain organizational outcomes. It is often asserted that turf protection is a central feature of bureaucratic life. Does turf protection operate to hinder coordination in a network of nonprofit agencies that deliver services under contract to a state agency? We do not know, and the experientialists have no way of telling us because they ignore institutional context.

Public management has ignored the fiscal structure within which public services are delivered. The literature in economics and public finance demonstrates that fiscal structure affects behavior and that there is great variation in the effects of different fiscal instruments. Changing instruments will likely change the set of incentives and perhaps the behavior of public managers. How can this be accounted for in cases dealing with leadership and the identification of best practice?

We may also find that the wise practitioner is just as subject to error as any other human. In a recent study of service integration among sets of service providers in four cities, Keith Provan and I found relatively high rates of integration in all four sites on a set of linkage measures (Provan and Milward, 1995). However, each and every one of the two hundred managers interviewed claimed that fragmentation of services was a big problem in their community mental health network. Many told compelling stories of clients who had fallen through the cracks. The problem articulated may be one of a system overwhelmed by large numbers of multiproblem clients, poor quality services, and inadequate resources, but it is not a problem of a fragmented system of service providers.

In the same study, case managers had very different views of what constituted success than did the seriously mentally ill clients and their families. The case managers placed a high value on allowing the client to function in a deinstitutionalized environment. They viewed success as being able to negotiate the set of services the clients needed, even if the client had to transfer twice to get there by bus. This definition of success was viewed by families and clients as burdensome, and they preferred services located in close proximity for ease of access. Some case managers dismissed this as "open air institutionalization." Whose view of success do we accept, the wise case manager or the client and family who must deal with the system? While success is difficult to measure,

I would prefer to let those with a problem define it before allowing the definition to come from professional ideology.

Almost all the leading practitioners in mental health have advocated that a community mental health system be governed by a local mental health authority. The idea is to blend flexibility with accountability, with the authority having its hands on all of the money coming into the system while being close enough to the problem to be able to distribute it wisely through a set of contracts. In our study (Provan and Milward, 1995) and one conducted of the Robert Wood Johnson Foundation's demonstration program (Morrissey et al., 1994), which used the local mental health authority model, there was no relationship between the model and successful outcomes. In our study, the model that worked the best was a direct relationship between the state funding agency and the local providers. Just as agency theory predicts, direct monitoring by a funder is likely to be more successful than imposing an intermediary between the principal and the agent. By assuming that practitioners know what is wrong with an organization or a delivery system, scholars abdicate their role as analysts and researchers. Would any of these wise practitioners' solutions be found wanting without systematic empirical research? All theories are subject to restricted determinacy, that is, they apply in some places and times better than others, but theories can be falsified; practitioner wisdom cannot. Systematic research can increase the probability that reform efforts, when enacted, will not assume that the world works the way practitioners think it does or should.

Those who teach management of either government or business are often drawn to successful practitioners. At present, this focus on the executive runs counter to the emphasis on the customer that underlies Vice President Gore's National Performance Review and state and local reinventing government efforts. James Q. Wilson (1994) points out that the current round of reform—reinventing government—is at odds with all prior reform efforts. All the previous attempts were designed as ways of increasing the power of the chief executive. This round of reform is focused on empowering the customer in an attempt to sell government back to the American people. Thus, the "best practice" approach to public management is out of alignment with the zeitgeist. While there are worse fates, it means that the power of this approach is unlikely to carry the day if it does not provide answers that are perceived as useful. This may be one reason that public management scholars played almost no role in the National Performance Review.

Two types of questions beg for answers today. These questions relate to *performance* and *governance:* Performance in the sense of how we can improve the efficiency and effectiveness of taxpayer-funded services in various institutional settings; governance in regard to the effects of the new kinds of arrangements (privatization, public-private partnerships, contracting out) on equity, responsiveness, and accountability in a world of empowered public managers.

In my opinion, public management research has little to say on either score. The success of the last few years in getting public management researchers to take social theory seriously has not allowed enough time for these researchers to make progress on a research agenda that would illuminate these questions. In Lynn's article (1994) and the comment that follows by Jane Fountain (1994), they discuss the utility of game theory, the new economics of organizations, institutional theory, and social network analysis for understanding the organizational, structural, and incentive problems in the management of public and nonprofit organizations. The chapters in this volume on the relative contributions of economics (Weimer and Vining), political science (Ellwood), psychology (Weiss), and sociology (Kaboolian) represent an important attempt to seriously evaluate what these social sciences have to offer the public management scholar. Other chapters also explicitly struggle with these issues. O'Toole evaluates and Koremenos and Lynn utilize game theoretic approaches to public management research. Taken together, these studies are an important demonstration that the link between public management and deductive, rational approaches with sets of a priori assumptions can be useful in analyzing organizational and incentive problems in public organizations and networks of organizations. They also point to the work that remains to be done if public management research is to provide answers or advice to the world of practice.

If the link between social theory and public management is one theme of this book, then a second is how to manage change in the face of increasing demands for performance. A number of the chapters take this as their theme. In these, the issue is not the link to social science theory, rather it is the necessity of focusing on systematic change within a set or network of organizations. Bardach and Radin deal with how to integrate services within a network of services. Their perspective forces us to consider issues that go beyond a single bureaucracy or organization and its manager. What incentives exist to enhance cooperation among a set of interdependent and sometimes competing organizations? Brudney adds a related concern: As we move away from a reliance on public organizations and public servants to deliver taxpayer-supported services, how do we integrate volunteers into our privatized service delivery systems?

Thompson and Ingraham and Bryson, Ackerman, Eden, and Finn devote their chapters to examples of how large-scale redesign of the public sector has been conducted and what we can learn from these efforts. The entire book is framed by Peters's systematic consideration of the changing nature of public management and public managers as seen from the perspective of the fundamental changes affecting both the nature of the state and governance as a process.

For those of us who have contributed to the effort to redefine public management theory, this volume is a step on the evolutionary journey of a quite young and diverse field. There is still a long way to go and many difficult issues to face. How close a link do we need to the social sciences? Clearly, understanding is important, but what can we say about why certain organizations perform better than others? Can we move from a generalized study of the role of norms and values in the management of public organizations to a discussion of what norms and values lead to better outcomes than others? In our concern to understand the nature of the new organizational forms and mechanisms that are emerging to deliver public goods and services in ways that are only loosely linked to the state, what can we say about governance in this hollow state? How do we deal with the normative issues that revolve around public management in ways that simply are not similar to the scholarly concerns of social sciences, where value considerations are either not as important or, as in economics, they constitute a set of prior assumptions about the way the world does and should work. Those of us who are committed to a program of systematic, empirical study of public organizations cannot and should not avoid these issues as we press our research agenda forward.

References

Behn, Robert D. 1988. "Management by Groping Along." *Journal of Policy Analysis and Management* 7, no. 3: 643–663.

———. 1991. *Leadership Counts: Lessons for Public Managers from the Massachusetts Welfare, Training, and Employment Program.* Cambridge: Harvard University Press.

Bozeman, Barry. 1993. "Conclusion: Searching for the Core of Public Management," in Barry Bozeman, ed., *Public Management: The State of the Art,* pp. 361–363. San Francisco: Jossey-Bass.

Fountain, Jane E. 1994. "Comment: Disciplining Public Management Research." *Journal of Policy Analysis and Management* 13, no. 2: 269–277.

Lynn, Laurence E., Jr. 1993. "Policy Achievement as a Collective Good: A Strategic Perspective on Managing Social Programs," in Barry Bozeman, ed., *Public Management: The State of the Art,* pp. 108–133. San Francisco: Jossey-Bass.

———. 1994. "Public Management Research: The Triumph of Art over Science." *Journal of Policy Analysis and Management* 13, no. 2: 231–259.

Morrissey, J. P., M. Calloway, W. T. Bartko, M. S. Ridgely, H. S. Goldman, and R. I. Paulson. 1994. "Local Mental Health Authorities and Service System Change: Evidence from the Robert Wood Johnson Program on Chronic Mental Illness." *The Millbank Quarterly* 72, no. 1: 49–80.

Provan, Keith, and H. Brinton Milward. 1995. "A Preliminary Theory of Network Effectiveness: The Case of Community Mental Health Systems." *Administrative Science Quarterly* 40, no. 1: 1–33.

Wilson, James Q. 1994. "Reinventing Public Administration." *PS: Political Science and Politics* 27, no. 4: 667–673.

Notes on Contributors

Fran Ackerman is a lecturer in the Department of Management Science at the University of Strathclyde, Glasgow, Scotland. She is writing a book with Colin Eden on managing organizational change through the use of computer-assisted and non-computer-assisted group support technologies.

Eugene Bardach is Professor of Public Policy at the Graduate School of Public Policy, University of California, Berkeley. He is writing a book on the challenges of interorganizational collaboration in the public sector.

Jeffrey L. Brudney is Professor of Political Science and Director of the Doctor of Public Administration (DPA) program at the University of Georgia. He is the author of *Fostering Volunteer Programs in the Public Sector: Planning, Initiating, and Managing Voluntary Activities* and winner of the John Grenzebach Award for Outstanding Research in Philanthropy for Education. He is coauthor of *Applied Statistics for Public Administration* and the author of numerous other publications. In 1994, Dr. Brudney was the Fulbright-Kahanoff Scholar at York University (Toronto, Canada) in the Voluntary Sector Management Program.

John M. Bryson is Professor of Planning and Public Affairs at the Hubert H. Humphrey Institute of Public Affairs at the University of Minnesota. He is the author of *Strategic Planning for Public and Nonprofit Organizations* and coauthor (with Barbara C. Crosby) of *Leadership for the Common Good*. He is working on a book about facilitating large-scale public and nonprofit organizational change.

Colin Eden is a professor and head of the Department of Management Science at the University of Strathclyde, Glasgow, Scotland. He is the coauthor (with Sue Jones and David Sims) of *Thinking in Organizations* and *Messing about in Problems*. He is working on a book with Fran Ackerman about managing organizational change through the use of computer-assisted and non-computer-assisted group support technologies.

John W. Ellwood is Professor of Public Policy at the Graduate School of Public Policy of the University of California, Berkeley. Professor Ellwood's scholarship and writings have centered on the congressional budget process, legislative behavior, and corporate governance mechanisms. Among his publications are the books *Limiting Congress' Budget Making Power* and *Reductions in U.S. Domestic Spending: How They*

Affect State and Local Governments, and the articles "The Politics of the Enactment and Implementation of Gramm Rudman Hollings: Why Congress Cannot Address the Deficit Dilemma," "The Current Recession and California's Structural Budget Deficit: Its Causes and Consequences," and "In Praise of Pork."

Charles B. Finn is fellow and Director of Information Services at the Hubert H. Humphrey Institute of Public Affairs at the University of Minnesota. He is working on a book about strategic planning and management from a stakeholder perspective.

Patricia W. Ingraham is Professor of Public Administration and Political Science at the Maxwell School of Citizenship and Public Affairs at Syracuse University. She is the author of *The Foundations of Merit: Public Service in American Democracy,* and she has edited five other books. Her research interests focus on managing change and reform in public organizations.

Linda Kaboolian is an assistant professor at the Kennedy School of Government, Harvard University. Her research is on service delivery systems and customer service to diverse communities. She is involved with efforts to infuse innovation into traditional labor-management relations in the public sector.

Donald F. Kettl is Professor of Political Science and Public Affairs at the University of Wisconsin-Madison and Nonresident Senior Fellow at the Brookings Institution. Kettl contributed to and edited *Inside the Reinvention Machine.* He is a student of public policy and public management, specializing in the design and performance of public organizations.

Barbara Koremenos is a graduate of the Harris Graduate School of Public Policy Studies at the University of Chicago. She is pursuing her Ph.D. in Political Science at the University of Chicago. Besides her interest in public management research, she is also engaged in research applying game theory to the study of international relations.

Laurence E. Lynn Jr. is a professor at the Harris Graduate School of Public Policy Studies and in the School of Social Service Administration at the University of Chicago. His most recent book is *Public Management as Art, Science, and Profession.* His current research is concerned with public management theory and its application to issues of human services and education administration.

H. Brinton Milward is Professor of Public Administration and Policy and Director of the School of Public Administration and Policy, University of Arizona, Tucson. His current research focuses on the relationship between interorganizational networks and the state regarding issues of governance. Recent publications include "A Preliminary Theory of Interorganizational Effectiveness" (with Keith G. Provan), "Human Services

Contracting and Coordination: The Market for Mental Health Services," "Nonprofit Contracting and the Hollow State," "Contracting for the Hollow State," and "What Does the Hollow State Look Like?" He received his Ph.D. in public administration from Ohio State University.

Laurence J. O'Toole Jr. is Professor of Political Science and a research associate of the Institute of Community and Area Development at the University of Georgia. He has also held visiting appointments at scholarly institutions in Germany and the Netherlands. He has written and edited a number of books and articles on public policy implementation in network settings and is currently exploring this subject in the field of water policy.

B. Guy Peters is Maurice Falk Professor of American Government at the University of Pittsburgh. A student of public policy and comparative governance, Peters has held Fulbright Fellowships at the University of Strathclyde (Scotland) and the Hoschschule St. Gallen (Switzerland), as well as other positions in Norway, Sweden, Mexico, and the Netherlands. He is the author of many books, including *The Politics of Bureaucracy* and *American Public Policy: Promise and Performance.*

Beryl A. Radin is Professor of Public Administration and Policy in the Graduate School of Public Affairs at Rockefeller College of the State University of New York at Albany. She is currently president of the Association for Public Policy Analysis and Management. Her work has focused on intergovernmental and federalism issues in a number of policy areas. She has been a consultant to a wide range of government agencies, including the U.S. Department of Agriculture, the World Bank, the National Institute of Mental Health, the Department of Health and Human Services, and NASA.

James R. Thompson is a doctoral student in public administration at the Maxwell School of Citizenship and Public Affairs at Syracuse University. The title of his dissertation is "Organizational Innovation in the Federal Government: A Political Perspective." It investigates issues of organizational politics that surround attempts at change in the federal reinvention laboratories.

Aidan R. Vining joined the Faculty of Business Administration, Simon Fraser University, in 1984. His areas of expertise are public policy analysis, including state-owned and mixed enterprise, conceptual issues in policy analysis, criminal justice policy, and business strategy. He has published many articles on policy analysis and has presented his papers at numerous international conferences. His most recent book is *Cost-Benefit Analysis: Concepts and Practice* (with A. Boardman, D. Greenberg, and D. Weimer).

David L. Weimer is Professor of Political Science and Public Policy at the University of Rochester. He writes in the areas of policy analysis and political economy. His recent books include *Institutional Design* and *Policy Analysis and Economics: Developments, Tensions, Prospects.*

Janet A. Weiss is Associate Dean and Professor of Organizational Behavior and Public Policy at the University of Michigan, jointly appointed in the Business School and the School of Public Policy. Her research explores the role of ideas in public policy and public management. Having sunk below the rigorous training in psychology she received in graduate school, she now uses the perspectives of several disciplines.

Index

Page references to figures are printed in italic type.